LABOR, CRAFTS AND COMMERCE IN ANCIENT ISRAEL

To Joshua and David

MOSHE ABERBACH

Labor, Crafts and Commerce in Ancient Israel

THE MAGNES PRESS, THE HEBREW UNIVERSITY, JERUSALEM

Published with the assistance of the
Dr. Louis L. Kaplan Rebbe's Fund, Baltimore

Distributed by The Magnes Press, P.O. Box 7695, Jerusalem 91076, Israel

BM
509
.E27
A23
1994

ISBN 965-223-860-0

Printed in Israel
at Ben-Zvi Printing Enterprises, Jerusalem

Contents

PREFACE   IX

CHAPTER I: Labor, Crafts and Trade in the Bible   1
1. Sheep and Cattle Raising 1;   2. Agriculture 4;   3. Arts and
Crafts 7;   4. The Medical Profession 9;   5. The Wailing
Women 21;   6. Levites and Priests 22;   7. Traders and
Peddlers 23;   8. Scribes 24;   9. Indolence Condemned 25.

CHAPTER II: Industry and Trade in the Hellenistic Age   28
1. Ecclesiastes on Labor 28;   2. Ben Sira's Views on Labor, Commerce
and Crafts 29;   3. Economic Progress during the Hasmonean Age 37.

CHAPTER III: Occupational Structure of the Rabbis   38
1. General Characteristics of the Rabbinate 38;   2. Rabbis in Agriculture and Industry 39;   3. Viniculture 54;   4. Rabbinic Land Surveyor — Rab Adda 55;   5. Woodchopper and Shepherd — R. Akiba 55;   6. Animal Hire Service — R. Jose of Yodkart 56; 7. Rabbis
and Agricultural Laborers 57;   8. Rabbis in Business — Silk Trade
and Other Commercial Activities 58; 9. Rabbis as Schoolteachers and
Educators 68;   10. Rabbis as Professional Preachers 71;   11. Rabbinic Scribes 71;   12. Rabbis as Physicians 77;   13. Rabbinic Craftsmen 82; 14. Miscellaneous Rabbinic Occupations 85;   15. Occupations of Early Christians 89.

CHAPTER IV: Rabbinic Attitude to Physical Labor   91
1. Moral Value of Work 91;   2. Divine Blessings depend on Human
Efforts 91;   3. Work essential for Human Dignity 92;   4. Merit of
Labor more potent than Fathers' Merit 92;   5. Miracles due to
Work 93;   6. Labor as Part of Divine Plan since Adam 94; 7. Abra-
ham and Isaac — Labor in the Promised Land 95; 8. Israel's Work on
the Tabernacle — Condition of Divine Presence 95;
9. "Six Days you shall Labor" 96;   10. Tree-Planting in the Land of
Israel 96;   11. The Divine Worker — The Craftsman's Pride in his
Work 99;   12. Craftsmen, Scholars and Pilgrims 100;   13. Legal
Privileges of Craftsmen and Laborers 100;   14. Work as a Social
Necessity 101;   15. Torah and a Worldly Occupation 102;
16. Work Obligatory for Wives 102;   17. Work Essential for Prolonging Life 102; 18. "Love Work" 103;   19. He who will not work,
neither shall he eat 104;   20. Monotonous and Uninteresting Work
not to be shunned 104;   21. Indolence Condemned 105;
22. How to "find" Work 105;   23. Labor honors the worker 105;

24. Hard Work as a Cure for Colds 106; 25. Dissenting Views due to Hellenistic Influence 106; 26. Importance of Craft Skills 107; 27. Craft Skill as Social Security 107; 28. Craft Education 108; 29. Son should follow Father's trade 108; 30. Study and Work — Antidote to Sin 109; 31. Work in the Scheme of Life 110; 32. Maimonides and the Three-Hour Workday 111; 33. Equality of Laborer and Scholar 111; 34. Minimum of Study — Maximum of Work 112; 35. Abandonment of Studies for Vocational Career 112; 36. Torah Study as Exclusive or Principal Vocation 113; 37. Study and Work in Equal Proportions 117; 38. Torah and Commerce 118; 39. Higher Education for "Eaters of Manna" 119; 40. Torah for Israel, Labor for Gentiles 119; 41. No Blessing in Manual Work 120; 42. Dislike of Economic Activity due to Self-Sacrifice for Torah 121; 43. Prosperous and Poverty-stricken Students 121; 44. Want and Destitution for the Sake of Learning 122; 45. Martyrdom on the Altar of Torah 124.

CHAPTER V: The Occupational Structure of the Jews in the Talmudic Age   126

1. Agriculture 126; 2. Building 127; 3. Textile Industry 131; 4. Pottery 134; 5. Glass Industry 136; 6. Metal Industry and Arms Manufacture 140; 7. Marketing and Trading Activities 141; 8. Commercial Ethics — Price Control 144; 9. Private Enterprise — Legal Problems 148; 10. Jewish Occupations in the Roman-Hellenistic Dispora 151.

CHAPTER VI: Recommended and Undesirable Trades   159

1. "Clean and Easy" Crafts 159; 2. Commerce and Business Education 160; 3. Trading in Sacred Commodities 163; 4. Bookkeeping and Accountancy 164; 5. Agriculture 164; 6. Sheep and Goat Breeding 179; 7. Medicine 181; 8. Morally Undesirable Trades 201; 9. Bloodletting 203; 10. Prison Administration 205; 11. Peddlers 205; 12. Tanners 207; 13. Weavers 209; 14. Artistic Weavers 212; 15. Launderers 214; 16. Transport Workers — Ass-Drivers and Camel-Drivers 220; 17. Herdsmen and Shepherds 224; 18. Storekeepers 231; 19. Sailors 232; 20. Ritual Slaughterers and Butchers 233; 21. Hunters 236; 22. Fishermen 239.

CHAPTER VII: Vocational Training — Masters and Apprentices 241

1. Biblical and Hellenistic Periods 241; 2. Shepherd Apprentices 241; 3. Roman Age 241; 4. Apprenticeship Agreements 242; 5. Unsuitable Applicants for Apprenticeship 243; 6. Duration of Apprenticeship 243; 7. Relationship between Master and Apprentice 244; 8. Refusal to teach a Craft 246.

Bibliography 251

List of Abbreviations 256

General Index 258

Sources 280

Hebrew Bible 280
Apocrypha and Pseudepigrapha 283
New Testament 284
Hellenistic-Jewish Literature 284
Rabbinic Literature 285

Preface

Among the many spurious arguments used by modern anti-Semitism, that of Jewish parasitism and unwillingness to work has probably been the most widely disseminated and the most dangerous. The concentration of Jews in commerce, banking and the free professions, and their virtual absence (outside of Israel) from agriculture, mining and heavy industry, tended to lend credibility to the charge that the Jews avoided productive labor. Even Jews were sometimes inclined to believe this unfounded accusation.

The truth of the matter, as students of Jewish history and sociology have long known, is that Judaism, so far from frowning on manual work, encourages it, not only as a necessary means of earning one's livelihood but as a moral value in its own right. In pre-medieval Europe, Jews were well represented in agriculture as well as in many branches of industry. It was Christian intolerance that effectively excluded the Jews from feudal agriculture and the guild-dominated craft trades. Driven to commerce and banking, Jews excelled and prospered because they had to excel and prosper in order to survive. The "miracle" of Jewish survival — albeit in a sadly decimated state — after 1,500 years of almost incessant discrimination and persecution was due to the vital economic functions performed by the Jews. At the time when the Dark Ages were at their darkest, and Europe's economy had sunk to the level of village autarky, adventurous Jewish merchants — the so-called Radanites — pioneered international commerce, extending from France and Spain to India and China.

Driven from these profitable operations by the superior competition of the commercial republics of Italy and the Hanseatic League in Germany, the Jews employed their accumulated capital in banking — which is what Jewish "usury" really was. The rise of royal power in Western Europe, a necessary beneficial development favoring the creation of the modern national state, can be directly traced to the heavy contributions levied on the Jews for the royal exchequer.

The wealth that Jewish merchants and bankers created for Europe — though kings and emperors squandered much of it on fratricidal and foreign wars, on Crusades and luxurious edifices — was nevertheless the economic basis of Europe's recovery from the Dark Ages and of the magnificent Renaissance which began in the twelfth and thirteenth centuries.

Much has been written about the Jewish contribution to modern capitalism,[1] and while it must be admitted that there has been some exaggeration of the Jewish role in the rise of capitalism — the impoverished Jews of sixteenth and seventeenth century Europe lacked the capital for the decisive role attributed to them — the Jews did play their part, and played it well. A few financial geniuses, in the eighteenth and early nineteenth centuries, rose from obscurity to dominate the money markets of Europe. But even the Rothschilds, at the height of their power, were able to function in the way they did only because their activities were wholesome and essential. Their wise employment of capital was just as necessary for the unprecedented expansion of nineteenth century trade and industry as the labor of entrepreneurs, scientists, engineers and skilled workmen.

If this study emphasizes the role of manual work in Jewish history, it is thus by no means an essay in apologetics, as if to say, "The Jews are not quite so bad as they are made out to be. They have not always been shady traders, usurers and slum landlords. When they lived under normal political and economic conditions or were given a chance by friendly rulers, they also engaged in agriculture, crafts and all kinds of manual labor". This was, indeed, the common approach fostered by the inferiority complex of the newly liberated ghetto Jew in the early years of Jewish emancipation. German and Austrian Jews were particularly adept at this kind of indirect self-flagellation, continuing in this vein down to the Hitler period. Granted that the Jewish economic structure was lopsided and unhealthy, there were no grounds for Jews chiding

---

1   Cf., in particular, Werner Sombart, *The Jews and Modern Capitalism* (Eng. translation, Glencoe, Ill., 1951).

themselves for historic developments for which they were manifestly not responsible. Whatever the faults of individual Jews, as a group the Jews have always played a beneficial role in society, irrespective of their economic activities and occupations.

What, then, is the purpose of this study, if we refuse to make excuses for Jewish preponderance in other spheres? It is, briefly stated, to correct widespread misconceptions concerning Jewish economic activities throughout history; to demonstrate Jewish participation in every facet of economic life open to them; and above all, to emphasize the moral significance attached to labor in biblical and rabbinic literature alike.

In this century, indeed, pioneers of the Israeli labor movement — such as A.D. Gordon, Berl Katzenelson, David Ben-Gurion and many others — created what has rightly been called a "Religion of Labor", not simply because they hated and despised Jewish "huckstering" and petty trading in the Diaspora, but because they were inspired idealists who correctly realized that without a vast Jewish labor movement the Zionist dream would remain just that — a dream. They and thousands like them — students, engineers, and intellectuals of every hue — sacrificed promising careers in the Diaspora and went to a desert called Palestine to reclaim by their labor the eroded soil of the mountains and malaria-infested swamps for the Jewish people. It was their sweat and blood, freely given to their nation, that created the state of Israel. In the entire history of mankind, there is no parallel to such heroism shouldered not by individuals but by an entire movement. Without the inspiration derived from the ethical sources of the Jewish faith, it is very doubtful whether the *Halutzim*, the pioneers who braved all obstacles to rebuild their country and their people, would have found the moral stamina that sustained them against incredible odds.

This study is an attempt to lay bare and analyze these valuable sources, scattered as they are in the vast sea of biblical and rabbinic literature. While every attempt has been made to follow strict scholarly criteria in evaluating the source material, a work of this type should not be designed for the exclusive use of historians and theologians. It is to be hoped that the presentation of the material in a readable as well as scholarly manner, will make it suitable for interesting reading by intelligent laymen whose standards are sometimes no less exacting than those of professional students of religion or history.

It is in line with this aim that, with some exceptions, no attempt has been made to describe the technical details of the production of raw materials and manufactured articles in ancient Israel. Not only would such descriptions greatly have expanded the scope and size of this book, but they would have been of little interest to non-specialist general readers who rarely wish to immerse themselves in detailed portrayals of ancient tools and manufacturing processes.

Finally, it is my pleasure to acknowledge with gratitude the assistance generously provided by all those who have helped to make the writing and publication of this work possible. First and foremost, I am indebted to Mr. Leon Lerner, formerly director of the Baltimore branch of the B'nai B'rith Vocational Service, who originally commissioned me to write a pamphlet on the Jewish attitude to labor and craft education. It was this pamphlet, intended primarily for a lecture at an inter-denominational conference in New Orleans, that provided the impetus for additional research in this vast but relatively neglected area of Jewish social and economic history in ancient times. Mr. Lerner encouraged me to continue this research, and he generously provided all the necessary technical assistance.

I would also like to express my thanks to Dr. Louis L. Kaplan, former President of the Baltimore Hebrew College for his financial support through his Rebbe's Fund. Acknowledgements are also due to the Baltimore Hebrew University Herman and Rosa Lebovitz Cohen Fund, which provided the resources for the preparation of the final draft of the book. I am also grateful to Dr. Shmuel Avitzur who read the manuscript for The Magnes Press and made a number of useful suggestions and corrections. Last, but not least, thanks are due to Mr. Dan Benovici, director of The Magnes Press, whose ideas and patience have brought this project to final fruition.

Moshe Aberbach

Heshvan 5754 – November 1993

Chapter One

Labor, Crafts and Trade in the Bible

1. Sheep and Cattle Raising

If it is true that the Bible reflects the life and culture of the people of ancient Israel over a period of well over a thousand years, we should rightly expect to find biblical references concerning the manner in which the people earned their daily bread.

Throughout their earliest history — in patriarchal times, in the course of their sojourn in the land of Goshen in Egypt, and during their wanderings in the Sinai Desert — the Hebrews were shepherds, tending sheep and cattle. Occasionally, they might settle down temporarily and engage in some primitive form of agriculture, presumably on uncultivated land acquired from their neighbors.[2] Under Egyptian bondage, the Israelite slaves were employed as brickmakers,[3] and their temporary work stoppage at the instigation of Moses and Aaron[4] must be one of the first recorded strikes in history. Likewise, Pharaoh's violent reaction[5] may well be the first known case of successful strike breaking.

None of this, however, altered the basic structure of Israelite society, which was essentially nomadic and based primarily on sheepbreeding and the raising of cattle. Occasionally, there was not enough pasture for all the members of the tribe to stay together. Part of the tribe would have to separate from the rest and seek new grazing grounds.[6] In time, there seems to have developed an acute shortage of suitable pasture land. Thus in the famous Joseph story, Jacob had to send his favorite son all the way from the vicinity of Hebron to Shechem — a distance of almost 50 miles

---

2   See Gen. 26:12; 33:19; 37:7.
3   Exod. 5:7ff.
4   Ibid. 5:4f.
5   Ibid. 5:6ff.
6   Gen. 13:5ff.; 36:6ff.

as the crow flies — to find Joseph's brothers, who were pasturing their sheep there.[7] When Joseph arrived at the place, they had moved still farther north and were at Dothan, nearly 14 miles north of Shechem.[8]

Despite these difficulties and occasional famines, which eventually forced the Israelites to settle in Egypt because of lack of pasture land in Canaan,[9] sheep and cattle (as well as camels[10] and asses) continued to be the main wealth of the Patriarchs as it had been in the past.[11] What was originally a necessity for nomadic tribes became in time an idealized way of life, in which the simple virtues flourished, untainted by the idolatry and immorality of agricultural civilizations. Thus Joseph proudly instructed his brothers how to reply to Pharaoh's question, "What is your occupation?" They were to answer, "Your servants have been keepers of cattle from our youth, even until now, both we and our father".[12]

Sheep and cattle raising continued to be the occupation of at least some Israelites even under the Egyptian bondage;[13] and when they left, they took with them "very many cattle, both flocks and herds".[14] Moses himself had been a shepherd,[15] and, with his brother Aaron, he led God's people "like a flock".[16] King David, too, had been a shepherd[17] before he was taken "from the sheepfolds ... to be the shepherd of Jacob his people, and Israel his inheritance".[18] The shepherd — whose occupation

---

7   Ibid. 37:13.
8   Ibid. v. 17.
9   Cf. ibid. 47:4.
10   See ibid. 12:16; 24:10–46; 30:43; 31:17; 32:8,16. W.F. Albright, *From the Stone Age to Christianity* (Baltimore, 1940), pp. 120, 196, and 219; also idem, *The Archaeology of Palestine* (London, 1954; revised and reprinted 1960), p. 206, suggests that camels had not yet been domesticated in the patriarchal age, and their mention in the patriarchal narratives is therefore an anachronism. However, this view has met with a good deal of opposition, and there is extensive controversy on the subject; see *The Interpreter's Dictionary of the Bible*, vol. I (Nashville–New York, 1962), p. 492. See, esp., S.Z. Leiman, "The Camel in the Patriarchal Narrative", in *Yavneh Review*, 1967, pp. 16–26.
11   Cf. Gen. 12:16; 13:2; 24:10–46; 26:14; 30:43; 31:17; 32:8,15,16; 45:10; 46:32; 47:1; 50:8.
12   Ibid. 46:33–34.
13   Exod. 9:4ff.; 10:9; 12:32.
14   Ibid. 12:38.
15   Ibid. 3:1.
16   Pss. 77:21.
17   I Sam. 16:11,19; 17:15,28,34.
18   Pss. 78:70f.; cf. II Sam. 5:2; 7:8; I Chron. 11:2; 17:7.

in ancient Egypt and, later, in Roman times, was a distinctly despised one[19] — was in the biblical age synonymous with leader.[20] Even the Almighty Himself was praised as the shepherd of His people,[21] including, in particular, of such national heroes as the patriarch Jacob[22] and King David, who immortalized this concept of the Divine Shepherd in the famous hymn, "The Lord is my shepherd, I shall not want".[23]

No wonder, then, that in the story of Cain and Abel, the "good guy" whose offering was willingly accepted by the Lord was the shepherd Abel, while the "bad guy" whose produce was rejected by God was the farmer Cain, who in his jealousy slew his brother.[24] Implicit in this legend is the idea that the Creator was not too pleased with the agricultural habits of men.[25] He had indeed "cursed" the earth ever since Adam and Eve had eaten the forbidden fruit[26] — suggesting that agricultural labor was not as acceptable as shepherding.

Even when the Israelites had long been rooted in the land flowing with milk and honey, there was still a pious sect, the so-called Rechabites, who in addition to abstaining from wine would also refrain from building houses or engaging in any agricultural pursuits. Instead, they would "dwell in tents" — i.e., live as nomadic shepherds.[27] The prophet Jeremiah — who himself owned land[28] and predicted among the future blessings of the Land of Israel that fields and vineyards would yet be purchased after the return from captivity[29] — nevertheless bestowed

---

19 Gen. 46:34; *Midr. Pss.* 23:2, edit. Buber, p. 198. For a full discussion of the social position of the shepherd and cowherd in the Talmudic age, see Chapter Six.
20 Num. 27:17; II Sam. 7:7; I Kings 22:17; Is. 44:20; 63:11; Jer. 2:8; 3:15; 10:21; 23:1ff.; 25:34ff.; 50:6; Ezek. 34:2–31; 37:24; Mic. 5:4; Nah. 3:18; Zech. 10:2f.; 11:3–17; 13:7; I Chron. 17:6; II Chron. 18:16.
21 Pss. 74:1; 79:13; 80:2; 95:7; 100:3; cf. Is. 40:11; Jer. 13:17; 31:10; Ezek. 34:11ff.; Hos. 4:16; Mic. 7:14.
22 Gen. 48:15.
23 Pss. 23:1.
24 Gen. 4:2ff.
25 See *Gen. Rabba* 22, 3; 36.3; *Tanh.* Noah 13. See also M. Radin, *The Life of the People in Biblical Times* (Philadelphia, 1943), p. 147.
26 Gen. 3:17; 5:29.
27 Jer. 35:6ff.
28 Ibid. 32:7ff.
29 Ibid. 32:15,43f.

high praise upon the Rechabites for their loyalty to their ancestral customs and their abstemious way of life.[30]

2. Agriculture

Whatever the theory of moralists and pious men, life proved too potent for the overwhelming majority of the Israelite people. True, the land was flowing with milk and honey rather than with wheat and barley; but this did not deter the Israelite conquerors from settling down side by side with the Canaanites, learning their ways, both good and bad, and tending with love and devotion the land that the Lord had given them for possession. Thus despite the nostalgic yearning for the days of Israel's youth, when the people followed their God "in the wilderness, in a land that was not sown",[31] the vast majority of the Israelites preferred to be simple farmers, cultivating their small — and often far from adequate — plots of land to eke out a bare living from the parched mountainous soil. The self-sufficient village communities were at first rarely in need of the skill of the craftsman, and there are but few monuments to remind us of the artistic achievements of the ancient Israelites. Their pottery was primitive, or else it was imported; and their stern code prohibiting the making of images rendered impossible the development of religious art, which was the basis of all ancient art.

Indeed, not only the village community, but the family unit — the farmer, with his wife and children and an occasional servant or hired laborer — tended to be self-sufficient. Most, if not all, of the needs of the family were provided at home without recourse to specialized artisans. After the harvest, the farmer, together with the members of his family, would thresh and winnow the grain, and his wife would grind it into flour and bake it into thin leavened or unleavened loaves of bread,[32] mostly small thin rolls, resembling our cakes or biscuits. On the relatively few occasions when he wanted to eat meat — for example, during festivals, pilgrimages to sacred shrines or when celebrating happy family events or the arrival of guests — the farmer (or his servant) would kill a sheep,[33] a

---

30   Ibid. 35:13ff.
31   Ibid. 2:2.   32   Radin, *op. cit.*, pp. 148ff.
33   Cf. II Sam. 12:1–4 for the parable of the poor man's lamb slaughtered by a rich man to entertain his guest.

goat or an ox, and he and his wife would personally see to the cooking, roasting and baking.

An instructive example is the story of the visit of the three "angels" to Abraham, who was not, to be sure, a settled farmer but conducted himself with characteristic hospitality. He first ordered his wife Sarah to "make ready quickly three measures of fine flour, knead it, and make cakes".[34] Abraham himself "ran to the herd and took a calf, tender and choice, and gave it to the servant, who hastened to prepare it. Then he took curds and milk, and the calf which he had prepared, and set it before them".[35] The entire process of catering for the guests is carried out at home, without any recourse to outside assistance.

Of all the domestic chores, perhaps the most difficult was that of grinding the grain into flour. It was hard labor, done by placing the grains between rectangular millstones (with rounded corners), which were then manipulated so as to crush the grains into flour. Alternatively, the grains might be placed in a earthenware pot or mortar, where they were pounded and ground with a wooden pestle until the husk was separated from the kernel.[36] This method was so laborious that possession of millstones was considered vital even for the poorest, and neither the upper nor the lower millstone were ever to be taken in pledge for a debt, since "he would be taking a life in pledge".[37]

Because grinding was such hard work, it was, in a male-oriented society, usually given to women, especially female slaves.[38] In Isaiah (47:2), fallen Babylon is depicted as reduced to menial slavery: "Take the millstones and grind meal".[39] However, male prisoners might be humiliated in the same manner, and one of the most tragic biblical scenes is that of the blind and weakened Samson forced to grind in the prison of Gaza.[40]

Despite such occasional incidents, grinding remained by and large a female monopoly. In the story of the siege of the tower of Thebez, we are told that when Abimelech king of Shechem approached the tower, trying

---

34   Gen. 18:6. The "cakes" were probably flat wafers.
35   Ibid. vss. 7–8.
36   Radin, *The Life of the People in Biblical Times* (Philadelphia, 1943), p. 149.
37   Deut. 24:6.
38   Exod. 11:5.
39   Radin, *op. cit.*, p. 150.
40   Jud. 16:21.

to set it on fire, a woman threw a millstone on Abimelech's head and crushed his skull.[41] In Radin's words: "She took the weapon nearest to her hand".[42]

Fortunately for women, grinding was not their main occupation. For most of their time the farmer's wife and daughters were usually engaged in spinning and weaving clothes for the family. In later times, the ideal "woman of worth" (whose total accomplishments were closer to a male dream than to a female reality) would herself be a "craftsman" (or "craftsperson") of no mean accomplishments. She would sew, spin and weave "with willing hands",[43] providing garments for her household, especially, we are told, winter clothing, so that "she is not afraid of snow".[44] In addition, she would make the coverings and clothing of fine linen or purple, including linen garments and girdles for sale to the foreign (Canaanite or Phoenician) merchant.[45]

Of course, before the worthy lady of the house could begin her spinning and weaving, a good deal of preliminary work had to be done to provide her with the raw material for the exercise of her nimble fingers. Shepherds had to shear the fleece from the sheep — usually a major occasion in the somewhat monotonous life of the shepherds, culminating in a great feast with drinking galore.[46] The wool had to be sorted out according to color and quality, washed and dried. It then had to be carded — i.e., separated into single fibers, which in turn were combed into straight yarn. All this was done by men; but once the yarn was ready, it was usually spun and woven by women into garments — as well as hangings, coverings, draperies and rugs. In later times, however, with increasing specialization and a growing demand for artistic weaving and embroidery, male weavers and artists took over much of the better-class work.[47]

Although primitive agriculture and home industries continued to be the main source of livelihood for the masses, the period of the monarchy witnessed a more highly developed system of managing large estates and,

---

41   Ibid. 10:53.
42   *Op. cit.*, p. 150.
43   Prov. 31:13.
44   Ibid. v. 21.
45   Ibid. vss. 19–24.
46   I Sam. 25:2ff.; ibid. 25:36; cf. Gen. 31:19.
47   Cf. Radin. *op. cit.*, pp. 154f.

in particular, royal lands. The various branches of agriculture were organized along "modern" and presumably more rational lines. King David, for example, created an entire bureaucracy to be in charge of the royal estates and to supervise agricultural laborers in the fields and vineyards; wine and olive presses; as well as the royal herds, flocks, asses and camels.[48]

Some two and a half centuries later, King Uzziah of Judah, who was a lineal descendant of King David, distinguished himself as a large-scale farmer — "for he loved husbandry".[49] Among his possessions were "large (herds of) cattle", for whom "he hewed out many cisterns",[50] and extensive estates "in the hill-country and in the fertile lands".[51] The cultivation of the olive would also seem to have been a large-scale operation. The production of olive oil was often undertaken in veritable factories, as recent excavations in Ekron (Tel Miqne) have amply demonstrated.[52] The large number of olive presses discovered there and occasionally elsewhere points to the existence of a major industry. The huge amounts of olives needed to keep the olive presses busy could hardly have been supplied by small individual farmers. We may assume that among the Israelites, as among the Philistines, large agricultural estates were gradually becoming more common. Nevertheless, such large-scale agriculture (including olive growing), requiring a considerable labor force,[53] was the exception not the rule. The masses no doubt continued to cultivate their land or tend their herds in the ancient, primitive, time-honored manner.

3. Arts and Crafts

While the simple life of the Israelites — "a people that dwells alone and is not reckoned among the nations"[54] — inevitably slowed down the

---

48 I Chron. 27:25–31.
49 II Chron. 26:10.
50 Ibid.
51 Ibid.
52 Oral communication from Dr. Barry M. Gittlen, a distinguished archaeologist, who is Field Archaeologist at the Tel Miqne excavations.
53 Ibid.
54 Num. 23:9.

process of learning from artistic but pagan neighbors, there was no lack of appreciation for the art of the craftsman. The Hebrew language itself gave due recognition to the close association between craft and art (compare English *art* — *artisan*), and the two most commonly used words for craftsman — *harash* [55] and *omman* (or *umman*) — also signify the artist who was held in high esteem.

As early as in the fourth chapter of Genesis, some of the legendary pioneers of art and craftsmanship are commemorated, despite the fact that they and their descendants played no discernible role in Israel's history. Thus, Jubal, a descendant of Cain, was said to have been the ancestor "of all those who played the lyre and the pipe"; [56] while his half-brother, Tubal-Cain, is the first man recorded to have been a "forger of all instruments of bronze and iron". [57] The craft of the smith who knew how to weld iron and brass into swords and plowshares, utensils, receptacles and chariots was, in fact, one of the oldest of all specialized crafts, vital alike in peace and war. [58]

In early biblical times, the nomadic tribe of the Kenites — who were closely associated with the Israelites, specifically with the tribe of Judah, and were even related by marriage to Moses [59] — were itinerant smiths or tinkers, practicing their craft in southern Judah, the Negev and the Aravah. It has been suggested that they may have introduced the crafts of mining and metallurgy to the Israelites, and that Moses may have learned from them the art of making the bronze serpent which miraculously healed the Israelites who had been bitten by snakes. [60]

During the reign of King Solomon — probably even earlier — copper mining and smelting became a highly sophisticated industry, which enabled Solomon to have the bronze pillars of the Temple and its vessels cast by skilled workmen. [61] We are told that there was such an abundance of bronze that the total weight of the numerous bronze Temple vessels

---

55 *Harash* was originally associated with woodwork, and only later did it include the metalworker, too; cf. M. Wischnitzer, *A History of Jewish Crafts and Guilds* (New York, 1965), p. 2.
56 Gen. 4:21.
57 Ibid. v. 22.
58 Cf. Radin, *op. cit.*, p. 161.
59 Judges 1:16; 4:11; I Sam. 15:6.
60 Num. 21:6–9; cf. G.M. Landes, *The Interpreter's Dictionary of the Bible*, vol. 3 (Nashville–New York, 1962), pp. 6f.
61 I Kings 7:15ff.; II Chron. 3:15ff.; 4:1ff.

was unknown.[62] During the excavations, in 1938–40, at Tell el-Kheleifeh, at the southern end of the Aravah desert, the largest ancient copper refinery in the entire Near East was uncovered.[63] The refinery was in all probability worked by slave labor recruited from prisoners-of-war[64] — a practice initiated by King David when he enslaved the vanquished Ammonites.[65] Although morally deplorable, it was an improvement on the more primitive and cruel practice of murdering prisoners-of-war.

Solomon made lavish use of copper and bronze in the adornment of the Temple.[66] His chief architect was Hiram (or Huram) of Tyre, the son of an Israelite mother and a Tyrian father, "a worker in bronze", from whom he probably learned his craft expertise.[67] Hiram is described as "full of wisdom, understanding and skill, for making any work in bronze".[68]

The casting of the bronze pillars and vessels of the Temple was done in the Jordan valley "in the clay ground between Succoth and Zarethan"[69] — identified by Albright as the valley east of the Jordan and north of the river Jabbok.[70] The reason for this location was presumably the existence of a long-established metal refinery in the area.

Hiram was by no means the only Temple architect in Israel. Long before him, we hear of a great Israelite sanctuary builder, Bezalel son of Uri. Special praise was accorded to him when he, together with Oholiab son of Ahisamach, built the tabernacle in the wilderness. Bezalel is described as having been "filled ... with the spirit of God, with ability, with intelligence, with knowledge and with all craftsmanship, ... to devise artistic designs, to work in gold and silver and bronze, in cutting stones for setting and in carving wood for work in every skilled craft".[71]

62 I Kings 7:47; II Chron. 4:18.
63 Cf. N. Glueck, "The Excavations of Solomon's Seaport: Ezion-geber" in *Annual Report of the Smithsonian Institution*, 1941, pp. 453–478.
64 Cf. M. Wischnitzer, *op. cit.*, p. 3.
65 II Sam. 12:31.
66 I Kings 7:15ff.; II Chron. 3:15ff.; 4:1ff.; cf. F.V. Winnett, *The Interpreter's Dictionary of the Bible*, vol. I, s.v. Bronze, p. 467.
67 I Kings 7:13f.; II Chron. 2:12f.
68 I Kings 7:14; cf. II Chron. ibid.
69 I Kings 7:45–46; cf. II Chron. 4:17.
70 W.F. Albright, *Archaeology and Religion of Israel* (Baltimore, 1942), p. 137.
71 Exod. 35:30–33; cf. ibid., 31:2ff.

Oholiab is depicted as "a craftsman, and a skillful workman, and a weaver in colors, in blue, and in purple, and in scarlet, and fine linen".[72] Both Bezalel and Oholiab were endowed with the "ability to do every sort of work done by the craftsmen or by the designer, or by an embroiderer in blue and purple and scarlet yarns, and in fine linen".[73] In addition, they were both "inspired ... to teach" their crafts to students.[74] Significantly, the first art school ever established in modern Jerusalem was named Bezalel after the great architect of the first sanctuary of Israel.

The skill of dyeing clothes in many colors as well as embroidery and artistic weaving, in which women would seem to have excelled,[75] was a highly developed art in ancient Israel. The beautiful multi-colored patterns of embroidered apparel which were produced, no doubt, by gifted Israelite women, enjoyed a great reputation even outside the borders of Israel. Thus, we are told, in Deborah's Song, one of the most ancient poems in biblical literature, how Sisera's mother was anxiously awaiting her son's return from the war against Israel, laden with spoils "of dyed garments embroidered".[76] Not only Sisera, but also his men were to return with "two pieces of dyed work embroidered for the neck of every spoiler".[77]

Not everybody could afford the luxury of artistically woven garments, which are not often mentioned in the Bible, and then mainly in connection with the making of the Tabernacle.[78] Wealthier aristocrats, however, did make sure that their wives and daughters were dressed in the best that money could buy. The austere prophet Isaiah, denouncing the haughty and wanton "daughters of Zion" with their mincing gait, "making a tinkling with their feet",[79] lists what looks like a women's department store inventory of exquisite garments and ornaments of which the vain luxury-loving women would be stripped. The expensive garments include veils, turbans, tiaras, armlets, sashes, kerchiefs, aprons, mantles, shawls, lace gowns and gauze robes. The ornaments of which

---

72   Ibid. 38:23.
73   Ibid. 35:35.
74   Ibid. v. 34.
75   Cf. Radin, *op. cit.*, p. 157.
76   Jud. 5:30.
77   Ibid.
78   Exod. 26:1 ff.; ibid. vss. 31–37; 35:5; ibid. vss. 23–26; 35; 36:8 ff.; ibid. v. 35; 38:9 ff.; ibid. v. 23; 39:1 ff.; ibid. vss. 22–29.
79   Isaiah 3:16.

they would be deprived comprised anklets, fillets, crescents, pendants, bracelets, amulets, signet rings and nose jewels.[80]

In a parable of the loving husband (God) who provides his beloved (Israel) with the richest apparel obtainable, the prophet Ezekiel represents God as saying to Israel:

> I clothed you also with embroidered cloth and shod you with leather, I swathed you in fine linen and covered you with silk. And I decked you with ornaments, and put bracelets on your arms, and a chain on your neck. And I put a ring on your nose, and earrings in your ears, and a beautiful crown on your head. Thus you were decked with gold and silver; and your raiment was of fine linen, and silk, and embroidered cloth. ...[81]

It is evident that such costly apparel was worn only by wealthy women. Hence, to satisfy this limited but growing market, skillful artists must have been at work producing exquisite garments of every description. Despite these proofs of artistic activities in later times, in other respects the Israelites were extremely backward compared with Egyptians, Babylonians, Phoenicians, Canaanites, Philistines and other Near Eastern peoples.

When King David wanted to build his palace, he had to get craftsmen from Tyre because he could not find any in Israel.[82] As already mentioned, King Solomon, too, had to invite a master builder from Tyre to build the Temple of Jerusalem.[83] Solomon even had to get Phoenician woodcutters to cut cedars from the Lebanon because, as he frankly admitted, "there is no one among us who knows how to cut timber like the Sidonians".[84]

In the pre-monarchic age there was not even an arms industry to speak of in Israel. The Philistines made sure — apparently by excluding the Israelites from the iron market which the Philistines controlled — that "there was no smith to be found throughout all the land of Israel; for the Philistines said, 'Lest the Hebrews make themselves swords and spears' ".[85] Inevitably, the Hebrews became totally dependent on the Philistines for the repair of agricultural implements.[86]

---

80 Ibid. 3:18–24.   81 Ezek. 16:10–13.   82 II Sam. 5:11.
83 I Kings 7:13f.; II Chron. 2:6, 12f.
84 I Kings 5:20; cf. II Chron. 2:7f.
85 I Sam. 13:19; cf. M. Wischnitzer, *op. cit.*, p. 2.
86 I Sam. 13:20. M. Wischnitzer, *op. cit.*, p. 6, points out that "the workmen and the merchants who procured stone and timber were paid in cash" by the foremen who

This dismal state of affairs soon came to an end under the monarchy. The Israelites soon learned some of the arts and crafts in which their neighbors excelled, and as trade developed, and the economy expanded, Israelite master craftsmen made their appearance. About a century after Solomon, large-scale Temple repairs were efficiently carried out by native builders, carpenters, masons and stonecutters.[87] Around 621 B.C.E., similar repairs were undertaken by local carpenters, builders and masons.[88] By the end of the First Commonwealth, craftsmen and smiths formed such an important social class in Jerusalem that Nebuchadnezzar, King of Babylonia, specially selected them for deportation[89] — partly perhaps because they were considered the aristocrats of labor,[90] but mainly, no doubt, in order to prevent the large-scale manufacture of arms by the Judaeans.

The Bible mentions a considerable number of craft tools, such as the hammer, the anvil, the ax, the tongs (or pincers), the plane, compasses, blowers and the engraving tool.[91] We hear also of copper mining,[92] stone-hewing (or quarrying),[93] stone-engraving and seal-engraving.[94]

Seals were carefully guarded and cherished as prized possessions.[95] Thus, the shepherdess of the Song of Songs asks her beloved, "Set me as a seal upon your heart, as a seal upon your arm".[96] For the most part, however, seals were worn only by distinguished persons such as tribal chieftains and kings.[97] During the Israelite monarchy, seals became

supervised the repair work and were trusted by the workers — a procedure repeated during the reign of Josiah. The priests, according to Wischnitzer, "were removed from the role of employers and thus prevented from spending Temple money on articles of luxury".

87 II Kings 12:2; II Chron. 24:12f.
88 II Kings 22:5–6; II Chron. 34:11.
89 II Kings 24:14,16; Jer. 29:2.
90 Cf. Radin, op. cit., p. 162.
91 Cf. Exod. 25:38; 32:4; 37:23; Num. 4:9; Deut. 19:5; 20:19; Jud. 4:21; I Kings 6:7; 7:49; Is. 6:6; 8:1; 10:15; 41:7; 44:12f.; Jer. 6:29; 10:3f.; 23:29; II Chron. 4:29.
92 Deut. 8:9.
93 Cf. Exod. 34:1ff.; I Kings 5:29; II Kings 12:13; 22:6; Ezra 3:7; I Chron. 22:2,15; II Chron. 2:1,17; 24:12; 34:11.
94 Exod. 28:11,21,36; 39:6,14,30.
95 Jer. 22:24; Hag. 2:23.
96 Cant. 8:6.
97 Cf. Gen. 38:18,25; I Kings 21:8; Esth. 3:12; 8:8,10.

increasingly common, and the large number of seals, including personal name seals, found in the course of archaeological excavations, testifies to the large-scale manufacture and use of seals.[98]

During prosperous times, there was a growing demand for luxury items such as ivory, which was carved for inlaid decorations. King Solomon had a "throne of ivory";[99] while King Ahab's extravagance surpassed even that of Solomon when he had an "ivory house" built for himself.[100] A royal wedding poem preserved in the book of Psalms speaks of "ivory palaces"[101] — indicating that some kings may have had more than one ivory-inlaid palace built to satisfy vanity and enhance glory.

The luxury-loving upper classes were not slow to imitate royal extravagance. The prophet Amos excoriates "those who lie upon beds of ivory"[102] and threatens that "the houses of ivory shall perish"[103] — presumably along with their fat drunken denizens who indulged their luxurious tastes at the expense of the poor.[104]

Prophetic disapproval notwithstanding, craftsmen and artists must have been employed in considerable numbers to fashion such enormously expensive items for the rich. The archaeological evidence attests to the widespread use of ivory among the upper classes.[105] They were not, however, permitted to enjoy their luxurious lifestyle for very long. The Assyrian conquerors were insatiable, and they included ivory, gold and silver among their spoils. About 700 B.C.E., Sennacherib King of Assyria claims in an inscription to have received an enormous amount of tribute from Hezekiah King of Judah, including couches and chairs inlaid with ivory as well as other treasures of every kind.[106] Undoubtedly,

---

98   Cf. A. Reifenberg, *Ancient Hebrew Arts* (New York, 1950), pp. 31–37. Of special interest is the discovery, some years ago, of a seal belonging to Baruch son of Neriah, Jeremiah's faithful disciple. Cf. N. Avigad, "Baruch the Scribe and Jerahmeel the King's Son", in *Israel Exploration Journal*, vol. 28 (1978), pp. 52 ff.

99   I Kings 10:18; II Chron. 9:17.

100 I Kings 22:39.

101 Psalms 45:9.

102 Amos 6:4.

103 Ibid. 3:15.

104 Cf. ibid. 4:1.

105 Cf. J.B. Pritchard, in *The Interpreter's Dictionary of the Bible*, vol. 2 (Nashville-New York, 1962), pp. 774 f.

106 J.B. Pritchard, *Ancient Near Eastern Texts*, 3rd edition (Princeton, 1969), p. 288.

the aristocracy and other wealthy elements did not fare any better than the king. One way or another, their extravagant and often ill-gotten riches were carried off by foreign conquerors.

Both luxury and ordinary crafts required expert workmen who lived, for the most part, in large or medium sized cities where there was a market for their manufactured goods. We hear about stone masons[107] who apparently made, among other things, ornamental stone pillars; gold and silver smiths;[108] and carpenters or wood workers,[109] who built houses, made furniture and carved pictures and statues — the latter two mainly for religious cultic purposes. Both stone masons and carpenters are mentioned in connection with the preparations for the building of Solomon's Temple[110] as well as the Second Temple (c. 520 B.C.E.). On the latter occasion, we are told that these indispensable artisans were paid in cash, while the Phoenician workmen, who transported timber from the Lebanon by sea to Jaffa, were remunerated in kind — food, drink and olive oil.[111] Evidently, the skilled stone masons and carpenters were valued more highly than the relatively unskilled Phoenician porters and maritime transport workers.

Last but not least, there was the blacksmith, who, in addition to his ordinary work, also took a modest share in making inexpensive idols for those who could not afford high quality ones.[112] Such was the importance attached to the blacksmith that in Deutero-Isaiah he is depicted as having been specially created by God:

"Behold, I have created the smith who blows the fire of coals and produces an instrument (or weapon) for its own purpose".[113]

The manufacture of idols seems to have been a major craft industry to the very end of the First Commonwealth. In Isaiah 40:19f. and 44:12–19, we find graphic descriptions of the manufacture of idols. The gold, silver and iron smiths played a particularly important role in the manufacture of both secular ornaments and precious and artistically beautiful cult objects, including idols.[114]

---

107 Cf. Exod. 28:11;31:5;35:33; II Sam. 5:11; I Chron. 14:1;22:15; II Chron. 24:12.

108 Cf. Jud. 17:4; Is. 40:19; 41:7; 46:6; Jer. 6:29; 10:9,14; 51:7; Mal. 3:3; Prov. 25:4; Neh. 3:8,31,32; I Chron. 29:5.

109 Cf. II Sam. 5:11; II Kings 12:12; Is. 40:20; 44:13; Jer. 10:3; I Chron. 14:1; 22:15; cf. Exod. 31:5; 35:33.

110 I Kings 5:32 [18].   111 Ezra 3:7; cf. Wischnitzer, *op. cit.*, p. 13.

112 Is. 44:12.   113 Ibid. 54:16.   114 Cf. ibid. 44:12.

The fact that so many craftsmen were engaged in what might be termed the cult industry, thus forming a vested interest in idolatry, may have influenced, more than we suspect, the resistance encountered by the iconoclastic Puritan prophetic party in its endless efforts to eradicate idolatry from Israel.[115]

So far, we have been dealing mainly with the major skills requiring some artistic talents. The Bible mentions, however, many common trades and crafts, which assumed increasing importance with the development of urban civilization in many parts of the Holy Land.

The walls and fortifications built by the kings of Israel and Judah required the employment of a large pool of skilled or semi-skilled labor — as well as the importation of materials and finished products from neighboring countries.[116] During the reigns of David, Solomon and some of the later kings of Israel and Judah, trade and industry flourished, providing employment for workers of all types.

Particularly widespread was the craft of the potter. Earthenware vessels were in universal demand — there is hardly an archaeological site in which ancient pottery has not been unearthed — and since such vessels were very fragile,[117] they needed constant replacement. No less than 34 Hebrew and Aramaic terms are applied to the pottery vessels of the Old Testament. They include bowls of every size and shape as well as cooking pots, frying pans, griddles, cups, plates, jars, pitchers, juglets and lamps. They were indispensable for daily life, and occasionally were given artistic form, decorated, stamped, and made into objects of beauty.[118] There were also writing tablets, children's toys and numerous Canaanite cult objects (including household fertility idols!) made of clay — a practice which was anathema to Judaism but nonetheless indulged in by the Israelites throughout the First Commonwealth.

---

115 Cf. Acts 19:23ff. for the similar opposition of the silversmiths of Ephesus who objected to the apostle Paul's preaching against idolatry which threatened the livelihood of the idol manufacturers.
116 Cf. M. Wischnitzer, *op. cit.*, p. 4; W.F. Albright, *The Archaeology of Palestine* (London, 1949), p. 122; Y. Yadin, "The Fourth Season of Excavations at Hazor", *Biblical Archaeologist* xxii, 1 (Feb. 1959), fig. 11.
117 Cf. Is. 30:14; Pss. 2:9; Lam. 4:2.
118 Cf. J. L. Kelso, art. "Pottery," in *The Interpreter's Dictionary of the Bible*, vol. 3 (Nashville–New York, 1962), pp. 846–853.

So important was the pottery industry that royal potteries were established[119] for the large-scale manufacture of official government storage jars, partly for commercial purposes and partly for the payment of taxes in produce. The jars were stamped with Hebrew letters reading *LAMELECH* — "For the king" or "Belonging to the king" — followed by the name of the city where they were produced or stored.[120]

The Valley of Hinnom, which is rich in clay and close to water supplies, was a center of pottery manufacture, and the nearest city gate in Jerusalem was therefore called "the Potsherd Gate".[121] It was there that Jeremiah denounced the atrocities committed in the Hinnom Valley, where child sacrifices in honor of pagan deities were still being offered in the early days of Jeremiah's ministry.[122] To illustrate the doom predicted by the prophet, he broke an earthenware flask, saying, "Thus says the Lord of hosts: So will I break this place and this city, as one breaks a potter's vessel, so that it can never be mended".[123] Similarly, Deutero-Isaiah depicted the Persian conqueror Cyrus as trampling on rulers "as on mortar, as the potter treads clay".[124]

Mass production of pottery — necessitated by its fragile nature — was greatly facilitated by the invention of the improved double wheel and the use of cheaper clay. Better techniques reduced production costs and lowered prices.[125]

Potters were nevertheless very particular about the manner in which they executed their work, and if the pottery produced was not up to mark, they would have no hesitation in breaking it and making another vessel out of the same material. The prophet Jeremiah specially went to a "potter's house" (i.e. workshop) to watch the process, and his description of the potter's work and the moral that he drew from it, became a classic statement frequently cited in later literature:

> I went down to the potter's house, and there he was working at his wheel. And whenever the vessel he was making of clay was spoiled in the potter's hand, he reworked it into another vessel, as it

119 I Chron. 4:23.
120 M. Wischnitzer, *op. cit.*, p. 9.
121 Jer. 19:2; cf. M. Wischnitzer, *op. cit.*, p. 8.
122 Jer. 19:3ff.
123 Ibid. 19:10–11.
124 Isaiah 41:25.
125 Cf. M. Wischnitzer, *op. cit.*, pp. 8–9.

seemed good to the potter to do.[126] Then the word of the Lord came to me, saying: "O house of Israel, can I not do with you as this potter has done? says the Lord. Behold, like the clay in the potter's hand, so are you in my hand, O house of Israel".[127]

Jeremiah's "clay in the potter's hand" probably supplied one of the titles given to God who is frequently referred to as the *Yozer* ("potter" or one who forms or shapes an object) of the world, of man, of Israel or even of individuals. God the Creator (*Boré*) is also the *Yozer*, and the two terms are often used as synonyms, though they are actually different in meaning.[128] In this way the humble trade of the potter was elevated into a divine calling.

In all fairness, though, it must be added that God was invested with titles to other trades as well. He was the first *Shadchan* (matchmaker), since it was He who introduced Adam and Eve to each other,[129] and, according to the rabbis, He has continued to occupy Himself with matchmaking ever since.[130] Indeed, God did not deem it beneath His dignity to adorn brides so as to make them more attractive to their prospective husbands.[131]

God was also the first tailor, clothing Adam and Eve in skin garments[132] which, though perhaps not quite suited to modern tastes and certainly not in accordance with the latest fashion, were an immense improvement on the girdles of fig leaves made in all haste by the first

---

126 A similar scene was witnessed by a modern writer, W.M. Thomson, who watched an Arab potter at work: "From some defect in the clay, or because he had taken too little, the potter suddenly changed his mind, crushed his growing jar instantly into a shapeless mass of mud, and beginning anew, fashioned it into a totally different vessel" (Jeremiah, Soncino edition, London, 1949, p. 125).

127 Jer. 18:3–6. The metaphor of clay in the hand of the potter as a symbol of complete impotence before a higher power became quite popular (cf., e.g., Is. 45:9; 64:7) and inspired a beautiful Hebrew liturgical poem sung during the Day of Atonement evening service:

> Lo! as the potter mouldeth plastic clay
> To form his varying fancy doth display;
> So in thy hand, O God of love, are we;
> Thy bond regard, let sin be veiled from Thee.

128 Cf., e.g., Is. 45:7: "I *form* light and *create* darkness".

129 Gen. 2:18–22.

130 Cf. *Gen. R.* 68, 4; *Lev. R.* 8, 1, *et al.*

131 Cf. *Eccl. R.* 7, 2–3.

132 Gen. 3:21.

human pair.[133] God was also a desert guide for the Israelites[134] — an extremely important function at the time — and a physician — "I am the Lord your healer".[135] In time of war, God could be a warrior, too — "The Lord is a man of war";[136] and when the Canaanite general, Sisera, was defeated by the Israelites, "they fought from heaven, the stars in their courses fought against Sisera".[137]

All this should not be regarded as humorous asides, but as serious evidence of the high regard in which certain crafts or trades were held. If they were important enough for the community, it was not beneath the dignity of God to become not just a sort of divine patron saint, but an active participant in the pursuit of such trades.

Other crafts and trades mentioned in the Bible include those of the washermen or "fullers",[138] who used a special field outside the city where they washed, beat and stretched their woolen products,[139] as well as cooks, bakers and perfumers — the latter, for the most part, were women employed in wealthy homes or royal courts.[140] Later, however, with increasing urbanization and commercialization, male bakers and perfumers[141] became more frequent.[142] At the time when Samuel and Saul met for the first time, Samuel seems to have employed a male cook to prepare the festive banquet;[143] but since the Hebrew for "cook" *tabbah* can also mean "slaughterer", we may suspect that our worthy cook and others like him, had to do some "moonlighting" in order to make ends meet. We do not hear of washerwomen, though they undoubtedly existed and are mentioned in rabbinic literature.[144] In major cities there were

---

133 Ibid. 3:7.
134 Exod. 13:21; Num. 10:33.
135 Exod. 15:27.
136 Exod. 15:3; cf. also ibid. 14:14:"The Lord shall fight for you"; cf. ibid. 14:25; *et al.*
137 Jud. 5:20.
138 Is. 7:3.
139 Cf. Radin, *op. cit.*, p. 160.
140 I Sam. 8:13.
141 Cf. Jer. 37:21; Neh. 3:8.
142 Cf. Radin, *op. cit.*, p. 152, who does not, however, distinguish between the early and late biblical periods. His assumption that baking was almost a male monopoly is most improbable, especially in the rural districts, where baking had been done by the women of the household since time immemorial.
143 I Sam. 9:23f.
144 Cf., e.g., *T.Y. Ned.* V, 1, 39a; *T.B. Mak.* 24a.

entire streets or quarters in which members of a guild lived and worked.[145] Thus, in Jerusalem there was a bakers' street from which Jeremiah obtained his bread ration during the siege of Jerusalem by the Babylonians.[146]

4. The Medical Profession

The medical profession enjoyed a certain reputation, though, at times, it was associated with magic practices.[147] Joseph had his Egyptian "physicians"; but characteristically he is recorded as having required their attendance not while his father Jacob was alive and sick, but only after his death when the services of "physicians" were required for embalming Jacob's body.[148] Like everybody else in ancient Egypt, the medical profession, too, cared more about the dead than about the living.

In the Land of Israel, however, the physicians, some of whom combined their practice with the priesthood (especially in the diagnosis of certain leprous and skin diseases involving problems of ritual purity), would seem to have been familiar with the medicinal properties of herbs, and they knew how to dress wounds. Thus, when the prophet Isaiah tried to describe the diseased state of the nation, he depicted it as full of "bruises and sores and festering wounds; they have not been pressed out, or bound up, or softened with oil".[149] Isaiah himself seems to have been familiar with the art of healing; for when Hezekiah King of Judah became dangerously ill with a boil which apparently grew septic and

---

145 Cf. Radin, *op. cit.*, p. 160; I. Mendelsohn, "Guilds in Ancient Palestine", *Bulletin of the American Schools of Oriental Research*, 8 (Dec. 1940), pp. 17–21.

146 Jer. 37:21.

147 Cf. Radin, *op. cit.*, p. 171.

148 Gen. 50:2. According to Julius Preuss, *Biblisch-talmudische Medizin*, third edition (Berlin, 1923), p. 18, Joseph's *roph'im* (= healers, physicians) were not necessarily real physicians. The term may have been borrowed to denote embalmers because the Hebrews did not embalm their dead — hence they lacked a specific term for this practice. However, since the Hebrews were frequently in contact with Egypt and lived there for centuries, they could hardly have been ignorant of the widespread Egyptian practice of embalming the dead.The use of the term *roph'im* for embalmers indicates that physicians were familiar with the art of embalming. It may well have been the most profitable part of their practice.

149 Is. 1:6.

poisoned his blood-system, the prophet, who had at first predicted the king's early demise,[150] hit on a cure which is known to have been used by veterinary surgeons in Ugarit, Northern Syria, as early as the fourteenth century B.C.E. It was a remedy made of boiled figs which was applied to the wound or the boil. Its mollifying effect and healing properties helped to cure the king of his malady, and he lived for another 15 years.[151]

The prophet Jeremiah, too, appears to have known something of contemporary medicine. Bewailing the sickness of Judaean society, he bitterly lamented, "Is there no balm in Gilead? Is there no physician there?"[152] Thus, Gilead in Transjordan had the distinction of producing balm (or balsam), which has a mollifying effect on wounds and was widely used to soothe sores and inflammations of all kinds. Hence also the relative abundance of physicians in Gilead.

Needless to say, the physicians were not always successful in their efforts. The Code of Hammurabi, which is known to have exercised considerable influence on the legal system of the Hebrews, prescribes some stiff penalties for medical malpractice if the victim happened to be a freeman. Thus, if a surgeon performed a major operation "with a bronze lancet", causing a "seignior's" death or, if he "opened up the eye-socket of a seignior" and thereby destroyed the patient's eye, the surgeon's hand was to be cut off.[153]

Biblical physicians, though not subjected to such ruthless punishment, were not exactly held in high esteem. When Job had had his fill of suffering, and his friends were trying to brainwash him that it must all be his own fault, since it was inconceivable that a perfect God should punish an innocent man, the unhappy man almost insulted his friends, shouting at them, "Worthless physicians are you all".[154]

A similar experience must have befallen King Asa of Judah who, "sought help from physicians" against a severe disease which affected both his feet.[155] The pious Chronicler, who must have been a forerunner

---

150 II Kings 20:1; Isaiah 38:1.
151 II Kings 20:6f.; Isaiah 38:5,21.
152 Jer. 8:22.
153 Cf. James B. Pritchard, *Ancient Near Eastern Texts relating to the Old Testament*, third edition (Princeton, 1969), p. 175.
154 Job 13:4.
155 II Chron. 16:12f.

of the Christian Scientists, considered such medical consultations worse than useless. Asa should have consulted God, and since he did not, it served him right that he died within a couple of years after the onset of his illness.[156] To some extent, however he was compensated for his suffering; for, we are told, "they laid him on a bier which had been filled with various kinds of spices prepared by the perfumer's art; and they made a very great fire in his honor".[157] One can only hope that the physicians had a hand in all this. One likes to think that they made themselves useful after all. Like the perfumers, they would take care of patients when they were dead, no less than when they were alive, perhaps even more so.

The somewhat low esteem in which physicians were held at times may have been due to a perception that their therapeutic activities amounted to usurping a divine prerogative. "I am the Lord your healer",[158] said the Almighty, promising "I will put none of the diseases upon you which I put upon the Egyptians" — provided Israel was obedient to the divine will.[159] When men, in their folly, sinned and were punished with sickness, all they needed to recover was to cry to the Lord in their trouble, and He "sent forth his word, and healed them".[160] Ideally, therefore, supplication and prayer were better healing agents than physicians and medicines.[161]

5. The Wailing Women

The wailing women, on the other hand, confined their art to funerals, leaving the living in peace, except perhaps when they were teaching their daughters or neighbors to utter doleful dirges for the departed. These wailing women were no amateurs, and their profession was highly regarded in a society which honored the dead much more than it ever did the living. No one, not even the poorest in Israel, could be buried without suitable lamentation and weeping. Unfortunately, relatives could not

156 Ibid. v. 13.
157 Ibid. v. 14.
158 Exod. 15:26; cf. also Deut. 23:39, Job 5:18.
159 Exod. 15:26.
160 Psalms 107:17–19.
161 Cf. Preuss, *op. cit.*, pp. 23f.

always be trusted to weep with feeling and utter heart-rending cries to bring tears into other people's eyes. Hence, it was incumbent to hire at least one wailing woman,[162] whose fountain of tears could always be turned on and off at will (depending presumably on the size of the fees). This institution, which was naturally a female monopoly, has survived down to modern times, and in its heyday it represented a skilled craft in which one had to be carefully trained — just as nowadays actors and actresses have to be taught how to portray various emotions. Thus, in an instructive passage, Jeremiah called upon the women of the Land of Judah, "Teach your daughters a lament, and each to her neighbor a dirge. For death has come up into our windows, it has entered our palaces...".[163]

Incidentally, we learn from this passage that daughters would follow in their mothers' footsteps and pursue the same career. The same was usually true of sons, too.[164] In biblical times, at least, it was most unusual for sons of farmers and craftsmen to desert their fathers' occupations. Only in times of crisis do we find unemployed young men looking for any job going — including, if necessary, illegal occupations. Thus, Moses' grandson, Jonathan, a young unemployed Levite from Bethlehem, went North in search of a job, and after a stint as an idolatrous priest at a private shrine, he ended up as chief priest of the tribe of Dan.[165]

6. Levites and Priests

Jonathan was probably not the only one whose career was dramatically changed in times of unrest. The entire tribe of Levi, along with that of Simeon, is originally depicted as a robber tribe wielding "weapons of violence", and Jacob curses their anger and condemns them to be divided in Jacob and scattered in Israel.[166] By the time of Moses' blessing, the Levites who, shortly after the Exodus, had ruthlessly slain the golden calf worshippers,[167] had become respectable and

162 M. Ket. IV, 4.
163 Jer. 10:20f.
164 Cf. Radin, op. cit., p. 16.; R. de Vaux, Ancient Israel, vol. I, p. 77.
165 Jud., Chaps. 17–18.
166 Gen. 49:5ff.
167 Exod. 32:26ff.

dedicated priests who observed the divine precepts, taught them to the people, offered incense and sacrifices and deserved to have their enemies, whoever these might be, destroyed, so that they may rise no more.[168]

7. Traders and Peddlers

Another career of doubtful moral standing was trading and peddling. During early biblical times, there were hardly any Israelite traders, and the very word used for merchant — "Canaanite" — indicates clearly enough that the merchant was a foreigner, most probably a Phoenician who in language, religion and culture was virtually identical with the biblical Canaanites. Thus, as already mentioned, the "woman of worth" "makes linen garments and sells them; she delivers girdles to the merchant" ("the Canaanite").[169] Although she is a woman of exceptional talent and ability, she would not dream of engaging in the hurlyburly business of the market place. She, like most of her Israelite contemporaries, is a primary producer, and it is the foreign merchant who disposes of her products in the market.[170] Only small-scale local markets, where craftsmen and peasants sold their wares and products, may have been in the hands of native Israelites.[170a]

Merchants, most of whom were really peddlers and hucksters, had a bad reputation as gossipers and purveyors of saucy (and often untrue) tales about other people's affairs — so much so that the Hebrew words for "peddler" (*Rokhel*) and "bearing tales" (*Rakhil* — hence also *Rekhilut*) are almost identical. Traders were also distrusted on account of their notorious dishonesty.[171] In the uncomplimentary words of the prophet Hosea, the trader "in whose hands are false balances; he loves to oppress" (i.e., to deceive).[172] There was thus little to attract the ancient Israelites to a business career, and only during the Second Temple period, in the time of Nehemiah (c. 444 B.C.E.), do we hear of a native

---

168 Deut. 33:8ff.
169 Prov. 31:24.
170 Cf. Radin, *op. cit.*, p. 163.
170a Cf. de Vaux, *op. cit.*, p. 78.
171 Cf. Radin, *op. cit.*, p. 165.
172 Hosea 12:8.

trading class which showed its patriotism by participating in the repair of the walls of Jerusalem.[173]

8. Scribes

Finally, we learn about the existence of families or guilds[174] of scribes (*Sopherim*) — mostly Levites and teetotalling Rechabites[175] — who seem to have jealously kept their craft within their own group. Naturally, they tended to live together in certain places, such as Jabez,[176] which was also the name of a clan in southern Judah.[177] Apparently they or, more probably, their Canaanite predecessors bestowed their trademark upon the South Judaean city of Kiriath Sepher (The City of the Scroll or Book), later renamed Debir,[178] possibly because the Canaanite scribes disappeared or lost their functions after the Judahite conquest. Scribes were employed in a variety of jobs:

a) As court scribes, drawing up legal documents, recording business transactions, marriages, divorces, and so on.

b) As royal scribes and recorders, whose function it was to act as royal secretaries and to record the annals and chronicles of the kings. To them we owe some of the historical books of the Bible such as the greater part of Samuel and Kings.

c) As Temple scribes, writing, copying or editing the religious and cultic literature of the nation. There is hardly a book of the Hebrew Bible to which they did not contribute either original material or editorial arrangement. During the Second Commonwealth, these scribes — no longer confined to the Temple (though priests and Levites seem to have specialized as scribes)[179] — engaged in teaching as well as writing, so that the word *Sopher* came to mean school teacher as well as scribe. The violent attacks in the New Testament on the "Pharisees and scribes"[180] were due not to their alleged hypocrisy, but to their exalted status as

173 Neh. 3:31f.
174 Cf. M. Wischnitzer, *op. cit.*, p. 12.
175 Cf. I Chron. 2:55; II Chron. 34:13; cf. also Jer. 35:1ff.
176 I Chron. 2:55.
177 Ibid. 4:9f.
178 Jos. 15:15f.; Jud. 1:11.
179 Cf., e.g., Ezra 7:1-6; I Chron. 24:6.
180 Cf. especially, Matt. chap. 23.

intellectual leaders of the Jewish people. It was under their guidance that the vast majority of the Jews refused to accept Christianity, which appealed only to relatively uneducated Messianic enthusiasts, mainly in Galilee, where Pharisaic and scribal influence had not yet become fully established.

In addition, there were prophetic scribes who recorded the words and deeds of their masters — the Prophets. This is expressly stated in the case of Baruch, Jeremiah's disciple, to whom we owe the book of Jeremiah in its polished literary form.[181] There is, however, little doubt that most of the prophetic books of the Bible were preserved in a similar manner.

9. Indolence condemned

Whatever one's station in life, one was expected to be hard-working and diligent. Laziness was condemned as anti-social, dangerous and intolerable. Wisdom literature, and especially the book of Proverbs — which concludes with the eulogy of the ideal "woman of worth" who "does not eat the bread of idleness",[182] who "rises while it is yet night",[183] and whose "lamp does not go out at night"[184] — is replete with maxims and slogans in favor of regular, diligent work. Industrious activity, we are told, is the only source of wealth, for only "the hand of the diligent makes rich".[185]

At the same time, the book of Proverbs firmly sets itself against any kind of idle indulgence. The sluggard is condemned as an unreliable worker or agent: "Like vinegar to the teeth, and smoke to the eyes, so is the sluggard to those who sent him".[186]

The idler is also warned of the dire fate in store for him if he persists in his unwholesome conduct. Persistent inactivity is bound to result in what might be termed a lethargic, sleepy disposition,[187] so that ultimately the sluggish person would be unable to rouse himself sufficiently for any

181 Jer. 36:32.
182 Prov. 31:27.
183 Ibid. v. 15.
184 Ibid. v. 18.
185 Ibid. 10:4.
186 Ibid. 10:26.
187 Cf. ibid. 19:15.

kind of work. He is therefore warned, "Love not sleep lest you be impoverished: open your eyes, and you will have plenty of bread".[188] In more concrete terms, the sluggard is told that if he refuses to plow in the autumn or winter and then expects to harvest in the summer, he is in for an unpleasant surprise; for he will find nothing to gather in.[189]

Sleepiness was apparently the characteristic quality of the indolent; for we are informed that "as a door turns on its hinges, so does the sluggard on his bed".[190] The sage author of Proverbs, whom we may imagine to have always been up with the lark, gravely admonishes the somnolent idler:

"How long will you lie there, O sluggard? When will you arise from your sleep? A little sleep, a little slumber, a little folding of the hands to rest, and poverty will come upon you as a vagabond, and want as an armed man".[191]

Even those who inherit property from their ancestors must not imagine that they can afford to loaf and do nothing. Relating what was evidently a common experience, the Wisdom teacher tells his disciples:

"I passed by the field of a sluggard, and by the vineyard of a man without sense; and lo, it was all overgrown with thorns; the ground was covered with nettles, and its stone wall was broken down".[192]

The idler is told to take an example from the ant and "consider her ways and be wise"; for "without having any chief, officer or ruler, she prepares her food in the summer and gathers her sustenance in the harvest".[193]

The contrast between the success of the diligent worker and the disgraceful failure of the indolent loafer is vividly drawn in a series of proverbs, which, separated though they are from each other, have this in common that they all aim at arousing the lazy good-for-nothing from his dangerous lethargy:

"A wise son gathers in summer; but he that sleeps in harvest time brings shame".[194] "He that tills his land shall have plenty of land, but he

---

188 Ibid. 20:13.
189 Cf. ibid. 20:4.
190 Ibid. 26:14.
191 Ibid. 6:9–11; cf. 24:33f.
192 Ibid. 24:30f.
193 Ibid. 6:6–8.
194 Ibid. 10:5.

that follows worthless pursuits has no sense".[195] "The soul (i.e., the appetite) of the sluggard craves, and gets nothing; but the soul of the diligent shall be abundantly gratified".[196]

Finally, the arrows of satire are brought to bear upon the lazy drone who will clutch at any excuse to justify his refusal to go out and do an honest day's work: "The sluggard says, 'There is a lion outside! I shall be slain in the streets!' ".[197]

The indolence of the loafer is portrayed in deliberately exaggerated terms, suggesting that he is too lazy even to eat:

"The sluggard buries his hand in the dish; it wears him out to bring it back to his mouth".[198]

The trouble with the indolent is that he cannot even be lectured because he is convinced of his own intellectual superiority: "The sluggard is wiser in his own eyes than seven men who give sensible answers".[199]

These constant warnings against idleness were not academic exercises for the benefit of hypothetical idlers. They reflect a genuine concern with a growing social malaise, which seems to have become a serious problem in Hellenistic times when urbanization and the prevalence of Greek concepts and Greek values tended to undermine the traditional occupations and work habits of the middle and upper class Jewish farmer. There was a serious danger that he would prefer commerce and urban comfort to the backbreaking toil on the land. The Wisdom writers sensed the perils threatening the nation and sought to stem the tide of careless indolence and pleasure-seeking which may have engulfed a considerable section of Jewish youth. It was essential to preserve and restore pristine virtues, of which the work ethic was not the least important.[199a]

---

195 Ibid. 12:11.
196 Ibid. 13:4.
197 Ibid. 22:13.
198 Ibid. 26:15.
199 Ibid. 26:16.
199a It has been plausibly suggested that during the Persian period Zoroastrianism, with its emphasis on the diligent cultivation of the land, may have influenced Judaism in the same direction. The Zoroastrian religion stated that "Whoever sows grain sows holiness". This concept is indirectly echoed by Deutero-Isaiah (45:18), "He (viz. God) did not create it (i.e. the earth) a chaos, He formed it to be inhabited" — an idea which implies cultivation of the land. Cf. H. Weinheimer, Geschichte des Volkes Israel, vol. II (Berlin, 1911), pp. 29–30.

Chapter Two

Industry and Trade in the Hellenistic Age

1. Ecclesiastes on Labor

We do not know to what extent the moralistic preaching of the early Wisdom writers was successful. During the Hellenistic period when Greek influence pervaded every facet of Jewish life, physical labor, which in Greece was performed mainly by women and slaves, was sometimes looked down upon as degrading and unworthy of a man of good breeding. Nevertheless, in later Jewish Wisdom literature, physical work is still valued as a healthy and essential activity. In Koheleth (Ecclesiastes), attributed to King Solomon, but actually written towards the end of the third century B.C.E., the pessimistic spirit of the Hellenistic world is indeed prevalent, so that "all is vanity"; [200] and yet, in spite of this, "Sweet is the sleep of a laboring man, whether he eats little or much". [201] One should never cease from laboring in one's field: "In the morning sow your seed, and at evening withhold not your hand; for you do not know which will prosper, this or that, or whether both alike will be good". [202] Little prospect of success is offered to the idle dreamer: "He who observes the wind will not sow; and he who regards the clouds will not reap". [203] Unwillingness to perform one's work is bound to be disastrous: "Through sloth the roof sinks in, and through idleness of the hands the house leaks". [204]

The evidence of contemporary literature confirms that the masses of the people did, indeed, diligently engage in physical labor — in the

200 Eccles. 1:1; 12:8.
201 Ibid. 5:11.
202 Ibid. 11:6.
203 Ibid. v. 4.
204 Ibid. 10:18.

countryside primarily agriculture, and in cities, arts and crafts as well as commerce. Thus, in the Letter of Aristeas, which appears to have been written in the late third century B.C.E., the Land of Israel is described as "well adapted not only for agriculture but also for commerce", while Jerusalem is depicted as a "city rich in crafts".[205] The people in the countryside have to cultivate the soil, and they enjoy abundant harvests.[206] The author of the Letter of Aristeas valued artisans highly, and opposed the exploitation of workers, advocating instead fair wages for arduous toil.[207]

While the author of the Letter of Aristeas lived in Alexandria, the capital of Egypt, and is likely to have been influenced by the views prevalent among Alexandrian Jews, there is every reason to assume that his ethical views on the dignity of labor and justice for the workers were shared by the Jews of Eretz Israel, where physical labor was traditionally cherished and praised. Only a century before the beginning of the Hellenistic age, Nehemiah was able to mobilize the entire community, skilled as well as unskilled workers, to rebuild the walls of Jerusalem.[208] He could not have succeeded in such an enterprise without the wholehearted cooperation of a people accustomed to all kinds of physical labor.

2. Ben Sira's Views on Labor, Commerce, and Crafts:

a. Idleness

Koheleth's positive attitude to diligent manual work is to some extent shared by the book of Ecclesiasticus composed by Ben Sira about 200 B.C.E. There industriousness is esteemed as a valuable asset. Even hard manual and agricultural labors are not to be shunned, since they are allotted to man by God:

"Hate not laborious work; neither husbandry, which the Most High

205 *The Letter of Aristeas* 114.
206 Ibid. 107–8.
207 Ibid. 258–9.
208 Nehemiah, chapters 3 and 4.

has ordained".[209] Idleness, which "teaches much mischief",[210] is condemned as undesirable and offensive. The indolent, who must never be consulted about anything pertaining to work,[211] is in Ben Sira's eyes an abominable excrescence:

A slothful man is like a filthy stone,
And everyone will hiss at his disgrace.
A slothful man is like the filth of a dunghill,
Whoever takes it up will shake out his hand.[212]

b. Change of Occupation

With the increasing urbanization of Palestine and the new commercial opportunities in the numerous Hellenistic cities founded by the successors of Alexander the Great, there developed — to use a modern term — a new mobility of labor, characteristic of an expanding economy. Sons were no longer content to follow in their fathers' footsteps. The younger generation was excessively drawn to the cities and wanted to make use of the manifold opportunities provided by the huge "common market" established by the urban-centered Hellenistic empires. There was also the pursuit of pleasure in the cities, especially on the part of young aristocrats and men of wealth, though, in the words of the Letter of Aristeas, "every one has a natural tendency towards the pursuit of pleasure".[213] What was especially worrisome was the unplanned growth of cities owing to ever-increasing migration from the villages for the sake of greater opportunities and economic improvement. Egyptian agriculture was already showing signs of decline as a result of this trend, and measures were taken by the Ptolemaic government to control the influx to Alexandria of peasants from the countryside.[214] Since Judaea was under Egyptian rule throughout the third century B.C.E., similar trends were bound to affect the economy of the country.

209 Ecclus. 7:15.
210 Ibid. 33:27.
211 Ibid. 7:11.
212 Ibid. 22:1–2.
213 *The Letter of Aristeas* 108.
214 Ibid. 109 ff.

Ben Sira was none too pleased with these new developments. Conservative in outlook as he was, he loved the old ways and virtues, and preferred the young to follow in the footsteps of their fathers. He was opposed to changing one's occupation, advising his students to "grow old in your work".[215]

c. Commerce

Commercial activities, learned from the Phoenicians and Greeks,[215a] were intensely disliked by Ben Sira, who distrusted businessmen sufficiently to advise his disciples, "Take not counsel with a merchant about merchandise"[216] — no doubt because the inexperienced simpleton was bound to be outsmarted by the clever, unscrupulous merchant. Ben Sira was convinced that business was a tissue of lies and deceit, to which even honest men were bound to succumb once they are exposed to the temptations of profiteering:

A merchant shall hardly keep himself from wrongdoing,
And a huckster shall not be acquitted of sin.
Many have sinned for the sake of gain,
And he that seeks to multiply profit will turn his eye away
(*viz.*, from shady deals).

A nail will stick fast between the joinings of stones,
And sin will thrust itself between buying and selling.
Unless a man holds fast in the fear of the Lord,
His house shall speedily be overthrown.[217]

Ben Sira accordingly advised the budding man of affairs to restrain his greed and keep himself at least from excessive involvement in the complexities of business activity: "My son, why multiply thy business (unduly), seeing that he that hastens to increase gain, shall not go unpunished".[218] Thus, as far as Ben Sira was concerned, a commercial

---

215 Ecclus. 11:20.
215a On the prevalence of Greek loan words in commercial terminology during the Hellenistic–Roman period, cf. J. Klausner, *Ha-Bayit ha-Sheni bi-Gedulato*, pp. 68 ff. On the growth of commerce among the Jews of the Diaspora, cf. L. Herzfeld, *Handelsgeschichte der Juden des Altertums*,[2] pp. 194–270.
216 Ecclus. 37:11.
217 Ibid. 26:29; 27:1–3.
218 Ibid. 11:10.

career, however profitable, could not be recommended to any honest and God-fearing young man.

d. Physicians

Ben Sira had more respect for the physician whose social standing in Hellenistic society was very high, and whose professional services were valued even at royal courts. Unlike some Jewish predecessors of the Christian Scientists,[219] Ben Sira did not regard human healing as opposed to God's purpose.[220] On the contrary, the physician was endowed with the knowledge of his craft by God Himself, who also provided herbs with medicinal properties to cure the sick. Of course, as a religious Jew, Ben Sira did not regard medicine as a substitute for prayer, but he considered that both should be utilized on the principle that God helps those who help themselves:

Honor the physician before you have need of him;[221]
For him also has God allotted.
It is from God that the physician gets wisdom,
And from the King he receives gifts.
The skill of the physician lifts up his head,
And before princes he shall stand.
God brings forth medicines out of the earth,
And let not the discerning man reject them.
Was not water made sweet with wood,
So that every man might be acquainted with His power...?
By means of them the physician assuages pain,
And likewise the apothecary prepares a confection...
My son, in sickness be not negligent;
Pray unto God, for He can heal...
And to the physician also give a place,
And let him not depart, for of him, too, there is need.
For there is a time when successful help is in his power,

---

219 Cf. II Chron. 16:12; see *supra*, Chapter One, p. 20f.
220 Cf. S. Schechter, *Studies in Judaism* (Philadelphia, 1945), II, 76.
221 Cf. *T.Y. Taan.* III, 6, 66d; *Exod. R.* 21, 7; and *Tanh.* Mikketz 10, where this verse is quoted as a popular proverb. Cf. also a similar proverb in Ben Sira 18:19 ("... before you fall ill, take care of your health").

For he also makes supplication to God...
He that sins before his Maker,
Is presumptuous before the physician.[222]

Significantly, the last two lines read in some versions:

He that sins before his Maker
Shall be delivered into the hands of the physician.

Evidently, a scribe who had experienced the misfortune of consulting an incompetent or grasping physician, made his literary revenge by altering the text to suit his purpose. We shall see later that during the Talmudic age the honorable profession of the physician, who is so highly praised by Ben Sira, declined somewhat, so that the altered text may well fit in with changed circumstances.[223]

e. Scribes

Ben Sira's highest praise was reserved for the professional scribes, who must, however, not be regarded as mere copiers of sacred texts. By that time, they were the leading intellectuals of the age, the spiritual leaders of the people, the predecessors of the rabbis, and the interpreters of the law. They were the synagogue preachers, the teachers of the masses, the founders of the Jewish educational system, which, in its essentials, has survived down to the present day. No doubt, their work as educators and teachers of the law required them to copy the books of the Torah, the Prophets, the Psalms, Proverbs, and the rest of the Hebrew Bible, which they gradually canonized. But this was only a means to a higher end — that of spreading the knowledge of Judaism among the people.

They also had to make a living, and most of them did some part-time work to earn their bread. With the increasing urbanization and commercialization of Judaea, the work of the courts increased, and there was a demand for scribes to draw up legal documents of various kinds. We may surmise that many scribes managed to gain a scanty livelihood from such uninspiring but necessary routine work. Fortunately, neither this nor any

---

222 Ecclus. 38:1-15.
223 W.O.E. Oesterley, *Ecclesiasticus* (Cambridge, 1912), p. 248, commenting on this verse, maintains that "the words are not to be understood as a disparagement of the physician." Rather, he considers them to underline the theological concept

other work they may have done occupied more than a small part of their time and attention. As Ben Sira saw them, they were men of leisure who could devote themselves to the acquisition and dissemination of wisdom in its widest sense:

> The wisdom of the scribe increases wisdom (*viz.* by teaching it to others). And (only) he that has little business can become wise.[224]

f. Miscellaneous Occupations and Acquisition of Wisdom

Although Ben Sira recognized that there were many essential arts and crafts, without which society could not survive, he felt — as did the ancient Greeks and a few rabbis — that learning and culture could thrive only through leisure, while the more or less full-time activity of the farmer and artisan would leave neither time nor energy for learning and wisdom. In his interesting discourse on this problem — which has not yet been solved, even in this age of automation — Ben Sira enumerates a whole series of contemporary occupations, and indicates their place in society:

> How can he become wise that holds the goad,
> And glories in the pitchfork winnowing in the tempest;
> Who leads cattle and turns about oxen,
> And whose discourse is with bullocks;
> Who sets his heart on harrowing the seed strips,
> And whose anxiety is to give his heifers their fodder?
> Likewise the craftsman and skilled artificer
> Who by night as by day has no rest,
> Who cuts engravings of signets,
> And whose art is to make variety of design;
> Who is careful to make the likeness true,
> And whose anxiety is to complete his work.

---

that "sickness is the punishment for sin." This interpretation not only lacks a sense of humor, but fails to take account of parallel rabbinic disparagements of the physician; cf. *M. Kid.* IV, 14 ("The best of physicians is destined for hell") and *infra*, Chapter Six, pp. 186 ff.

224 Ecclus. 38:24. Cf. *M. Aboth* II, 5; IV, 10; VI, 6. According to R.H. Charles, *Apocrypha and Pseudepigrapha* (Oxford, 1913), vol. I, p. 452, the earlier scribes depicted in Ben-Sira, "appear for the most part to have belonged to the upper and

So also the smith sitting by the anvil,
And considering the unwrought iron;
The vapor of the fire wastes his flesh,
And in the heat of the furnace he burns,
To the sound of the hammer he inclines his ear,
And to the pattern of the vessel are his eyes directed;
He sets his heart on completing his work,
And his anxiety is to make it well to serve its purpose.
So also the potter sitting at his work,
And turning the wheel about with his feet;
Who is always in anxiety over his work,
And all his handiwork is by number;
He fashions the clay with his arm,
And he bends its strength in front of his feet;
He is careful to complete the glazing,
And his anxiety is to clean the furnace.
All these are deft with their hands,
And each is well skilled in his work;
Without them a city cannot be inhabited,
And wherever they dwell they hunger not; [225]

wealthy classes, ... and to have been separated from the working classes ... by a wide social gulf. They were apparently a leisured class, raised above the necessity of earning a livelihood, who took the lead in public affairs and counsel, and acted as judges. ... They obviously belonged to the nobility, and perhaps to the noble families of the priesthood..."

However, Charles himself points to Ecclesiasticus 11:1 ("The wisdom of the poor man lifts up his head and causes him to sit among princes") as well as to Ecclesiastes 9:16 ("... the poor man's wisdom is despised, and his words are not heeded"), which seem to contradict his theory. There is little evidence that as a class wealthy Jews were more learned than poor Jews. On the contrary, there were High Priests who were ignorant of the Law (cf. *M. Yoma* I, 3, 6), and even the son-in-law of Judah the Patriarch was a rich, ignorant boor (*T.Y. M.K.* III, 1, 81c). There were impecunious scholars who became famous and wealthy, while others, equally famous, remained poor all their lives.

Although Charles's view is by and large supported by M.Z. Segal (*Sepher Ben-Sira Ha-Shalem* (Jerusalem, 1972), p. 253), it appears likely that only a small minority of the scribes were independently wealthy at any time — and that includes the age of Ben-Sira.

225 Cf. *T.B. Sanh.* 29a: "Although a famine may last for seven years, it does not pass the craftsman's gate."

But they are not required for the council of the people,
And in the assembly they do not hold high rank;
They do not sit on the seat of the judge,
And law and justice they do not understand;
They do not expound the instruction of wisdom,
And the parables of the wise they do not understand;
But they are skilled in the work they have wrought,
And their thought is on the practice of their craft.[226]

It is noteworthy that Ben Sira, an intellectual aristocrat not untouched by snobbery, denies the capacity of the farmer and craftsman to participate in public affairs. He concedes that "without them a city cannot be inhabited," and he realizes that many of them are not rough laborers, but highly skilled craftsmen. But he accepts the prevailing Hellenistic scale of values, which he evidently considers quite reasonable. The manual laborer is tied to his craft and is ignorant of the world. His mental horizon is bounded by his work. Inevitably, his social status is inferior, and he cannot participate in public affairs. His knowledge is too little, and his leisure too inadequate to enable him to acquire learning or take part in the deliberations of the city council. Objectively, Ben Sira's evaluation was true; but Judaism was never daunted by unfavorable circumstances. If conditions were not conducive to the dissemination of learning, then conditions must be changed. Since the time of Ezra (5th cent. B.C.E.) attempts were made to spread the knowledge of the Torah among the masses, and the dream of universal education for all Jewish males was eventually realized by the rabbis. Many of the rabbis were farmers and artisans, and many earned only a scanty livelihood; but that did not stop them from devoting every spare minute to the acquisition of learning. Their contribution to the political and spiritual development of the Jewish people became one of the most decisive factors in Jewish history. All this would have seemed a pipedream to Ben Sira, whose intellectual horizon had been both widened and circumscribed by the powerful influence of Hellenistic civilization.

226 *Ecclus.* 38:25–34.

3. Economic Progress during the Hasmonean Age.

The Hellenistic age also included the relatively short period of Jewish independence under the Hasmonean rulers (141–63 B.C.E.). The territorial expansion of the Judaean state during the Hasmonean age brought most of the seacoast of Palestine under Jewish rule. The port of Jaffa was fortified,[227] and its harbor was rebuilt or extended by Simon the Hasmonean, with a view to increasing maritime trade, which in turn helped to promote the development of crafts.[228] The importance of the maritime trade is indicated on the Hasmonean coins which include a ship's anchor among the symbols minted on them.[228a]

The interdependence of commerce and crafts is well illustrated in the great Hasmonean sepulcher in Modiin, which was clearly aimed at fostering seaborne commerce;[229] for on the monument "were carved ships so that they could be seen by all who sail the sea."[230] The erection of the monument required the employment of builders, sculptors and numerous skilled artisans.[231]

227 Cf. *I Maccabees* 14:34.
228 Cf. ibid. 14:5; M. Wischnitzer, *op. cit.*, pp. 16f.
228a Cf. *Encyclopaedia Judaica*, vol. 5, s.v. Coins and Currency, cols. 699 and 716. For the extensive bibliography on the subject, see ibid., col. 731; also B. Kanael, *Altjüdische Münzen* (Sonderdruck aus *Jahrbuch für Numismatik und Geldgeschichte*, 17. Jahrgang, 1967), pp. 228–237.
229 M. Wischnitzer, *op. cit.*; cf. also J. Klausner, *Ha-Bayit ha-Sheni bi-Gedulato*, p. 89.
230 *I Maccabees* 13:29.
231 M. Wischnitzer, *op. cit.*, p. 17.

Chapter Three

Occupational Structure of the Rabbis

1. General Characteristics of the Rabbinate

Although Hellenistic influences affected rabbinic thinking throughout the Talmudic age, the rabbis, with few exceptions, radically disagreed with the Greek concepts relating to work and trade. Greek civilization was based on slave labor, and the complete freedom of the intelligentsia from manual work was the indispensable condition for the creation of art, literature, science and all the other accomplishments of Hellenistic civilization.

In Palestine and Babylonia, however, Jewish civilization, based as it was on high ethical norms, could not flourish through slavery. The institution as such existed, of course, as it did throughout the ancient and medieval world right down to modern times; but its economic role was limited, and slaves never constituted an appreciable part of the Jewish population. Hebrew slavery was virtually extinct, and non-Jewish slaves were converted to Judaism (which meant that they were expected to keep most of the religious laws, including Sabbath observance) and provided with so many legal safeguards that they became, in effect, domestic servants rather than slaves in the usual sense of the word. Only the wealthy could afford to keep slaves, while the economy as a whole was based on the free labor of farmers, agricultural laborers and urban craftsmen and traders.

Under such conditions there was no room for a leisured class of intellectuals and spiritual leaders, producing cultural values, thanks to the compulsory labor of others. The rabbinate was a calling, not a profession; an honor, not a source of livelihood; a part-time voluntary activity carried on by high-minded self-sacrificing men, rather than a career with substantial material emoluments. There were, of course, exceptions; but they formed an insignificant minority. The predominant view was that one must not make the Torah "a spade to dig therewith",[232] and the vast majority of the rabbis had to earn their living like everybody else. Their preaching and teaching was done during their spare time, including a good part of the night. This basic fact of life exercised a powerful influence on rabbinic thinking in regard to labor in general and specific occupations in particular. The rabbis were eminently qualified to deal with all aspects of life precisely because they were active participants in every phase of legitimate human activity. Thanks to "repentant sinners" who joined their ranks, the rabbis were not ignorant even of the problems of sin and crime. The Talmud and Midrash — indeed, the entire range of rabbinic literature — provide an inexhaustible source on the social and economic as well as religious and cultural life of the Jewish people. The rabbis, none of whom lived in ivory towers, were not only spiritual guides and religious leaders, but farmers and workmen, craftsmen and traders, and therefore familiar with every aspect of the daily life of the people. It was from this that their tremendous moral influence on the people derived.

2. Rabbis in Agriculture and Industry

Just as the majority of the Jewish people in Palestine and Babylonia were farmers or landless agricultural laborers, so, according to all indications, were most of the rabbis. A survey of rabbis whose occupations are listed indicates that a majority of them were engaged in agricultural activities of one sort or another.

i Abba Hilkiah
The earliest recorded case of a rabbi working in a field is that of Abba Hilkiah, a saintly man who lived around the beginning of the Common Era. His reputation as a miracle worker and rain-maker was such that during a drought a delegation of scholars specially came to ask him to pray for rain. They found him ploughing, and when they greeted him, he refused to reply; for, as he explained later, as a hired day laborer, he was not entitled to interrupt his work even for a moment.[233]

232 *M. Aboth* IV, 5.
233 *T.B. Taan.* 23 a–b.

ii R. Eliezer ben Hyrcanus

In contrast to the poor saint who feared he might be cheating his employer if he so much as exchanged a greeting during work time, R. Eliezer ben Hyrcanus, a prominent rabbi during the last decades of the first century C.E., was a wealthy landowner who began his career doing his own ploughing. Longing to study the Torah, he ran away from home and almost starved to death until he was provided with food by his teacher, R. Johanan ben Zakkai. (This is probably the first recorded case of a "scholarship" grant). His father, Hyrcanus, who did not appreciate learning, specially traveled to Jerusalem to disown and disinherit his fugitive son; but after hearing him preach a brilliant sermon, he changed his mind and left him his entire fortune. Henceforth, R. Eliezer was able to combine his favorite occupation, the study of the Law, with that of a rich country squire.[234]

iii R. Eleazar ben Azariah

Another wealthy scholar and landowner was R. Eleazar ben Azariah who became prominent around 100 C.E. when he was appointed President of the Sanhedrin, the High Court and supreme legislative body of the Jewish community.[235] He appreciated the importance of economic independence for successful and thorough study, and one of his most widely quoted maxims is that, "if there is no flour (i.e., bread), there can be no Torah".[236]

iv R. Tarfon

R. Eleazar's contemporary, R. Tarfon, was also a rich landowner; but he left the cultivation of his land to servants or tenant farmers who hardly knew him by sight. On one occasion, he went to his estate and picked himself some figs. He was apprehended by one of his own tenants or employees who suspected him of being identical with a regular thief whom they had been unable to catch. R. Tarfon had to betray his identity to save his life — an act which he always regretted because he felt he had derived a material advantage from his scholarly

---

234 *ARN.* Vers. I, ch. 6, edit. Schechter, pp. 30f.; *Gen. R.* 42, 1; *PRE* 1.
235 *T.B. Ber.* 27b; 57b; *Kid.* 49b.
236 *M. Aboth* III, 17.

reputation. In his view, learning must be done for its own sake, not for any practical purpose.[237]

v R. Eleazar ben Harsom

A similar accident once befell an older contemporary rabbi, Eleazar ben Harsom, who was said to have been left a fabulous fortune by his father. He was not only a great landowner (hyperbolically reported to have owned a thousand villages),[237a] but he was also a shipping magnate — a sort of Jewish Onassis — controlling a fleet of a thousand ships — no doubt an exaggerated number. Yet, he took no interest in his vast possessions, but "would take a sack of flour on his shoulder (presumably, to bake his own bread) and go from city to city and from province to province to study the Torah". One day he was seized by his own servants whom he had never seen, and they forced him to perform "public service" for the Romans — forced labor which the Romans and their helpers usually imposed on the poor.[238] Sad to relate, all his wealth was destroyed in the course of the Roman-Jewish wars.[239]

vi R. Hiyya, his Sons and R. Simeon ben Halafta

Around 200 C.E., we learn about a famous rabbi, R. Hiyya, who was not only a landowner, but also a silk and linen [239a] merchant. He does not appear to have had the time or the inclination to cultivate the land himself, and he is reported to have leased the field to his business partner, R. Simeon b. Halafta. The expected yield did not, however, materialize.[240] R. Hiyya's sons, Hezekiah and Judah, who were also scholars of note, reversed their father's course, and left their college to work on their estates, which had apparently been badly neglected. Their time was so completely taken up that they were forced to neglect their studies. Before long, they had forgotten whatever they had learned. In the course of their desperate efforts to recall their learning, they speculated whether their father, who was no longer among the living, was, in

237 *T.Y. Sheb.* IV, 2, 35b; *T.B. Ned.* 62a.
237a *T.B. Yoma* 35b, where Heb. עיירות literally means "cities". However, the "cities", whatever their number, are more likely to have been villages.
238 *T.B. Yoma* 35b.
239 *T.Y. Taan.* IV, 8, 69a.
239a *Gen. R.* 77, 2; *T.Y. Baba Metsia* V, 8, 10c; VI, 1, 10d.
240 *Ruth R.* 5, 12.

the other world, aware of his sons' troubles.[241] Hezekiah, incidentally, was the author of a famous maxim, namely that just as it was the father's duty to teach his son Torah, so he was in duty bound to teach him a trade.[242] His own action, in devoting himself to agriculture was in line with this tendency.

vii R. Johanan

Not all rabbis, however, were willing to forsake learning for the sake of their economic wellbeing. Thus, the greatest of the Third Century Palestinian rabbis, R. Johanan, sold all his fields, vineyards, and olive yards, so that he might be able to devote himself entirely to the study of the Law.[243]

viii R. Simon

The problem of cultivating land while at the same time devoting the necessary time and energy for the study of the law, continued to beset the rabbis, especially during the third century, which was noted for its prolonged economic crisis throughout the Roman Empire. R. Simon had an estate which he was unable to manage, and since he was apparently unable or unwilling to sell it, he tried to lease it. But the only potential customers were Gentiles, and in view of the gradual displacement of the Jews from the land of their fathers, the rabbis objected to selling or even leasing Jewish land to non-Jews. R. Johanan, accordingly, advised R. Simon to leave the land uncultivated.[244]

ix Abba bar Abba and his son Samuel

In Babylonia, too, the rabbis owned fields which they either cultivated themselves or else leased to tenant sharecroppers who were expected to look after the land, cultivate it, and pay an agreed portion of the crop to the owner. Before long, the rabbis discovered that this was no sinecure, but required constant attention; otherwise, serious losses, through damage or theft, were likely to be incurred.

---

241 *T.B. Ber.* 18b.
242 *T.B. Kid.* 30b.
243 *Lev. R.* 30, 1; *Cant. R.* 8, 7, 1; *Exod. R.* 47, 5; *Tanh.* edit. Buber, Ki Tissa 19, p. 60a (119).
244 *T.Y. Demai* VI, 1, 25a–b.

Abba bar Abba (c. 200 C.E.) was in the habit of inspecting his property twice a day. His son, Samuel, however, who was one of the greatest and most scientific scholars in Babylonia and who was, among other things, a competent physician and astronomer, found time to inspect his estate only once a day. He wisely stated that "He who inspects his property daily will find a coin" (i.e. derive profit from such an inspection).[245] His care seems to have paid off at least indirectly; for, we are told, when a tenant farmer of his brought him some dates, which had the taste of wine, he discovered that the reason was that the date trees had been planted between vines. Realizing that the date trees were weakening the vines (which, in Babylonia, were much more valuable), he had the palm trees uprooted.[246]

x Rab Assi
Other Babylonian landowner rabbis discovered the soundness of Samuel's maxim. Rab Assi (early 3rd cent. C.E.) used to inspect his estate day by day without discovering anything amiss. Impatiently, he asked, "Where are all those coins promised by Master Samuel?" One day he saw that an irrigation pipe had burst on his land which was rapidly being flooded. He quickly took off his coat, rolled it up, and stuffed it into the hole. Having taken such indispensable emergency measures, he summoned help, and the pipe was repaired. He then gratefully acknowledged, "Now I have found all those coins promised by master Samuel!".[247]

xi Abaye
About a century later, one of the foremost Babylonian rabbis, Abaye, discovered, during one of his daily inspections, that his tenant farmer was stealing a bundle of twigs. Abaye put an end to such petty pilfering.[248]

Abaye became in due course a wealthy landowner employing laborers and tenant farmers to cultivate his fields.[249] Earlier, however, he had a hard struggle to combine his devoted study of the Torah with his agricultural duties. A student by the name of R. Shimi ben Ashi once presented himself, requesting that Abaye give him lessons. The latter,

245 *T.B. Hul.* 105a.
246 *T.B. Baba Kamma* 92a.
247 *T.B. Hul.* 105a.
248 Ibid.
249 *T.B. Ber.* 45b; *Ket.* 60b.

however, had to do his own studying and could not accede to this request. When R. Shimi suggested that the lesson be held at night, Abaye excused himself explaining that he had to do irrigation work at night. R. Shimi offered to do the irrigation work himself by day, and study under the great master at night. Abaye agreed, but the over-eager R. Shimi disregarded the interests of others who had to use the water, and Abaye scrupulously refused even to taste of the produce of that year.[250]

xii R. Abba bar Abina, Rab Hisda, Rab Joseph and
Rabba bar Rab Huna — Legal Problems
Occasionally, rabbis might have legal problems with the tenant farmers who looked after their estates. Thus, when some pigeons were found on a palm tree leased by R. Abba bar Abina to a tenant, the question as to who owned the pigeons presented some difficulties.[251] Rab Hisda had to evict a tenant farmer who, it appears, was in the habit of cheating him.[252] Some rabbis seem to have had some very strange "tenants". In Third Century Babylonia, for example, Rab Joseph permitted some cuppers, who "cured" people of diverse ailments by bleeding them, to perform their none too pleasant art under his date trees. The blood drawn from the patients attracted ravens who would suck it up and then perch on Rab Joseph's date trees and damage them. Rab Joseph tried to order the cuppers to transfer their operations elsewhere. This caused some controversy, since Rab Joseph was trying to upset an established privilege. He claimed, however, that there was no legal title to activities causing damage, either directly or indirectly.[253]

Another legal problem besetting rabbinic as well as other landowners was that of land-clearing near the bank of a river or canal. Thus, Rabbah bar Rab Huna (3rd cent. C.E.) owned a forest by a river bank. When asked to make a clearing by the water's edge, to enable bargees who pulled laden boats (like the famed Volga boatmen) to walk along the river, he refused to do so. His reason was that it was not really necessary, and that in any case the neighboring forest belonged to a nobleman who

---

250 *T.B. Git.* 60b.
251 *T.Y. B.M.* I, 4, 7d–8a.
252 *T.B. B.K.* 119a.
253 *B.B.* 22b–23a.

could not be compelled to cut down any part of his forest. His own clearing would, therefore, be useless. Eventually, however, the edge of his forest was cut down by order of Rabbah bar Rab Nahman — to the intense displeasure of the owner.[254]

xiii Rab Hilkiah bar Tobi

Some of the rabbinical farmers in Babylonia could point to real success stories in both the economic and spiritual spheres. In the third century C.E., Rab Hilkiah bar Tobi used special methods of cultivation, adapted to some extent from earlier prototypes used in Palestine,[255] to obtain higher and better yields. He owned a small piece of land which he divided into two sections. He would plough one half and leave it barren for one year while sowing the other half. In the following year he would reverse the process. Thus he managed to obtain a twofold yield, and his wheat was of such good quality that he was able to sell it for high-priced fine flour.[256]

xiv Rab Huna

Rab Hilkiah's famous contemporary, Rab Huna, started rather modestly as a poor student and farm laborer. Once he appeared before his teacher, Rab, girded with a string instead of a belt. When Rab expressed his astonishment at his poverty-stricken appearance, Huna explained that, finding himself short of wine for kiddush (the ceremony of Sabbath "sanctification"), he had to pawn his belt to be able to purchase the kiddush wine. Rab blessed him that he should one day be smothered, as it were, in silk. Many years later, this came true.[257]

Rab Huna had to labor in the fields, and even carry his own spade on his shoulder, when he was already recognized as a rabbi. When a younger scholar offered to carry it for him, Rab Huna insisted that he should not do so if he was not accustomed to this, since he himself did not want to be treated with respect at the cost of someone else's degradation.[258]

According to one account, Rab Huna was a herdsman, too busy looking after cattle even to have time to appear in court as a witness.

254 B.M. 107b.
255 Cf. M. Men. VIII, 2; T. Men. IX, 3.
256 T.B. Men. 85b.
257 T.B. Meg. 27b.
258 Ibid. 28a.

When requested by someone to testify on his behalf, he asked to be compensated for his loss of working time.[259] Even when Rab Huna had become an authorized judge, he was reluctant to preside over a court of law, which was usually an unpaid honor, because it inevitably cost him loss of working time: "Provide me with a man", he said, "who will draw the (irrigation) water in my place, and I will pronounce judgment for you".[260]

Eventually, however, Rab Huna did become a very wealthy man who not only presided over the college of Sura, probably the greatest Talmudic academy of all time, but actually maintained 800 full-time students.[261] Since college presidents were not paid in those days, Rab Huna must have derived his huge income from vast estates and, possibly, from certain commercial operations, as well as donations from philanthropic well-wishers.

Despite his prosperity, or perhaps because of it, Rab Huna had some trouble with his tenant farmers. One of them used to steal so much from him that he retaliated by refusing to let him have his lawful share. When subsequently hundreds of jars of wine turned sour, it was suggested to him that this was a divine punishment for what we would today call "over-reacting". Stealing from a thief, it was pointed out, could not be justified. Rab Huna thereupon gave a pledge never again to withhold what was due to his tenant farmers. The story has a happy ending. According to one legendary version, the wine which had become vinegar miraculously became wine again. Another more sober version relates that the price of vinegar rose so high that it was as dear as wine. In either case, Rab Huna recouped his losses.[262]

xv Rab Hisda

Another successful farmer rabbi was Rab Huna's junior colleague, Rab Hisda,[262a] who was quite an expert on various aspects of agriculture and cattle raising. Like Master Samuel before him, he discovered that his tenant farmers had planted palm trees among vines, which were very expensive in Babylonia, whereas date trees were extremely common and

259   *T.Y. Sanh.* I, 1, 18b.
260   *T.B. Ket.* 105 a.
261   Ibid. 106a.
262   *T.B. Ber.* 5b.
262a See also *supra*, p. 44.

inexpensive.[263] Rab Hisda gave instructions to have the palm trees cut down, roots and all.[264] As already mentioned, he got rid of a tenant farmer who had regularly swindled him whenever he shared out the crops between himself and his landlord. As a result, the tenant lost even that part of the crop which would have been rightfully his.[265]

Rab Hisda was also familiar with cattle raising. He seems to have had certain color "prejudices" in regard to the quality of oxen. One of his maxims was, "A black ox (is superior to others) because of its hide, a red one (is superior to others) because of its flesh, a white one (is superior to others) for ploughing".[266] Far more explosive, however, is his statement that, "black oxen amongst white ones spoil the herd (because, as the commentators explain, black oxen are inferior to white ones). White patches on black oxen are a blemish",[267] evidently because "black is beautiful" only when not tinged with white. (Incidentally, the translation followed here is rather free and in accordance with the real meaning of Rab Hisda's saying. The actual words used could well be the slogan of modern segregationists: "Black among white is a blemish; white among black is a blemish").

Like a real gentleman farmer, Rab Hisda also had storehouses in which he kept his produce. He was in the habit of leaving the keys to the storehouses with the servants, except for the key to the timberstore, which he would keep himself,[268] — no doubt to prevent pilfering of a commodity which was rather scarce in Babylonia.

Despite all his agricultural interests, the main source of Rab Hisda's wealth, and also of his charitable endeavors was what we would today call his liquor business. According to his own testimony, "If I had not been a beer manufacturer, I would not have become rich".[269] The beer produced by him was probably a concoction of fermented dates and/or barley probably grown by himself. It was a strong, intoxicating drink, not unlike the modern arak. Since viniculture is most suitable in hilly terrain, while Babylonia (Iraq) is predominantly a flat plain suitable for

263 *T.B. Taan.* 9b.
264 *T.B. Baba Kamma* 92a.
265 Ibid. 119a.
266 *T.B. Nazir* 31b.
267 Ibid.
268 *T.B. Git.* 56a.
269 *T.B. Pes.* 113a. Cf. also *T.B. M.K.* 28a. On the wealth of some Babylonian rabbis, see Y. Gafni, *Yehudey Bavel bi-Tekufat ha-Talmud* (Jerusalem, 1990), p. 129; M. Beer, *Amora'ey Bavel* (Ramat-Gan, 1975), pp. 258–271.

the cultivation of date-bearing palm trees, date beer became the most popular drink of the country, and those who produced good quality beer in large quantities were sure to make a fortune.

xvi Rab Papa

Rab Hisda's emphasis on beer manufacture as the primary source of his wealth was echoed a couple of generations later by Rab Papa[270] who was not only very rich,[271] but seems to have anticipated Madison Avenue techniques of advertising and salesmanship. He proudly boasted, "My beer will not deteriorate",[272] and even dealt with the competition of wine by flatly declaring that when one can drink beer (which was inexpensive) and drinks wine one is guilty of wasteful extravagance.[273] Other rabbis, however, disagreed. Failure to drink wine, which was regarded as better and healthier than beer, was harmful to one's physical wellbeing, so that, despite the higher cost, the consumption of wine was preferable.[274]

Incidentally, even as late as the eleventh century, we find the famous French Jewish Bible and Talmud commentator, R. Solomon Yitzhaki, better known as Rashi, explaining a Talmudic passage in accordance with his own economic interests. He owned a vineyard and was a wine producer in Troyes, the capital of the French Champagne which was, and still is, a famous wine producing area. Commenting on a Talmudic suggestion that drinking a jar of water every morning was good for one's health, Rashi explains, as would any full-blooded modern Frenchman, that this applies only to one who has no wine.[275]

Both Rab Hisda and Rab Papa seem to have supplemented their agricultural and industrial ventures with some commercial and banking enterprises. They certainly displayed remarkable knowledge in such matters. Thus, Rab Hisda advised students what food, fuel and linen to buy in the market, and how to preserve clothes to last for a long time.[276]

270 Ibid.
271 Cf. *B.M.* 46a.
272 Ibid. 65a.
273 *T.B. Shab.* 140b. R. Samuel Edels, known as the Maharsha, aptly comments on Rab Papa's "commercial" (*ad loc.*): "Rab Papa said it for his own benefit, since he was a beer manufacturer".
274 Ibid.
275 *B.M.* 107b.
276 *T.B. Shab.* 140b.

In addition, he was also what we would today call a marriage counselor, and he advised his daughters how to conduct themselves with a view to keeping the affection of their husbands.[277] It is highly probable that his daughters were not the sole beneficiaries of his sage counsel.

Rab Papa, too, gave advice — though in his case, it was banking and large-scale commerce that occupied his attention. He had, for example, little trust in the repayment of outstanding debts and he, accordingly, pointed out that "Every bill requires collecting (in other words, don't count your chickens before they are hatched); in every credit sale it is doubtful whether payment will be forthcoming or not; and when it is forthcoming, it may be bad money" (i.e., either poor quality coins or in such small installments that the money is frittered away and cannot be accumulated for future investments).[278] Despite such caution, Rab Papa would sell his beer on credit, charging, however, a higher price because of delayed payment.[279]

Like any modern entrepreneur, Rab Papa formed a partnership with a colleague of his, Rab Huna son of Rab Joshua, and their operations extended to both the commercial and agricultural spheres. For example, we find them purchasing some land[280] as well as a considerable quantity of sesame; and they had to hire some boatmen to transport it across a canal. Again, like modern shippers, they took out an accident insurance policy. Despite all the precautions, things did not turn out well; for the canal was stopped up — an accident considered so unusual that their policy, according to a court decision, did not cover it. Their demand that the boatmen should hire asses and deliver the stuff as stipulated was, accordingly, rejected.[281]

Other joint operations of theirs were, however, more successful. They acquired real estate, probably for commercial or industrial exploitation, and seem to have done well. At any rate, they expressed their satisfaction with their purchases.[282] However, since their fields adjoined one another, a disagreement arose between them with regard to Rab Huna's right to

---

277 Ibid.
278 *T.B. Pes.* 113a.
279 *T.B. B.M.* 65a.
280 *T.B. Hor.* 10b.
281 *T.B. Git.* 73a.
282 *T.B. Hor.* 10b.

dig and cut out the roots of Rab Papa's date trees which had spread into the land owned by Rab Huna.[283]

Rab Papa also engaged in the seemingly more modest business of leasing land for growing fodder, either for his own herds or for sale to other farmers. When his lease was up, he shrewdly demanded compensation for "improvement" — some trees had sprung up during the period of the lease — on the grounds that he had leased the field for precisely such a contingency. His claim was, however, only partly successful, and all he was able to get was the value of the timber.[284]

xvii Rab Papi

A couple of generations later, another Babylonian rabbi and head of a Talmudic Academy, Rab Papi, combined his teaching activities with extensive land holdings. His estates were cultivated by tenants, and it would seem that a paternalistic relationship developed between him and his tenants. Thus, on Friday evening, Rab Papi would recite the "sanctification" blessing (the so-called *kiddush*) for his students and subsequently repeat it for the benefit of his tenants who came from the fields a little later.[285] Since the *kiddush* is usually a family ceremony, the fact that Rab Papi recited it for his tenants indicates a close relationship between the rabbinic squire and his tenant farmers.

xviii Rab Bibi bar Abaye — Problems of Ethics

Despite such friendly personal relations, Rab Papi strictly enforced the legal rights of the lessors against tenants who, incidentally, were usually sharecroppers and might claim compensation for improvements. When, for example, Rab Bibi bar Abaye, who had leased a field and surrounded it with a ridge on which sorb bushes had sprouted forth, demanded compensation for the improvement he had effected, Rab Papi rudely brushed his claim aside, describing it as "words of no substance".[286]

Rab Bibi bar Abaye, on his part, was not above sharp practices when it came to looking after his own interests. We are told of a woman who

283 *T.B. B.B.* 26a–b.
284 *T.B. B.M.* 109a.
285 *T.B. R.H.* 29b.
286 *T.B. B.M.* 109a.

owned a palm tree on land belonging to him; but whenever she went to cut her tree, he resented her "trespassing" on his land, although she presumably must have had right of access to her tree. The woman was so upset that, to avoid further unpleasantries, she made the tree over to him for life on the understanding that after his death it would revert to her or to her heirs. He thereupon made the tree over to his little son, so that the woman should not be able to claim it after his own death. Rab Bibi's legal trick did not, however, avail him anything. On the contrary, he was sharply rebuked by the judge, Rab Huna son of Rab Joshua, and the palm tree eventually reverted to its original owner.[287]

xix Rab Joseph — Problems of Ethics
That some Babylonian Rabbis who were also well-to-do farmers and businessmen were liable to use their knowledge of the law to promote their own interests without considering the moral issues involved, is also indicated in the following story. Rab Joseph (late 3rd cent. C.E.), who eventually became head of the academy of Pumbeditha, owned a vegetable plot which was looked after by a gardener who worked for half of the profit. When the gardener died and his five sons-in-law tried to take over, Rab Joseph argued that the old man, who had had no one to rely on, had worked hard; whereas now, with the gardening divided between five, each would rely on the others to do the work, thus causing him financial loss. Acting on this doubtful presumption, he gave them an ultimatum: they could either accept improvement compensation due to them and quit, or else he would evict them without paying them any compensation. Rab Joseph cited the authority of earlier Babylonian rabbis who had laid down a rule that "if a gardener dies, his heirs may be evicted without receiving compensation for improvement". We do not know how this particular case was resolved — Rab Joseph probably won it — but the Talmud concludes the story with a significant postscript: "This ruling (concerning the right of evicting the heirs of a deceased gardener) is incorrect".[288] Since no explanation is given why the ruling is incorrect, we are justified in assuming that the moral aspect of the matter was ultimately given preference over what was, at best, a law of doubtful fairness.

287 *T.B. B.B.* 137b.
288 *T.B. B.M.* 109a.

Rab Joseph was also involved in another dispute, this time with his neighbor, Raba son of Rab Hanan, who owned date trees adjoining Rab Joseph's vineyard. Birds roosting on the date trees would fly down and damage the costly vines of Rab Joseph. He therefore demanded that Raba cut down his date trees, so that the birds should not have a base from which to damage his vineyard. Raba refused on the grounds that date trees, which were a vital source of food, must not be cut down. He did, however, give Rab Joseph permission to do so, and face the moral and religious consequences.[289]

xx Rabina — Problems of Ethics
Another rabbinic garden-plot owner in Babylonia who employed a gardener to tend his plot was Rabina (4th cent. C.E.). Unfortunately, the gardener was incompetent and spoiled the garden. Rabina instantly fired him; but the gardener complained before Raba, the greatest legal authority of his time, that he had been unfairly treated. Raba pointed out that Rabina had acted within his rights. The gardener protested that he had not been given any warning. Raba, however, retorted that no warning was necessary. Gardeners as well as schoolteachers, butchers and certain other tradesmen are employed on the implicit understanding that if they fail to give satisfactory service, they are liable to be dismissed without notice.[290]

Despite such cases of a lack in moral sensitivity, there is some evidence that there was also a counter-tendency at work insisting on ethical rather than strictly legal considerations. For example, we are told of a third century Babylonian rabbi — his identity is not quite certain — who employed porters to transport a heavy jar of wine. As it happened, they were negligent and broke the jar, spilling its contents. Their rabbinic employer, aware that they were too poor ever to repay him for the loss he had incurred, seized their upper garments which they had taken off before starting work. If he could not get full compensation, he wanted to secure at least partial reimbursement, presumably on the principle that "possession is nine-tenths of the law". The porters, however, complained to Rab who ordered the rabbi to return the garments. They then pointed out that they were poor men living from hand to mouth — porters were

289 *T.B. B.B.* 26a.
290 *T.B. B.M.* 109a–b.

usually indigent — that they had worked all day and badly needed their wages which their employer had naturally withheld. Rab ordered him to pay them their wages; and when the astonished rabbi asked Rab on what legal foundation his verdict was based, the latter cited Proverbs 2:20, "So you will walk in the way of good men and keep to the paths of the righteous". In other words, there are times when one must not insist on the strict letter of the law but rather apply its humane spirit.[291]

A similar case is reported in the Talmud of Palestine (the so-called Jerusalem Talmud) where the rabbis were more inclined to heed ethical considerations. A certain trader in pots and pans handed his wares to a porter to transport them for him. When the porter broke the pots in his care, presumably through negligence, his employer confiscated his coat as part-compensation. The porter complained before R. Jose bar Hanina (3rd cent. C.E.), described elsewhere as "a judge able to penetrate to the innermost intention (or: deeper meaning) of the Law".[292] R. Jose ran true to form and told the porter to go to his employer and demand not only the return of his coat but also payment of his wages, again on the basis of Proverbs 2:20. Although the trader was not personally present in court, he yielded on both counts.[293] This story differs from the previous one, since in this case the judge himself spontaneously advised the plaintiff to demand his wages, whereas in the previous account Rab merely responded to the porters' request.

It was in line with this enlightened theory of law that R. Johanan (3rd cent. C.E.) stated that Jerusalem had been destroyed only because judicial verdicts were issued there which were strictly in accordance with the law, instead of going beyond the requirements of the law.[294]

xxi Student Agriculturists

By the fourth century, students and rabbis who combined their studies at the Babylonian academies with agricultural activities were so numerous that Raba, one of the leading Babylonian rabbis, advised his students to stay away from their studies during the months of Nisan (March/April) and Tishri (September/October), because these were the busiest months

291 *T.B. B.M.* 83a.
292 *T.B. B.K.* 39a.
293 *T.Y. B.M.* VI, 8, 11a.
294 *T.B. B.M.* 30b.

of the agricultural year. Nisan was the time of the ripening of the grain, while in Tishri the vintage and olive pressing had to be done.[295]

xxii R. Ishmael, son of R. Jose

Those who engaged in agriculture frequently specialized in spheres other than grain-growing. In second century Palestine, for example, R. Ishmael son of R. Jose owned a fruit orchard, which was looked after by a tenant gardener who regularly every Friday used to bring R. Ishmael a basket full of fruit. On one occasion, when the gardener had a lawsuit, he brought the basket a day earlier. R. Ishmael thereupon refused to accept the basket and disqualified himself from acting as judge in this case because the earlier delivery of the fruit constituted a subtle form of bribery.[296]

In Babylonia, too, there were small-scale gardener rabbis such as Rab Daniel bar Rab Ketina who carefully tended his garden every day, and was said to have had the miraculous ability to bring rain precisely to those beds that required it.[297] Some, like Rab Joseph and Rabina (mentioned previously), were prosperous garden plot owners employing hired labor or sharecroppers to tend their gardens.

3. Viniculture

i R. Jannai

Some Palestinian rabbis specialized in viniculture which required relatively less laborious work and also left more time for study. Thus, in the third century C.E., R. Jannai was hyperbolically said to have planted no less than 400 vineyards, but such a statement simply meant that he was the owner of a number of vineyards.[298]

ii R. Hiyya bar Adda

Another third century Palestinian rabbi, Hiyya bar Adda, combined viniculture with tutoring. On one occasion, he took a three-days' vaca-

---

295 *T.B. Ber.* 35b.
296 *T.B. Ket.* 105b.
297 *T.B. Taan.* 9b.
298 *T.B. B.B.* 14a.

tion for the vintage, which turned out to be a fabulously rich one. Evidently, he could manage with a relatively brief interruption of his regular teaching activity to tend his small vineyard. However, we are told that R. Simeon ben Lakish, whose children were being tutored by R. Hiyya bar Adda, took it rather amiss that his children's education had been neglected, and he chided R. Hiyya, asserting that if he had not taken a vacation from teaching, the grape harvest would have been even more successful.[299]

iii Rab Joseph

About the same time, we find that the Babylonian teacher, Rab Joseph, whom we have already met as an owner of date trees, was also an expert viniculturist. By giving his small vineyard an extra hoeing, he was able to produce wine that was twice as strong as the usual brand.[300]

4. Rabbinic Land Surveyor — Rab Adda

In Babylonia, where agriculture was highly developed, we even hear about a rabbi who was a land surveyor. Rab Adda (3rd cent. C.E.) would measure out land in business transactions, divided inheritances, etc., and he would appear to have been a very busy man. He was advised by Rab Judah to do his work with the utmost care, and not to neglect even minor parcels of land because, as Rab Judah put it, "every bit of ground is fit for garden saffron" and therefore of some value.[301]

5. Woodchopper and Shepherd — R. Akiba

Far less profitable were the trades of the woodchopper and shepherd. Yet, we find that one of the greatest rabbis of all times, R. Akiba, earned his scanty living precisely from these rather despised occupations. His

---

299 T.B. Ket. 111b. On the historical background of this story, cf. M. Aberbach, "Who was the Teacher of Resh Lakish's Children?" (in Hebrew), Sinai, vol. 53, No. 3, Sivan 1963.
300 T.B. Men. 87a.
301 T.B. B.M. 107b.

poverty was such that he and his wife had to sleep on straw because they could not afford a bed or a mattress.

During the years he had to spend away from home studying under the leading teachers of his time, his wife would sell the locks of her hair and send him the proceeds to maintain himself. Eventually, R. Akiba not only became a great scholar, but inherited considerable wealth, so that he could afford rare luxuries, including an extraordinarily expensive "Jerusalem of gold" — a golden ornament on which the picture of Jerusalem was engraved — which he bought for his loyal and long-suffering wife.[302] Poverty similar to that endured by R. Akiba in his early years was also the lot of the famous Hillel who lived during Herodian times and who labored at some unspecified occupation. According to a tradition recorded by Maimonides[303] Hillel was a woodchopper earning a pittance, half of which he had to spend on his education. Once he earned nothing and, unable to gain admittance to the college, he followed the lectures all through the night from a skylight on the roof. As it happened, there was a heavy snowfall and he was almost buried under the snow. Fortunately, he was noticed and rescued next morning.[304]

6. Animal Hire Service — R. Jose of Yodkart

A sideline in connection with agricultural activities was to hire out animals for work with farmers and others who did not possess such beasts of burden. The fourth century rabbi, Jose of Yodkart, had a she-ass which he used to hire out. The animal was apparently trained to go home on her own at the end of her work day. To save time, those who hired her would place the hire-money on her back before she went home. Since her owner had a legendary reputation as a miracle worker, his ass was popularly credited with such unusual intelligence that — so the story goes — she would not budge if the amount placed on her back was either too much or too little. One day,

---

302 T.B. Ket. 62b–63a; Ned. 50a–b; Shab. 59a–b; T.Y. Shab. VI, 1, 7d; ARN, Vers. I, 6, edit. Schechter, pp. 15a–b (29–30).
303 Maimonides, Commentary on the Mishnah, Aboth IV, 7.
304 T.B. Yoma 35b.

we are told, a pair of sandals was left on her back, and she refused to move until the sandals were taken off.[305]

7. Rabbis and Agricultural Laborers

i R. Jose of Yodkart

Despite his miraculous powers, R. Jose engaged in ordinary farming and even employed laborers whom, in accordance with contemporary custom, he would provide with food. Once he was late, and the laborers complained to his son that they were hungry. According to the story, R. Jose's son was also endowed with miracle-working powers, and he ordered a nearby fig-tree to bring forth its fruit "so that the laborers of my father may eat". The fig-tree obligingly did as commanded, and the laborers got their meal. When R. Jose arrived, he profusely apologized for the delay, but was informed that his son had already taken care of the laborers. R. Jose was extraordinarily annoyed at what he considered an abuse of miraculous powers.[306]

ii R. Johanan ben Mathia

The above-mentioned custom of providing food for agricultural laborers, who usually toiled in the field from sunrise to sunset,[307] could at times create special problems, though legally one was supposed to follow local custom. Thus, the second century Palestinian Rabbi, R. Johanan ben Mathia, once told his son to hire laborers to help out in the field. R. Johanan's son did as he had been bidden, and agreed to supply the laborers with food. When his father learned of this, he told him, "My son, even if you were to prepare for them a banquet like Solomon's in his glory, you would still be unable to fulfill your undertakings; for they are the children of Abraham, Isaac and Jacob".[308]

R. Johanan, accordingly, instructed his son to stipulate that they could claim only bread and pulse for their meal, and nothing else.[309]

---

305 *T.B. Taan.* 24a.
306 Ibid. 24a.
307 *T.B. B.M.* 83b; cf. *Pss.* 104:23.
308 Abraham was said to have provided banquets superior to those of King Solomon; cf. *T.B. B.M.* 86b.
309 *Mishnah B.M.* VII, 1.

8. Rabbis in Business — Silk Trade and Other Commercial Activities

i R. Johanan ben Zakkai

Incidents such as those mentioned above show us the ancient rabbis in their daily life, which, as appears from all indications, was concentrated primarily on agriculture and ancillary occupations. Nevertheless, as we have already seen, some rabbis were no strangers to the world of business and industry. For example, in the first century C.E., we find R. Johanan ben Zakkai engaged in unspecified commercial activities long before he became the head of the Sanhedrin in Yavneh.[310]

ii R. Hiyya, R. Simeon son of Judah the Patriarch, and R. Simeon ben Halafta

Over a century later, we find R. Hiyya and R. Simeon son of Judah the Patriarch, both of whom were also well-to-do landowners, engaged jointly in the highly profitable silk trade, apparently between Babylonia and Palestine.[311] On one occasion, after pursuing their business activities at Tyre, one of the foremost trading centers of antiquity, they departed from the city, but decided to turn back and check once more if they had left anything behind. Their wise precaution was well rewarded; for they found a bale of silk which they had forgotten.[312]

On another occasion, R. Hiyya and R. Simeon ben Halafta, both of whom were also engaged in agriculture, went to an Arab market, apparently Hegra, in Northern Arabia, where they learned the meaning of certain difficult biblical words by listening to conversations in the local Aramaic dialect.[313] The primary purpose of their journey to Arabia was no doubt commercial.

iii Abba bar Abba and R. Judah ben Bathyra II

Two other contemporary rabbis, both of them Babylonians, were likewise engaged in the silk trade. Abba bar Abba, whom we have already met as a meticulously circumspect landowner,[313a] was also moonlighting

---

310 *Sifre, Deut.* 357, edit. Friedmann, p. 150a; edit. Horovitz-Finkelstein, p. 429; *T.B. Sanh.* 41a; *R.H.* 31b.
311 Cf. Jacob Neusner, *A History of the Jews in Babylonia* (Leiden, 1965), I, 88f.
312 *Gen. R.* 77, 2.   313 Ibid. 79, 7.   313a See *supra*, p. 43.

as a silk merchant, and he sent some of his merchandise to R. Judah ben Bathyra II who resided at Nisibis, Syria, near the upper Euphrates, and was presumably also a silk merchant.[314]

iv R. Abba

One or two generations later, we find R. Abba, a Babylonian rabbi who had settled in Palestine but continued to travel between the two countries,[315] engaged in the silk trade. At any rate, it is certain that he owned a valuable silk ornament which a certain unscrupulous man recommended to ruffians as a worthwhile article to be purloined by them. Eventually they stole it and the man who had drawn their attention to it, was sentenced to pay for the loss.[316]

v Babylonian Rabbis and Silk Merchants in Palestine

One of the characteristic features of the history of third and fourth century Palestine was the constant migration of Babylonian students and scholars to Palestinian academies. Yet this was a period of constant decline in Palestine, while the Babylonian academies were flourishing and going from strength to strength. What is more, the waves of immigration to Palestine were more than offset by the fairly large-scale emigration movement which was caused by the steadily deteriorating economic situation in Palestine. All the more surprising, therefore, are the constant waves of immigration from prosperous Babylonia. It has rightly been surmised that, in addition to "Zionist" motives, the Babylonian immigrants — who incidentally continued to travel back and forth between the two countries — were also part-time businessmen, and that they went to Palestine partly in order to develop Mediterranean markets for their trade in silk and other wares.[317]

vi Silk Merchants as Missionaries and Converts

Even much earlier, while the Temple of Jerusalem was still standing in all its glory, Jewish merchants, who had the knowledge and prestige of

---

314 *Midr. Sam.* 10, 3, edit. Buber, p. 35.
315 Cf. *T.B. Kid.* 59a.
316 *T.B. B.K.* 117b.
317 Cf. Neusner, *op. cit.*

rabbis even though they may not have been active as such, participated in the international silk trade, traveling all over Western Asia, buying and selling, while at the same time spreading their religious views among the pagans.[318] These wealthy men who had connections in the highest circles were religious missionaries no less than merchants. Business provided them with a livelihood; but spreading the message of Judaism was the very essence of their lives. One such merchant, Ananias (Hananiah), was instrumental in the conversion to Judaism of the royal family of Adiabene — the modern Kurdistan in Northern Iraq — an achievement of profound political as well as religious implications.[319]

Significantly, these learned silk merchants were so anxious to win over the pagans that they were willing to compromise even on essential principles in order to gain converts. The same Ananias who had taught the Jewish faith to the royal family of Adiabene, strongly advised one of his royal disciples to refrain from undergoing the rite of circumcision, since such an act, which was completely alien to the local tradition, was likely to arouse opposition or even rebellion. Ananias claimed that one could worship God even without being circumcised, and in any case God would forgive an act of omission which was due to necessity.[320] Eventually, the male members of the family underwent circumcision without any untoward consequences.

This incident showed that the rabbinic traders turned missionaries tended to religious liberalism, especially where Gentiles were concerned. This brought them dangerously close to Pauline Christianity, which likewise required little in the way of practical observance of the laws of the Torah, particularly on the part of Gentile converts. Within a couple of centuries, the conversion to Christianity of the people of Edessa, a city on the main Asiatic trade route near the Euphrates, involved also Jewish silk merchants:

"Even Jews skilled in the law and the Prophets, who traded in silks, they too were convinced and became disciples, and confessed Christ that he is the son of the living God".[321]

318 Neusner, *op. cit.*, p. 89.
319 Josephus, *Ant.* XX, 2, 3, 34f.
320 Ibid. 2, 4, 38–42.
321 Doctrine of Addaeus the Apostle, cited in William Cureton, *Ancient Syrian Documents* (London, 1864), p. 14.

vii Commercial Ethics — R. Hanina

Needless to say, such converts among learned merchant rabbis were exceptions. With the exception of a third century rabbi, Ilfa, who abandoned his studies in order to devote himself to a commercial career,[322] all other rabbis who were in business continued both studying and teaching. They also scrupulously applied Jewish religious and legal principles to the conduct of their own businesses, making sure that their honesty should be above reproach. Thus, in the third century, R. Hanina, one of the foremost Palestinian scholars of his time, was, among other things, a trader in honey. Usually he sold bee honey, but on one occasion he erroneously sold date honey. Later he told his customers, "Since I do not want to deceive you, I want you to know that the honey I sold you was date honey". Although they were by no means displeased, but on the contrary claimed that for their purpose this was just what they required, R. Hanina was too conscientious to permit himself to derive benefit from an error. He accordingly used the proceeds to build a *Beth Midrash* (House of Study) in Sepphoris.[323]

viii R. Zera

A couple of generations later, we meet with another extraordinarily conscientious scholar merchant. R. Zera, a Babylonian who emigrated to Palestine where he earned his living as a linen merchant, consulted R. Abbahu, the leading scholar of his age, whether he was permitted to adorn his goods to give them an improved appearance, thereby attracting customers. He was told he could do so in view of the fact that he was selling only new materials, not second-hand stuff, where appearances could be deceptive.[324]

ix R. Abbahu

R. Abbahu himself traded in fine veils which he may have produced at his own workshop. Once he consulted R. Jose ben Hanina whether he might beautify the veils he was offering for sale. He, too, was assured that this was a legitimate practice.[325]

---

322 *T.B. Taan.* 21a.
323 *T.Y. Peah* VII, 4, 20b.
324 *T.Y. B.M.* IV, 9, 9d.
325 Ibid.

x Simeon ben Shetah

Some rabbis went to inordinate lengths to conduct their business in a manner which was not only above reproach, but strove for exemplary, indeed perfect, honesty. Simeon ben Shetah, a leader of the Pharisees in the first half of the first century B.C.E., was a linen (or flax) merchant. To ease his burden, his disciples purchased a donkey from an Arab trader. Subsequently they discovered that a precious stone was suspended from the animal's neck. Although Simeon was urged by his disciples to keep the stone to which he was legally entitled, he indignantly rejected their suggestion. "What do you think?" he asked, "Is Simeon son of Shetah a barbarian?" When the stone was returned, the grateful Arab trader exclaimed, "Blessed be the God of the Jews!" or, according to another version, "Blessed be the God of Simeon son of Shetah!"[326]

xi Abba Shaul ben Botnith and R. Eleazar ben R. Zadok

Similar tales of rabbis who were honest in their business dealings beyond the requirements of the law are quite frequent in the Talmud. We are told of two pious storekeepers, Abba Shaul ben Botnith and R. Eleazar ben R. Zadok, who flourished in Jerusalem around the middle of the first century C.E., that they would take extraordinary care to avoid the possibility of giving their customers less than the proper amounts. When they nevertheless found that because of the foam on top of the measures they had saved a considerable amount of wine, they donated it for "public purposes".[327]

xii Commercial Ethics and Gentiles — General Rabbinic Attitude

Even in later centuries, when relations between Jews and pagans had sadly deteriorated, the rabbis took care to return lost articles or money to gentiles as well as to Jews and to adhere to a code of commercial ethics under all circumstances. We are told that some rabbis had purchased wheat from soldiers or, according to another interpretation, from money-lenders, and found money among the wheat. According to the letter of the law, they were entitled to keep the find. However, they

---

326 T.Y. B.M. II, 5, 8c; *Deut. R.* 3, 3.
327 *M. Bez.* III, 8; *T. Yom Tob* III, 8; *T.Y. Bez.* III, 9, 62b; *T.B. Bez.* 29a; cf. A. Büchler, *Types of Jewish-Palestinian Piety from 70 B.C.E. to 70 C.E.* (London, 1912), p. 144.

returned it to its owners, who thereupon enthusiastically praised the God of the Jews.[328]

While such moralizing stories are not without some legendary elements, they were no doubt designed to promote commercial honesty (which was certainly far from universal), and they reflect the prevailing rabbinic attitude. This must have impressed itself upon the popular consciousness, bearing in mind the enormous spiritual influence exercised by the rabbis.

xiii R. Abdima and R. Hiyya bar Joseph — Unethical Business Practices
Only one or two merchant rabbis had to be taken to task for what was considered an unethical practice. A certain R. Abdima, who sold and probably produced ships' sails, would steep them in water to improve their appearance. For some reason or other this was not considered permissible, and he was criticized by the third century rabbi, Jacob bar Aha.[329] According to a different interpretation, R. Abdima was a salt merchant who was in the habit of steeping his sieves in water, so that the rough salt should have a clean and purified appearance after being sifted. There is even a third explanation of this obscure passage, according to which he was a butcher who steeped clean meat in water, with a view to making it look bloated and fat, which was evidently preferred by contemporary housewives. If this is correct, R. Jacob bar Aha's criticism becomes intelligible and was indeed fully justified.

If R. Abdima was indeed a salt merchant, as has been suggested, he was not the only rabbi-merchant engaged in this field. A younger Palestinian contemporary of his, R. Hiyya bar Joseph, was a salt merchant, and, like R. Abdima, he became involved in some questionable commercial ethics, though in his case he just managed to avoid censure by timely consultation. A customer of his gave him advance payment — though apparently only a deposit — for a quantity of salt. Before he had managed to deliver the salt, it rose in price, and R. Hiyya was tempted to withdraw from the transaction since he could now obtain a higher price than originally stipulated. He decided, however, to consult R. Johanan who told him in no uncertain

328 *T.Y. B.M.* II, 5, 8c.
329 Ibid. IV, 9, 9d.

terms that despite the fact that no legally binding contract had been concluded, he was morally obliged to abide by the verbal agreement.[330]

xiv Rab Hama and Rab Dimi — Market Privileges for Scholars
In Babylonia, where the Exilarch (the civil ruler of the Jewish community) was closely associated by family ties and general interests with the scholarly community, rabbis were granted certain exclusive commercial privileges which provided them with considerable advantages over competitors. Thus, on market days, scholar merchants enjoyed a monopoly of the market, no one else being allowed to offer the same goods for sale unless and until the scholars had sold their entire stock. Rabbis were also exempt from the usual tolls and taxes imposed on imports and exports. They were thus able to charge an increased credit price, which was a concealed form of interest, generally at a higher rate than was customary because, as the fourth century Babylonian scholar merchant Rab Hama explained, his customers actually benefited from dealing with him despite the higher cost of the merchandise. This was because the goods which he sold them for export remained nominally in his possession until they were resold elsewhere, and in the meantime he was responsible for any losses incurred, while his customers were released from tolls and similar charges on his goods and were, moreover, granted a market monopoly usually reserved for rabbis. They were consequently able to make a considerable profit on the merchandise purchased from Rab Hama.[331]

The market privileges granted to rabbis were, to be sure, by no means automatic. A rabbi who was not a recognized scholar had to prove his worth before gaining the coveted market monopoly. An interesting case was that of Rab Dimi of Nehardea (4th cent. C.E.) who once imported a load of figs in a boat. The Exilarch was in no hurry to grant him market privileges. Instead, he arranged for a scholar to be sent to test his knowledge. Rab Adda bar Abba who was given this assignment gave Rab Dimi a difficult test, asking him only a single question which the latter could not answer. Rab Adda thereupon failed him on the spot and gave him, moreover, a none too gentle hint that he would do well to go elsewhere. Needless to say, the market was not reserved for him, and his

---

330 *T.B. B.M.* 48b.
331 Ibid. 65a.

figs were a dead loss since he could not sell them in time before they became rotten. He then appealed to Rab Joseph, the head of the academy of Pumbeditha, who strongly sympathized with Rab Dimi and called for divine punishment on those who had wronged him. Sure enough, Rab Adda bar Abba died shortly thereafter.[332]

xv Rab Safra — Business Disputes

Rabbis involved in business disputes and litigation were occasionally given some legal advantages not granted to others. Thus, Rab Safra, a fourth century Babylonian rabbi, was left some money by his father which he was supposed to share with his brothers. However, before the division of the estate could be effected, Rab Safra invested the money in his business. His brothers then sued him for a share in the business profits; but Raba, who was generally in the habit of favoring scholars in lawsuits,[333] decided the case in favor of Rab Safra. "Rab Safra", he said, explaining his decision, "is a great man; he cannot be expected to leave his studies in order to toil for others".[334] On another occasion, however, Rab Safra was less fortunate. Having entered a business partnership with a certain Issur,[335] Rab Safra divided the stock without Issur's knowledge in the presence of two witnesses. He intended to dissolve the partnership, but in order to do so legally, three witnesses or a properly constituted court were required. Although he tried to argue that two witnesses were sufficient, he was overruled.[336]

xvi R. Hiyya and R. Eleazar — Bankers and Money-changers

Closely associated with commerce was banking, which in antiquity comprised primarily changing money and coins for a small fee. In Temple times money-changers were essential for the thousands of pilgrims who came to Jerusalem from all over the Roman and Parthian empires. Not surprisingly, there were money-changers in the Temple area,[337] where they enjoyed a brisk trade all year round, but especially

---

332 *T.B. B.B.* 22a.
333 *T.B. Shab.* 119a.
334 *T.B. B.B.* 144a.
335 Whether he is identical with Issur the money-changer (see *infra*, p. 68; *T.B. B.K.* 99b) or with Issur the Proselyte (cf. *T.B. B.B.* 149a; *Ket.* 23a) is uncertain.
336 *T.B. B.M.* 31b–32a.
337 *Matt.* 21:12f.; *Mark* 11:15; *John* 2:15f.

during the three pilgrim festivals — Passover, Pentecost and Tabernacles. So essential were their services that, when preparations for the
rebuilding of the Temple were made in the early years of Hadrian's reign,
money-changers' tables were set up for the convenience of the anticipated throngs of pilgrims along the entire sea-coast between Antioch in
Northern Syria and Acco (Acre) near the northern border of Palestine.[338]

By and large, bankers and money-changers must have been highly
skilled men who had to determine on the spot the real value of the coins
offered to them.[339] If they failed to satisfy their customers or otherwise
made a mistake, they had to bear the loss.[340] R. Hiyya who, as we have
seen, was a landowner and silk merchant, but seems to have pursued
some banking business as a sideline, was once consulted by a woman as
to the genuineness of a coin. He assured her that it was solid currency;
but it turned out that it was bad (i.e., either mixed with inferior alloy or
clipped or otherwise damaged) and could not be used or exchanged
anywhere. R. Hiyya then ordered his nephew Rab, who assisted him in
his business, to change the woman's bad coin for a good one and to
register the transaction as "a bad business".[341]

Later, in the third century, a similar stroke of bad luck befell R. Eleazar, who was shown a *sela* (= four *denarii*) by a customer. He pronounced it genuine. When it turned out to be worthless, he was
summoned before R. Simeon ben Lakish, who sentenced him to pay for
his mistake.[342] On another occasion, R. Simeon ben Lakish himself
consulted R. Eleazar concerning a doubtful *denarius*. Again, R. Eleazar
considered it to be genuine and passable; but this time R. Simeon
intimated that he was relying on his (R. Eleazar's) judgment, and that he
would hold him responsible if anything went wrong. R. Eleazar tried to
argue that he could not be held accountable for any error of judgment,
but R. Simeon insisted that he was responsible.[343] We are not told how it
turned out eventually. One can only hope that R. Eleazar, who was a very
poor man,[344] was right for a change.

---

338 *Gen. R.* 64, 10.
339 Krauss, *Talm. Arch.*, II, 412.
340 *Tos. B.K.* X, 10.
341 *T.B. B.K.* 99b.
342 *T.Y. Kil.* VII, 4, 31d.
343 *T.B. B.K.* 100a.
344 *T.B. Ber.* 5b.

While R. Eleazar may not have been a very proficient or successful money-changer, it would seem that for the most part able bankers and money-changers were prosperous and rich. In a Midrashic parable we are told of a wealthy moneychanger who stays at home or in his place of business waiting for customers. In sharp contrast, it is the itinerant money-changer who looks for business when none is brought to him.[345]

xvii Dishonest Money-Changers
For the non-expert, money-changing could thus be a precarious and risky business. In addition, there was the ever-present temptation to commit fraud, especially when one was dealing with travellers, pilgrims and other strangers whom one was unlikely to encounter again. Evidently some money-changers succumbed to such temptations, for the reputation of the profession was none too high. The apparent ease with which Jesus managed to overturn the tables of the money-changers near the Temple,[346] while the authorities took no action whatsoever, indicates that he had popular sympathy on his side. Again, the fact that the hated Balaam, the rabbinic prototype of the evil seducer, is compared in the Midrash to a money-changer[347] points to a low opinion of the profession on the part of the rabbis. In another passage, moreover, Balaam is expressly linked to a fraudulent money-changer who falsifies his weights. He is detected by the market chief and when charged with deception, insolently announces that he has already sent an appropriate bribe to the chief's house.[348]

Another homiletic parable tells us of a banker and money-changer who had come under suspicion of fraud, whereupon the king ordered him to be dismissed and replaced by another who was then commanded to refund the debts incurred by his predecessor.[349]

It was mainly because of the doubtful honesty and the generally poor reputation of the money-changer that relatively few rabbis entered what could have been a lucrative profession for qualified people. Besides, money-changing and banking could be carried on only in major urban centers, for the most part in Hellenistic cities, which were rarely centers

---

345 *Sifre Deut.* 13, edit. Friedmann 67b–68a; edit. Horovitz-Finkelstein, p. 22.
346 *Matt.* 21:12f.; *Mark* 11:15; *John* 2:14ff.
347 *Num. R.* 20, 7; *Tanh.* Balak 4, edit. Buber IV, 134.
348 *Num. R.* 20, 18; *Tanh.* Balak 12, edit. Buber IV, 141.
349 *Num. R.* 4, 8.

of rabbinic learning. Hence, apart from the few rabbis mentioned, there were hardly any rabbinic money-changers or bankers during the Talmudic period. We hear of a R. Hana the money-changer (3rd cent. C.E.) who was once asked for a special *denarius* for measuring the extent of a defect in an animal.[350] About the same time, there were two highly expert money-changers in Babylonia, named Dankcho and Issur;[351] but whether they were scholars is uncertain. Most rabbis who had a flair for business preferred to enter commerce rather than banking.

9. Rabbis as Schoolteachers and Educators

i R. Hiyya

Next to commerce, schoolteaching (which ideally was supposed to be done free of charge, but in practice had to be remunerated),[352] seems to have provided a natural outlet to rabbinic scholars. Although hardly a profitable occupation — most schoolteachers were notoriously poor — it required neither capital nor ownership of land nor any particular skill (other than natural aptitude) which rabbis did not already possess by virtue of their religious training. Then, as now, it was usually assumed that, while most schoolteachers were not qualified to be rabbis, all rabbis were qualified to be schoolteachers. Pedagogic skill was not yet taught as a subject, and was certainly not a primary requirement for a teacher.

The teaching profession was thus an open field, and anyone who wished to open a school at his own home could do so, earlier objections being overruled in the interest of education.[353] The rabbis were far from being incompetent teachers. Some of the rabbinic schoolteachers were outstanding pedagogues, who used educational methods which seem surprisingly modern. After the rabbinic exhortations to parents to let their children attend school had begun to bear fruit, there was, to begin with, a desperate shortage of schoolteachers. Around 200 C.E., R. Hiyya, who was a landowner and silk merchant, passionately devoted himself to the cause of elementary education. He trained a number of pupil

350 *T.B. Hul.* 54b.
351 *T.B. B.K.* 99b. See *supra*, p. 65.
352 *T.B. Ned.* 37a.
353 *T.B. B.B.* 21a–b.

teachers who were to teach each other whatever they had learned, eventually, no doubt, teaching other young students as well. R. Hiyya also provided all the necessary teaching aids, and the ingenious manner in which he set about his task is described by R. Hiyya in what has become a classical passage in the history of Jewish education.

"I bring flax seed, sow it, and weave nets (viz. from the plant). With these I hunt stags with whose flesh I feed orphans. From the skins of the stags I prepare scrolls, and then I go to a town where there are no teachers of young children. I then copy the five books of the Pentateuch for five children (respectively), and teach another six children (respectively) the six orders of the Mishnah (= the basic part of the Talmud). Then I tell each one, 'Teach your section to your fellow students' ".[354]

The Patriarch, R. Judah I, paid ungrudging tribute to R. Hiyya's self-sacrificing work in the cause of education: "How great are the deeds of Hiyya!" he exclaimed with admiration.[355]

ii Samuel bar Shilath

A generation later, we hear of the Babylonian rabbi, Samuel bar Shilath, who was such a devoted schoolteacher that for thirteen years he could not find time to visit his garden. Even when at last he took time off for this purpose, he claimed that his thoughts were with the children.[356] Rab, the spiritual leader of Babylonian Jewry, praised him highly, applying to him the biblical verse, "They that turn many to righteousness shall be like stars for ever and ever".[357]

iii Rab

Rab himself was an outstanding educator whose ideas can only be described as ultra-modern. He was opposed to corporal punishment of schoolchildren[358] and advised Rab Samuel bar Shilath to use nothing bigger than shoelaces for punishing his pupils. This was, of course, only a symbolic punishment, and meant in effect that schoolchildren were not to be physically hurt. He was also concerned about the mental health of ill-adjusted children. Accordingly, he advised Samuel bar Shilath to

354 *T.B. Ket.* 103b; *B.M.* 85b.
355 Ibid.; ibid.
356 *T.B. B.B.* 8b.
357 Ibid.; cf. Daniel 12:3.
358 *T.B. Shab.* 119b.

refrain from admitting children under the age of six to his school, since the hard program of study was too much for young children. Those who were inattentive or could not keep up with the rest of the class, were not to be excluded or expelled, but were to be seated next to good students so that they might learn from their good example.[359] Of course, there was the possibility that the good pupils would be adversely affected by the bad ones; but Rab evidently felt that on balance it was preferable not to reject a child because of his inadequate or late development.

On the other had, unlike so many modern educators, who tend to regard the elementary school as a playground or as a center for socializing, in fact anything except serious study, Rab considered the elementary school to be precisely what it was meant to be in the first place — an institution for the study of the Bible to be attended by students up to the age of ten. Learning to read and understand the Hebrew Bible was therefore the most essential aspect of the elementary school curriculum. Once a child was old enough to attend school — usually at the age of six or seven — he should be stuffed with Torah (according to Rab's advice) "like an ox" (*viz.*, with fodder).[360]

iv Levi bar Sisi

An unsuccessful rabbi turned schoolteacher was Levi bar Sisi who was sent by R. Judah the Patriarch to the Galilean town of Simonia. His failure had nothing to do with teaching. The townspeople were able or willing to provide the salary of only one communal official. They, therefore, asked the Patriarch for a candidate who would be able to fulfill every conceivable communal function, including preacher, judge, synagogue supervisor as well as Bible and Mishnah teacher. Just in case any other function might crop up, they stipulated that the successful candidate must be prepared to "carry out all our functions". In other words, he must be a communal maid-of-all-work.[361] The Patriarch obligingly sent Levi bar Sisi to assume the burdens of office. On arrival, he was placed on a high platform and showered with questions of every description.

---

359 *T.B. Ket.* 50a; *B.B.* 21a.
360 Ibid.; ibid.
361 Incidentally, such exaggerated demands were by no means an isolated phenomenon. A generation later, the same versatile qualifications were required by the well-to-do community of Bostra in Transjordan; cf. *T.Y. Sheb.* VI, 1, 36d; *Lev. R.* 5,4; *Lam. R.* 3, 16.

Possibly because of nervousness and excitement, he was unable to answer — whereupon he was instantly fired. On his return to the Patriarch, the latter discovered that Levi actually knew all the answers, but by then it was too late.[362]

10. Rabbis as Professional Preachers

A congenial occupation for a rabbi was that of preacher. Although for the most part unpaid, some professional preachers, as well as those who combined this occupation with other communal functions, were paid. Thus, in third century Palestine, there are known to have been two preachers who substituted for R. Johanan whenever he was away from his synagogue. We are even told that they were paid two *sela's* a week each, which was by all indications a very modest salary indeed.[363]

11. Rabbinic Scribes

i Nahum
Another traditional occupation for a rabbi was that of scribe. Even in Temple times professional scribes were, as a rule, learned men; and even if their authority as religious leaders of the community was circumscribed — a limitation which would certainly apply to scribes specializing in writing legal documents rather than copying sacred texts — they were nevertheless close enough to rabbinical rank to be linked with the Pharisees in New Testament denunciations.[364] We learn of expert scribes known as "the family of Hagira" in Jerusalem.[365] The Jerusalem scribes, who evidently enjoyed a high reputation, followed special methods in writing Torah scrolls.[366] One of these learned scribes was a certain Nahum "the Libellar(ius)" (i.e., a scribe who would usually write legal documents as well as biblical scrolls) who lived in Jerusalem and was

362 *T.Y. Yeb.* XII, 6, 13a; *Gen. R.* 81, 2.
363 *T.Y. Suk.* V, 1, 55a; *Gen. R.* 98, 11.
364 Cf. especially, *Matt.* chapter 23.
365 *T.Y. Meg.* I, 11, 71d.
366 *T.B. Baba Bathra* 14a.

well versed in religious traditions which he could trace back to hoary antiquity.[367]

ii Court Scribes — Ben Karara

The Sanhedrin or High Court as well as provincial courts employed professional scribes to record the names of the judges and their individual opinions regarding the innocence or guilt of the accused.[368] Although we are not told so explicitly, we may assume that such court scribes were not mere "court reporters", but scholars familiar with legal and religious cases argued before the court. Even scribes who specialized in writing bills of divorce[369] — they apparently had their "headquarters" in the market somewhat like scribes in Arab markets down to modern times[370] — were, it seems, men of learning.[371] One such learned scribe, Ben Karara (or, according to another reading, Ben Kadara), practiced his trade during the latter half of the first century C.E. in the Galilean town of Arab, but some of his divorce-bill techniques did not meet with the approval of the majority of rabbis.[372]

iii R. Yeshebab the Scribe

A generation later, we hear of R. Yeshebab the Scribe who was said to have given away his entire property to the poor;[373] though, according to another account, he only intended to donate beyond the permissible limit of one fifth of his estate to charity, but was prevented by his colleague R. Akiba from carrying out his well-meant but improvident plan.[374] Unfortunately, his goodhearted nature did not save him from suffering a martyr's death during the Hadrianic persecutions.[375]

iv Nakai the Scribe

A younger contemporary of R. Yeshebab was Nakai the Scribe who participated in the rabbinic decision to declare the city of Tiberias clean

---

367 *M. Peah* II, 6.
368 *M. Sanh.* IV, 3.
369 Cf. *T.B. Git.* 84b.
370 Cf. *M. Git.* III, 1; *Sifre Deut.* 269, edit. Friedmann, p. 122a; edit. Horovitz-Finkelstein, p. 288.
371 Cf. Krauss, *Talm. Arch.* III, 320, n. 282.
372 *Tos. Git.* II, 10.
373 *T.Y. Peah* I, 1, 15b.   374 *T.B. Ket.* 50a.   375 *Lam. R.* 2, 2.

despite the fact that it had originally been built on a gravesite.[376] The effect of the decision was to open this important center to Jews of priestly descent as well as to scholars who insisted on residing only in levitically purified localities. Nakai would appear to have regretted this decision; for he criticized R. Simeon bar Yohai for initiating the city's purification. The story concludes with the account of the miraculous and untimely decease of Nakai, allegedly because he had opposed R. Simeon and his colleagues.[377]

v R. Ammi

A century later we learn concerning R. Ammi, a leading Palestinian rabbi of his time, that he wrote no less than four hundred scrolls of the Law. This, if true, would place him among the most productive scribes of all times. However, even in the Talmud this hyperbolic statement is deflated into four hundred verses — a suggestion equally untenable.[378] R. Ammi's output was neither so prodigious nor so exiguous as later speculation intimated. "Four hundred" is a recognized Talmudic figure for "large number", and the tradition simply indicates that R. Ammi was a diligent and fast-working scribe.

vi Rab Huna

R. Ammi's older Babylonian contemporary, Rab Huna, a wealthy man who certainly did not require any moonlighting job, is nevertheless supposed to have written seventy scrolls of the Law.[379] If this were accurate, it would have left him precious little time for his numerous other activities, which included the presidency of the great academy of Sura. No doubt, the round number seventy is a characteristic exaggeration of a fair number, which was however, certainly no more than a small fraction of seventy.

vii Rab Aha bar Jacob

One of Rab Huna's students, Rab Aha Bar Jacob, wrote a single Torah scroll on calf's skin parchment and managed it in such a way that its

---

376 Cf. Josephus, *Ant.* XVIII, 2, 2 (38).
377 *Gen. R.* 79, 6.
378 *T.B. Baba Bathra* 14a.
379 Ibid.

length from top to bottom and circumference were exactly equal — the ideal manner in which a scroll of the Law was supposed to be produced. In practice, however, only rarely did anyone succeed in balancing length and circumference exactly — Rab Huna had managed it only once. Rab Aha's feat became an object of envy, and when he died shortly afterwards, his premature end was attributed to the "evil eye".[380]

viii R. Hanina the Writer

A little later, we hear of a R. Hanina the Writer (viz. of legal documents), who was also a scholar, transmitting a rabbinic opinion concerning the liability of a High Priest to incur the penalty of flagellation.[381] This instance is interesting since it shows that even ordinary scribes who did not as a rule specialize in writing Torah scrolls could be rabbis and men of some scholarship.

ix R. Meir and Rab Hananel

By far the most important, and probably the most skillful, of rabbinic scribes was R. Meir who flourished in Palestine in the middle of the second century C.E. He produced an improved ink by adding vitriol to the ink then commonly in use, with the result that the writing was safeguarded against accidental erasure.[382] Despite his skill, he was warned by his teacher, R. Ishmael, to be extremely meticulous in his work because a single error committed in what was after all a sacred calling could amount to accidental blasphemy, depicted in the colorful language of the time as "destroying the entire universe".[383]

Despite this dire warning, the sacred scrolls written by R. Meir were said to have contained curious marginal annotations which, judging by what often happened in similar cases, could all too easily have crept into the text itself — and perhaps even did so.[384]

R. Meir was also somewhat careless about the regulation that sacred texts must be copied, not written by heart (which could introduce

---

380 Ibid.
381 *T.Y. Sanh.* II, 1, 19d.
382 *T.B. Erub.* 13a; *T.B. Sot.* 20a. On the technical aspects of the manufacture of writing materials, cf. L. Löw, *Graphische Requisiten und Erzeugnisse bei den Juden. Gesammelte Schriften* (Szegedin, 1889–1900).
383 Ibid.; ibid.
384 *Gen. R.* 9, 5; 20, 12; *T.Y. Taan.* I, 1, 64a.

irreversible errors into the text). On one occasion he spent the festival of Purim in the province of Asia in what is today western Turkey, and, unable to find there a scroll of the book of Esther, he wrote one from memory. Although this was excused on the grounds that he had no alternative if he was to carry out the obligatory reading of the scroll of Esther, this did not deter Rab Hananel, a third century Babylonian scribe, from writing Bible scrolls by heart even though there was no emergency. He was, however, tactfully advised that he was transgressing a rabbinic regulation, no matter how wonderful his memory.[385]

R. Meir's unorthodoxy extended to his manner of disposing of his earnings. Although justly described as a "skillful scribe", his earnings amounted to only three *sela's* a week — roughly sixty dollars today, though the cost of living as well as the standard of living were much lower in those days. He spent his wages in equal proportions on food and drink; on clothing; and on the support of poor scholars. All this apparently covered only his personal expenses — including presumably the maintenance of his wife. He did not, however, provide for his children, and when asked why he refused to do so, his reply was truly astonishing:

"If they are righteous, then it will be as David said, 'Yet have I not seen the righteous forsaken, nor his seed begging bread'.[386] If they are not righteous, why should I leave my possessions to the enemies of God?"[387]

x Income and Status of Scribes

If the income of a skillful scribe amounted to so little that two thirds of it were absorbed by basic necessities, such as food and clothing for one or two persons, it is evident, as has already been pointed out in Chapter Two, that the average scribe would invariably be a poor man. This is expressly stated in the Talmud, according to which the wages of scribes never contain a sign of blessing.[388] More explicitly, we are told that scribes of sacred texts and those who trade in such holy articles "never see a sign of blessing".[389] To rationalize this apparent injustice it was pointed out, not without subtle irony, that "the Men of the Great Assem-

---

385 *T.B. Meg.* 18b.
386 *Pss.* 37:25.
387 *Eccl. R.* 2, 18.
388 *T.B. Pes.* 50b.
389 Ibid.; *T. Bik.* II, 15.

bly", which was a legislative-judicial assembly of scribes and teachers of the Law said to have been organized by Ezra, had observed twenty-four fasts, praying that scribes should not grow rich lest they cease to pursue their calling.[390] The Men of the Great Assembly could have saved themselves the trouble. There was no danger that scribes would get wealthy by pursuing their trade. Only if they had other sources of income could they grow prosperous.

In addition to inexorable economic realities, the basic reason for what was only slightly concealed rabbinic opposition to the economic well-being of scribes was the dislike of the rabbis for those who were using the Torah as "a spade to dig therewith",[391] i.e. exploiting a religious act, which ideally should be done free of charge, for financial gain. Hence also the extension of the lack of blessing to traders in sacred articles. In theory, this should have exempted scribes who specialized in writing legal documents from the curse of poverty; and it would indeed seem that such necessary work was adequately and instantly paid.[392] Nevertheless, since the preparation of legal documents was in all probability a seasonal occupation, busy periods alternating with slack ones, it may readily be assumed that scribes specializing in divorce bills and similar legal documents utilized their spare time to write sacred texts which they would then sell for whatever price they could get.

Thus, despite the active participation of scholars and rabbis in this sacred profession — which was so essential that scholars were not supposed to reside in a town where no scribe was living[393] — the status of the scribe was never high in post-Temple times.[394] He is even listed among hewers of wood and drawers of water who undoubtedly belonged to the lowest social category.[395]

It is therefore not altogether surprising that the scribe was included in a list of seven professional people who were to be deprived of their share in the world-to-come.[396] Although the commentators attribute this condemnation to the carelessness with which some scribes performed their

---

390 T.B. Pes. 50b.
391 M. Aboth IV, 5.
392 Cf., e.g., Deut. R. 3, 17.
393 T.B. Sanh. 17b.
394 Cf. Krauss, op. cit. III, 171.
395 Num. R. 8, 4; cf. Jos. 9:23–27.
396 Aboth R.N., edit. Schechter, Vers. I, ch. 36, p. 108.

work — R. Ishmael's above-mentioned warning to R. Meir is generally cited in this connection — it is probably the financial abuse of a sacred activity which lies at the root of the matter.

12. Rabbis as Physicians

i Relative Neglect of Medical Profession

While there is a good deal of medical advice in the Talmud, there were very few rabbis who could be considered professional physicians, which is all the more remarkable in view of the fact that during the Middle Ages literally hundreds of rabbis became distinguished practitioners of medicine. The neglect of the medical profession by the early rabbis was probably due to the lack of training facilities. Moreover, the emphasis set on the exclusive study of the Torah effectively denied the time required for mastering the art of healing. Last, but not least, the impoverished Jews of Palestine were evidently unable to afford the fees to be paid to the physicians, and while the Babylonian Jews were somewhat better off, their preoccupation with agriculture and their characteristic superstitions, made them a less than attractive prospect for the would-be physician.

ii Mar Samuel

The only outstanding rabbi-physician of the Talmudic age was Mar Samuel (3rd cent. C.E.) whom we have already mentioned as a careful landowner who daily inspected his estate. His versatility was such that, in addition to his rabbinical and medical accomplishments, he was also a calendar expert [397] and astronomer of note who claimed that he was as familiar with the paths of heaven as with the streets of his native Nehardea in central Babylonia. [398] Because of his outstanding astronomical knowledge he was surnamed Yarhina'ah (lit., the lunar expert) — a title not accorded to any other rabbi. [399]

As a physician, Mar Samuel specialized in ophthalmology, and he even invented an eye salve which was named after him, and was in

397 *T.B. Hul.* 95b; R.H. 20b.
398 *T.B. Ber.* 58b.
399 *T.B. B.M.* 85b.

demand even in the Land of Israel.[400] His ruling that an inflamed eye should be treated even on the Sabbath[401] was generally accepted both in Babylonia and in the Holy Land.[402] His most prominent patient was the Patriarch R. Judah I. When the latter contracted an eye disease, Mar Samuel offered to bathe it with a lotion or, alternatively, to apply an ointment to it; but the Patriarch, who was extremely sensitive to pain, said he could bear neither lotions nor ointments. Mar Samuel then placed a phial of chemicals under the Patriarch's pillow. The vapor of the chemicals, though not applied directly to the eye, seems to have been sufficiently powerful to penetrate and heal the eye.[403]

Despite his success, Mar Samuel realized that eye salves could have undesirable side effects, and he frankly conceded that the various liquids used for salves, while they could heal certain eye diseases, also had the effect of dimming the eyesight — the only exception being pure water which could sometimes heal (through bathing the eyes) but caused no ill-effects.[404] In line with his preference for water, Mar Samuel declared that "a drop of cold water in the morning, and bathing the hands and feet in hot water in the evening, is better than all the eye-salves in the world".[405]

He also realized the influence of air or wind on health,[406] and he traced skin diseases to lack of proper hygiene.[407] Pointing out the danger of leaving wounds exposed to infection, he suggested various methods of treatment.[408] He rightly attributed many digestive ailments to inappropriate or radical changes of diet;[409] and he cured his friend and colleague Rab, who was suffering from stomach trouble, by providing him with laxative food and drink.[410] Even the value of exercise after meals was recognized by Mar Samuel who claimed to know cures for virtually all diseases, except for three, one of which was due to lack of exercise.[411]

---

400 T.B. Shab. 108b.
401 T.B. A.Z. 28b.
402 Ibid.; T.Y. Shab. XIV, 4, 14d; T.Y. A.Z. II, 2, 40d.
403 T.B. B.M. 85b.
404 T.B. Shab. 78a.
405 Ibid. 108b.
406 T.B. B.M. 107b.
407 T.B. Shab. 133b.
408 T.B. A.Z. 28a.
409 T.B. B.M. 113b; B.B. 146a.
410 T.B. Shab. 108a.
411 T.B. B.M. 113b.

iii R. Hanina

Samuel's Palestinian contemporary, R. Hanina, whose main livelihood was derived from trading, was also a part-time physician, though it is doubtful whether he obtained any income from this profession. He seems to have favored natural, preventive treatment from earliest childhood such as hot baths and anointing the body with olive-oil which, he maintained, would assure a hale and healthy old age. In his own words, "The warm baths and the oil with which my mother anointed me in my youth have stood me in good stead in my old age".[412] His vigor in old age was such that when he was already eighty years old, he was able to stand on one foot and put on or take off his shoe. This he regarded as the true criterion of youth.[413]

R. Hanina was consulted on a variety of diseases, but apparently he had quite a few cases of mule-bite wounds, some of which he considered to be incurable. At any rate, he maintained that none of his patients who had been injured by white mule bites had ever recovered.[414]

Samuel and R. Hanina agreed that ninety-nine percent of all deaths were due to colds[415] — a somewhat exaggerated estimate due perhaps to frequent outbreaks of fever epidemics at that time which could be attributed to "colds". R. Hanina, moreover, lived in Sepphoris, a Galilean hill fortress exposed to winter storms, so that its inhabitants were, as pointed out in the Palestinian Talmud,[416] highly susceptible to colds.

R. Hanina also maintained high standards of medical ethics. In line with rabbinic ideas on the subject, he refused to sanction saving one life by taking or even endangering the life of someone else.[417] It was because of his high regard for human life and his consistent endeavors to minimize suffering that he, along with his colleague, R. Jonathan, permitted the desecration of the Sabbath by grinding cress and putting it into old wine as a remedy for colic.[418]

---

412 *T.B. Hul.* 24b.
413 Ibid.
414 *T.B. Yoma* 49a.
415 *T.Y. Shab.* XIV, 3, 14c.
416 Ibid.
417 *T.Y. A.Z.* II, 2, 40d; cf. *M. Ohol.* VII, 6.
418 *T.Y. Shab.* XIV, 4, 14d; *T.Y. A.Z.* II, 2, 40d.

iv R. Johanan

R. Hanina's pupil, R. Johanan, whose professional competence is uncertain, nevertheless appears to have moonlighted as a physician. Like his teacher, he insisted that danger to life or limb was a major consideration permitting the Sabbath rest to be set aside. For example, a malfunctioning eye; injury to or inflammation of the back of the hand or the leg; and gum trouble due to scurvy — though none of these posed any direct danger to life — should, according to R. Johanan, be treated on the Sabbath.[419] He took a serious view of severe inflammatory fever, which he regarded as equivalent to an internal injury, and hence sufficiently dangerous to permit treatment even on the Sabbath.[420] He also suggested that the best way of warming up a sufferer from jaundice was to wrap him well, or rub him, in his sheet.[421] As we shall see, he also prescribed certain cures, though apparently for hypothetical cases only.[422]

The treatment must have been effective; for we are told that in Babylonia Rab Kahana (circa 300 C.E.) applied R. Johanan's prescription to a distinguished patient who duly recovered.[423]

Even the Palestinian patriarchs, most of whom were also scholars, were familiar with some medical lore.[424] The last of the Patriarchs, Gamaliel VI (died 426 C.E.), was a professional physician who discovered a remedy for disease of the spleen.[425]

v Preventive Medicine — R. Hiyya, Mar Ukba, Rab Judah,
  R. Johanan and Rabbah bar Rab Huna
Other rabbis, while in all probability not qualified physicians, displayed a considerable amount of medical knowledge. Samuel's older contemporary, R. Hiyya, although hardly a professional physician in view of his preoccupation with agricultural and mercantile activities, showed remarkable familiarity with the science of embryology.[426] He may have practiced preventive medicine. At any rate, his advice on how to prevent

---

419 Ibid.; ibid.
420 *T.B. A.Z.* 28a.
421 *T.B. Shab.* 110b.
422 *T.B. Git.* 69a.
423 *T.B. Shab.* 110b.
424 Cf., e.g., *T.B. Nid.* 63b.
425 Cf. Krauss, *op. cit.* I, 719, n. 608.
426 *T.B. Nid.* 25a.

stomach trouble[427] is, in spite of its obvious limitations, quite sound even by modern standards.

There were also some other rabbis who dabbled in the art of preventive medicine. For example, in third century Babylonia, Mar Ukba and Rab Judah pointed out that certain unwholesome practices could cause general debility.[428] Rab Judah, following the example of his teacher, Mar Samuel, seems to have been familiar with methods of treating eye diseases.[429] He also prescribed remedies for wasp bites, scorpion bites, thorn pricks, fever and shivers.[430]

Some rabbis whether medically qualified or not, taught certain cures to their disciples who, although still in the best of health, might one day profit from the advice of their masters. Thus, in third century Palestine, R. Johanan prescribed a herbal cure for swollen glands or, according to another interpretation, swollen jaws.[431] He also warned against drinking lukewarm water, which he considered extremely dangerous.[432] A generation or so later, Rabbah bar Rab Huna, a Babylonian rabbi, offered some suggestions on how to cure a toothache.[433]

Occasionally one comes across cases of rabbis with semi-medical qualifications who specialized in the art of circumcision. We hear of a R. Judah the Circumciser, who was consulted on problems of circumcision on the Sabbath.[434] Another member of the same profession, R. Judan or R. Judah, who apparently flourished in Palestine at a later date, seems to have had wider interests, discussing as he did calendar problems as well as aggadic stories and folklore.[435]

13. Rabbinic Craftsmen

i Construction Worker — Shammai

Significantly, the rabbis were by no means confined to "intellectual", commercial or agricultural occupations. There is evidence that they were

---

427 *T.B. Git.* 70a.
428 Ibid.
429 *T.B. A.Z.* 28b.
430 Ibid.
431 *T.B. Git.* 69a.   432 *T.B. B.M.* 29b.   433 Ibid.
434 *T.B. Shab.* 130b; *T.Y. Shab.* XIX, 1, 16d.
435 *T.Y. R.H.* III, 9, 59a; *Meg.* I, 7, 71a.

familiar with the entire range of contemporary crafts, thus representing a genuine cross-section of the population. As far back as the beginning of the Common Era, Shammai, who became the founder of a school which tended to be rather strict in the interpretation of the law, was a construction worker by trade. He was not too friendly to pagans who wanted to convert to Judaism but stipulated impossible or unacceptable conditions. On that famous occasion when a non-Jew asked to be converted on the condition that he be taught the whole Torah while standing on one foot, Shammai, thinking that the man was trying to make a fool of him, pushed him back with his builder's measuring-rod. Actually, the would-be proselyte meant that he wanted to be taught the central message or the very essence of Judaism, and this was well understood by Shammai's liberally minded colleague Hillel, who told the heathen rejected by Shammai, "What is hateful to you, do not do to your fellow-man: that is the whole Torah. The rest is commentary, go and learn it".[436]

Shammai used his measuring-rod for a similar purpose when a simple-minded pagan, who had heard about the rich garments worn by the high priests, asked to be converted on condition that he be appointed High Priest. Shammai, convinced that the non-Jew was deriding and mocking him, pushed him out of the house with his measuring-rod. Eventually, however, Hillel, realizing that the pagan was a simple honest man who was in any case attracted to Judaism, accepted his condition until the pagan discovered for himself that he was ineligible for the priesthood, not to mention the High Priestly office.[437]

ii Carpenter — R. Abin

Closely associated with the building trade was that of the carpenter. In third century Babylonia we hear about a R. Abin the Carpenter who was in the habit of honoring the Sabbath by kindling many lights. For this, he was blessed by Rab Huna to have great men descended from him. The blessing was duly fulfilled, and his two sons both became learned rabbis.[438]

---

436 *T.B. Shab.* 31a.
437 Ibid.
438 Ibid. 23b.

iii Needlemaker — R. Joshua

A humble trade, which was nevertheless practiced by one of the greatest rabbis of the late first and early second centuries C.E., was that of needlemaker. R. Joshua ben Hananiah, who was even for a time head of the Sanhedrin, and was highly respected by Jews and Romans alike because of his extraordinary intelligence and learning, was able to scratch only a bare living from his trade (which he practiced at home), and lived all his life in poverty. Once he was visited by the wealthy Patriarch, Rabban Gamaliel II, who was shocked to discover that the walls of R. Joshua's home were black. "From the walls of your house, it is apparent that you are a charcoal-burner", exclaimed the astonished Patriarch. R. Joshua, whose craft required him to burn charcoal for shaping the needles, angrily replied, "Alas for the generation of which you are the leader; for you know nothing of the troubles of the scholars, of their struggles to support and sustain themselves". The "class struggle" among poor and wealthy scholars could not have been expressed more eloquently. Nevertheless, when Rabban Gamaliel humbly apologized, R. Joshua, after some hesitation, forgave him.[439]

iv Blacksmith — R. Yitzhak Nappaha

Closely related to R. Joshua's trade was that of the blacksmith, and we do indeed learn about a R. Yitzhak Nappaha (the blacksmith) who flourished in Usha, Galilee, during the second century C.E. Unlike R. Joshua, he seems to have been a prosperous man who owned five courtyards and, in all probability, the houses roundabout.[440] Evidently, he must have been a master craftsman employing apprentices or laborers who worked under his direction. A descendant and namesake of his who lived in the third century was apparently not a blacksmith by trade, but proudly carried the family title "Nappaha" — proof that it was an honored craft carrying no social stigma whatsoever. A famous contemporary of his, R. Johanan, is known throughout rabbinic literature as Bar Nappaha, "the son of a blacksmith", which is unmistakable evidence that leading rabbis were not at all ashamed of their humble origins.

439 *T.B. Ber.* 28a; *T.Y. Ber.* IV, 1, 7d.
440 *Tos. Erubin* VII, 7.

v Tanner — R. Jose

In a similar vein, we find R. Ishmael son of R. Jose reporting, without embarrassment, that his father had been a tanner by occupation[441] — notwithstanding the fact that the tanner's trade was perhaps the most unpleasant and despised profession among the ancient Jews (see below, Chapter Five).

vi Sandal-maker — R. Johanan

Another trade which was far from prestigious was that of sandal-maker or cobbler. Yet R. Johanan the sandal-maker, the devoted disciple of R. Akiba, was referred to by his craft title.[442] Despite his humble trade, he was a man of great intelligence and courage. When R. Akiba was arrested by the Romans during the Hadrianic persecutions, a religious problem came up which required R. Akiba's decision. Any communication on a Jewish religious matter was, however, strictly prohibited, and any attempt to contravene the interdict was punishable by death. R. Johanan the sandal-maker accordingly disguised himself as a peddler, and offered his wares to the prisoners; but in between the usual questions and answers on the transactions, he slipped in the religious problem that had arisen. R. Akiba replied with equal cunning in between the business discussions.[443]

vii Cobblers and Tailors — R. Abba bar Zemina,
    R. Judah the Tailor, R. Hanina and R. Oshaia

Towards the end of the third century C.E., R. Abba bar Zemina seems to have combined the trade of the cobbler with that of tailor — possibly a logical development since shoes were, in fact, sewn together with threads very much like clothes. For a time, he plied his trade in Rome where he was sewing at the house of a non-Jew. When he was offered non-kosher meat, he declined to eat it despite threats to his life. The Roman then explained that he had really meant to test his devotion to his faith and that he would have killed him if he had violated the Law; for, as the Roman explained, every man must observe the rules of his religion; the Jew must be a loyal Jew, the Gentile — a loyal Gentile.[444]

441 *T.B. Shab.* 49a–b.
442 *T.B. Ber.* 22a; *T.Y. Hag.* III, 1, 78d.
443 *T.Y. Yeb.* XII, 6, 12d.
444 *T.Y. Kil.* IX, 5, 32d; *T.Y. Sheb.* IV, 2, 35a–b.

A few generations earlier, we hear of a R. Judah the Tailor who seems to have combined his trade (which was presumably not very lucrative) with that of scribe, which was, as we have seen, even less profitable. In that capacity he wrote both legal deeds and scriptural scrolls. The manner in which he did the former did not meet R. Judah the Patriarch's approval; but the Patriarch rebuked his son Simeon for informing him concerning the authorship of a certain deed written by R. Judah the Tailor. "Keep away from talebearing", the Patriarch exclaimed angrily. He also disliked being told by his son that a well-written scroll of the book of Psalms had been prepared by R. Judah the Tailor. Although in this case Simeon's intention had been to praise him, it was better to avoid speaking highly of a person because inevitably disparaging remarks would follow.[445]

Cobblers and shoemakers could not always pick and choose the area where they wished to follow their trade. One had to look for neighborhoods where there was a demand for shoes or for the repair of footwear. Thus, two pious third century rabbis, R. Hanina and R. Oshaia, worked as shoemakers in a "red light" district inhabited by harlots. The latter were indeed regular customers, and the rabbinical shoemakers often had to deliver the finished goods to the homes of the prostitutes. They managed, however, to avoid even looking at their enticing customers, who, in turn, respected them as holy men.[446]

14. Miscellaneous Rabbinic Occupations

i Tax-collector — R. Zera's Father

Occasionally we come across some unusual occupations for Jews which were nevertheless practiced by scholars or members of their families. Thus, in third century Babylonia, the father of R. Zera was employed by the government as tax-collector. He was, however, a most unusual revenue officer. Knowing, as he did, the rapacity of government officials who often fleeced the people to a much greater extent than even the heavy-handed government required, R. Zera's father would go out of his way to protect the taxpayers. For example, he would subtly warn the towns-

445 *T.B. B.B.* 164b.
446 *T.B. Pes.* 113b.

people to hide for a while whenever the district supervisor would come to town. Naturally, the amount collected fell far short of expectations. But when the inspector tried to accuse him of failing in his duty, he had a ready answer: "Of whom shall I demand payment?"[447] Since the Persians who ruled Babylonia at the time had no efficient census returns, they tended to judge by sight, and, with most people in hiding, even heavily populated areas looked almost uninhabited.

ii Detectives — R. Eleazar son of R. Simeon and R. Ishmael son of R. Jose

The idea of a detective rabbi has only recently become popular thanks to some best-selling novels. In second century Palestine, however, rabbis who were also detectives and police officers were not subjects for imaginative fiction, but a highly controversial reality. Thus, R. Eleazar son of R. Simeon once met a Roman police detective who had been sent to arrest thieves and burglars. R. Eleazar pointed out to him that his methods of catching the thieves were unreliable, since he did not really know how to detect them. It could well be that he caught the innocent and let the guilty escape. The police officer agreed that he could not really be sure, but since it was his duty to make an arrest, he had no alternative but to do so, even though he might have little but a hunch to go upon. R. Eleazar then suggested the following method of detection:

"Go into a tavern at the fourth hour of the day (i.e., between 9 and 10 a.m., the usual time for breakfast). If you see a man dozing with a cup of wine in his hand, make inquiries concerning him. If he is a scholar, you may assume that he rose early to pursue his studies. If he is a day laborer, he must have been up early to do his work. If his work is of the kind that is done at night, he might have been rolling thin metal (so that he made no noise which would have provided an alibi). But if he is none of these, he must be a thief (who "works" by night and sleeps during the day); so you may arrest him".[448]

This advice impressed the Roman authorities who promptly appointed R. Eleazar himself as a police detective. In this capacity, he was quite successful — in fact too successful for the liking of his patriotic fellow Jews, who were not happy at the idea of delivering Jewish thieves

447 *T.B. Sanh.* 25b–26a.
448 *T.B. B.M.* 83b.

and burglars to the Romans to be cruelly executed. Moreover, some of these thieves were, in fact, anti-Roman guerillas, and R. Eleazar's collaboration with the enemy seemed all the more reprehensible in view of his father's uncompromising hostility to the Romans. Before long, R. Joshua ben Korha sent him a scathing message: "Vinegar son of wine (i.e., a degenerate son of a righteous father)! How long will you deliver up the people of our God for slaughter?!" R. Eleazar replied in picturesque style, "I am weeding out the thorns from the vineyard". R. Joshua, however, retorted, "Let the owner of the vineyard (God or the Roman authorities) himself come and weed out the thorns".[449]

The same insulting epithet — "vinegar son of wine" — was hurled at R. Eleazar by a fuller. The rabbi, annoyed by what he considered insufferable insolence, had the man arrested. Subsequently, realizing the full implications of what he had done, he tried to secure the fuller's release. By then, however, it was too late. The Romans executed him by "hanging" which most probably meant that he was crucified. R. Eleazar was deeply upset about this incident, and although he was assured that the victim had been an abominable character, the rabbi turned detective remained inconsolable; for his conscience gave him no rest. Many stories were told about his self-afflictions which he personally "summoned" to purge himself of his sin.[450]

Another rabbi turned detective was R. Ishmael son of R. Jose, a highly respected colleague of R. Eleazar. Although no one dared openly criticize R. Ishmael, a characteristic legend reflects the dissatisfaction felt in patriotic Jewish circles. Accordingly, the prophet Elijah appeared to him and rebuked him for handing over Jewish people to the Romans for execution. R. Ishmael tried to excuse himself by pointing out that he was obliged to play his unpleasant role because he was under government orders to do so. Elijah, however, told him that he should rather have fled than collaborate in this manner with the enemy.[451]

iii Gladiator — R. Simeon ben Lakish

If some years ago, a rabbi who earned his living by professional wrestling created a sensation, the case of R. Simeon ben Lakish, a third century

449 Ibid.
450 Ibid.
451 Ibid. 83b–84a.

Palestinian rabbi who became a professional gladiator, should have served as a suitable precedent. R. Simeon, who was endowed with uncommon strength, found it difficult to make ends meet, and so, in his extremity, he abandoned his studies and sold himself to the so-called "ludarii"[452] — apparently impresarios who arranged gladiatorial contests and wild beast fights for the delectation of the bloodthirsty Greek and Roman mobs. The "ludarii" would hire or buy gladiators — in the latter case they were of course slaves — whose job it was either to fight against the wild beasts themselves or, more usually, to finish off the raging beasts whenever they threatened the assembled people.[453] For this purpose, knives and swords had to be used, and those who wielded these weapons had to have both skill and brawn if they expected to survive the ordeal. Even so, theirs was a short life, and sooner or later they were bound to make a fatal mistake and be torn up by the deliberately starved and enraged beasts. Only sheer desperation could drive a man to an occupation which, though well paid,[454] was in the last resort a permanent rendezvous with death.

Not surprisingly, the rabbis looked askance at Jews who recklessly threw away their lives on such a dangerous gamble. Such desperadoes were not considered worthy of ransoming if they had sold themselves,[455] although generally redemption of Jewish slaves and captives was a primary religious obligation. No doubt, the rabbis considered that people who sold their lives for money were bound to repeat the offense, and the community could not reasonably be expected to shoulder indefinitely such a heavy financial burden. Nevertheless, there were rabbis who sympathized with their fallen brethren, although these were usually of the dregs of society and religiously non-observant. Despite the law, some rabbis went out of their way to help these doomed men and have them ransomed.[456]

In view of the horror in which the circus games were held among Jews,[457] it is all the more surprising that an outstanding scholar of the

---

452 *T.B. Git.* 47a.
453 Cf. Graetz, *Geschichte der Juden* IV, (4th edit.), p. 238; Bacher, *Die Agada der Pal. Amor.* I, 342ff.; Krauss, *Talm. Arch.* I, 701, n. 366; *J.E.* V, 675.
454 Cf. *T.Y. Ter.* VIII, 5, 45d.
455 *T.Y. Git.* IV, 9, 46b.
456 Ibid.; *T.B. Git.* 46b–47a.
457 Cf. Josephus, *Ant.* XV, 8, 1 (274f.)

stature of R. Simeon ben Lakish should have sold himself to a life of constant peril and almost certain death. The only acceptable explanation is that his economic circumstances must have become so utterly hopeless that, short of begging for bread, he had no conceivable alternative.

Somehow or other, R. Simeon managed to escape from the "ludarii." According to a legendary story, he tricked his guards and killed them one by one.[458] There was also a widespread notion that in his youth he had been a robber chief and was "converted" by R. Johanan bar Nappaha, who subsequently became his teacher, colleague and brother-in-law.[459] All these legends are probably based on his circus exploits — an experience which left its mark on him for many years to come. Thus, he once gave a knock-out blow to a Samaritan who was blaspheming against rabbinic Judaism.[460] Owing to the starvation diet of his youth, he became later, when he could afford it, a voracious eater, with very peculiar habits which he had obviously picked up among the circus gladiators. He would sit on the floor while eating,[461] and sometimes also during his studies at the *Beth Hamidrash* (college).[462] He was endowed with a portly paunch, and he would frequently lie on his stomach while eating or studying.[463] Like a true gladiator, he never worried about the morrow, but spent all he had without bothering to leave anything for the future. At his death, all he left for his family was a small measure of saffron.[464] The improvident gladiator rabbi had come to his rest.

15. Occupations of Early Christians

In conclusion, it is worth noting that the earliest teachers and missionaries of the Christian church, who, by background and training, did not essentially differ from their rabbinic opponents, were also men who had their special crafts and evidently continued to pursue them, as far as possible, even after they had embarked on converting both Jews and

458 *T.B. Git.* 47a.
459 *B.M.* 84a.
460 *T.Y. M.K.* III, 7, 83b.
461 *T.B. Git.* 47a.
462 *T.B. Zeb.* 5a.
463 Ibid.; *T.B. Git.* 47a.
464 *T.B. Git.* 47a.

Gentiles to their beliefs. Jesus himself, like his father Joseph, was a carpenter,[465] and his first disciples whom he gathered around him were fishermen who plied their trade in the Sea of Galilee. Jesus, who wanted them to follow him, promised to make them "fishers of men".[466] Paul, by far the most successful propagandist of Christianity, was a tentmaker by trade, which he and some of his associates continued to practice even during his numerous missionary journeys.[467] Of the Gospel writers, Matthew was a tax-collector,[468] while Luke was a physician.[469]

465 *Matt.* 13:55; *Mark* 6:3.
466 *Matt.* 4:18ff.; *Mark* 1:16ff.; *Luke* 5:2ff.
467 *Acts* 18:3.
468 *Matt.* 10:3.
469 *Col.* 4:14.

Chapter Four

Rabbinic Attitude to Physical Labor

1. Moral Value of Work

The immense versatility of the rabbis in the Talmudic age enabled them to appreciate the importance and dignity of labor. With few exceptions, they looked upon physical as well as intellectual work from the point of view of men who had had first-hand experience and were in fact directly engaged in work of one kind or another, including, in many cases, humble crafts yielding only a bare livelihood.

In line with their social background, the rabbis expressed their concept of the moral value of work in truly superlative terms. Thus, according to the third century Babylonian rabbi, Ulla, "He that lives on his labor is greater than a God-fearing man".[470]

This attitude is all the more remarkable in view of the all-pervading Hellenistic influences during the Talmudic age. The Greeks regarded physical labor as an activity fit only for slaves, women, and the lowest class of freemen. The Greek philosophers, scientists and other intellectuals considered unlimited leisure to be an essential privilege and vitally necessary for any intellectual activity. By and large, the rabbinic view was diametrically opposed to such concepts. The entire spirit of Judaism, both biblical and rabbinic, favored honest labor in all its forms, regarding it as part of the divinely instituted order of the universe.

2. Divine Blessings depend on Human Efforts

Although the rabbis were well aware that the divine blessings promised in the Bible were usually conditional on the observance of the Torah and its precepts, and did not depend on any human efforts, there were some

---

470 *T.B. Ber.* 8a.

who went beyond the requirements of the Law and demanded that man himself must, as it were, create the divine blessings by his own unstinted labor. Interpreting Deuteronomy 14:29 — "that the Lord your God may bless you in all the work of your hands that you do" — a late Midrash states, "It might be thought God's blessing would be granted even if one sits in idleness. Therefore Scripture says, "in all the work of your hands that you do". If a man "does" (i.e., works), he will be blessed; otherwise, he will not be blessed".[471]

3. Work essential for Human Dignity

Work in the rabbinic view was essential for human dignity and independence. However strange, hard or unpleasant, work was still preferable to relying on public or private assistance. To be a welfare case was the worst humiliation, and almost any alternative was better than living on charity. As Rab, the founder of the Academy of Sura, once said to Rab Kahana, "Flay a carcass in the market place and earn wages, and do not say, 'I am a priest and a great man, and the work is degrading to me' ".[472]

A later Midrash explained the prevailing rabbinic view with even greater force:

"If perchance a man were to say, 'I am of noble descent, a member of a great family. It is not fitting that I should perform (manual) work and degrade myself, we say to him, 'Fool, your Creator has already preceded you, even before you came into the world, as it is written, (He rested on the seventh day) from all the work which he had done' ".[473]

4. Merit of Labor more potent than Fathers' Merit

The rabbis were particularly concerned to counter a fatalistic tendency current in pietistic and sectarian circles that there was no need to do anything since God knows man's needs and will therefore miraculously

---

471 *Midr. Pss.* 136, 10, edit. Buber 261a; *Seder Eliahu R.* 14, edit. Friedmann, p. 71; *Yalkut* II, 899, par. 690.
472 *T.B. Pes.* 113a; *B.B.* 110a.
473 *Midrash Ne'elam*; cf. Gen. 2:2.

supply them to the righteous believers, even if they do nothing to maintain themselves.[474] Referring to Genesis 31:42 — "If the God of my father, the God of Abraham and the Fear of Isaac, had not been on my side, surely now you would have sent me away empty-handed. But God saw my plight and the labor of my hands, and He gave judgment last night" — the Midrash infers that the merit of labor is more potent than the merit of one's fathers. For the latter merely preserved Jacob's property, whereas the former preserved his life. "This teaches that man should not say, 'I will eat and drink and have a good time, and I will not trouble myself to do anything, and Heaven will have mercy'. Therefore, it is written, 'You have blessed the work of his hands'.[475] Man must labor and work with both his hands, and the Holy One, blessed by He, will send His blessings".[476]

5. Miracles due to Work

As an illustration of this principle, the remarkable case of R. Hanina ben Dosa (1st cent. C.E.) was cited by the rabbis. R. Hanina, who had a great reputation as a miracle-worker, was nevertheless poverty-stricken all his life, subsisting on a small quantity of carobs ("boxers" or "St. John's bread") which grew freely in the Land of Israel and are usually eaten by goats. Evidently miracles were not paid for, and nobody could make a living by performing them, still less by relying on them. Once he noticed that his fellow townsmen were taking gifts and offerings to the Temple of Jerusalem. Unwilling to forego the privilege of personally bringing a gift of his to the Temple, he got hold of a large stone, and chipped, chiselled and polished it, thus transforming it into a presentable gift. However, it was far too heavy to carry by himself; so he looked for porters to bring the stone to Jerusalem. Eventually, he got hold of five men who were willing to carry the stone for him; but then R. Hanina discovered that he had no money to pay the men. Naturally, they were unwilling to work for nothing, and so they left him. At this point, so the story goes, God

---

474 For a characteristic example of this tendency, cf. *Matt.* 6:25–34. It was not unknown even in rabbinic circles; see *infra*, pp. 113 ff.
475 Job 1:10.
476 *Gen. R.* 74, 12; *Tanh. Wayetse* 13.

arranged for five angels disguised as men to appear before him. Asked by R. Hanina to carry the stone for him, they agreed to do so on the same terms as the other five laborers, though they did not insist on immediate payment. On the other hand, they did insist that R. Hanina lend them a hand. He placed his hand under the stone to help them carry it, but, miraculously, he suddenly found himself in Jerusalem. Having somehow earned enough money to pay the porters, he looked for them, but could not find them.[477] The moral of the story is clear: even miracles do not happen unless one works to achieve them.

6. Labor as Part of Divine Plan since Adam

Other historical or legendary examples were frequently cited to prove that human labor was part of the divine purpose from the very beginning. Even in paradise, man was not supposed to idle his time away, but was required, as it were, to earn his keep. According to R. Eliezer (c. 100 C.E.) and R. Simeon ben Eleazar (c. 200 C.E.), "even Adam, the first man, did not taste any food until he had done some work, as it is stated, 'He (viz. God) placed him in the Garden of Eden to till it and tend it'.[478] Only then was he told, 'Of every tree of the garden you may freely eat' ".[479]

Even the curse pronounced by God against Adam — "By the sweat of your brow you shall eat bread"[480] — was transformed by the rabbis into a disguised blessing:

"When the Holy One, blessed by He, said to Adam, 'Thorns and thistles it shall bring forth to you',[481] tears flowed from his eyes, and he pleaded before Him, 'Sovereign of the Universe! Shall I and my ass eat out of the same crib?!' But as soon as He said to him, 'By the sweat of your brow, you shall eat bread',[482] his mind was set at rest".[483] The

477 *Eccl. R.* 1, 1.
478 Gen. 2:15.
479 Ibid. v. 16; *Aboth R.N.*, Vers. I, chap. 11; Vers. II, chap. 21, edit. Schechter, p. 23a.
480 Gen. 3:19.
481 Ibid. 3:18.
482 Ibid. 3:19.
483 *T.B. Pes.* 118a; cf. *Aboth R.N.* Vers. I, chap. 1, edit. Schechter, p. 4a (7).

implied meaning of this highly significant Aggadic passage is that labor, however hard, is essential for the dignity of man. It is the material basis of civilization, one of the vital elements distinguishing man from the animals which do, indeed, work instinctively but without the active intelligence employed by man.

7. Abraham and Isaac — Labor in the Promised Land

Abraham, too, discovered that the Promised Land was a home not for idlers, but for hard-working people — which made it all the more attractive to him:

"When Abraham was traveling through Aram Naharaim and Aram Nahor (Mesopotamia and Syria), he saw the inhabitants eating and drinking and reveling. 'May my portion not be in this country!' he exclaimed. But when he reached the promontory of Tyre (i.e., the northern frontier of the Land of Israel) and saw them engaged in weeding and hoeing at the proper seasons, he said, 'Would that my portion might be in this country!' "[484]

In this manner, then, did the Land of Canaan become the promised heritage of the Hebrew people. Just as Abraham appreciated the value and dignity of labor, so did his son Isaac. Although he was the chosen recipient of divine blessings,[485] he realized that "the blessing rests only upon the work of one's hands", and so he sowed the land "and reaped a hundredfold".[486]

8. Israel's Work on the Tabernacle — Condition of Divine Presence

The same lesson that the divine blessing ultimately depends on diligent human endeavor was also stressed in a Midrashic comment on the making of the Tabernacle. "Even the Holy One, blessed be He, did not cause His presence to dwell in Israel until they had performed some

---

484 *Gen. R.* 39, 8.
485 Gen. 26:24.
486 Ibid. v. 12; *Tos. Ber.* VII (VI), 8.

work, as it is stated, 'And let them make Me a sanctuary, that I may dwell among them' ".[487]

As long as the Israelites were busy making the Tent of Assembly — the portable sanctuary used in the wilderness and, later, in the land of Canaan during the period of the Judges they were quite happy and did not complain; but whenever they had nothing to do, they got themselves into trouble[488] a subtle psychological observation which has been proved true throughout recorded history. Those who are busy working have neither time nor inclination to get into mischief. Unemployment, on the other hand, is a road certain to lead to trouble.

9. "Six Days you shall Labor"

Even when the Israelites were commanded to observe the Sabbath and rest from their work, they were also told, "Six days you shall labor and do all your work"[489] — a statement which the rabbis considered to be an independent precept rather than an introduction to the prohibition of work on the Sabbath.[490] Some went even further, regarding work as being of such overriding importance that in their view, anyone who did not work during the week, would end up working on the Sabbath.[491]

It was in line with this reasoning that R. Josiah, a second century Palestinian rabbi, would move garments or utensils shortly before the commencement of the Sabbath from one house to another or from one corner to another, so that the Sabbath should be clearly distinguishable as a day of rest.[492]

10. Tree-Planting in the Land of Israel

In a similar vein, the rabbis believed that the Israelites were enjoined to till the soil and, in particular, to plant trees when they entered the

487 *Exod.* 25:8; *Aboth R.N.*, edit. Schechter, Vers. I, chap. 11, p. 23a; Vers. II, chap. 21, p. 22b (44); *Mekil. R. Sim.*, edit. Hoffman, p. 107; edit. Epstein, p. 149.
488 *Pesik. R.* V, 20b; cf. *Tanh.* Naso, 12.
489 Exod. 20:9; Deut. 5:13.
490 *Aboth R.N.*, Vers. I, chap. 11 and Vers. II, chap. 21, edit. Schechter, p. 22b (44); cf. also Philo, *De Legibus* XX, 98.
491 Cf. *Aboth R.N.* ibid; ibid.
492 Ibid., Vers. II, chap. 21, edit. Schechter, p. 23a (45).

Promised Land, even if there was no immediate need for such work. In an edifying parable, the Israelites were compared to the chicks of a hen who are cared for by their mother, but must eventually learn to fend for themselves:

"The hen, when her young are tiny, gathers them together and places them beneath her wings, warming them and grubbing for them. But when they are grown up, if one of them wants to get near her, she pecks it on the head and says to it, 'Go and grub in your own dunghill!' So during the forty years that the Israelites were in the wilderness, their manna fell, the well came up for them, the quails were at hand for them, the clouds of glory encircled them, and the pillar of clouds led the way before them. When the Israelites were about to enter the (Promised) Land, Moses said to them, 'Let every one of you take up his spade and go out and plant trees.' "[493]

Not only Moses, but God Himself was depicted as being concerned with planting trees in the Land of Israel. The verse, "When you enter the land and plant any tree for food"[494] — was interpreted not merely as a conditional clause, but as a meritorious act, indeed, as a divine precept. As the Midrash puts it, "The Holy One, blessed be He, said to Israel, 'Learn from me. If it were possible to say so, even I need (*viz.* to plant), even as it is written, 'The Lord God planted a garden in Eden, in the East' ".[495]

In the same passage, God is represented as saying to Israel, "Although you will find the land full of good things, do not say, 'We shall dwell there and plant nothing', but take care and plant. ... Just as you entered and found trees planted by others, so shall you plant for your children. No man should say, 'I am old, tomorrow I die. Why should I bother to labor for others?' ".[496]

The same Midrash explains that it was precisely for this reason that man was denied advance knowledge of the day of his death. For such knowledge was bound to render him unwilling to perform work from which he would derive no benefit:

---

493 *Lev. R.* 25, 5.
494 Leviticus 19:23.
495 Gen. 2:8; *Tanhuma*, Kedoshim, 8.
496 Ibid.

"The Holy One, blessed be He, made the hearts of men ignorant of (the day of) death, so that man should build and plant. If he is worthy, (the fruits of his labor) will be his; if he is not worthy, they shall belong to others".[497]

As an illustration of this principle, the Midrash tells a legendary story of the Emperor Hadrian, who once met an old man planting fig trees. Hadrian asked him how old he was, and when he was told that he was a hundred years of age, the Emperor expressed surprise that the old man was toiling away to produce figs which he was very unlikely to eat himself. The graybeard replied with exemplary dignity, "If I am worthy, I shall eat;[498] if not, then as my forefathers have labored for me, so I am toiling for my children". Hadrian, thereupon, asked the old man to let him know if he should be privileged to eat of his figs. When, in due course, the fig-trees produced their fruit, the graybeard presented a basket of his figs to the Emperor who honored him and rewarded him by having the basket filled with *denarii*.

Subsequently, the jealous wife of a neighbor of the old man persuaded her husband to present the Emperor with a sack of figs, in the hope that he would exchange them for *denarii*. The henpecked husband obediently did as he was bidden by his domineering wife, and brought a sack of figs to the imperial palace. There he naively explained, "I heard that the King (i.e., the Emperor) is fond of figs and exchanges them for *denarii*". Hadrian gave orders that the impertinent visitor be made to stand at the palace gate, and that every one entering or leaving should throw a fig in his face. By nightfall, they had emptied his sack, and he was allowed to go home, his face swollen from the impact of the figs that had been thrown at him. He bitterly complained to his wife, "I have to thank you for all of this honor!" Quite unabashed, she retorted, "Go and tell it to your mother. You are fortunate that they were figs and not citrons, and that they were ripe and not hard!".[499]

The moral of the story is obvious. Honest, selfless work is ultimately rewarded. Jealous greed, on the other hand, is duly punished.

---

497 Ibid.
498 *Viz.* of the fruit of the fig-trees.
499 *Lev. R.* 25, 5; *Eccl. R.* 2, 2, 20; *Tanh.*, ibid.

The tremendous emphasis in rabbinic literature on planting trees has inspired modern Zionism and, in particular, the Jewish National Fund, which has used those ancient texts to bolster its afforestation efforts. Thanks to these fine endeavors, the long process of soil erosion in Israel has been halted, and the very climate has been changed for the better. The exhortations and parables, the stories and legends have borne fruit some two thousand years later.

11. The Divine Worker — The Craftsman's Pride in his Work

If, according to the rabbis, God was the first planter, He was also the first worker when He created the world; and when He finished the work of Creation, "He rested on the seventh day from all *His work* which He had done".[500] If God took pride in His work, how much more so was man to appreciate the dignity of his labor. And, indeed, the ancient artisans were conscious of the value and importance of their craft. According to Rab's interpretation of Ecclesiastes 3:11 — "He has made everything beautiful in its time" — God "made every man's trade seem fine in his own eyes".[501] Such a statement could never have been made in the modern industrial age, which has virtually destroyed the functions of craftsmen, thereby undermining man's interest and pride in his work.

Around 100 C.E., R. Eleazar ben Azariah pointed out that every craftsman, showed his pride in his trade by displaying some object characteristic of his craft. Thus, a weaver would carry a small distaff behind the ear; a wood dyer would go out with a dyed sample of wool tied on to his ear; while a scribe would carry a reed pen stuck behind his ear.[502] Elsewhere, we learn that the tailor would have his needle stuck in his garment; the carpenter would go out with a chip of wood behind his ear; the wool corder would have a cord tied on his ear; the money-changer would walk about with a *denarius* dangling from his ear; while the dyer might carry a sample of his work around his neck (presumably, if it was too big to tie onto his ear).[503]

500 Gen. 2:2; *Aboth R.N.*, Vers. II, chap. 21, edit. Schechter, p. 23a (45).
501 *T.B. Ber.* 43b.
502 *Aboth R.N.*, ad loc.
503 *Tos. Shab.* I, 8; *M. Shab.* I, 3; *T.B. Shab.* 11b.

12. Craftsmen, Scholars and Pilgrims

It was in line with the importance attributed to craftsmanship in antiquity that, while the general public and even senior students were expected to display their reverence towards rabbis and scholars by rising at their approach, craftsmen, during their working hours, were expressly exempted from this requirement.[504] On the other hand, during special celebrations, such as the bringing of the first fruits to the Temple when large numbers of pilgrims would make their way to Jerusalem, it was customary for the craftsmen of Jerusalem to rise in honor of the pilgrims and welcome them to the city.[505] However, since pilgrims and other tourist were a source of tremendous revenue to the people of Jerusalem, welcoming the pilgrims could be regarded as good public relations, a tourist attraction of considerable importance. "Visit Jerusalem and its magnificent Temple and enjoy a royal welcome from the friendly people of the Holy City" might well have been the text of travel posters in ancient Alexandria, Athens or Rome.

Even "white collar" workers, such as bankers or money-changers were regarded as "craftsmen" or specialists who were not expected to rise before scholars while engaged in their work. R. Hana, the moneychanger, whom we have already met in the previous chapter, was once approached by Bar Nappaha, in all probability R. Johanan, by far the most outstanding of the third century Palestinian rabbis. Since R. Hana was evidently only a junior rabbi and not actively engaged in public teaching or preaching, he wanted to show his respect for the leading rabbi of his time by rising from his chair. Bar Nappaha, however, would not permit him to do so. "Sit down, my son", he said to R. Hana, "sit down. Craftsmen are not allowed to rise before scholars while occupied with their work".[506]

13. Legal Privileges of Craftsmen and Laborers

The importance and dignity of labor was also given due legal emphasis. It was pointed out that, while anyone, no matter how highly placed, who

---

504 *T.B. Kid.* 33a; *Hul.* 54b; *T.Y. Bik.* III, 3, 65c.
505 *M. Bik.* III, 3.
506 *T.B. Hul.* 54b.

misappropriated or derived any benefit from sacred money or Temple funds, was guilty of an extremely serious offense, the workers and craftsmen employed by the Temple administration could be paid with sacred money, which they were free to use for their own purposes without compunction.[507]

Similarly, it was emphasized that, while a person who robbed someone even of a penny's worth was obliged to restore it to him even if it meant traveling to the ends of the earth, a laborer picking dates for the owner was entitled to eat of them during working hours, even if each date was worth a *denarius*.[508]

In a similar vein, it was pointed out that despite the fact that the generation of the Flood had been doomed because of robbery, an agricultural laborer working for a landowner was free to eat of the produce of the field without incurring any penalty.[509]

14. Work as a Social Necessity

The rabbis saw in work more than a physical necessity or a source of material advantages. "Great is work" is a frequently used rabbinic expression which meant much more than it actually said. Pursuit of a craft was a social necessity; for, as R. Judah the Patriarch put it, "Great is work; for he who does not engage in work becomes a subject of (unfavorable) comment among people (who ask), 'From where does this man take the means to obtain food; from where does he take the means to obtain drink?' ".[510]

The Patriarch may well have had in mind some of the students and scholars who were maintained by him. No doubt he felt that not all were so distinguished as to deserve the ancient equivalent of scholarships and fellowships. Their privileged position, which included exemption from certain taxes and compulsory labor service, evidently aroused some jealousy among the masses, and R. Judah no doubt felt that these privileges could not be maintained indefinitely.

---

507 *Aboth R.N.*, Vers. I, chap. 11, edit. Schechter, p. 22b (44); Vers. II, chap. 21, p. 23a.
508 Ibid., Vers. II, chap. 21, p. 23a.
509 *T.Y. Maas.* II, 6, 50a.
510 *Aboth R.N.*, Vers. II, chap. 21, edit. Schechter, p. 22b (44).

15. Torah and a Worldly Occupation

His son, Rabban Gamaliel III, who lived at a time of growing economic crisis which was to grip the entire Roman Empire during the third century C.E., continued and, indeed, intensified his father's warnings. In a famous maxim of his, he stated, "An excellent thing is the study of the Torah combined with a worldly occupation; for the labor required for them both causes sin to be forgotten (i.e., there will be no time left for sinful pursuits). But any study of the Torah without following some craft will in the end be futile and lead to sin".[511]

16. Work Obligatory for Wives

According to this view, labor is not merely a social or economic necessity, but a moral imperative. It is vital for maintaining an unblemished character. It was partly for this reason that a wife was legally required to work for her husband — at least according to one opinion — even if she provided him with a dowry or with bondwomen who could do the work for her. No matter how wealthy a woman was, if she had nothing to do, she was bound to become bored and thus easily led into amorous adventures with other men. Generally, wives were expected to grind wheat (only in a handmill), do washing, baking, and cooking, feed her children, make her husband's bed, and work in wool (i.e., spinning and weaving). The latter, according to R. Eliezer, she was required to do even if she brought him a hundred bondwomen, "since idleness leads to immorality". A generation later, Rabban Simeon ben Gamaliel would not allow a marriage to continue if the husband refused to permit his wife to perform some work; "for idleness leads to idiocy".[512]

17. Work Essential for Prolonging Life

However, quite apart from problems of morality or the risk of mental retardation, the rabbis realized a fact which has been fully confirmed by

511 *M. Aboth* II, 2.
512 *M. Ket.* V, 5.

modern research and experience — namely that work of some kind is an indispensable necessity for prolonging life. Idleness, it was realized some two millennia ago, was a sure prescription for early decease: "Great is work, for anyone who fails to occupy himself with it, risks his life".[513] And again, "No man dies except in idleness"[514] was a rabbinic adage repeated in many forms, and its slight exaggeration does not affect its essential correctness.

To illustrate the truth that work means life and idleness death, the rabbis told an Aesop-type fable about a man who had a sow, a she-ass, and a filly. While he allowed the sow to eat to her heart's delight, he strictly rationed the ass and the filly. The latter complained to the ass, "What is this lunatic doing? To us who do the work of the master he gives food by measure, but to the sow which does nothing he gives as much as she wants!" The ass, who on this occasion displayed greater intelligence than one is wont to attribute to this species, sagely replied, "The hour will come when you will see her downfall; for they are feeding her up not for the sake of honoring her, but for her own hurt". When the next feast day came around, they took the sow and stabbed her to death. When afterwards they placed barley before the filly, she was sniffing at it but was afraid to eat. However, the ass reassured her, "My dear, it is not the eating which leads to slaughter, but the idleness".[515]

18. "Love Work"

Significantly, one of the earliest rabbinic maxims recorded deals with man's attitude to labor. Shemayah, a Pharisaic leader, who flourished about the middle of the first century B.C.E., preached that one should "love work and hate lordship".[516] Thus, the natural inclination of some people to dislike their work and seek positions of power where they could compel others to work for them, was condemned as not conducive to genuine happiness and human progress.

---

513 Aboth R. Nathan, edit. Schechter, Vers. II, chap. 21, p. 22b (44).
514 Ibid.; Vers. I, chap. 11, p. 23a (45).
515 *Esther R.* 7, 1.
516 *M. Aboth* I, 10.

19. He who will not work, neither shall he eat

If work was essential for life in a general sense, it certainly was indispensable for *homo economicus* who has to make a living. The principle that "he who does not work, neither shall he eat",[517] was enunciated by the rabbis in a somewhat different form but basically in accordance with the same philosophy:

"If a man does not prepare (food) for himself while he is on dry land, what will he eat when at sea?... If a man does not prepare (food) for himself while he is in a settled area, what will he eat in the wilderness?".[518] More concretely, the question was put, "If a man does not plow, and sow, and reap, and harvest, and gather the grapes during the summer season, what will he eat in the rainy season?".[519]

20. Monotonous and Uninteresting Work not to be shunned

The modern problem of dull, uninteresting work performed without joy or pleasure of any sort was somehow anticipated by the rabbis, probably as a result of the development of large-scale agricultural and manufacturing operations introduced by the Romans. Under the new conditions, division of labor became a practical reality, so that the sense of creative work and individual craftsmanship was lost. The rabbinic view was that where one's livelihood was concerned, one could not pick and choose. If the work, as such, offered no interest, then the wages must serve as the incentive:

"Do not refrain from undertaking a pursuit which is limitless or a task which is endless. This can be compared to a man who was (hired) to carry away sea-water to pour it out on the dry land. The sea did not grow less nor was the dry land filled up; so the man became dispirited (or: aggravated). Thereupon, people said to him, 'You fool! Why are you dispirited (or: aggravated)? Continue to draw your pay of one golden *denarius* daily' ".[520]

---

517 Cf. *II Thessal.* 3:10.
518 *Eccl. R.* I, 15; cf. *A.Z.* 3a; *Midr. Prov.* 6, edit. Buber, p. 28a (55).
519 *Midr. Prov.* 6, edit. Buber, p. 28a (55).
520 *Aboth R.N.* Vers. I, chap. 27, edit. Schechter, p. 42b. (84).

21. Indolence Condemned

The author of this parable was the wealthy Rabbi Tarfon whom we have already mentioned as a great landowner who was once beaten by his servants or tenants to whom, it seems, he was completely unknown. Eventually, however, he knew his laborers well enough to criticize their unwillingness to exert themselves in their work. A parable of his depicting the brevity of life and the pious tasks waiting to be performed was undoubtedly taken from personal experience. Representing only the employer's point of view, he stated, "The day is short, and the work (to be performed) is much, and the laborers are indolent, but the reward is great and the landlord urges on (to complete the work)".[521]

The indolence of some people, so sharply denounced in the Bible, was also criticized in rabbinic literature. About 200 C.E., R. Simeon ben Eleazar, commenting on Proverbs 6:6 ("Go to the ant, O sluggard; consider her ways and be wise"), declared, "It was sufficient humiliation for man that he had to learn from the ant. Even if he had learned and acted accordingly, he would have been humiliated; but although he should have learned from the ways of the ant, he did not".[522]

22. How to "find" Work

In accordance with the concept of treating physical labor not as a necessary evil but as a blessing for man, the rabbis suggested various ways of "finding" work, even if there was no immediate need for it:

"What should a man do when he has no work to do? If he has a dilapidated courtyard or a waste field, let him go and attend to it. ..."[523]

23. Labor honors the Worker

If it was impossible to find work of major importance, one could always do some minor work so as to bear in mind the value and dignity of labor.

521 *M. Aboth* II, 15.
522 *Sifre, Deut.* 306, edit. Friedmann 130b; edit. Horovitz-Finkelstein, p. 324.
523 *Aboth R.N.*, Vers. I, chap. 11, edit. Schechter, p. 23a (45); cf. ibid. Vers. II, chap. 21, where a "waste" garden is added.

Thus, R. Judah bar Ilai, who was extremely poor, was in the habit of carrying a jug on his shoulders to the ill-furnished House of Study, where he would use it as a substitute for a seat since, evidently, he could not afford a better one. But so far from regarding this as a menial task beneath his dignity, R. Judah was quite proud of his "work": "Great is labor", he said, "for it honors the worker".[524] The same attitude was taken by his contemporary, R. Simeon bar Yohai, who would bring a basket to the House of Study for the purpose of using it as a seat.[525] In both these cases, the "honor" was quite concrete. Their "work" enabled them to avoid having to squat on the floor — a posture common among students, but unbecoming to great masters of the Law.

24. Hard Work as a Cure for Colds

Similar "fringe benefits" from physical labor were depicted by fourth century Babylonian rabbis. Rab Joseph, for example, used to cure colds by working at the mill; while Rab Shesheth tried to obtain the same effect by carrying heavy beams. The principle underlying these curious methods was that the exertion of hard labor was bound to cause perspiration and warm the body, thus gradually overcoming the shivers of the cold. As Rab Shesheth explained it, "Work is a splendid thing to make one warm".[526]

25. Dissenting Views due to Hellenistic Influence

Despite this overwhelming approval of work — any kind of honest work — some rabbis could not entirely escape Hellenistic influences which regarded physical labor, if not with outright contempt, at any rate as unfit for a man of distinction. Thus, in third century Babylonia, Mar Samuel, who had studied in Palestine, declared that "once a person is appointed leader of a community, he must not perform manual labor in the presence of three people".[527] His Palestinian contemporary, R. Jo-

---

524 *T.B. Ned.* 49b.
525 Ibid.
526 *T.B. Git.* 67b.
527 *T.B. Kid.* 70a.

hanan, went even further and told a certain R. Hanina bar Sisi whom he saw chopping wood, "This is not in accordance with your dignity!" When the latter replied, "What can I do? I have no one to serve me", R. Johanan retorted, "If you have no one to serve you, you should not have accepted an official appointment" (*viz.*, ordination as rabbi).[528] Such attitudes were however, rare and certainly not characteristic.

26. Importance of Craft Skills

Important as physical labor in general was, it was preferable to learn a skilled craft rather than rely exclusively on brawn. The rabbis considered it essential for economic security to have a trade in hand. A craft was more than just a means of earning one's livelihood. It was life itself. The biblical exhortation, "And you shall choose life",[529] which was originally, no doubt, meant as an ethical-moral precept, was interpreted by the rabbis to mean "Choose a craft".[530] More concretely, it was pointed out that if a man learns a craft, God Himself, as it were, would provide for his sustenance, so that he may live.[531]

27. Craft Skill as Social Security

Unlike modern times, crafts were never out of date or even temporarily outmoded. Once a craft had been mastered, it could be practiced throughout one's life: "No craft ever disappears from the world"[532] was a sound motto in the pre-industrial age. A popular proverb in Babylonia stated, "Even if a famine lasts seven years, it does not pass the artisan's gate".[533] Much earlier, R. Judah the Patriarch had expressed his admiration for craftsmanship, claiming, not without exaggeration, that anyone engaged in such work would never be short of money.[534]

528 *T.Y. Sanh.* II, 6, 20c–d.
529 Deut. 30:19.
530 *T.Y. Peah* I. i, 15c.
531 *Eccl. R.* 6, 8.
532 *T. Kid.* V, 14; *T.B. Kid.* 82b.
533 *T.B. Sanh.* 29a.
534 *Aboth R.N.*, Vers. II, chap 21, edit. Schechter, p. 22b (44).

Indeed, as early as 100 C.E., Rabban Gamaliel II gave a picturesque description of the tremendous advantages and security conferred by skilled craftsmanship: "Whoever knows a craft ... resembles a vineyard surrounded by a fence and a furrowed field surrounded by a hedge. ... He is like a fenced vineyard which cannot be invaded by cattle and beasts, and whose fruit cannot be eaten by those who pass by, neither can they see what is in it. But whoever knows no craft ... resembles a vineyard whose fence is broken down, so that cattle and beasts invade it, and passers-by eat its fruit and see what is in it".[535]

28. Craft Education

Because of the vital importance of craft education for earning one's living, the rabbis agreed that it was the father's duty to teach his son, not only the Torah, but also a craft or to arrange for his training with a master craftsman, if he could not teach him himself.[536] Failure on the part of the father to provide for his son's craft training was stigmatized as education for brigandage.[537] To learn a trade was held to be of such vital importance that terms between the trainee's parents and the master craftsman could be settled even on the Sabbath when otherwise anything even remotely associated with work was strictly prohibited.[538]

29. Son should follow Father's Trade

In choosing one's occupation, it was thought desirable that a son should follow his father's trade — and stick to it for the rest of his life.[539] This highly conservative attitude could not be maintained indefinitely. It reflects a state of affairs admirably suited to a static society. The fact that the father was expected to teach his son a trade, indicates that this was indeed the usual practice. However, the mere fact that the desirability of keeping to one's ancestral craft had to be specially stressed indicates that,

535 *T. Kid.* I, 11.
536 *Mekilta Bo* 18 (on Exod. 13:13); *Tos. Kid.* I, 11; *T.B. Kid.* 29a; 30b.
537 *Tos. Kid.* I, 11; *T.B. Kid.* 29a, 30b.
538 *T.B. Shab.* 150a; *Ket.* 5a.
539 *T.B. Men.* 16b; *Arak.* 16b.

with the growing urbanization of Palestine, the time-honored custom was honored more in the breach than in the observance. The importance attributed to the arrangement of training apprentices with master craftsmen rather than with parents points in the same direction.

30. Study and Work — Antidote to Sin

One of the major problems the rabbis had to contend with was to reconcile the religious requirement of Torah study (often in its widest sense of the sum total of human wisdom applied to religious life) with the unavoidable necessity of earning one's living. Although the rabbis elevated the study of the Torah to the point where it became the ultimate object in life, they realized that, "if there is no flour (for baking bread) there can be no Torah".[540] However, they also insisted that, "If there is no Torah, there will be no flour"[541] — or, in other words, the Almighty would withhold His blessing, so that the ignorant who refused to study would ultimately find that their goal of material prosperity had eluded them. This truth has only in recent years become evident, and today no one doubts the necessity of years of intensive study for launching a successful career.

In the Talmudic age, on the other hand, study of the Torah rarely provided one with a livelihood — unless, indeed, one became a schoolteacher, a Torah scribe, or a professional judge. It was, therefore, necessary to find ways and means of combining study with work. The overwhelming majority of rabbis agreed with the above-quoted opinion of Rabban Gamaliel III that the study of the Torah combined with a worldly occupation was an excellent thing.[542] Even earlier, a saintly group of rabbis who were known as "The Holy Brotherhood" had preached, "Acquire a craft for yourself together with Torah".[543] This was approvingly cited by Rabban Gamaliel's father, Judah the Patriarch,[544] who, as editor of the Mishnah (the basic part of the Talmud), stated that "whoever is conversant with Bible, Mishnah and a worldly occupation, will not speedily sin".[545]

540 *M. Aboth* III, 17.
541 Ibid.
542 Ibid. II, 2.
543 *Eccl. R.* 9, 9.
544 Ibid.
545 M. *Kid.* I, 10; cf. *Tos. Kid.* I, 16.

This sentiment, as we have seen, was echoed by his son, and subsequently in a different form by an anonymous rabbi who interpreted Lamentations 3:27 — "It is good for a man that he bear the yoke in his youth" — as referring to "the yoke of the Torah, the yoke of a wife, and the yoke of labor".[546] Although this may sound uncomplimentary to women, it is actually a statement of fact, namely that marriage involved responsibilities, and in the circumstances existing at the time, it was evidently wise to study, work and marry early in life.

31. Work in the Scheme of Life

In the twelfth century, the Jewish philosopher Maimonides suggested the exact order of preparing for life. After studying in one's youth, one should find work, then buy a home, and only then should one get married. Fools, on the other hand, marry first (he must have had some of our college students in mind); then they buy a home if they have the money; and only late in life do they try to find a job — or else they live on charity.[547] Nowadays, they simply sponge on doting parents.

Since craftsmen did not work fixed hours in workshops or factories, but were for the most part independent tradesmen, the question how much time should be allocated to study and work, respectively, was of some importance. Ancient craftsmen, unlike modern Americans, were hardly inclined to work themselves to death for the sake of a few extra shekels, and the independence of which they were proud included the right to close shop at any time they felt like it. Rabbinical workmen often anticipated the concept of leisure suited to the age of automation. Thus, R. Jose ben Meshullam and R. Simeon ben Manasia, two saintly rabbis who belonged to the above-mentioned "Holy Brotherhood", used to divide the day into three parts — a third for the study of the Torah, a third for prayer, and a third for work. According to another account, which is more probable, "they labored in the Torah throughout the winter and in their work throughout the summer".[548] In agriculture as well as in other occupations summer tended to be the busy season.

---

546 *Lam. R.* 3:27.
547 *Yad*, Hil. Deot V, 11.
548 *Eccl. R.* 9, 9.

32. Maimonides and the Three-Hour Workday

Maimonides, precise as he was in everything, was probably the first to propose a three-hour workday, the remaining nine hours of the day (on the assumption that the total working day has twelve hours) to be devoted to the study of the Torah.[549] Modern concepts of leisure have yet to devise a better use of one's spare time — a problem which, with the spread of automation, is likely to become increasingly acute.

33. Equality of Laborer and Scholar

The high value accorded to "worldly occupations" implied the recognition of the personality and rights of craftsmen and, indeed, of any manual workers. In spite of the dislike of the ignorant *Am Ha-'areṣ* (peasants) current among many scholars, we are told that the "Rabbis of Jabneh" had a favorite saying which demonstrated their belief in the full equality of the laborer, however minute his knowledge of the Law: "I am (God's) creature and my (non-scholarly) fellow-man is God's creature. My work is in the town (*viz.* in the House of Study), and his work is in the field. I rise early for my work and he rises early for his work. Just as he does not excel in my work (*viz.* the study of the Torah) so I do not excel in his work. But should you say perchance that I do much (in studying the Torah) and he does little, (I can retort that) we have learned: Whether one does much or little, it is all the same, provided he directs his heart to Heaven".[550]

Thus, the laborer was elevated to the status of a scholar — a remarkable *tour de force* on the part of scholars for whom the study of the Torah was the very essence of life. Some rabbis were, indeed, prepared to go a long way in making concessions to those who could not devote much time to study. According to R. Joshua, "If man studies two (Jewish religious) laws in the morning and another two in the evening, while occupying himself with his work all day long, it is accounted unto him as if had fulfilled the whole Torah".[551] A similar view was expressed by a

---

549 *Yad,* Talm. Tor. I, 12.
550 *T.B. Ber.* 17a.
551 *Mekil.* on Exod. 15:4; edit. Friedmann 47b; edit. Lauterbach II, 103f.; edit.
     Horovitz-Rabin, p. 161; *Tanh.* Beshallah, 20.

third century scholar, R. Ammi, who stated, "Even though a man learns only one chapter (*viz.* of the Mishnah) in the morning and one chapter in the evening, he has fulfilled the precept (recorded in *Joshua* 1:8), 'This book of the law shall not depart out of your mouth' ".[552]

34. Minimum of Study — Maximum of Work

Even R. Simeon bar Yohai (2nd cent. C.E.), normally the most uncompromising exponent of exclusive Torah study (see below),[552a] agreed that, in principle, it was possible to fulfill the obligation of studying Torah by reading the *Shema*[553] morning and evening, though he significantly added that this must not be mentioned to the ignorant common people who might thereby be encouraged to neglect their children's education.[554]

A century later, R. Johanan, by far the most learned Palestinian Jew of his time, who, as we shall see, sacrificed everything for the sake of study, nevertheless made the hyperbolic statement that "Whoever studies the Torah even one day in the year, Scripture accounts it unto him as if he had done so throughout the year".[555] While this must not be regarded as the consensus opinion of the rabbis, who certainly would not have considered an annual day of study as even remotely satisfactory, the basic tendency is unmistakable. For the common man it was essential to follow a trade, and that, inevitably, left little time for study. However little time one was able to squeeze in was to be welcomed.

35. Abandonment of Studies for Vocational Careers

Occasionally one meets with extremists who were altogether set on vocational careers and material gain, to the exclusion of all intellectual activities. Some of the senior disciples of the rabbis abandoned their studies altogether, causing disappointment and grief to their teachers.[556]

---

552 *T.B. Men.* 99b.
552a Pp. 113f.
553 Deut. 6:4–9.
554 *T.B. Men.* 99b.
555 *T.B. Hag.* 5b.
556 Ibid. 9b.

We even hear of a brilliant original scholar, R. Eleazar ben Arach, who had been highly praised by R. Johanan ben Zakkai,[557] abandoning his studies and consequently forgetting everything he had ever learned.[558]

The most remarkable example of a scholar who not only forsook his studies but also lost his religious faith and became a militant propagandist, agitating in favor of pursuing a trade instead of "wasting" one's time on religious studies, was Elisha ben Abuyah (2nd cent. C.E.). He would enter schools, and when he saw the students being instructed by their teacher, he would say, "Why are they sitting here and what are they doing here? This one should follow the builder's craft; this one's trade is carpentry; this one is a hunter by profession; and this one should become a tailor". We are told that the students, probably poor youngsters who suffered great hardships trying to pursue their studies, let themselves be enticed by the persuasive ex-rabbi to abandon their studies and become craftsmen as suggested by him.[559]

36. Torah Study as Exclusive or Principal Vocation

It was perhaps by way of reaction to such fanatical anti-intellectualism that some rabbis went to the other extreme, and opposed, in principle at least, all work which was not absolutely essential in preference for what was to be one's primary occupation — the study of the Torah. Firmly believing that where there was a will, there was a way, they rejected the concept of Torah with a worldly occupation, opting instead for a life devoted exclusively to religious studies which, in their opinion, was the only purpose for which the Jewish people had been created. The most prominent representative of this school of thought was R. Simeon bar Yohai who, with his son R. Eleazar, spent some twelve years in a cave hiding from the Romans, studying Torah and subsisting on carobs and water. When at length they were able to leave their hiding place, they were, according to legend, deeply aggrieved that, while they had suffered so much for the sake of the Torah, the world was continuing along its

557 *M. Aboth* II, 8–9.
558 *Aboth R. Nathan*, edit. Schechter, Vers. I, chap. 14 end, p. 30a (59); *T.B. Shab.* 147b; *Eccl. R.* 7, 7.
559 *T.Y. Hag.* II, 1, 77b.

usual course, the masses of the people being engaged in the usual agricultural activities — ploughing, sowing and reaping. In their unreasoning anger, R. Simeon and his son "flashed their eyes" with deadly effect on those they saw "forsaking eternal life and occupying themselves with the temporary needs of life".[560]

The Talmudic legend accurately conveys the attitude of the saintly type of scholar — an attitude strongly disapproved of by the overwhelming majority of rabbis. The same story which glorifies R. Simeon bar Yohai relates that, following his (and his son's) destructive "eyeing" of those engaged in agriculture, a heavenly voice echoed: "Have you emerged to destroy my world? Return to your cave!"[561] There they stayed for another year until they finally made their peace with the world. Clearly, the "heavenly voice" echoes the opinion of the moderate majority which refused to sanction extremism. Nevertheless, the extreme minority must not be thought to have consisted of unreasoning fanatics. R. Simeon bar Yohai explained that the Torah was one of the precious gifts bestowed on Israel by the Almighty; but, like all valuable gifts, it could be acquired only through suffering.[562] This implied, among other things, economic sacrifices and willingness to be satisfied with little in order to be able to devote one's entire life to study. R. Simeon's dedication to study was such that he once declared that, had he been at Mt. Sinai at the time when the Torah was given to Israel, he would have asked the divine Lawgiver to provide man with two mouths, one to be used continuously and exclusively for the oral study of the Torah.[563] The classical argument against combining study with work was formulated by R. Simeon bar Yohai in the following words:

"If a man ploughs in the ploughing season, and sows in the sowing season, and reaps in the reaping season, and threshes in the threshing season, and winnows when there is a wind, what is to become of the Torah?"[564]

This by no means unreasonable argument which was anticipated, as we have seen, by Ben Sira, was supported by R. Nehorai, a contemporary of R. Simeon, who put forward an even more idealistic view of the

---

560 T.B. Shab. 33b; cf. T.Y. Shebiith IX, 1, 38d.
561 T.B. Shab. 33b.
562 T.B. Ber. 5a.
563 T.Y. Shab. I, 2, 3a–b.
564 T.B. Ber. 35b.

advantages of exclusive Torah education: "I would set aside every trade in the world," he declared, "and teach my son nothing but the Torah; for man enjoys its reward in this world, while the principal remains for the world-to-come. But with all other trades it is not so; for every trade in the world can support a man only in the days of his youth and while his strength is with him, but when a man falls into sickness or old age or suffering, and is unable to engage in his work, he dies of hunger. But with the Torah it is not so; for it guards him from all evil in his youth, and grants him a future and hope in his old age".[565]

R. Nehorai had no illusions on the difficulties likely to be encountered in attempting to master the Torah. More often than not it was necessary, as R. Nehorai himself pointed out, to leave one's home and go to a distant place where the study of the Torah flourished.[566] But, whatever the sacrifice, he felt that in the long run it was well worthwhile.

Such unstinted devotion to study, which inevitably implied neglect of ordinary work, was not confined to a handful of exceptional scholars. We find a surprisingly large number of rabbis who tended to agree with this attitude, even if they stressed the importance and dignity of labor. Thus, about 100 C.E., a generation or two before R. Simeon bar Yohai, R. Eliezer, despite his praise for labor,[567] nevertheless expressed himself in terms which hardly differed from R. Simeon's opinions. Attributing his own views to the prophet Jeremiah, he stated, "When Jeremiah said to Israel, 'Why do you not occupy yourselves with the study of the Torah?' they replied, 'How shall we find our sustenance?' At that moment he brought forth a jar of manna,[568] and said unto them, ... 'Your forefathers who engaged in the study of the Torah, see from where they obtained their sustenance! You, too, occupy yourselves with the study of the Torah, and I shall give you your sustenance out of this (jar)' ".[569]

That R. Eliezer fully shared these sentiments can be proved not only by his self-sacrificing career of study,[570] but also by his notorious outburst against those who left his day-long lecture on a festival in order to eat and

---

565 *Tos. Kid.* V, 15; *M. Kid.* IV, 14; *T.B. Kid.* 82b.
566 *M. Aboth* IV, 14.
567 *Aboth R.N.*, edit. Schechter, Vers. II, chap. 21, pp. 22b(44)–23a(45).
568 Cf. *Exod.* 16:33.
569 *Tanh.* Beshallah 21; *Mekil.* on Exod. 16:33, edit. Friedmann 51b; edit. Lauterbach II, 126; edit. Horovitz-Rabin, p. 172.
570 Cf. *Aboth R.N.*, edit. Schechter, Vers. I, chap. 6, pp. 15b(30)–16a(31)

drink. According to the uncompromising R. Eliezer, they were "forsaking everlasting life and occupying themselves with temporal life".[571] R. Eliezer's colleague, R. Joshua, apparently went even further, and specifically advised against teaching a trade to one's son "in order that he should not neglect the words of the Torah".[572] A generation later, we find Ben Zoma praising God for having created the laboring classes to minister to his needs, so that he should find everything ready for him, and dispense with the innumerable labors required to satisfy one's material requirements.[573]

R. Simeon's colleague, R. Judah bar Ilai, who had insisted on the dignity of labor,[574] and declared that whoever did not teach his son a craft virtually taught him how to become a brigand,[575] emphasized nonetheless that labor should merely be a temporary activity, while one's main occupation should be confined to the study of the Torah. To illustrate how successful such a combination could be, he pointed out that "the earlier generations made the study of the Torah their main concern, and their ordinary work a subsidiary occupation, and both prospered in their hands; while later generations made their ordinary work their main concern, and their study of the Torah a subsidiary occupation, and neither prospered in their hands".[576]

R. Judah, indeed, raised this problem to the point where it assumed a theological significance:

"Whoever makes the study of the Torah his primary occupation, and his ordinary work his secondary occupation, will become a person of primary importance in the world-to-come. But one who makes the study of the Torah his secondary occupation, and his ordinary work, his primary occupation, he will become a person of secondary importance in the world-to-come".[577]

---

571 *T.B. Bezah* 15b.
572 *Midr. Pss.* 1:17, edit. Buber 8b. The text may not be accurate, and, according to Solomon Buber, *ad loc.*, should be emended to agree with a different version in *T.Y. Sot.* IX, 10, 23c, according to which R. Joshua objected only to studying "Greek wisdom", since both day and night should be devoted to the study of Torah.
573 *T.B. Ber.* 58a; Tos. ibid. VI, 2.
574 *T.B. Ned.* 49b.
575 *T.B. Kid.* 29a.
576 *T.B. Ber.* 35b.
577 *Aboth R.N.*, edit. Schechter, Vers. I, chap. 28, p. 43b (86).

A century later, we find a certain R. Simon opposing the very concept of limiting the time allocated to the study of the Torah: "He that
makes the study of the Law a matter of time (i.e., sets time limits to his
study sessions) destroys the Covenant (*viz.* between God and Israel).[578]
R. Simon's younger contemporary, R. Eleazar, maintained that "every
man in Israel must labor in the Torah all hours of the day".[579] R. Johanan, a teacher and colleague of R. Eleazar, not only quoted R. Judah's
above-cited opinion with approval,[580] but even sold his entire estate in
order to be able to devote himself entirely to Torah study, thus avoiding
the temptation of "neglecting everlasting life and occupying oneself with
temporal life".[581] Alluding perhaps to his erstwhile fellow student Ilfa
who had abandoned learning for a business career,[582] R. Johanan ex-
pounded Deuteronomy 30:13: "Neither is it beyond the sea", in the
sense that knowledge of the Torah is not to be found among merchants or
dealers" (some of whom would engage in maritime trade).[583]

In some respects, such preference for almost exclusive Torah study
was shared by the moderates who did not relish the idea that labor
should interfere unduly with one's Torah studies. Thus, Hillel, undoubtedly the most moderate of scholars, insisted that one who occupied
himself unduly with business could not become wise (i.e., a scholar).[584]
This was also the view of R. Simeon's and R. Judah's contemporary,
R. Meir, who stated, "Reduce your business and occupy yourself with
study".[585] It was probably he, too, who included "diminution of business" and "diminution of a worldly occupation" among the forty-eight
qualifications necessary for the acquisition of Torah.[586]

37. Study and Work in Equal Proportions

Although such views emphasizing study in preference to labor or business continued to meet with favor in later times, they were not found to

578 *T.Y. Ber.* IX, 5, 14d.
579 Ibid.
580 *T.B. Ber.* 35b.
581 *T.B. Taan.* 21a; *Pesik. R.K.* 28, edit. Buber, p. 178b; *Exod. R.* 47, 5; *Lev. R.* 30, 1.
582 Cf. *T.B. Taan.* 21a.
583 *T.B. Erub.* 55a.   584 *M. Aboth* II, 5.
585 Ibid. IV, 10.   586 Ibid. VI, 6.

be safe guides for a practical way of life for the majority of the scholars, still less for the masses of the people. Only those who, like R. Jose ben Meshullam and R. Simeon ben Manasia, genuinely tried to practice R. Ishmael's advice to "combine the study of the Torah with a worldly occupation"[587] which implied approximately equal proportions between the two, were successful in their efforts in both directions. Those, on the other hand, who attempted the herculean task of avoiding physical labor and devoting their entire lives to the study of the Torah, failed to pass the test. As Abaye in fourth century Babylonia put it, "many have acted in accordance with R. Ishmael's counsel and were successful. Others have acted according to R. Simeon's advice and were unsuccessful".[588] Not to everyone was it given to live in caves and subsist on carobs and water.

Rabbis with a more practical frame of mind would sometimes endeavor to restrain excessive devotion to study which could be economically ruinous. Thus, (as has already been mentioned in Chapter Three), Abaye's colleague, Raba, almost implored his students not to neglect their agricultural pursuits during the height of the season in the spring and the autumn: "I beg of you *not* to appear before me during Nisan (March/April when the harvest began) and Tishri (September/October, the time of the grape harvest and olive pressing), so that you may not be anxious about your food supply during the rest of the year".[589]

38. Torah and Commerce

A similar attitude is also to be found in the Targum (Aramaic translation) to Ecclesiastes 7:18. The Hebrew text: "It is good that you should take hold of one, but neither let go of the other" is rendered as follows in the Aramaic Targum:

"It is good that you should be engaged in the affairs of this world to do yourself good by way of commerce (*lit.*, in the way [or manner] of merchants), but neither forsake your portion in this book of the Law".

This concept of combining religious studies not just with any kind of work but specifically with commercial activities was destined to be

---

587 *T.B. Ber.* 35b.
588 Ibid.
589 Ibid.

characteristic of the late medieval and modern Central and East European Jewish communities where business rather than manual labor was the hallmark of respectability, and was often combined with a high level of Talmudic scholarship.

39. Higher Education for "Eaters of Manna"

Extremists who insisted on full-time study of the Torah to the exclusion of everything else were hard put to it to offer a rational answer to the inevitable question — how to provide one's necessities while neglecting all economic activities for the sake of the Torah. As already pointed out, the personal achievement of exceptional men like R. Simeon bar Yohai and his son was no criterion for universal application. A few individuals, no doubt, could solve the problem of maintenance during study either by enduring extreme privations or by obtaining assistance from well-wishers. Significantly, appeals for *Yeshivot* (Talmudical Academies) are known to have been conducted in wealthy Diaspora centers as early as the first century C.E.[590] For the vast majority of students and scholars such solutions were not really feasible — not to mention the broad masses who were indeed supposed to study the Torah, but not to the exclusion of every other activity. In fact, even R. Simeon bar Yohai, the High Priest of pure scholarship as the only permissible profession, realized that only a tiny minority could live up to his standards. He was candid enough to admit that in the conditions of his time, higher education was to all intents and purposes reserved for the economically privileged "eaters of manna", in other words, to persons of independent means "who did not need to engage in labor or commerce" to earn a living.[591]

40. Torah for Israel, Labor for Gentiles

Nevertheless, some theoretical justification for the extremist theory had to be formulated, and R. Simeon bar Yohai, therefore, put forward an

590 For a list of such appeals during the Talmudic age, cf. M. Aberbach, in *Essays presented to Chief Rabbi Israel Brodie on the occasion of his seventieth birthday* (London, 1967), p. 4, n. 31.
591 *Mekilta* (on *Exod.* 13:17; 16:4); IV, 2, edit. Friedmann, 23b; 47b; edit. Lauterbach I, 171; II, 104; edit. Horovitz-Rubin, pp. 76, 161; *Tanh.* Beshallah 20.

ingenious argument, albeit based on faith rather than practical reasoning, to persuade the elect, if not the people as a whole, that it was possible to combine the study of the Torah with a reasonable standard of living without any need to spend precious time and energy on exhausting labors: "When Israel perform the will of the Omnipresent", he stated emphatically, "their work is performed by others".[592] His idea, then, was that Israel should become a nation of scholars whose material needs would be freely supplied by non-Jewish labor. This was no wild dream of a visionary remote from the realities of life, nor was it necessarily an expression of hatred and contempt for the Gentiles, though R. Simeon, a disciple of the martyred R. Akiba, was a life-long enemy of the Romans.[593] Although he based his prediction on Isaiah 61:5f.,[593a] it may well be that he envisaged a state of affairs which actually prevailed in certain areas of Europe during part of the Middle Ages when restricted economic activity on the part of the Jews with concentration on commerce and banking provided the practical basis for the magnificent development of Jewish learning on a scale which had never been possible in antiquity when agriculture and craftsmanship absorbed Jewish energies.

41. No Blessing in Manual Work

There was also another school of thought which accepted the basic principle enunciated by R. Simeon that exclusive study of the Torah was a desirable ideal, but was realistic enough to consider the necessity of labor an inescapable curse laid upon man as a punishment for his misdeeds. The need to combine a worldly occupation with study was, therefore, tacitly accepted, but neither blessing nor dignity was found in manual labor.

The foremost representative of this original, if somewhat fatalistic, approach to the problem of Torah and life was R. Simeon ben Eleazar

---

592 *T.B. Ber.* 35b.
593 Cf. *Shab.* 33b; *Mekilta* on Exod. 14:7, edit. Friedmann 27a; edit. Horovitz-Rabin, p. 89a.
593a Is. 61:5f.: "Aliens shall stand and pasture your flocks, foreigners shall be your plowmen and vinedressers; but you shall be called 'Priests of the Lord'..."

who, in words reminiscent of a well-known New Testament passage,[594] asked pathetically, "Have you ever seen an animal or a bird practicing a trade? Yet they have their sustenance without anxiety. And were they created for any other purpose but to serve me? But I was created to serve my Master. Surely, then, I ought to have my sustenance without anxiety. But I have committed evil deeds and forfeited my (right to) sustenance (without care).[595] According to another version, R. Simeon b. Eleazar said, "Never in my life have I seen a deer engaged in gathering fruits, a lion carrying loads, or a fox as a storekeeper. Yet they have sustenance without anxiety, although they were created only to serve me. ..."[596]

42. Dislike of Economic Activity due to Self-Sacrifice for Torah

This idealization of animal and bird life, did not, of course, correspond to the harsh reality of nature. At the same time, it must be stated that the dislike of economic activity evinced by some scholars (which, incidentally, was not confined to manual labor, but included, as already pointed out, even profitable commercial activities) was not due to any unwillingness to work for one's living. They were motivated by a sense of values which was radically different from the commonly accepted ideas. They were self-sacrificing men who were willing to forgo everything and suffer any hardships and privations for the sake of their ideal — the study of the Torah both day and night.

43. Prosperous and Poverty-stricken Students

Only a small minority of students could readily afford to study in comfort, being endowed with private means or married to wealthy wives. Occasionally, students would even stipulate in their marriage contracts that their wives should maintain them during several years of study,[597] which was a common practice during the Middle Ages right down to the nineteenth century, and is still quite common in ultra-orthodox circles.

594 *Matt.* 6:26 ff.
595 *M. Kid.* IV, 14; *Tos. Kid.* V, 15.
596 *T.B. Kid.* 82b.
597 *Tos. Ket.* IV, 7; *T.Y. Ket.* V, 2, 29d.

Students and scholars who were less fortunate and had to earn their living and maintain their families would indeed work for their livelihood; but, like Hillel or R. Akiba, they would confine their "worldly occupations" to the minimum, while concentrating nearly all their efforts on their studies. Such an arrangement was hardly sufficient to provide them with the barest necessities of life. In times of stress — as, for instance, in the years of economic crisis following the Bar Kochba rising (132–135 C.E.) — students were reduced to such extreme poverty that many of them had to share their outer garments with each other:

"Six disciples would cover themselves with one garment between them; yet they would occupy themselves with the study of the Torah".[598]

In the third century C.E. — a period of grave crisis throughout the Roman empire — there were even cases of students (as well as others) who had to spend every night, including the Sabbath, in darkness because they lacked the means to fulfill the universally observed Jewish custom of kindling the Sabbath lights.[599]

The self-sacrificing spirit of such students was so great that it was hyperbolically said that even the Almighty was moved to tears at the sight of scholars who lacked the wherewithal for studying the Torah, but still persisted in doing so.[600]

As usual, ancient Jewish history was drawn upon to illustrate a state of affairs characteristic of the Talmudic Age. In a speech attributed to Moses, the prototype of the Jewish scholar, he is said to have told the Israelites what enormous sacrifices he had made for the Torah:

"How much pain have I taken over the Torah, how much labor have I devoted to it, and how much toil have I given to it! ... I have sacrificed my life for it. My blood I have given for it!"[601]

44. Want and Destitution for the Sake of Learning

This was no exaggeration. It accurately reflected the life of the average student for whom no sacrifice was too great in his search for knowledge.

---

598 *T.B. Sanh.* 20a; cf. A. Büchler, *The Jewish Community of Sepphoris*, pp. 67 ff.
599 *T.B. Shab.* 25b.
600 *T.B. Hag.* 5b.
601 *Sifre, Deut.* 306; edit. Friedmann, p. 131b; edit. Horovitz-Finkelstein, p. 337.

Likewise, the solemn precept given by Moses to Israel to be ready to endure every form of hardship for the sake of the Torah,[602] faithfully echoed the sentiments of the Talmudic scholars who felt that the Torah could be acquired only by cheerfully accepting suffering.[603] After all, as the old rabbinic saying has it, "according to the suffering (or: labor) is the reward",[604] and centuries earlier the Psalmist had confessed, "It is good for me that I was afflicted, that I might learn your statutes".[605] The rabbis certainly agreed that learning could not be fully absorbed without sacrifices. In a famous passage, the rabbis, accordingly, advised:

"This is the way of (studying) the Torah: A morsel of bread with salt you shall eat, and water by measure you shall drink, and on the ground you shall sleep, and a life of privation you shall live; yet in the Torah you shall labor. If you do thus, you shall be happy in this world, and it shall be well with you in the world to come".[606]

Poverty and hardship mattered little in the rabbinic view, for "Only he who lacks knowledge is poor".[607] To eliminate the dearth of spiritual riches, it was well worth while to endure material destitution, which was, indeed, a characteristic attribute of the majority of scholars: "The words of the Torah", it was emphasized, "remain only with him who renders himself naked (*viz.* of material goods) on their behalf".[608] Stark poverty was thus, according to some rabbis, almost essential for attaining and preserving knowledge of the Torah. As the second century scholar Ben Azzai put it, "If a man debases himself for the sake of the Torah, eats dry dates, wears shabby clothes, and sits and keeps guard at the door of the sages (i.e., of the meeting place of the sages), though every passer-by may say, 'Perhaps this man is a fool', in the end you will find that the whole Torah is entirely at his command".[609]

Elsewhere, too, we find that many rabbis regarded a comfortable mode of life as incompatible with advanced Torah study: "Whoever loves wealth and pleasure cannot learn the Oral Law (i.e., the Talmud); for it

---

602 Ibid.
603 *Aboth* VI, 5.
604 Ibid. V, 23.
605 *Pss.* 119:71.
606 *Aboth* VI, 5.
607 *T.B. Ned.* 41a.
608 *T.B. Sot.* 21b.
609 *Aboth R. Nathan*, edit. Schechter, Vers. I, chap. 11, p. 23b (46).

involves much painstaking effort and doing without sleep, and sometimes one wears himself out and debases himself for it. Therefore, the
reward granted for the study of the Torah is (only) in the world to
come".[610]

Some rabbis went even further, regarding poverty as an indispensable
condition for maintaining one's scholarship: "Why are they (viz. scholars) poor in this world? In order that they should not occupy themselves
with other matters, thus forgetting the Torah".[611] There were even some
who elevated scholarly poverty to the status of a basic virtue essential for
a noble character:

"The Torah said before the Holy One, blessed be He: 'O Lord of the
Universe, grant it that my portion be among a poverty-stricken tribe; for
if rich people occupy themselves with me, they will become haughty, but
when poor people engage in studying me, they know that they are
starving and humble' ".[612]

45. Martyrdom on the Altar of Torah

Not only destitution and hunger, but even death itself held no terrors for
rabbis and students, many of whom deliberately courted martyrdom in
their search for knowledge.[613] R. Simeon bar Yohai, who, as we have
already seen, was the most outstanding representative of the extremist
point of view that the study of the Torah should be man's exclusive
occupation, displayed his contempt for death even while he was still a
student, and his teacher, R. Akiba, was imprisoned during the Hadrianic
proscription of Judaism (135–138 C.E.). Braving almost certain death,
the young Simeon visited his master in prison and demanded to be
taught Torah in the very dungeon in which R. Akiba was kept. The latter
refused to risk his pupil's life — his own he had already forfeited — and
only when Simeon expressed himself willing to take the risk, did
R. Akiba consent to teach him some general wisdom which the Romans
could be expected to tolerate.[614]

610 *Tanh.* Noah 3.
611 *Yalkut Prov.*, II, par. 934, p. 973.
612 *Yalkut Ruth*, II, par. 597, p. 1039.
613 Cf., e.g., *T.B. Ber.* 61b; *A.Z.* 18a.
614 *T.B. Pes.* 112a.

It was in reference to such students and rabbis that the view was expressed that they "killed themselves for the words of the Torah",[615] which, indeed, could be preserved only through one who "kills himself for their sake".[616]

Admittedly, such utter self-sacrificing devotion, was not a practical aim for the majority of students, most of whom had to find a way of reconciling their love of learning with their material needs. But for a substantial minority, whose thirst for knowledge was greater than their hunger for bread, self-immolation on the altar of the Torah was a necessity lovingly undertaken in the hope that it would serve as an example for future generations.

---

615 *T.B. Git.* 57b.
616 Ibid.; *T.B. Ber.* 63b; *Shab.* 83b.

Chapter Five

The Occupational Structure of the Jews in the Talmudic Age

1. Agriculture

The Jews of Palestine and Babylonia, and to some extent also in the Hellenistic Diaspora, lived relatively normal lives, and their occupational structure does not seem to have differed substantially from that prevailing among their non-Jewish neighbors. Predominantly, they were agriculturists, as is expressly stated by the great first century historian Josephus. Explaining why Greek historians knew so little about ancient Jewish history, he writes:

"Ours is not a maritime country.[617] Neither commerce nor the intercourse which it promotes with the outside world has any attraction for us. Our cities are built inland, remote from the sea; and we devote ourselves to the cultivation of the productive country with which we are blessed".[618]

Allowing for a measure of exaggeration[618a] — for even Palestinian Jews were at least beginning to engage in commerce, and handicrafts were certainly widespread throughout the country — it is clear that at least 80 percent, possibly 90 percent, of the population continued to be engaged in agricultural pursuits.[618b]

---

617 Ancient Judaea was confined mainly to the inland mountainous areas of Palestine.

618 *I Apion* 12 (60).

618a Cf. J. Klausner, *Ha-Bayit ha-Sheni bi-Gedulato* (Tel-Aviv, 1930), p. 42.

618b The overwhelming concentration on agriculture is also indicated in Josephus' vivid description of Galilee, which he depicts as being "entirely under cultivation" and "everywhere fruitful", without any wasteland, so that "even the villages, thanks to the fertility of the soil, ... are all ... densely populated" (Bell. III, 3, 2, par. 43; 3, 3, par. 44).

King Herod of Judaea (37–4 B.C.E.), who was a capable administrator despite his numerous crimes, extended and developed agriculture even in areas which had previously been uncultivated. This was especially true in the Jordan valley and in the wild areas of Northern Transjordan which had previously been the habitat of outlaws and bandits. To maintain order and guard his frontiers against Arab marauders — a problem which was not created by modern Israel but has existed since time immemorial — Herod invited and successfully settled in Trachonitis, N.E. of the Lake of Galilee, a considerable number of warlike Babylonian Jews, who performed exactly the same functions that are carried out today by military settlements in the Golan Heights and elsewhere along the frontiers of Israel.[619]

2. Building

i Temple Builders
Despite the prevalence of agriculture in Palestine, there was also a growing urban population, practicing various crafts, so many indeed that it would be tedious to enumerate all of them.[620] The more significant and interesting industries, however, deserve mention. During the Herodian regime the most remarkable development took place in the building industry. King Herod of Judaea was one of the greatest builders of all time. Suffice it to say that two of the most important sights in modern Israel — the Western (Wailing) Wall and the fortress of Masada — were both built by Herod, not to mention the port of Caesarea, the cities of Samaria and Neapolis (today Nablus) and a host of other cities, fortresses, and palaces.

All this feverish building activity, financed by heavy taxes paid in the main by the peasantry, provided employment for many thousands of workmen. In connection with Herod's magnificent rebuilding of the Temple of Jerusalem, we are informed, that "he prepared a thousand wagons to carry the stones, selected ten thousand of the most skilled

---

619 Josephus, *Ant.* XVII, 2, 1–2, 23 ff.
620 For a large but still incomplete list of manufactured articles produced in Palestine during the Talmudic age, cf. L. Herzfeld, *Handelsgeschichte der Juden des Altertums* (Braunschweig, 1879), pp. 129–130.

workmen, purchased priestly (actually, workmen's) robes for a thousand priests, and trained some as masons, and others as carpenters".[621]

The courts and porticoes around the Temple continued to be built by vast numbers of workmen for many decades after Herod's death. The Temple treasury was rich, receiving vast amounts of contributions from Jews all over the world. A full treasury was a permanent temptation to avaricious Roman governors, and the Jewish authorities felt that they might as well spend the money for a good purpose rather than let the Romans lay hands on it. By the 60's of the first century C.E., over 18,000 workmen were employed by the Temple — a dangerous proletariate if they ever became unemployed. Both employers and employees did their best to spin out the work around the Temple until eventually the shortest working day in history was duly introduced. In Josephus's own words, "If any one worked for but one hour of the day, he received his pay immediately".[622]

Despite this liberal policy, the day was bound to come when all the structures around the Temple would be completed. This actually happened in 64 C.E., and overnight no less than 18,000 workmen found themselves out of work. The Temple authorities, who were also in charge of the municipality of Jerusalem, urged King Agrippa II (who was the official Curator of the Temple) to pull down one of the porticoes and have it rebuilt to a greater height. The King, who was not exactly a social reformer, objected on the ground that, "it is always easy to demolish a structure, but hard to erect (a new) one"; but what really worried him was the great cost of the project which he, accordingly, vetoed. He did not, however, prevent the authorities from providing alternative employment to the displaced workers. Jerusalem was, therefore, paved with white stone — a luxury which only the richest cities could afford.[623] For the time being at least, 18,000 jobs were saved by what may well have been the first "New Deal" in history.

Herod's grandson, Agrippa I, continued his grandfather's building activities, the most notable of which was Jerusalem's third wall north of the city, the completion of which was prevented by the Romans.[624]

---

621 Josephus, *Ant.* XV, 11, 2, 390.
622 *Ant.* XX, 9, 7, 220.
623 Ibid. 219 ff.
624 Ibid. XIX, 7, 2, 326 f.; *Bell.* II, 11, 6, 218; ibid. V, 4, 2, 147–155.

Agrippa II was also engaged in extensive building activities, including major Temple repairs, which were, however, never completed owing to the outbreak of the Roman-Jewish war in 66 C.E.[625] Queen Helena of Adiabene, a convert to Judaism, had a palace built in Jerusalem[626] as well as a mausoleum for herself and her family.[627]

ii Stone masons
Large-scale building operations generally required a large number of workmen; for, in addition to skilled masons on the job itself, there were many preliminary operations before the actual work could be started. The big heavy stones had to be quarried in the mountains, and transported by wagons or by camel (or by pack animals such as mules) to the chiseller whose skill was not considered inferior to that of the builder himself.[628]

A Talmudic parable gives us an interesting description of some of the methods used by stone masons in their work:

"A stone mason....was quarrying stones in a mountain. One day, he took his pickaxe in his hand, went out and sat on the mountain and chipped away small stones. When people came and asked him, 'What are you doing?' he told them, 'I am about to uproot the mountain and cast it into the Jordan'. They said to him, 'You cannot possibly uproot the whole mountain'. Nevertheless, he continued chipping away until he reached a large rock (or: until it became the size of a large boulder). He penetrated beneath it, broke it loose, uprooted it, and cast it into the Jordan, saying, 'This is not your place, but there (is your place)' ".[629]

According to another version of the same parable, the stone mason was quarrying small stones and casting them into the Jordan, and when he reached large boulders, he cut them loose with an iron mattock and cast them into the Jordan.[630]

Before such stones or boulders could be used for building, they had to be smoothed to some extent; but, for important luxurious buildings, the

625 Bell. V, 1, 5, 36.
626 Ibid. V, 6, 1, 253.
627 Ibid. V, 2, 2, 55; V, 4, 2, 147.
628 *T.Y. B.M.* X, 7, 12c; *Tos. B.M.* XI, 5; *Tos. Kelim B.M.* IV, 6; *M. Shab.* XII, 1; cf.
   S. Krauss, *Talmudische Archäologie* I, 12.
629 *Aboth R. Nathan*, edit. Schechter, Vers. I, ch. 6, p. 15a.
630 Ibid., Vers. II, ch. 12, p. 15a.

stones had to be polished fine before being used. Thus, we are informed that on the Temple Mount there were large beams on the top of which expert stone masons would sit and polish the stones.[631]

iii Major Building Organization

The organization of major building operations was surprisingly modern. There was usually a contractor who was in charge of the entire operation and responsible for obtaining the labor force and building materials.[632] During their working hours, laborers and craftsmen were permitted to recite the brief *Shema* prayer, but not the much longer *Amida* prayer, since they were paid to work, not to pray.[633] Large buildings were, of course, carefully planned by architects; but the fact that the words used to describe these highly skilled men are Greek[634] would seem to indicate that they were, for the most part, non-Jews, who often worked together with Jewish artisans.[635] All types of craftsmen, including masons, plasterers and carpenters, were employed in addition to unskilled laborers, such as porters etc., who were engaged in auxiliary capacities; and there were oral or written agreements regulating wages and working conditions, as was also customary in the Roman-Hellenistic world.[636] In antiquity, as in modern times, building operations were expensive and risky, and master builders were often ruined as a result of ill-considered ventures. "Whoever engages in building becomes poor"[637] was a popular proverb, and there can be little doubt as to its truth.

iv Building Laborers

If master builders or contractors were assuming considerable risks, the ordinary laborer was even worse off, and it made little difference whether he was skilled or unskilled. In addition to the usual accident dangers faced by building workers at all times, much of the work, which involved carrying heavy loads of bricks or stone, tended to be extremely hard and physically exhausting. According to the Midrash, "there is no harder

---

631 *Tos. Kel. B.B.* II, 2.
632 *M. Sheb.* III, 9.
633 *M. Ber.* II, 4.
634 *T.Y. Ber.* IX, I, 13a; *Gen. R.* 24, 1; Tanhuma, Naso 5; edit. Buber 8, Num. 30.
635 Cf. M. Wischnitzer, *op. cit.*, p. 19.
636 Krauss, *Talm. Arch.* I, 20f.; 301f.
637 *T.B. Yeb.* 63a; *Sot.* 11a; *Exod. R.* 1, 10.

labor than that of handling clay.[638] It was one of Moses' greatest merits for which he deserved to be given the leadership of Israel that he not only "looked on their burdens",[639] i.e., sympathized with the hapless Israelite slaves, but actually helped to shoulder the burdens of each one, as they were carrying their heavy loads of mortar and bricks.[640]

v Decline of Building Industry
With the decline of Jewish Palestine in the course of the numerous wars and rebellions against the Romans, building became a relatively less important industry, and in a list (which was apparently compiled in the late second century C.E.) of thirty-nine principal activities prohibited on the Sabbath, only two — erecting a structure or pulling it down (for the purpose of rebuilding) — are connected with the building industry.[641]

3. Textile Industry

While agriculture continued to be the backbone of the economic life of the country, with no less than 18 labors enumerated in the above-mentioned list being associated with agriculture and food supply, the textile industry assumed increasing importance. Our list of activities forbidden on the Sabbath contains some thirteen processes connected with spinning, weaving, sewing and so on. In Jerusalem, there was a street of wool-shops as well as a clothes-market where locally manufactured textile goods were offered for sale.[641a] Galilee, where most of the Palestinian Jews were concentrated after the disastrous Bar Kochba war, was close to the great and ancient Phoenician trading centers, so that home-produced textiles could be readily marketed or shipped overseas.[641b] Women were active as weavers, working not only for their

638 *Exod. R.* 1, 27.
639 *Exod.* 2:11.
640 *Exod. R.* 1, 27.
641 *M. Shab.* VII, 2.
641a Josephus, *Bell.* V, 8, 1, par. 331; *M. Erub.* X, 9.
641b J. Klausner, *Ha-Bayit ha-Sheni bi-Gedulato*, p. 56, assumes too readily that Jewish craftsmen could not compete with foreign imports — hence the prevalence in the Talmud and Midrash of Greek and Latin terms for articles of daily use, including high quality clothes, etc. However, in view of the existence of densely populated Hellenistic cities in Palestine, and the enormous influence of

families but also to supply woolen and linen goods to a growing market.[642] The Upper Galilean town of Gush Halav (Giscala) was a silk-manufacturing center.[643] Fine linen cloth, which during the Second Commonwealth, had to be imported from India and Pelusium, Egypt,[644] was manufactured at Beth Shean, Beth Mehoza and Usha during the second and third centuries of the Common Era.[645]

The workmanship of the fine linen garments manufactured at Beth Shean was of such high quality, and so comfortable were they for the skin that one was hardly conscious of wearing them.[646] One rabbi even suggested that the "garments of skin" made by God for Adam and Eve[647] had the same smooth texture as the best textile products of Beth Shean.[648] Beth Shean's textiles were so highly valued that, around 300 C.E., R. Bibi specially sent R. Zera to Beth Shean to buy him a small finely spun fabric at the pagan fair of the *Saturnalia* despite the fact that, strictly speaking, observant Jews were not supposed to do business with pagans during heathen festivities.[649]

Far more important, from the business angle, than rabbinical appreciation of Beth Shean's fine linen products was the high price set on them by the Romans who encouraged the export of Beth Shean's manufactures to every corner of the Roman empire.[650] The Roman emperor Diocletian, who ruled the Roman empire with an iron hand (284–305 C.E.) and made a determined effort to halt inflation by

Hellenistic civilization throughout the eastern part of the Roman Empire, the use of foreign terms for manufactured articles does not prove that they were of foreign origin.

642 Cf. M. Wischnitzer, *op. cit.*, p. 20, where Mishnah B.K. X, 9 and Ket. V, 5 as well as T.B. Ket. 106a are cited as evidence that women were employed as weavers. Wischnitzer (*op. cit.*, p. 21) also quotes a poignant passage from the Syriac Apocalypse of Baruch (10, 19) calling upon the "virgins who weave fine linen and silk with gold of Ophir" to take them and "cast (them) into the fire ... lest the enemy get possession of them."

643 *Eccl. R.* II, 8, 2.

644 Cf. *M. Yoma* III, 7.

645 *Gen. R.* 19, 1; *Eccl. R.* 1, 18; *T.Y. Ket.* VII, 9, 31c; *T.Y. Kid.* II, 5, 62c; cf. M. Avi-Yonah, *Bimei Roma U-Bizantyon*, 4th edition (Jerusalem, 1970), p. 27.

646 *T.Y. Ket.* VII, 9, 31c; *T.Y. Kid.* II, 5, 62c; *Gen. R.* 21, 12; *Tanh. B. Gen.* 9a–b (17–18).

647 *Gen.* 3:21.

648 *Gen. R.* 20, 12.

649 *T.Y. A.Z.* I, 2, 39c.

650 *Totius orbis descriptio*, ch. 29.

means of strict price control designed to freeze prices at arbitrarily fixed levels, nevertheless allowed, in 301 C.E., very high prices to be charged for the high class manufactures of Beth Shean or, as it was called in Greek, Scythopolis.[651]

In contrast to Beth Shean's excellence, the linen garments produced at Arbel, in Galilee, were coarse and cheap.[652] This was also true of Egyptian linen manufactures, and it is significant that Clement of Alexandria (c. 150–c. 215 C.E.) found it necessary to chide the luxury-loving men of his city who preferred the fine imports from other countries, especially Palestine, to the coarse home-produced textiles of Egypt.[653]

Considerable differences in quality were also noted in other areas of industry. Thus, in Usha and Tiberias, which were among the most important Jewish centers in Galilee, reed-mats were produced, but those manufactured at Usha were soft and used as mattresses, while the mats of Tiberias were usually hard and uncomfortable.[654]

Among the specialized crafts was silk weaving, which flourished in Upper Galilee, most notably in the town of Giscala, whose products were sold in the great trading center of Tyre.[655] In Jerusalem there was a clothes market and wool-shops,[656] and there was even a special synagogue (which may also have served as a guild meeting place) of the *tarsiim*, who were probably artistic weavers of cloth from Tarsus, an important center of the linen industry in Asia Minor. There was also a synagogue of weavers in Lydda.[657]

The profitability of the textile industry was not without serious disadvantages. It became more profitable to turn good agricutural soil into pasture land than to continue the back-breaking toil associated with agricultural labor.[658] This, in turn, resulted in food shortages and the consequent rise in the price of basic foods, such as bread and vegetables.

651 G. Allon, *Toledot*, I, 102.
652 *Gen. R.* 19, 1; *Eccl. R.* I, 18.
653 Allon, *op. cit.*, I, 103.
654 *T.Y. Suk.* I, II, 52c; *T.B. Suk.* 20a–b.
655 Cf. M. Wischnitzer, *op. cit.*, pp. 29 f.
656 Cf. Josephus, *Bell.* V, 8, 1 (331).
657 Cf. T.B. Meg. 26a; S. Krauss, *op. cit.*, II, 258 and 625, notes 67a, 68 and 69; cf. also S. Krauss, *Synagogale Altertümer*, p. 209.
658 Cf. M. Avi-Yonah, *op. cit.*, pp. 27 and 41.

This problem and rabbinic attempts to deal with it will be discussed in Chapter Six.[659]

4. Pottery

A significant role in the economy of Galilee was played by potters who tended not only to concentrate in streets of their own, but seem to have dominated entire villages such as Kephar Hananiah, Kephar Shihin and Kephar Signa.[660] Even in modern times, earthenware vessels are produced in those same Upper Galilean areas rich in black earth, which in turn serves as raw material for the entire industry. In the absence of modern methods of refrigeration, these earthenware vessels are still very useful to keep water and wine fresh and cool. Somewhat rarer was "white" earth, which was presumably of a light reddish hue, and vessels made out of it were correspondingly more expensive.[661]

While Kephar Signa seems to have specialized in the manufacture of baking ovens,[662] Kephar Hananiah and Kephar Shihin were famous for their pottery, which was of such high quality that it was regarded as fireproof and unlikely to burst even in extreme heat.[663] In quantity too, the production of pottery in that area, and especially in Kephar Hananiah, was, it seems, enormous. "Would you bring pitchers to Kephar Hananiah?"[664] was a common proverb, equivalent to "taking coal to Newcastle" or "bringing water into the sea". So famous were the pots of Kephar Hananiah that they were widely sold all over the country, including southern Palestine (Judah), where they were used, among other things, for cooking or frying leeks.[665]

---

659 See *infra*, pp. 180 f.
660 Cf. M. Avi-Yonah, *op. cit*, p. 29; M. Wischnitzer, *op. cit.*, p. 30, who also mentions Lydda (= Lod), Bethlehem and Naaran as centers of the pottery industry, as indicated by excavations of numerous jars, amphores and oil lamps. In Gerasa, in Transjordan, there was even a guild of potters; cf. F.M. Heichelheim, "Roman Syria", *An Economic Survey of Ancient Rome*, T. Frank edit. (Baltimore, 1938), vol. II, p. 208.
661 Krauss, *Talm. Arch.* II, 272, 636; *Tos. B.M.* VI, 3; VIII, 27; *T.B.* ibid. 74a.
662 Cf. *M. Kel.* V, 4.
663 *T.B. Shab.* 120b.
664 *Gen. R.* 86, 5.
665 *Midr. Zuta Lam.* I, 5.

Despite a fair level of industrialization, the quality of the products was by no means uniform. In the case of baking ovens, we are expressly told that they varied in quality,[666] and Passover ovens used for roasting the Pascal lamb were liable to fall apart if exposed to rain.[667] Pottery, too, was of uneven quality. A Midrashic parable tells us that "a potter does not test defective vessels, because he cannot give them a single blow without breaking them".[668] The jars produced in the maritime plain of Sharon, though apparently considered to be of good quality,[669] were nevertheless far from perfect, and if one bought these jars, some ten percent of them were usually in faulty condition, apparently because the local clay was of inferior quality and did not get sufficiently dry to harden the finished product.[670] It has been surmised that the production of jars in Sharon was a subsidiary industry to wine production, and that the jars served to preserve the locally produced wine.[671]

The size of the pots and jars produced in the various pottery manufacturing centers differed considerably, and it seems that there were places which specialized in producing particular sizes. In some areas of Galilee, small jars and cruses were manufactured. Jars produced in Lod (Lydda) were of average size, while in Bethlehem, Galilee (not to be confused with the famous Bethlehem south of Jerusalem) rather large jars were produced — and there were even bigger jars in some areas.[672]

The lumps of clay which were shaped by potters into pots and pans of every imaginable form, looked like eggs in their raw form, and seem to have had some value;[673] for we are told in a parable that an apprentice found it worthwhile to steal a lump of potter's clay.[674] Even broken pieces of pottery, especially potsherds which could still be used as containers, had some value.[675] Indeed, we are told that broken pottery might be used to make new vessels or containers which were presumably cheap but by no means worthless.[676]

666 M. Pes. III, 4.
667 M. Taan. III, 8.
668 Gen. R. 32, 3; 34, 2.
669 Cf. Allon, op. cit., I, 104.
670 Mishnah B.B. VI, 2.
671 Allon, op. cit.; cf. M. Nid. II, 7; T.B. Nid. 21a.
672 M. Kel. II, 2; Sifra Shemini VII, 3, edit. Weiss 53b.
673 Cf., e.g., Tos. B.M. VI, 3; T.B. ibid. 74a.
674 Lev. R. 23, 12.
675 T. Kel. B.K. VII, 17.   676 T. Kel. B.M. I, 3.

Although we may assume that potters had a regular home like everybody else, they also had workshops combined with temporary living quarters and a storage room. These workshops, which were probably used only during the dry season, between April and October, consisted of two booths, the outer one serving as workshop and market store where the finished product was exhibited for sale, while the inner booth served as a storage chamber and, during the busy summer season, as living quarters.[677]

Like most artisans, potters were not exactly prosperous. A far from sumptuous ossuary discovered in Jerusalem in 1969, bearing the inscription of "Jonathan the Potter", indicates that even in large cities potters could not afford expensive burials which were commonplace among the well-to-do classes. Socially, potters seem to have occupied an inferior position during the Talmudic period. A Midrashic parable tells us of a man who was skilled in three crafts, that of the goldsmith, the potter, and the glazier. His friends would call him "goldsmith"; his enemies — "potter"; while those who were neither friendly nor hostile would call him "glazier".[678] Of course, this represents only the popular attitude which, in turn, reflected the respective economic advantages of these crafts. The rabbinic attitude, as will be shown in the next chapter, was influenced much more by moral than by social or economic considerations, so that the socially superior goldsmith, whose products undoubtedly earned a good profit, was nevertheless regarded as undesirable because he made trinkets for women, and any trade involving too much contact with women was considered undesirable.[679]

5. Glass Industry

During the Roman period, glass manufacturing became an important industry, especially in Northern Palestine, near the Phoenician border where glass was produced since very early times. Josephus, the famous historian of the Jewish war against the Romans, describes the sand on the banks of the small stream Belus, near Ptolemais (= Acco), out of

677 *M. Maas.* III, 7; *T. Maas. R.* II, 21; *T.B. Suk.* 8b.
678 *Num. R.* 2, 17.
679 *M. Kid.* IV, 14.

which glass was made. When the sand was removed to be carried away by ships, presumably to a glass manufacturing town, it was replaced by the winds "which bring into it, as it were on purpose, the sand which lay remote, and was no more than bare common sand, while this mine (along the shores of the Belus) presently turns it into glassy sand".[680]

This area of Northwestern Palestine belonging to, or bordering on, the territory of the Israelite tribe of Zebulun, was always renowned for the manufacture of glassware, so much so that one of the Aramaic translations of Deuteronomy 33:19: "the hidden treasures of the sand" renders: "Out of the sand they produce mirrors and articles made of glass".[681] According to the Talmud,[682] Zebulun complained about the poor quality of the land allocated to the tribe of which he was the progenitor. He was, however, assured that he would be compensated by the sand found in his territory. Out of that sand, he was told, "white" (i.e., colorless) glass would be manufactured. This was a valuable source of wealth, for the ancients found it very hard to produce colorless glass.[683] Similar, though less valuable, glassware was manufactured in Tiberias, and we have a number of reference to Tiberian winecups, which were made of thin and transparent glass.[684]

Ancient Palestinian glassware of all sorts has been discovered in the course of numerous excavations in the Holy Land, including a perfect "lacrimatory" or tear bottle, which may have been used to "store" tears for religious or magical purposes. It is probably to this strange use of glass bottles that Psalms 56:8 alludes: "Put thou my tears in thy bottle".

In biblical times, glass was extremely expensive. When the author of Job wanted to express the incomparable value of wisdom, he wrote, "gold and glass cannot equal it".[685] In Talmudic times, the same verse was applied to "the words of the Torah, which are hard to acquire like vessels of fine gold, but are easily destroyed (i.e., forgotten) like vessels of glass".[686] Elsewhere, glass links, used as ornaments, are enumerated together with jewels and pearls.[687]

680 *Bell.* II, 10, 2 (190).
681 *Targ. Ps.-Jon., ad loc.*
682 *T.B. Meg.* 6a.
683 Cf. Krauss, *op. cit.*, II, 286.
684 *T.Y. Nid.* II, 6, 50b; *T.B. Nid.* 21a; *Midr. Pss.* 75, 4, edit. Buber, p. 339.
685 *Job* 28:17.
686 *T.B. Hag.* 15a.   687 *M. Kel.* XI, 8.

It was about the beginning of the Common Era that the Jews acquired the art of glassblowing,[688] which greatly stimulated the large-scale manufacture of glass articles. We also learn about pincers and tubes used by glass makers as well as goldsmiths and blacksmiths,[689] probably during the heating process, which is described in a somewhat simplified manner: "Sand is put into the fire and comes out as glass".[690]

Occasionally, glass makers would combine their trade with other related crafts. Thus, as already mentioned, we are told in a Midrashic parable about "a man who was skilled in three crafts, that of the goldsmith, the potter, and the glazier".[691] Elsewhere, too, glassmakers or glass-sellers are mentioned together with potters or pot-sellers[692] — proof that these two trades were closely associated.

As already pointed out, "white", colorless glass was extraordinarily expensive as well as fragile, so much so that a finder of vessels of glass was not supposed to touch them, even if the owner never showed up. The same rule applied if one found articles of gold.[693] One of the most humorous pieces of advice offered in the Talmud reads as follows:

"If a person is left money by his father and he wishes to dissipate it, let him wear linen garments, use glassware, and engage workmen and not be with them". The glassware is subsequently explained to refer to "white" glass.[694]

Hyperbolically, it was said that since the destruction of the Temple "white" glass had ceased to be used.[695] This was, of course, incorrect (except, possibly, for a very short time), and what the rabbis actually meant was that, like all articles of luxurious living, expensive glassware should have ceased to be used, as a symbol of mourning. In fourth century or early fifth century Babylonia, Rab Ashi, the leading scholar of his time, made a wedding feast for his son, and when he noticed that the guests were becoming unduly merry — which the serious-minded rabbis

---

688 Cf., e.g., T.Y. Shab. VII, 4, 10d.
689 *T. Kel. B.M.* III, 10–11.
690 *Num. R.* 2, 13.
691 Ibid. 2, 17.
692 Cf., e.g., *T.B. Baba Kama* 31a.
693 *M. Baba Metsia* II, 8.
694 *T.B. Hul.* 84b; *B.M.* 29b.
695 *T.Y. Suk.* IV, 7, 54d; *T.B. Sot.* 48b.

disliked in any case, especially since the Jews were supposed to be in a state of permanent mourning for the Temple — he brought a cup of "white" glass and smashed it before them. This act considerably dampened their spirits.[696] This is the origin of the Jewish custom of breaking a glass at the conclusion of the wedding ceremony. But if it was originally a sign of mourning for the departed glory of ancient Israel, hardly anyone is aware of this nowadays. On the contrary, it is the signal for rapturous Mazel-tov wishes by all who attend the ceremony.

To protect the valuable glassware, sellers of glass used special tables made like beds, with raised frames, between which the vessels were exhibited for sale. Thus, they were in no danger of dropping to the ground.[697] Theoretically, of course, even broken glass could be "repaired" by being melted down again, though in most cases, it would hardly have been worthwhile. Nevertheless, in a parable designed to prove the possibility of resurrection, the rabbis stated, "If glassware, which, though made by the breath of human beings (i.e., by blowing glass), can yet be repaired when broken, then how much more so man, created by the breath of the Holy One, blessed be He!".[698]

Not all glassware sellers were equally careful. Some apparently kept their wares in baskets where it was much less protected. A Midrashic parable tells us about a villager — according to another version, a blind man — who was passing near a glass store and with a stick he accidentally broke a basket full of goblets and cut-glassware. The storekeeper seized the poor careless fellow and told him, "I know that I can not obtain redress from you, but come and I will show you how much valuable stuff you have destroyed.[699]

Poorer people could not afford expensive glassware, and had to be satisfied with cheap colored glass articles and ornaments. Thus, according to regulations regarding eligibility for "welfare" aid, indigent persons who owned relatively more expensive metal utensils were required to sell them and use cheap colored glassware before they were entitled to appeal for public assistance.[700] However, while this was the legal position, in practice a far more liberal attitude prevailed.[701]

696 *T.B. Ber.* 31a.
697 *M. Kel.* XXIV, 8.
698 *T.B. Sanh.* 91a.
699 *Gen. R.* 19, 6.
700 *T. Peah* IV, 11.
701 Ibid. IV, 10–12.

The technique of glass manufacture was highly developed, and required considerable investment.[702] We have already seen that the Jews had mastered the art of glassblowing. We also hear of such technical operations as perforating glass vessels and pouring lead into them[703] or, for the manufacture of gold glass, pressing designs etched in gold leaf between two layers of transparent glass.[704] A good many articles were made wholly or partly of glass, including plates, trays, spoons, cups, flasks, bowls, beads and many others.[705] Colored glass ornaments were so cheap that they were sold by weight.[706] Mirrors were, for the most part, made of metal,[707] but more expensive glass mirrors were also produced.[708] In the Diaspora, too, Jews were active in the glass-manufacturing industry. For centuries, Jews practiced the craft of glassmaking in Tyre, perhaps the most important center of the glass industry in antiquity.[709]

6. Metal Industry and Arms Manufacture

In addition to goldsmiths and silversmiths, who produced household articles and highly priced ornaments such as the "Jerusalem of gold"[710] — described as "a normal crown imitating a wall encircling a city and fortified by battlements"[711] the metal trade included smelters, blacksmiths, coppersmiths, needlemakers and armorers.[712] Jewish metal workers, especially coppersmiths, were employed in southern Palestine at least up to the end of the fourth century C.E.[713] There were also Jewish

702 Cf. M. Wischnitzer, *op. cit.*, p. 30.
703 *T.B. Shab.* 15b.
704 Cf. M. Wischnitzer, *op. cit.*, p. 53.
705 Cf. *M. Kel.* XI, 8; XXX, 1–4.
706 Ibid. XXIX, 6; *T.B. B.B.* 89a.
707 *T.B. Shab.* 149a.
708 Ibid.; *M. Kel.* XXX, 2; *Targ. Ps-Jon.* to *Deut.* 33:19.
709 Cf. M. Wischnitzer, *op. cit.*, p. 52.
710 Cf. *Aboth-de-R. Nathan*, edit. Schechter, Vers. I, ch. 6, p. 30; *M. Kel.* XI, 8; *M. Shab.* VI, 1; *T.Y. Shab.* VI, 1, 7d; *T.B. Shab.* 59a–b; *T.B. Sot.* 49b. Cf. also S. Krauss, *op. cit.*, vol. I, pp. 662f., note 961.
711 M. Wischnitzer, *op. cit.*, p. 22.
712 Ibid.
713 *M. Ket.* VII, 10; Allon, *op. cit.*, pp. 104f.

weapon-makers, and it is noteworthy that the rabbis prohibited the sale of weapons to Gentiles,[714] no doubt because they realized that the weapons were liable to be used against Jews. This is one of the earliest examples of what is now known as "gun control" laws.

At the time of the outbreak of the Roman-Jewish war, in 66 C.E., Jerusalem's armorers were mobilized for the war effort. In Josephus's words, "In every quarter of the city, missiles and suits of armor were being forged".[715]

However, since Jewish arms producers enjoyed a great reputation for excellent workmanship, the Romans forced the Jewish weapon makers to produce arms for the Roman legions. Prior to the outbreak of the Bar Kochba rising (132–135 C.E.), the Jewish weapon makers turned the tables on the Romans and deliberately produced faulty weapons which the Romans, naturally, refused to accept. The Jews would then secretly repair the weapons and use them to equip the Jewish insurgent armies.[716]

7. Marketing and Trading Activities

Many small hardware and clothing producers as well as farmers would also market their produce. With the increasing urbanization of Palestine under Roman rule, it was possible for the producer to live in a market town and work there, often in his own home, or, in the case of farmers, in the immediate vicinity of the town. According to R. Jose, a resident of Sepphoris, which for a time served as the capital of Galilee, there were at one time no less than 180,000 markets for "pudding" dealers in the city.[717] This, of course, is not only an exaggeration, but pure fantasy. It, nevertheless, indicates that Sepphoris was a center of what we would, today, call the food industry. The "pudding" mentioned was quite unlike any modern pudding. It consisted of a variety of ingredients such as minced meat and spices, mixed with wine, and it sounds tasty, though from a hygienic point of view the preparation may have left much to be desired.

714 *Tos. A.Z.* II, 4; cf. *Mishnah A.Z.* I, 7 and commentaries.
715 *Bell.* II, 22, 1 (646).
716 *Dio Cassius* 69, 12.
717 *T.B. B.B.* 75b.

There were also many expert cooks and bakers who produced large varieties of dishes and confections.[718] Many, probably most of them, sold their own concoctions, and some seem to have "made" it, at least in death; for unlike the poor who could rarely afford a tombstone, we find a number of tombstones, especially in Jaffa, which were inscribed in Greek and commemorate bakers, a cumin seller, a junk dealer and even a fuller and an ordinary laborer.[719] In Caesarea, a tombstone of a Jewish sandalmaker was found.[720] Hence, it would appear that most craftsmen and traders were socially "integrated," at least in the sense that they enjoyed certain privileges which in early times had been the exclusive prerogative of the wealthier classes.

As Palestine became more and more urbanized, trading — whether with one's own products or with imported or exported goods — assumed an ever increasing importance which is fully reflected in the Talmud. A substantial proportion of the Talmud is devoted to commercial problems, and this together with the Rabbinic Codes and Responsa of the Middle Ages and modern times represent virtually inexhaustible sources on Jewish business and banking activities during the past two millennia.

Even as early as the first century C.E., trade had become sufficiently important in the life of the country so that the high priest would include in his special prayer in the Holy of Holies on the Day of Atonement a request that the coming year should be distinguished by successful business activity.[721] Later, public prayers were offered whenever there was a sudden, dangerous drop in prices which endangered the economic survival of the trading community.[722] For example, it was pointed out that if linen garments in Babylonia or wine and oil in Palestine became so cheap that traders would face ruin, it was time to hold special prayer meetings,[723] since other methods of regulating the essentially free market were, as yet, unknown. While originally the exact degree of the price collapse was not stipulated, it was suggested in the late third century that

---

718 *Eccl. R.* III, 1, 8, 2; *Lam. R.* 3, 17.
719 S. Klein, edit., *Sepher Ha-Yishuv* (Jerusalem, 1939), I, 82f.
720 M. Avi-Yonah, *op. cit.*, p. 27.
721 *T.Y. Yoma* V, 3, 42c.
722 *T.B. B.B.* 91a.
723 Ibid.

a 40 percent drop of prices constituted a perilous situation.[724] It is noteworthy that the problem of over-production (especially in the sphere of farming) and consequent collapse of prices, which bothers America today, occasionally plagued even ancient Israel, where scarcity was the more usual phenomenon.

The rabbis were not, in principle, opposed to low prices as such. On the contrary, they opposed arbitrary raising of prices and speculative hoarding of essential food by dealers who wanted to sell it at a higher price later on.[725] In third century Babylonia, Samuel Yarhinaa as well as his father made it a special rule to sell their produce cheap during periods of scarcity when prices were high.[726] With a view to preventing a shortage of necessities, the rabbis prohibited the export of wine, oil and flour from Palestine, though this rule was relaxed in the case of wine and, occasionally, where oil was plentiful, the export of this important commodity was permitted.[727] Profiteering in necessities was restricted and discouraged, though not always successfully.[728] Attempts were also made to cut out the intrusion of more than one middleman in the sale of certain products, such as eggs, so that the profits of the dealers — wholesalers and retailers — should not raise prices for consumers.[729]

Most rabbis, likewise, did not object to price cutting by storekeepers, although R. Judah considered this unfair competition. He was, however, overruled by the majority who stated, on the contrary, that a storekeeper who reduced his prices deserved to be remembered for good.[730]

Even the equivalent of trading stamps was not unknown in ancient Israel. Storekeepers tried to attract customers by distributing roasted ears of grain and nuts to children. R. Judah, consistent with his principles, considered this, too, to be unfair competition. His colleagues, however, permitted this practice because they felt that healthy competition was essential to protect consumer interests.[731] A storekeeper who objected to such practices could be told by his enterprising competitor to

724 Ibid.
725 Ibid. 90b.
726 Ibid.
727 Ibid., 91a; cf. *Tos. A.Z.* IV (V), 2.
728 B.B. ibid.; *Tos. A.Z.* ibid., 1.
729 B.B. ibid.
730 *M. Baba Metsia* IV, 12.
731 Ibid.

resort to similar gimmicks of his own: "I distribute nuts; you distribute plums".[732]

8. Commercial Ethics — Price Control

There was a striking contrast between the rabbinic attitude on price control and the prevailing Roman system which was market-orientated, without regard to the interests of the weaker parties, usually the consumers, or to any ethical considerations such as fair trading practices. In Roman law, the price of any given commodity was determined solely by the parties to the transaction and, short of outright deception, there was nothing the buyer could do if he was grossly overcharged for an article worth only a fraction of the price charged. Likewise, there was no protection for the inexperienced or needy seller who gave away valuable objects for a song. According to Paulus, a famous third century Roman jurist, it was a man's natural right to purchase for a small price that which is really valuable, and to sell at a higher price that which is less valuable, and both buyer and seller could try to overreach one another.[733]

Jewish law, on the other hand, explicitly prohibited such practices. Even biblical law had provided that "when you sell anything to your neighbor, or buy anything from your neighbor, you shall not wrong one another".[734] The rabbis accordingly enacted a number of provisions based on ethical considerations and designed to safeguard the interests of both sides. Profits in each transaction were limited, and while no rigid rules were imposed, and variations depending on circumstances were introduced, generally an overcharge of more than one sixth above the prevailing market price was considered sufficient to cancel the sale. Where it was exactly one sixth, the buyer could recover the excess payment. If it was less than one sixth, the natural flexibility of the market as well as common sense clearly indicated that no further action be taken.[735] The seller, too, was protected if through ignorance or carelessness, he had been cheated out of his goods at a price below the market

---

732 *T.B. Baba Metsia* 60a.
733 Justinian, *Digest* XIX, II, 22 (3).
734 *Lev.* 25:14.
735 *T.B. Baba Metsia* 50b.

value.[736] Even experienced merchants were supposed to enjoy this right, though R. Judah considered that dealers who sold below market value did so deliberately, with a view to raising capital for business operations; for example, in order to buy up bargains. They had therefore no right to claim that they had been defrauded.[737]

The rabbis also instituted a careful weights and measures inspection system. Dealers had to clean their weights and measures periodically: in the case of wholesalers once a month, while retail storekeepers, who sold many articles in small numbers, were required to clean their scales and weights twice a week. Weights were not to be made of metal which could easily wear out, but of granite, stone or glass.[738]

Storekeepers were also not supposed to give their goods a delusive appearance by displaying the best stuff on top and placing the inferior below. Old clothes or old furniture were not to be renovated and sold as new. Animals for sale were not to have their appearance improved by being specially brushed up or drugged so that they might appear young.[739]

Since there were bound to be attempts to defraud inexperienced buyers or sellers, market commissioners were appointed whose task it was to supervise the entire functioning of the market. They tested the quality of the food, liquors and other articles offered for sale, and they controlled weights and measures. In Jerusalem, market commissioners were functioning since very early times, but they were not supposed to control prices, for competition was to be free and unfettered.[740] Apparently, the same system applied in the rest of Palestine, too; but in the third century C.E., when the entire Roman Empire was in the grip of a most serious and prolonged economic crisis, resulting in the debasing of the coinage and a runaway inflation, the Patriarch made an attempt at price control, to be enforced by the market commissioners.[741] By all appearances, the new policy was not very successful. Prices continued to rise and contributed their fair share to the ultimate collapse of the Roman Empire.

736 *M. Baba Metsia* IV, 4.
737 Ibid.; *T.B. B.M.* 51a.
738 *T.B. Baba Bathra*, 89a–b.
739 *M. Baba Metsia* IV, 12; I. Epstein, *Social Legislation in the Talmud* (London, 1947), p. 12.
740 *Tos. Baba Metsia* VI, 14.
741 *T.B. Baba Bathra* 89a.

In Babylonia, the local rabbis could not agree whether price control was desirable or practical. Rab, for example, on arrival in Babylonia, in 219 C.E., was appointed market commissioner by the civil ruler of Babylonian Jewry, the so-called *Resh Galuta* (= Exilarch), who instructed him to supervise market prices. Rab was, however, what we would today call a liberal economist and refused to interfere with the free market. As a result, he was for a time imprisoned by the Exilarch, presumably for disobeying orders.[742]

Rab's colleague, Samuel, on the other hand, was more interested in safeguarding the interests of the consumer, and, as we have seen, he went out of his way to help reduce prices. Very significant was his reaction to an attempt by hardware dealers to charge exorbitant prices around Passover time when most people had to replace their old earthenware utensils which were considered *Hametz* (i.e., saturated with leavened food) and unfit for use even after Passover. Samuel threatened that he would alter the law and permit the use of the old earthenware vessels after Passover.[743] Although we are not told what effect his warning had, we may assume that it worked. He made a similar threat against myrtle dealers who charged excessive prices for myrtles at *Succot* time when myrtles were in great demand for ritual purposes.[744]

In Palestine, too, there were occasional cases of rabbinic collisions with traders. We are told that a certain ruling by R. Tarfon, which was favorable to traders because it raised the limit of permitted overcharge, was joyfully received by the traders of Lod (Lydda); but when they learned that R. Tarfon had also increased the time limit during which defrauded individuals could demand redress or annulment of the sale, the traders begged R. Tarfon to leave the previous law unchanged.[745]

Merchants in Palestine, as elsewhere, had a bad reputation. Some of them were profiteers who, as we have already seen, cashed in on the religious feelings of the people. In Jerusalem, the grocers would cry out on the eve of Passover, "Come and buy ingredients for your religious requirements".[746] They were selling, we are told, the ingredients used for

742 *T.Y. B.B.* V, 11, 15a–b.
743 *T.B. Pes.* 30a.
744 *T.B. Suk.* 34b.
745 *M. B.M.* IV, 3.
746 *T.B. Pes.* 116a.

Haroseth, a mixture of apples, nuts, almonds etc. which were (and still are) used at the *Seder* table. While this is indeed a venerable custom, it was hardly an obligatory religious requirement in ancient times.[747] However, the "commercial" had to have religious overtones to be successful.

The area around the Temple of Jerusalem was a beehive of commercial activity, and there can be little doubt that a considerable number of merchants, moneychangers and even ordinary peddlers derived their living from the Temple and the vast throngs of pilgrims from all over the world who visited the Temple.[748] While the traders and bankers were no doubt carrying on legitimate and essential business, some at least must have taken advantage of the pilgrims. As already mentioned in Chapter Three, Jesus, who was himself a Galilean pilgrim to Jerusalem, must have had public opinion on his side when — according to the Christian tradition — he drove out the merchants and moneychangers from the Temple, overturning their tables and seats and telling them that they had made the Temple a den of robbers.[749] As far as we know, no attempt was made to stop him, and he had, moreover, some Scriptural support (though the Christian tradition does not record that he actually cited it); for the last verse of the book of Zechariah (14:21) predicts that "there shall no longer be a trader in the house of the Lord of hosts on that day". The Messianic era, which so many believed to have dawned, was obviously a suitable time for getting rid of the corruption represented by profit-hungry elements.

Traders were often regarded as dishonest and deceitful,[750] as, indeed, they had been even in biblical times.[751] They were also considered to be greedy and insatiable. Ecclesiastes 5:9 — "He that loves money will not be satisfied with money" — is rendered by the Aramaic Targum (translation) in the following significant manner: "A man (who is) a trader who loves to acquire money and the owner(s) of merchandise will not be satisfied accumulating money". Thus, a general statement, applicable to anyone, was deliberately interpreted to apply to businessmen who were evidently hated for skinning their customers.

---

747 Cf. *M. Pes.* X, 3.
748 *M. Shek.* I, 3; IV, 9; VII, 2.
749 *Matt.* 21:12; 11:15ff.; *Luke* 19:45f.; *John* 2:14ff.
750 *Tos. B.M.* III, 19.
751 Cf. Hos. 12:8; Amos 8:4ff.; Micah 6:11.

Occasionally, however, we learn about merchants who were far from greedy. In Tiberias, traders imposed a voluntary restriction upon themselves not to do any business during the intermediate days of the festivals of Passover and Succot.[752] This must have been a genuine financial sacrifice, since it involved closing the stores for seven or eight successive days. In modern times, such voluntary closing could be interpreted as annual vacations; but in antiquity they probably did not think of it that way. Merchants would close their stores solely out of respect for the sanctity of the festival, including the intermediate days during which work essential for one's livlihood was actually permitted.

9. Private Enterprise — Legal Problems

The entire business of traders as well as that of craftsmen who sold their own produce presented an enormous range of legal problems, which are discussed at great length in the Talmud. Frequently, a business establishment in a residential area might be a nuisance or, alternatively, an invasion of the rights of existing establishments. The privileges of free enterprise had to be weighed against the injustice of unfair competition. The rabbis generally tried to hold the balance between such opposing claims, just as they were unprejudiced and fair in determining the legal relations between employers and workers. And if, occasionally, one rabbi tended to lean more in one direction, there was usually another rabbi who would defend the interests of the other side.

A few selected examples will help to illustrate the problems outlined above. A baker or a dyer was not permitted to open shop under a (second floor) storehouse because the heat of the bakery or from the dyer's ovens was liable to damage the food or goods stored above.[753] The tenants of a courtyard could prevent anyone from setting up shop in the courtyard, and even a single objection by one of the tenants, such as "I can not sleep because of the noise created by the coming and going of the customers", was sufficient to stop any such enterprise from being established. Even where there was some slight interference with access to the courtyard or

752   *T.B. Moed Kat.* 13b.
753   *M. Baba Bathra* II, 3.

the houses inside it, the objections of tenants were decisive to prevent a business establishment from being opened.

The same rule applied also to a physician, blood-letter, weaver, tailor or tanner — none of whom could set up shop, if the neighbors objected because of the constant coming and going of patients and customers. Likewise, the owner of the house could not rent it to these professional people.[754]

An existing store, on the other hand, could apparently not so easily be closed down because of the objections of the neighbors. Similarly, no one could stop a craftsman from producing his wares at home, as long as he did not sell them there. The noise made in the course of manufacturing, e.g., by the hammers or the grinding of handmills, though undoubtedly a nuisance, was regarded as unavoidable.[755] The fundamental principle, based no doubt on economic realities, was that the domestic manufacturing industries, such as pottery, glassmaking etc., were too vital for the economy to suffer interference because of inconvenience to neighbors. Trade, on the other hand, could be carried on in the public market, and there was no overwhelming need for a merchant or a craftsman to sell his wares at his home.

On the question of free enterprise versus established interests there was a clear difference of opinion among the rabbis, mainly because it was difficult to decide between the different and indeed contradictory principles involved. Thus, according to one opinion, "If a resident of an alley sets up a handmill and another resident of the alley wants to set up one next to him, the first has the right to stop him, because he can say to him, 'you are interfering with my livelihood' ".[756] As against that, another view was that, "a man may open a store next to another man's store or a (public) bathhouse next to another man's bathhouse, and the latter cannot object, because he can say to him, "I do what I like in my property, and you do what you like in yours' ".[757] It is noteworthy, though, that even if the law did not prevent unfair competition, it was in practice morally condemned, especially in the Middle Ages, when the regulation of competition among Jews was absolutely essential for the

754 *T.B. B.B.* 21a–b.
755 *M. Baba Bathra* II, 3; *Tos.* ibid. I, 4.
756 *T.B. B.B.* 21b.
757 Ibid.

wellbeing of the community, restricted as it was in its economic opportunities.

Residents of another town, who did not pay taxes in the town where
they wanted to do business, could be prevented from setting up shop
there.[758] Itinerant peddlers and spice-sellers, on the other hand, could not
prevent competition among themselves, evidently because their services
were required, "so that the daughters of Israel should be able to obtain
finery" — no doubt as inexpensively as possible, which could be
achieved only if there was unrestricted competition.[759] They were not,
however, permitted to settle in the towns they visited, which would have
injured local interests unduly. Only students who moonlighted as
peddlers were permitted to settle down, since they would otherwise have
been disturbed in their studies.[760]

The conflict of interests involved — which incidentally is exactly
parallel to a similar conflict in nineteenth century America between the
urban peddlers and the country storekeepers (who sold at higher prices
than the peddlers) — is well illustrated in the following recorded stories:

Certain basket-sellers from abroad imported baskets to Babylonia,
competing with local products. Since Babylonian Jews enjoyed complete
autonomy, the local interests managed to stop the foreigners — Jews like
themselves, but not of the home-grown variety — from selling their baskets. The importers, thereupon, appealed to Rabina, a late fourth century
Rabbi, who decided that the foreigners had a right to sell to foreign
residents in Babylonia. But even this restriction (which must have been
difficult to enforce), applied only on market days, and even then only in
the market itself. Door-to-door peddling could continue unrestrained.[761]

Rather less lucky were certain wool traders, who imported wool to the
Babylonian town of Pum Nahara. Again, competing local interests tried
to stop the unwelcome intruders, who in turn appealed to Rab Kahana.
The latter displayed little sympathy for the visitors. Referring to the local
people, he said to the foreigners, "They have a perfect right to stop you".
When the importers pointed out that money was owing to them by
certain people in Pum Nahara, and that they themselves had to make a

758 *T.B. B.B.* 21b.
759 Ibid. 22a.
760 Ibid.
761 Ibid.

living while waiting for the settlement of the debts, Rab Kahana grudgingly permitted them to sell just enough to enable them to get by until they had managed to collect the debts due to them. After that, they were told unequivocally, they must leave.[762]

10. Jewish Occupations in the Roman-Hellenistic Diaspora

i Alexandria

While trades and professions specially favored or disliked will be discussed in the next chapter, some notice must be taken of the Hellenistic and Roman Diaspora, where the Jews were by no means confined to what we would call "white-collar" occupations. On the contrary, the Jews were often despised for their poverty rather than envied for their wealth, though, as we shall see, there were some notable exceptions. Palestinian schools and institutions had often reason to be grateful for the ancient equivalent of the United Jewish Appeal, which was always enthusiastically supported by Jews of all classes in the lands of the Dispersion.

By far the most important Diaspora center was Alexandria, Egypt, for a long time the largest city in the world. In the Roman period, Alexandria was second only to Rome, with a population estimated at between 500,000 and 1,000,000.[762a] Two out of the five districts into which the city was divided were Jewish,[763] and the total Jewish population of Alexandria exceeded that of Jerusalem.

Alexandria had the distinction of having the largest and most beautiful synagogue in the world, though some think that it was really a *basilica*, i.e., a market and trade union meeting hall used also for religious services.[764] It was surrounded by a double colonnade, and according to one opinion, one who had not seen this magnificent building "has never seen the glory of Israel". Hyperbolically, it was claimed that it could hold 1,200,000 worshipers; that it contained 71 seats of gold; and that it was so huge that the voice of the cantor could not be heard, so that it was necessary for an attendant to stand on a platform in the middle of the

---

762 Ibid.
762a Cf. S.W. Baron, *A Social and Religious History of the Jews*, 2nd edit., vol. I, p. 171.
763 Cf. Philo, *In Flaccum* 8.
764 Cf. S. Krauss, *Synagogale Altertümer*, pp. 261 ff.

building and wave a scarf whenever the congregation was required to respond to a blessing with the traditional Amen. Of special significance is the fact that the congregation was not seated indiscriminately, but according to their respective trades: "goldsmiths separately, silversmiths separately, blacksmiths separately, weavers separately, and metal workers (or, more likely, artistic weavers) separately". Poor immigrants would thus have little difficulty in finding guild-organized members of their own trade who — like the American *Landsmanshaften* in the nineteenth and early twentieth centuries — provided the newcomers with work, lodging and any other assistance they might require. This great synagogue was destroyed and many of its worshipers massacred following the bitter war waged by the Egyptian Jews against the Greeks and Romans in 115–116 C.E.[765]

That a synagogue should have served as a market hall and trade union center or vice versa, should occasion no surprise. Originally, the synagogue was not meant to be a building, and the very name — both in Hebrew and in Greek — meant an assembly or meeting place which could be used for all kinds of purposes, of which prayer services were only the most important.

Jewish goldsmiths and silversmiths would seem to have been quite numerous in Alexandria and, possibly, in other parts of Egypt, too. A fanciful Midrashic story relates that when Alexander the Great conquered the Near East, the Egyptians submitted a claim for all the silver and gold the Israelites had taken with them when they left Egypt.[766] The Jewish spokesman then pointed out that the Israelites, some of whom were silversmiths or goldsmiths, had served the Egyptians without pay for some two hundred and ten years. The Jews would therefore submit a counter-claim for payment at the rate of one denarius a day. When the mathematicians calculated that the Egyptians would lose much more than they could gain on the strength of their claim, the Egyptian representatives "departed in shame".[767]

The story undoubtedly reflects the actual conditions in Alexandria where Jewish goldsmiths and silversmiths seem to have formed a substantial class of skilled craftsmen. The pay of one denarius per day

---

765 *Tos. Suk.* IV, 6; *T.Y. Suk.* V, 1, 55a–b; *T.B. Suk.* 51b.
766 Cf. Exod. 12:36.
767 *Gen. R.* 61, 7; *T.B. Sanh.* 91a.

was probably minimal; but in any case it represented a fair wage for craftsmen, even allowing for the inflation which gripped the Roman empire in the third century C.E.

Alexandrian textiles enjoyed a great reputation, and Jewish artistic weavers produced pictorial tapestries for which there was considerable demand. We hear of the *vela Iudaica*, i.e., curtains made by Jewish weavers, with figures of Indian monsters woven into them.[768] There was evidently no religious objection against this form of artistic activity.

When bronze doors were required for the great eastern gate of the Temple Court, a certain Nicanor — evidently a wealthy philanthropist, probably an Alexandrian residing in Jerusalem — went to Alexandria, where skilled coppersmiths made the doors of refined, light-weight Corinthian bronze, which had a golden hue and "shone like gold". The valuable bronze doors were transported on a ship, and Nicanor accompanied the precious cargo when a storm arose and threatened to sink the ship. "Thereupon they took one of the doors and cast it into the sea, but still the sea would not stop its rage. So they wanted to cast the other door (into the sea to lighten the weight of the ship's cargo), but he rose and clung to it, saying, 'Cast me in with it!' Immediately, the sea stopped its raging. He wàs, however, distressed because of the other door (which had been cast into the sea). When he arrived at the harbor of Acco, it (viz. the 'sunken' door) broke through (the surface of the sea) and came up from under the sides of the ship. Others say, a sea monster swallowed it and ejected it (lit. spat it out) unto dry land. ... Therefore, all the gates that were in the Temple were changed for golden (i.e., gilded) ones, except for the Nicanor gate because of the miracles wrought with it".[769]

For all their fame, the Alexandrian coppersmiths were not always successful. Thus, we are told that an ancient cymbal of bronze, believed to have been made in the days of Moses, became damaged and had to be repaired by expert craftsmen. The rabbinic sages, who controlled the Temple administration during the last years of the Temple's existence, sent for craftsmen from Alexandria, and they "mended" it in such a way that the sound of the cymbal was no longer pleasant: "Thereupon they

---

768 Cf. Claudian, *Against Eutropius* I, 356–357; M. Wischnitzer, *op. cit.*, p. 49.
769 Cf. *T.B. Yoma* 38a; *Tos. Yom Hakip.* II, 4; *M. Mid.* I, 4; II, 3; Josephus, *Bell.* V, 5, 3 (201).

removed the improvement, and its sound became as pleasant as it had been before."[770]

Equally unsuccessful were Alexandrian coppersmiths who were summoned to repair an ancient bronze mortar — also believed to have come down from the days of Moses — that was used for pounding and mixing the incense drugs. The mortar was damaged, and the Alexandrian craftsmen mended it. However, it no longer worked as well as it had done in the past. "Whereupon they removed the improvement and it would mix them well again as it had done before".[771]

In Alexandria, Jews were also active in the shipping industry, both as shipowners and as sailors. The Jewish shipowners had their own corporation of *navicularii* (skippers, shipowners) organized according to Roman law, and they had to endure heavy taxes specially imposed on them. Naturally, they tried their best to circumvent the regulations and dodge the tax burden which adversely affected their ability to stay in business. The Roman governor of Egypt thereupon imposed the shipowners' tax liability on the entire Jewish community of Alexandria. This illegal act was repealed, in 390 C.E., by a decree of Emperor Theodosius I.[772]

Synesius, Bishop of Cyrene in North Africa (today Libya) during the early part of the fifth century C.E., describes a voyage he made in a Jewish-owned ship from Alexandria to Cyrene in 404 C.E. The ship was not only owned by a Jew (incidentally, with the good Roman name of Amarantus), but most of the sailors, including the pilot, were also Jews. Because of poor profits, the ship had been badly neglected, and instead of the usual three anchors, only one was available on that ship. There were over fifty passengers, men and women, and the sexes were strictly segregated from one another. These Jewish sailors were clearly not of the type who had a girl in every port. One day a severe tempest arose and the ship was in grave peril. It so happened that it was a Friday afternoon, and no sooner did the Sabbath begin than the pilot let go of the helm, and there was no one to steer the ship through the stormy sea. The passengers, who were thoroughly frightened for their lives, begged the pilot to resume his work and try and steer the ship to safety, but he insisted

---

770 Cf. *Tos. Arakhin* II, 3; *T.B. Arakhin*, 10b.
771 Cf. *Tos. Arakhin* II, 4; *T.B. Arakhin* 10b.
772 Cf. *Codex Theodosianus* XIII, 5, 18; S. Dubnow, *Weltgeschichte des jüdischen Volkes* (Berlin, 1926), vol. III, p. 254.

that he would do no work on the Sabbath. Instead, he read aloud from the Bible, oblivious to the tempest and refusing to heed the appeals and threats of the passengers. Only at midnight when the ship was in imminent danger of sinking, did the pilot go back to work, arguing correctly that Jewish law permitted work on the Sabbath when one's life was imperilled.[773] Eventually, the storm subsided, and the pilot brought the ship safely to its destination.[774]

Although Alexandrian Jews were represented in a large variety of occupations, including many highly skilled crafts as well as in commerce,[775] the numerous papyri discovered in Egypt reveal very little about the existence of Jewish craftsmen and artisans in the rest of Egypt. The papyrological evidence points to the existence of Jewish agricultural laborers, soldiers, policemen, customs-officers, and government officials. There was also a small socio-economic elite which engaged in banking and moneylending, but never on such a scale as to cause Jews to be identified with moneylending or commerce. Even the vicious Alexandrian anti-Semites did not make an issue of that aspect of Jewish economic activities. On the whole, it would appear that the Jews of Egypt were active in every contemporary occupation, and played a major role in the economic life of the country.[776]

ii Cyrene

Very little is known about the occupational structure of the rest of the Hellenistic Diaspora. In Cyrene, where there was an important Jewish community since very early times, there was a good deal of unrest not only between Jews and Greeks, but also among the Jews themselves. After the destruction of the Temple, a certain Jonathan, who was a weaver and a violently anti-Roman Zealot, fled from Judaea to Cyrene and raised a rebellion among the poorer people, many of whom he led into the desert where no doubt they felt safer from the Romans. The leading wealthy Jews, evidently afraid of the consequences of this seditious activity, informed the Roman governor, Catullus, of what was

---

773 Cf. *Mekilta* on Exod. 31:13; Tos. Shab. XV (XVI), 16; T.B. Yoma 85a.
774 S. Dubnow, *op. cit.*, vol. III, pp. 254f.; J. Juster, *Les Juifs dans l'empire romain* (Paris, 1914), vol. I, p. 486.
775 Cf. Philo, *In Flaccum* 57; M. Wischnitzer, *op. cit.*, p. 50; Tcherikover, *Hellenistic Civilization and the Jews* (Philadelphia, 1959), pp. 338ff.
776 Cf. V. Tcherikover, *op. cit.*, pp. 334–343; M. Wischnitzer, *op. cit.*

afoot, and very soon the rising was ruthlessly put down. Jonathan, however, sought to avenge himself on the rich Jews who had betrayed him and his followers, and charged them with having instigated the rising. Catullus, thereupon impartially put to death both rich and poor.[777]

iii Minor Diaspora Communities

Much later, in the fourth century, we hear of a Jewish hawker of old clothes — a trade which was to become almost a hallmark of the degraded eighteenth century Ghetto Jew — and of Jewish sorcerers, especially in North Africa, while in Oxford, England, there is even a tombstone of a fourth century Jewish sausage-seller.[778] We are not informed whether the sausages were kosher or not.

A century earlier, a Palestinian rabbi, Hiyya bar Abba, paid a visit to Laodicea in Syria. There, he was royally entertained by a wealthy man, who used to be a butcher and had always distinguished himself by honoring the Sabbath, setting aside the best meat for this holy day.[779]

iv Rome

Religious customs were also observed with the utmost strictness by the Jews of Rome. We are told of a tailor who on the eve of the Day of Atonement went to buy a fish which was also wanted by a servant of a Roman nobleman. The tailor and the servant bid against each other until the price of the fish rose to twelve *denarii*, at which price the tailor bought it. When the Roman nobleman heard about this, he was amazed that a poor tailor should have outbidden the servant of a Roman nobleman. However, on learning that this was done in honor of the meal to be eaten prior to the Day of Atonement, he admired the religious devotion of the tailor.[780]

The Jewish community of Rome was always distinguished by the great variety of occupations represented among its members. In addition to tailors, there were butchers, tentmakers, lime burners, and painters, including some artists. There were even Jewish poets and actors, and we

---

777 Josephus, *Bell.* VII, 11, 1–2 (437–446).
778 J. Parkes, *The Conflict of the Church and the Synagogue* (1961), p. 192.
779 *Gen. R.* 11, 4.
780 Ibid.

hear of an actor by the name of Alityros (or: Aliturus) who stood in high favor with the Emperor Nero and his wife, the Empress Poppaea Sabina.[781] Since many Jews were buried at the Roman harbor city of Portus, it has been surmised that many Jews were engaged in navigation and commerce. The same conclusion seems indicated by the large number of Jews who lived at Puteoli, a great port near Naples which served not only Rome but all Italy as the major port for Roman commerce with Alexandria and the east.[782] In recent years the oldest synagogue in Europe was excavated at Ostia, near Portus.

There is ample evidence that some Roman Jews attained influence and wealth. The Talmud tells us of a certain Thaddeus (or: Theodos) of Rome who was a man of considerable influence and, though not much of a scholar himself, a generous supporter of rabbis and students in Palestine.[783] Such wealthy individuals were, however, the exception. The majority of Roman Jews eked out a bare living, and some were, indeed, at the lowest rung of the social ladder. During the early years of the Empire, there were quite a few Jewish slaves in Rome, some employed in aristocratic and even in the imperial households. There was a large number of Jewish peddlers, beggars and, especially among women, fortune-tellers and even prostitutes.[784] Some 1500 years later, the Jews of Rome and other Italian cities were still following the same pattern of precarious existence.

There were few scholars among the Roman Jews, though they seem to have been familiar with the Bible. The Oral Law, however, was, it seems, but poorly developed among them. Only one Roman rabbi is mentioned in the entire Talmud, R. Mattia (or: Mattithya) ben Cheresh, who was actually born in Palestine, but left the country, probably because of the Bar Kochba war and the religious persecution which followed it. In Rome, he founded a college which had quite a reputation — so much so that it was enumerated in a short list of specially recommended colleges.[785] He himself, however, had no illusions about the comparative standards of his college and those of the Land of Israel, and, eventually, it seems that he returned to the Holy Land where he was only a minor

781 Josephus, *Vita* 3 (16).
782 H. Vogelstein, *Rome* (Philadelphia, 1940), pp. 42 f.
783 *T.Y. Pes.* VII, 1, 34a; *T.B. Pes.* 53a–b, *et al.*
784 Vogelstein, *op. cit.*
785 *T.B. Sanh.* 32b.

scholar among the great second century rabbis. However, he felt that it was better to be "a tail to lions than a head to foxes".[786] By that he meant that it was preferable to be a minor luminary among the scholars of Palestine than a leading authority among the relatively ignorant Jews of Rome — a view incidentally shared by St. Jerome who criticized the lack of learning among the Roman Jews.[787]

Nevertheless, we find among the Roman tomb inscriptions a Jew by the name of Eusebius, who was a teacher and a Torah scholar; also a synagogue leader called Mniaseas (= Manasseh), who is described as "a student of the sages" — the equivalent of the Hebrew *Talmid Hakham.*[787a]

---

786   *M. Aboth* IV, 15.
787   Cf. H. Vogelstein, *op. cit.*, p. 104.
787a Cf. H.J. Leon, *The Jews of Ancient Rome* (Philadelphia, 1960), p. 233.

Chapter Six

Recommended and Undesirable Trades

1. "Clean and Easy" Crafts

Although, in theory, honest work of any kind was preferable to reliance on other people's charity — to be dependent on another man's table was to live in a world from which light and happiness had been banished, so that life was not worth living at all[788] — nevertheless, in practice, not every trade was of equal value. Since it was the duty of the father to teach his son a trade,[789] he might as well endeavor to teach him "a clean and easy craft"[790] — what would nowadays be called a white-collar job — so that his social status and prestige might be raised. As examples of such comfortable trades, embroidery and perfume-making are specifically mentioned.[791] As R. Meir, the author of this concept of craft education, put it, "A man can make a living from any trade; but happy is he who sees his parents in a superior craft, and woe to him who sees his parents in a mean craft. The (civilized) world cannot exist without a perfume-maker and without a tanner. Yet happy is he whose craft is that of a perfume maker, and woe to him who is a tanner by trade".[792]

R. Meir was himself, as we have seen, a skilled scribe,[793] and for those who had natural or acquired calligraphic talents, it was indeed "a clean and easy craft", though the remuneration, even for purely secular services, was not exactly munificent. Yet R. Meir attached great importance to any kind of work, including hard agricultural labor.[794] He also

---

788 *T.B. Bezah* 32b.
789 *T. Kid.* I, 11; *T.B. Kid.* 29a; 30b.
790 *M. Kid.* IV, 14; *T. Kid.* V, 15; *T.B. Kid.* 82a–b; *T.B. Ber.* 63a.
791 *T.B. Ber.* 63a; *T.B. Kid.* 82b.
792 *T.Y. Kid.* IV, 11, 66d; cf. *T. Kid.* V, 14; cf. also *T.B. Kid.* 82b, where this saying is attributed to the aristocratic and class-conscious R. Judah the Patriarch.
793 *T.B. Erub.* 13a; *T.B. Sot.* 20a; *Eccl. R.* 2, 18.
794 *T. Ber.* VII, 8; *T.B. Baba Kamma,* 79b.

recognized that even the so-called unprofitable trades were not necessarily so; "for there is no craft wherein there is no poverty and wealth, since neither poverty nor wealth are due to a man's craft, but all depend on one's merit".[795]

Nevertheless, the natural human tendency, especially in an increasingly urban environment, to ease the burdens of life by following an easy and profitable occupation could not be suppressed. If the animals and birds did not have to work for their living, surely it was man's privilege to earn his livelihood without engaging in hard labor; and if in practice this was not the case, it was a curse brought about by man's evil deeds.[796] At the very least, however, man had the right, and indeed the duty, to ease his lot by finding less back-breaking and more pleasant work, if at all possible.

2. Commerce and Business Education

By far the most profitable pursuit was commerce, and in comparison with agriculture, its advantages seemed overwhelming. As Rab once said when he saw ears of grain swaying in the wind, thus suggesting a swaggering motion and arrogant pride, "Swing as you will, engaging in business brings more profit than you can do".[797] A century later, these sentiments were echoed by Raba who pointedly stated, "A hundred zuz (a contemporary coin) in business means meat and wine every day; a hundred zuz in land, only salt and vegetables".[798]

Rab, who was himself a smart man of affairs as well as a great scholar, was probably the first teacher in Jewish history who is known to have provided what we would today call a business education. His first pupil was none other than his son Aibu whom he had tried to make into a scholar, but without success. He decided, therefore, to train him for business. His advice, couched in brief epigrammatic sentences, was certainly sound at the time, and may occasionally be applicable even today. Here are a few examples:

---

795 M. Kid. IV, 14; cf. T.Y. ibid.
796 Ibid.; ibid.
797 T.B. Yeb. 63a.
798 Ibid.

"Sell your wares while the sand is still on your feet";[799] in other words, immediately you return from buying abroad, sell, thus gaining time for additional business. In this way, he enunciated in effect the modern commercial concept that a large turnover at a low profit is preferable to a small turnover at a high profit.

"Everything you may sell and regret (*viz.* if prices advance after the sale), except wine which you can sell without regrets" (because it might easily become sour and turn into vinegar).[800] What was true of wine was equally true of many other perishable commodities, which should be sold as soon as possible, especially where refrigeration was not available.

"Untie your purse, and then open your sacks",[801] i.e., accept payment only in cash and do not deliver the goods before the money has been paid in full. This, of course, runs counter to modern credit-based business practices; but for a trader with limited capital it was no doubt unduly risky to rely on the full repayment of debts incurred as a result of making possibly excessive purchases.

"Better a *kab* (a small weight) from the ground than a *kor* (a large weight) from the roof".[802] This is the equivalent of the well-known "a bird in hand is worth two in the bush", and meant that it was better to earn little near home than much far away. While the enterprising businessmen might look askance at such a conservative business outlook, it was often quite sound during unsettled times when risks were too high to make the game worth while. As we shall see, other rabbis, too, held similar views, especially where overseas commerce was concerned.

"When the dates are in your bag, run to the brewery".[803] Since the brewing of date-beer was a most profitable occupation, it was no doubt preferable to use the dates for brewing rather than for food.

Other rabbis also offered commercial advice to their students. They were told, for example, to buy goods while they were cheap because, sooner or later, they would go up in price.[804] "If you see any merchandise low in price and despised, go and deal in it; for eventually it will rise in price, and you will make a profit".[805] Many fortunes have been made

799 *T.B. Pes.* 113a.
800 Ibid.
801 Ibid.
802 Ibid.
803 Ibid.
804 *T.B. Ber.* 63a.   805 *Tanh. Mishpatim* 5.

even in modern times — for example, in real estate and on the stock exchange — by following this sound maxim.

On the assumption that in the long run prices rise, it was stated, presumably in reference to land and merchandise of lasting value: "When you buy you gain ... He who sells loses".[806]

Where there were markets specializing in certain goods, they should be utilized in preference to general markets: "Bring vegetables to a center of vegetables".[807] As a rule, merchandise should be offered for sale at the place where there was likely to be a demand for it.[808] In contrast to the best modern business practice, traders would first display their inferior merchandise — to get rid of it as fast as possible, and only afterwards (or if the customer insisted) would they show their best stock for which there was always a ready market.[809]

The budding capitalist was advised not to squander his money on luxuries,[810] nor to display it too openly,[811] nor to put all his eggs in one basket;[812] but to invest one third of his capital in real estate, another third in merchandise, and to keep approximately one third in ready cash[813] — no doubt in order to be able to take advantage of any bargains that might come his way.

Despite all the fine opportunities offered by business, it still was a hazardous occupation — so hazardous indeed that R. Judah did not consider a business education an adequate preparation for life.[814] Overseas commerce, potentially a fortune winner, could also ruin a merchant if anything went wrong.[815] There was, of course, always the risk of loss through accidents and piracy at sea or war and robbery on land. Even if one could avoid losses and break even, it was hardly worthwhile being in business just for the sake of being called a businessman: "If one buys and sells (at the same price) — do you call him a merchant?!"[816]

---

806 *T.B. B.M.* 51a.
807 *T.B. Men.* 85a; *Exod. R.* 9, 4.
808 *Exod. R.* ibid.
809 *Num. R.* 16, 12; *Tanh. Shelach* 6.
810 *T.B. Hul.* 84b; *T.B. B.M.* 29b.
811 *T.B. Taan.* 8b; *T.B. B.M.* 42a.
812 *Gen. R.* 76, 3.
813 *T.B. B.M.* 42a.
814 *T.B. Kid.* 30b.
815 *T.B. Pes.* 50b.
816 *T.B. B.M.* 40b.

Some trading was too poor and despised to be profitable. Such was the trade in cane and jars which, as the rabbis warned anyone interested in such activities, would never show a sign of blessing, being destined to failure — theoretically because their large bulk caused the evil eye to have an exceptional spell over them,[817] but in reality because there were sound business reasons (such as transportation difficulties, breakages and other accidental destruction) for their unprofitability. Even worse than these was the trade in certain "dirty" articles such as animal fats, which only the poorest would bother to handle. Hyperbolically, it was said that but for David's prayer, all Israel would be sellers of such "rubbish" which caused one's garments to be stained and ruined.[818]

No profit was likely to be derived from business activities of doubtful propriety, especially where insufficient heed was paid to moral or religious scruples. Business dealings with orphans' trust money, as well as trading in the produce of the Sabbatical year, was unlikely to be lucrative, there being no blessing in such morally or religiously reprehensible activities.[819] According to one version, traders in market stands (where the evil eye was also supposed to be prominent) were also unlikely to see a blessing in their activities.[820] The true reason was probably that the traders in market stands were small scale dealers who lacked the necessary capital for successful business development. The rabbis also disapproved of those who lived on mill-rent income and on earnings derived from one's wife's peddling.[821]

3. Trading in Sacred Commodities

Trading in sacred commodities was also frowned upon as being unsuitable for private gain.[822] A semi-sacred profession like interpreting lectures and sermons before synagogue audiences was likewise supposed to be under a bane.[823] In fact, any kind of sacred work, including that of

---

817 Ibid.
818 *T.B. Sot.* 49a and Rashi *ad loc.*
819 *Tos. Bik.* II, 16; *T.B. Pes.* 50b.
820 *T.B. Pes.* ibid.
821 Ibid.
822 Ibid.; *Tos. Bik.* II, 15.
823 *T.B. Pes.* ibid.

scribes who write scrolls, phylacteries and *Mezuzzot*, was supposed to be performed without thought of financial profit, preferably altogether without remuneration. Hence, it was maintained that "those who write sacred scrolls, phylacteries, and *Mezuzzot* ... never see a sign of blessing".[824]

To reassure producers and purveyors of sacred literature, and to enable them to obtain some reward for their labor, an "escape clause" was inserted according to which they were considered to be under a blessing, if they performed their functions conscientiously and with due respect to the holiness of their task.[825] Nevertheless, sacred work remained unremunerative, and the Talmudic description of the lack of blessing attached to such occupations was a faithful reflection of reality.

4. Bookkeeping and Accountancy

Unlike scribes and secretaries whose livelihood was evidently precarious and inadequate, skilled bookkeepers who could be employed both in business and in major agricultural enterprises, were, it seems, highly regarded. For, according to some rabbis — as well as according to the Aramaic *Targum* ("translation") *Onkelos* to Gen. 39:11 — Joseph, so far from doing general (i.e., unskilled) "work" for his master Potiphar, was actually his bookkeeper, and it was to examine his master's accounts that he entered the house for that fateful encounter with Potiphar's wife.[826]

5. Agriculture

i Social and Economic Importance
Land ownership and agricultural labor, which continued to be the occupation of the majority of the Jewish population in Palestine and Babylonia, were subject to different views, reflecting different conditions at different times. Generally, ownership of land was a hallmark of wealth and respectability: "Whosoever is greedy and covetous for money, but

---

824 Ibid.; *Tos. Bik.* II, 15.
825 Ibid.; ibid.
826 *Gen. R.* 87, 7; *Cant. R.* 1, 1.

has no land, what benefit does he gain?"[827] Conversely, genuine riches could be attained only through largescale landed possessions. The question, "Who is wealthy?" was answered by R. Tarfon, an immensely prosperous second century rabbi, in these words: "He who possesses a hundred vineyards, a hundred fields and a hundred slaves working in them".[828] Agriculture was, moreover, considered vital for safeguarding one's food supply — an indispensable insurance policy against a precarious dependence on the vagaries of the market, with its fluctuations in supplies and prices. All too frequently, one was subject to the extortionate prices of unscrupulous dealers — so much so that Lamentations 1:14 — "The Lord has delivered me into the hands of those against whom I am not able to stand" — was applied to a landless person whose sustenance depended upon his money.[829]

Another biblical curse recorded in Deuteronomy 28:66 — "Your life shall hang in doubt before you; night and day you shall be in terror; and you shall have no assurance of your survival" — was referred to those who have to depend on periodic grain purchases, and especially to those who have to rely on bread dealers.[830] In a remarkably forceful statement it was pointed out that "he who buys grain in the market...is like a young child whose mother has died; and though it is taken around to the homes of nursing mothers, it is not satisfied. And he who buys bread in the market...is like a man who digs his own grave. But he who eats of his own produce is like a child reared at his mother's breasts".[831]

Even if one was able to buy more cheaply in the market than produce on one's own land, according to the rabbis, "a man prefers one measure of one's own produce to nine measures of his neighbor's".[832] The same idea was stated in different words by R. Papa, a fourth century Babylonian rabbi: "Sow, and do not buy (viz., food in the market), even if the cost is the same".[833]

The desirability of being in a position to provide one's basic food at all times without being dependent on markets, which in antiquity were

---

827 *Eccl. R.* 5, 8.
828 *T.B. Shab.* 25b.
829 *T.B. Yeb.* 63b,
830 *T.Y. Shek.* VIII, 1, 51a; *T.B. Men.* 103b.
831 *Aboth – R.N.*, edit. Schechter, Version I, ch. 30, p. 45b (90).
832 *T.B. B.M.* 38a.
833 *T.B. Yeb.* 63a.

hardly reliable sources of supply, is also indicated in the following sayings by several Babylonian rabbis: "One should always take care that there be grain in the house; for strife is prevalent in a man's home only on account of (lack of) grain (i.e., food) ... Hence the popular proverb: When the barley is gone by the pitcher, strife comes knocking at the door. ... One should always take care that there be grain at home; for Israel was called poor only because of (lack of) grain".[834]

In Palestine, too, where urbanization was causing an increasing number of Jews to abandon agriculture, R. Eleazar stated in characteristic hyperbolic fashion that "any man who owns no land is not a proper man".[835] He expressed the pious hope that "there will be a time when all craftsmen shall take up agriculture".[836]

ii Agricultural Laborers

Yet, this same lover of the soil had no illusions on the supposed advantages of agricultural labor. However intensive the cultivation of land might be, R. Eleazar candidly admitted, business was more profitable.[837] Indeed, he went so far as to declare that "no occupation is inferior to that of agricultural labor".[838]

It may well be that R. Eleazar drew a distinction between landowners — including small farmers known as *Baalei Battim*, who comprised the majority of the Jewish population of Palestine[838a] — and landless agricultural laborers. The former had a genuine stake in the land, which raised their social status and acted as a brake against their emigration from the country — a major problem during the second and third centuries C.E. Agricultural laborers, on the other hand, had no land of their own; their work was all too often seasonal, and they frequently suffered from the scourge of unemployment.[839] For the most part they were day laborers hired for specific jobs and extremely short periods.

834　*T.B. B.M.* 59a.
835　Ibid.
836　Ibid.
837　Ibid.
838　Ibid.
838a　Cf. J. Klausner, *op. cit.*, p. 57. The *Baalei Battim*, who were regarded as ignorant of the Torah (cf. ARN, Vers. II, ch. 31, edit S. Schechter, p. 67 (34a), may have been identical with the religiously uneducated *Am Ha'Areṣ* (lit., "people of the land").
839　Cf., e.g., *Mishnah B.M.* II, 9; Matt. 20:1–7.

Their pay was low, though they were sometimes given food — usually bread and pulse — in addition to their wages.[840] Occasionally, when working conditions were unusually depressed, they were not paid at all, and had to be satisfied with food alone.[841] Agricultural laborers were generally entitled to eat of the food of the harvest[842] — a right based on the law of the Torah[843] — though they were advised not to overeat, since they might as a result find themselves out of a job.[844]

They were nevertheless free men entitled to customary rights and privileges accorded to workmen;[845] and unlike modern employees who all too often are denied the privilege of striking, day laborers and, generally, workers who had not contracted to carry out a specified piece of work, were legally permitted to quit their jobs "even in the middle of the day".[846] Leviticus 25:55 — "For unto me the children of Israel are servants; they are my servants" was interpreted to mean, "but not servants to servants". The Hebrew laborer, however poor, was free to work or not to work as he pleased.[847]

In addition to the virtually penniless landless day laborers — who since biblical times had to be paid before sunset[848] because they never knew where their next meal was going to come from — there were other classes of agriculturists who did not own any land, but whose social and economic status was nevertheless higher than that of the day laborers. There were all sorts of tenant farmers and leaseholders who either paid an agreed percentage of the crops or a fixed measure of the grain in rent.[849] The Roman wars had caused many small farmers to forfeit their land, and, in addition to Roman state lands, which were at least partly cultivated by Jewish agriculturists — often by the former owners — there were also large Jewish-owned estates worked by tenants or hired laborers.[850] In the course of the fourth century this undesirable tendency,

---

840 *Mishnah B.M.* VII, 1.
841 *T.Y. Ber.* II, 5, 5a; *T.B. Ber.* 16a.
842 *Mishnah B.M.* VII, 2.
843 Ibid.; cf. *Deut.* 23:25f.
844 *Mishnah B.M.* VII, 5; cf. *Tos. B.M.* VIII, 8.
845 Cf., e.g., *Mishnah B.M.* VII, 1ff.; *T.B. B.M.* 86a; Epstein, *op. cit.*, p. 16.
846 *T.B. B.K.* 116b; B.M. 10a.
847 *T.B. Kid.* 22b; *B.K.* 116b; *B.M.* 10a.
848 Deut. 24:14–15.
849 *Mishnah B.M.* IX, 1ff.; *Tos. B.M.* IX, 1ff.
850 Cf. Allon, *op. cit.*, p. 95.

which undoubtedly led to large-scale emigration from Palestine, became increasingly acute. This was partly due to the fact that small farmers owning plots of four to eight acres[851] were unable to survive the ever-growing burden of taxation, aggravated as it was by frequent disorders and changes of government.

iii Tenant Farmers

Those farmers who wanted to stay on their ancestral lands but could not afford to own it would often sell it to wealthy neighbors on condition that they themselves should be permitted to stay on their beloved soil; cultivate it; and pay the new owners a fixed percentage of the crop — which varied from one quarter to one third and up to one half — or an agreed amount, either in money or in kind, as rent. This "privilege", which would often be inherited by the children of the leaseholders of tenant farmers,[852] had the advantage that the impoverished farmer was not driven off his land; but he also had to endure the disadvantage of being virtually condemned to life-long poverty.

Not all such tenant farmers were assured of their rights on a permanent basis. Some could stay only for a limited period, during which they were expected to cultivate and improve the land placed in their care. Once the agreed period of service was over, it could be either renewed or terminated. In the latter case the poor tenant farmer would have to leave and look for work elsewhere. If he did not find any, he was bound to emigrate, mostly to Babylonia where economic conditions were far more favorable.

Some of these tenant farmers were expert planters and gardeners who would prepare the soil for vegetable or fruit plantations. They were paid on somewhat better terms, and they were entitled to be compensated for improvement of the soil.[853]

iv Landless Ikkarim

A special class of farm laborers, whose status is not quite clear, were the so-called *Ikkarim* (lit., farmers) who not only worked for others but seemed to have been tied to their employers in a sort of semi-feudal

---

851 Cf. Allon, *op. cit.*, p. 94.
852 Ibid., p. 95; cf. *T.Y. Git.* V, 6, 47b.
853 *Tos. B.M.* IX, 17–18; *T.B. B.M.* 109a–b. On tenant farmers (or sharecroppers) in Babylonia, see Y. Gafni, *Yehudey Bavel bi-Tekufat ha-Talmud* (Jerusalem, 1990), p. 132.

relationship. At any rate, they were not regarded as independent contractors but rather as dependent laborers.[854] These poor farm workers were occasionally tempted to steal some of the produce. In fourth century Babylonia, for example, Rab Zebid, head of the great academy of Pumbeditha, rather harshly disqualified two of his farm laborers as witnesses because they had stolen, respectively, a small measure of barley and a cluster of unripe dates.[855]

That the social status of the *Ikkarim* was low even in biblical times is indicated by a passage in Isaiah (61:5): "Aliens shall stand and feed your flocks, foreigners shall be your plowmen (*Ikkareichem*) and vine-dressers". King Uzziah of Judah, we are told, had *Ikkarim* and vine-dressers "in the hills and in the fertile lands"[856] — evidently dependent or semi-dependent laborers. That the position of the *Ikkarim* must have been very unfavorable during the Talmudic age, too, is suggested by a Midrash, according to which the Egyptians were punished with the fifth plague which wiped out most of their cattle and flocks[857] because they had forced the Israelites to become *Ikkarim* raising wheat and barley.[858]

v Fixed-Term Laborers

Finally, there were also laborers who hired themselves out for a fixed period of time — customarily for three years, which appears to have been the rule in biblical times[859] and was probably continued during the Hellenistic and Roman age. During this three-year period the hired laborer had to be maintained by his employer, while his wife and children were, it seems, left to their own devices. At the end of the term of service, the employer, who had so far provided only board and lodging, would pay an agreed amount in money, produce or livestock, or a combination of these.

A remarkable, though probably far from typical, story is told in the Talmud of such a laborer who came down from Upper Galilee to southern Palestine and was engaged by a farmer for a three-year term. When he had completed his period of service, he asked his employer for

854 Allon, *op. cit.*, p. 96; *T.Y. M.K.* III, 5, 82b; *Tos. B.M.* XI, 9.
855 *T.B. Sanh.* 26b.
856 *II Chron.* 26:10.
857 Exod. 9:1–7.
858 Cited by Allon, *op. cit.*, p. 96.
859 Deut. 15:18; *Isaiah* 16:14.

his wages, so that he should be able to support his wife and children. The farmer replied that he had no money. The long-suffering hired laborer requested produce, land or cattle in lieu of money; but the employer adamantly maintained that he had nothing to offer him. Even when the laborer despairingly suggested that he be given at least some pillows and bedding, the farmer would not budge an inch.

Utterly disappointed and deeply dejected, the poor laborer returned to his family empty-handed. However, he did not doubt that his employer was really an honest man who had temporarily fallen on evil times. He turned out to be right; for after a while the farmer came to his house, paid him his wages and brought him three donkey loads of food, drink and sweetmeats. He was astonished to find that the pious laborer had not only never suspected him of trying to take advantage of him, but had actually guessed the reasons why he was for the moment unable to pay him or offer him any other compensation for his toil.[860]

vi Intensive Agriculture — Galilee

Despite the poverty of the various classes of agriculturists, and perhaps because of it, the Jewish masses in Palestine, and to a lesser extent in Babylonia, too, were deeply devoted to their small farms and cultivated them intensively, often by means of "mixed farming" of several crops such as wheat, barley, vines and olives.[861]

Mountainous Galilee in particular, which was, according to all accounts, very thickly inhabited, had to be carefully and intensively cultivated if it was to yield a living for its people.[862] Fortunately Galilee, where the majority of Palestine Jewry lived following the disastrous Roman wars which had devastated and partly depopulated southern Palestine, was noted for its fertility,[863] and its fruit and olive crops were legendary.[864]

vii Slaves

Slaves were relatively rare in the small-scale family-centered Palestinian agricultural economy, though they would seem to have been somewhat

860　*T.B. Shab.* 127b.
861　Allon, *op. cit.*, pp. 93f., 98ff.; *T.B. B.M.* 107a.
862　Cf., e.g., *Josephus, Bell.* III, 3, 2 (42ff.).
863　Ibid.
864　*T.B. Ber.* 44a; *Men.* 85b; *Sifre Deut.* 355, edit. Friedmann 148a; edit. Horovitz-Finkelstein, p. 421; *Gen. R.* 20, 6; cf. *Josephus, Bell.* II, 21, 2 (592).

more widely used in the more highly developed Babylonian farms. Nevertheless, even in Palestine there were some large estates belonging to wealthy individuals who employed either free hired laborers or slaves who were for the most part of "Canaanite", i.e., non-Jewish, origin. However, they were usually circumcised, though sometimes against their will,[865] and obliged to observe all the negative and some of the positive commandments of the Torah.[866] Ownership of slaves was the hallmark of wealth: "Who is wealthy? ... R. Tarfon said: He who has a hundred vineyards, a hundred fields and a hundred slaves working in them".[867]

Although slaves were a status symbol, they were no unmixed blessing. They were regarded as lazy: "Ten measures of sleep descended to the world; nine were taken by slaves";[868] untrustworthy: "Slaves are not to be believed";[869] untruthful;[870] and inclined to engage in theft and robbery or, in the case of female slaves, in immoral conduct: "The more bondwomen, the more lewdness;[870a] the more (male) slaves, the more robbery".[871] Moreover, they hated their master,[872] though this was hardly a universal trait. Bad slaves were also apt to do whatever they wanted, and ask for permission only after presenting their master with a *fait accompli*.[873]

In contrast to such deeply ingrained prejudices, there was a strong humanitarian tendency which favored the slaves despite their supposedly bad character. They were praised for their class solidarity. As in the case of proselytes, whom they resembled to some extent, there were powerful bonds of affection between them.[874]

Individual slaves who were distinguished for their piety, faithfulness and intelligence were accorded high praise. Rabban Gamaliel II, for

---

865 *Pirke de-R. Eliezer* 29. Although this is a late Midrash, in this instance it reflects a legal position which is likely to have prevailed in the Talmudic age, too.
866 *T.B. Hag.* 4a.
867 *T.B. Shab.* 25b.
868 *T.B. Kid.* 49b.
869 *T.B. B.M.* 86b.
870 *T.B. Pes.* 113b.
870a Female slaves were sometimes used by their masters for immoral purposes — a practice frowned upon by the rabbis; cf. *Lev. R.* 9, 5.
871 *M. Aboth* II, 7; cf. *T.B. Pes.* 113b.
872 *T.B. Pes.* ibid.
873 *T.B. B.B.* 4a.
874 *T.B. Pes.* 113b.

example, who was a wealthy landowner,[874a] used every opportunity to bestow marks of respect and affection on his slave Tabi, who was exceptionally lauded for his piety — e.g., he would put on phylacteries which slaves were not required to wear[875] — his learning, and for his devotion to scholarship.[876] Not only his master but even outsiders such as R. Eleazar ben Azariah respected him for his outstanding qualities. The latter even went so far as to state that, strictly speaking, Tabi ought to sit and he, R. Eleazar, ought to stand and serve him.[877] By universal consent it was agreed that if Tabi had not been a slave, he would have been fit to become a rabbi.[878] When he died, the mourning customs observed for close relatives were strictly followed by Rabban Gamaliel[879] despite the fact that formal mourning for slaves was not in accordance with the prevailing etiquette.[880] Although slaves were generally not given any titles or surnames, at the household and estate of Rabban Gamaliel II senior slaves were called Father or Mother[881] — titles indicating considerable respect for the personality of the slave. Only a minority of rabbis, however, favored special marks of honor for either living or deceased slaves, however distinguished in character.[882]

It was realized that the slave was laboring under severe legal disabilities since he had no property rights, and whatever he acquired belonged to his master.[883] He was considered his master's chattel, and in rather uncomplimentary language slaves were described as "people who are like the ass"[884] or "like a beast",[885] i.e., chattels to be bought and sold.

874a His estates were cultivated by landless laborers and tenant farmers; cf. M. Demai III, 1; M. Baba Metsia V, 8. On Rabban Gamaliel's wealth, cf. A. Büchler, *The Economic Conditions of Judaea after the Destruction of the Second Temple*, pp. 37–38.

875 *T.Y. Erub.* X, 1, 26a; *T.Y. Suk.* II, 1, 52d.

876 *T.Y. Suk.* ibid.; *M. Suk.* II, 1.

877 *Midr. Prov.* 9, edit. Buber, p. 63.   878 *T.B. Yoma* 87a.

879 *M. Ber.* II, 7.

880 Ibid.; *T.Y. Ber.* II, 8, 5b; *T.B. Ber.* 16b.

881 *T.Y. Nid.* I, 5, 49b; *T.B. Ber.* 16b.   882 *T.B. Ber.* ibid.

883 *T.B. Pes.* 88b; *Kid.* 23b; *Meg.* 16a, et al.

884 *T.B. Yeb.* 62a. In Babylonia, contempt for slaves reached the point where certain masters, citing the statement that slaves were "people who are like the ass", engaged in sexual intercourse with their wives in the presence of both male and female slaves; cf. T.B. Nid. 17a. On slaves as domestic servants, see J. Newman, *The Agricultural Life of the Jews in Babylonia* (London, 1932), p. 70. See also Y. Gafni, *op. cit.*, p. 136.

885 *T.Y. Ber. II, 8, 5b.*

Attempts were nevertheless made to improve the legal position of the slave. If he was taken captive, he had to be ransomed just as if he were a freeman.[886] The biblical law that the slave must be freed if his master destroys his eye or knocks out his tooth[887] was extended by rabbinic law to include any serious injury.[888] Despite some objections against manumission,[889] there was a marked tendency to grant slaves their freedom, especially if they had performed faithful service for which they deserved to be rewarded. The example of Joseph, who had been a slave in Egypt, was cited to prove that a slave who "serves his master as he should do eventually obtains his freedom".[890] In the same spirit, it was enacted that a slave belonging to two masters who was freed by one of them must be manumitted by the other, too.[891]

It apparently became customary for the master to provide his liberated slave with a sum of money, so that he should not be in want.[892] We know of at least one occasion when a rabbi freed his slave because he was needed to make up a quorum of ten adult free men required for a public prayer service.[893] The tendency to liberate slaves reached its climax in the proverbial saying, "If your daughter has attained puberty, free your slave and give him to her".[894] Of course, this could not have been a common practice, and one may legitimately doubt if it ever occurred at all; but the very sentiment of such an adage is significant. It was in line with this attitude that the potential purchaser of slaves was advised to restrict himself to buying a "Hebrew slave" whose term of service was limited to six years.[895]

viii Serfs

Some agricultural or semi-agricultural activities of a specialized type were, it seems, performed by slaves or serfs as well as free landless

---

886 *T.Y. Git.* IV, 4, 45d.
887 Exod. 21:26f.
888 *Mekilta* on Exod. 21:26–27, edit. Friedmann 85b; edit Lauterbach III, 69f.; edit. Horovitz-Rabin, pp. 278–280.
889 *T.B. Ber.* 47b.
890 *Cant. R.* 1, 1 beg.
891 *M. Git.* IV, 4; M. Eduyoth I, 13.
892 *T.B. Pes.* 116a; cf. Deut. 15:13–15.
893 *T.B. Ber.* 47b.
894 *T.B. Pes.* 113a.
895 *Sifre Deut.* 118, edit. Friedmann 98b; edit. Horovitz-Finkelstein, p. 177; cf. Exod. 21:2; Deut. 15:12.

laborers or leaseholders. Many of the laborers were, it seems, treated almost like slaves, though, unlike slaves, they were entitled to wages in accordance with the quality and quantity of their work. A homiletic parable speaks of "a king who had an orchard, in which he built a tall tower. Now the king commanded that laborers should be engaged to do his work there. The king said that whoever was proficient in his work would get his wages in full, but whoever was indolent in his work would be put in the public prison".[896] Despite the "full wages" for good work, the supervision of the laborers from a high tower (implied by the context of the parable) provides something close to a concentration camp atmosphere, strongly reinforced by the threat of arbitrary imprisonment for "indolence". It is difficult to avoid the impression that these laborers were in fact serfs who could be ill-treated with impunity by the "king", i.e., the aristocratic employers, most of whom were owners of large estates cultivated by slaves or half-free serfs.

Some of these serfs were employed to tend the famous government-owned balsam trees of Ein-Gedi, mentioned among others by Pliny[897] as well as those grown in the Jericho area and south of the Dead Sea. Most of the laborers were Jews who lived in those districts.[898]

The same source also reports the existence of Jews who resided along the seacoast of Palestine and engaged in catching a purple-fish called hilazon, which they manufactured into a peculiar kind of blue dye required for ritual fringes.[899] In sharp contrast to such skilled operations, there were much less highly regarded activities on the farms, such as were performed by carriers of manure and straw. These humble agricultural laborers would rise early in the morning and scour the fields for straw and manure, which were needed by farmers. Lowly though they were, their diligence was highly praised

896 *Exod. R.* 2, 2. According to another rendering, the indolent laborer was to be handed over to the authorities to serve as a slave; cf. *Midrash Rabbah Exodus*, Soncino edition (London, 1939), p. 48.
897 *Hist. Nat.* V, 17; cf. Strabo XVI, 763; Josephus, *Bell.* I, 6, 6 (138); 18, 5 (361); IV, 8, 3 (469); *Ant.* IX, 1, 2 (7); XIV, 4, 1 (54); XV, 4, 2 (96).
898 *T.B. Shab.* 26a; Allon, *op. cit.*, p. 97.
899 *T.B. Shab.* 26b; Allon, *op. cit.*, pp. 97f.; cf. *Num.* 15:38.

by R. Eleazar who would himself rise early to commence his studies but was once preceded by those poor but hard-working laborers.[900]

ix The Am Ha'areṣ — Disadvantages of Agriculture
In earlier times when Hellenistic influence was more predominant, the agriculturist, no matter whether he worked on his own land or not, was considered ignorant and therefore incapable of genuine piety which, in Judaism, required a knowledge of the Torah.[901] The Hebrew term for agriculturist — *Am Ha'areṣ* — became synonymous with "ignorant". Scholars and uneducated peasants remained socially apart,[902] even though it was the teachers and rabbis who taught the peasants their rudiments of the Jewish religion. The fact that some scholars were themselves landowners did not materially affect the attitude of the majority. However much one invested in land, the returns were too inadequate to justify the risk. A common proverb already cited in a different context put it in a nutshell: "A hundred *zuz* in land — only salt and vegetables".[903]

There were other disadvantages, too. For, apart from the hard life common to all agriculturists — one would often have to spend the night in the field to watch the crops — landownership involved constant dispute with neighbors who encroached on one's rights.[904] To maintain unimpaired one's title to the land, it was essential to be very powerful indeed. "The earth", it was pointed out by R. Eleazar, "was given only to the strong".[905]

Even if one was strong enough to assert one's rights successfully, the backbreaking toil associated with the tilling of the earth transformed man into a slave of the soil: "If one enslaves himself to his land, he shall have sufficiency of bread; but if not, he shall have no sufficiency of bread".[906]

Last, but not least, excessive devotion to agriculture was sometimes believed to have undesirable moral results. Cain, who slew his

---

900 *Cant. R.* I, 1, 9.
901 *M. Aboth* II, 6.
902 Cf. *M. Demai* I, 2–3; *Tos.* ibid. II, 2ff.; see especially *T.B. Pes.* 49a–b.
903 *T.B. Yeb.* 63a.
904 Ibid.
905 *T.B. Sanh.* 58b.
906 Ibid.

brother;[907] Noah who disgraced himself in his drunken state;[908] and Uzziah, King of Judah, who had the temerity to enter the Temple and burn incense on the altar[909] — they all shared a common trait in that they "had a passion for agriculture,[910] but no good was found in them".[911]

x Agricultural Counseling

Despite such occasional criticism, agriculture was the basis of the economies of both Palestine and Babylonia, and many rabbis took a profound interest in the various agricultural activities. Advice on several aspects of husbandry was repeatedly offered by rabbis, some of whom were genuine agricultural experts. For example, in third century Babylonia, Rab Judah advised a colleague not to buy a field that was near a town, theoretically because of the "evil eye", which meant in practical terms that the crops were liable to be stolen or damaged by the thieves and vandals who always proliferated in cities.[912]

Rab Judah's teacher, Rab, took, however, the opposite view. According to him, it was a blessing for the landowner to have his property near the town in which he lived,[913] no doubt because it was convenient to have easy access to one's estate, which could thus be more closely supervised. The rabbis tried to reconcile these opposing viewpoints by suggesting with some plausibility that Rab's opinion was meant to apply to fields surrounded by wall and hedge which protected them against damage; while Rab Judah's contrary view applied to open, unprotected fields.[914]

In Palestine, where viticulture and olive-growing were important branches of agriculture, R. Johanan (3rd cent. C.E.) advised that one's estate should be divided into three (approximately equal) sections — one for grain, one for vines, and one for olives.[915] It is not certain whether this was designed as a sort of primitive crop rotation system or, as seems more probable, an insurance policy through diversification in case one

907 *Gen.* 4:8.
908 Ibid. 9:21.
909 *II Chron.* 26:16ff.
910 Cf. *Gen.* 4:2; 9:20; *II Chron.* 26:10.
911 *Gen. R.* 22, 3.
912 *T.B. B.M.* 107a.
913 Ibid.
914 Ibid. 107b.
915 Ibid. 107a.

crop or another failed or could not be marketed. In that case, the farmer could avoid ruin by relying on his remaining crops.

xi Olive-Growing

Olives, which even today cover vast areas of Northern Israel, were a mainstay of the ancient Jewish economy. Olive trees were protected by law and could not be uprooted, "so that the Land of Israel may be well cultivated".[916] Fantastic stories were told about the "myriads of olive trees"[917] and the enormous amounts of oil produced in certain areas or by certain individuals. For example, on one occasion, the people of Laodicea, in Syria, were in need of oil, and they appointed an agent to purchase "a hundred myriad" (i.e., a million) *manehs* (= a hundred million *denarii*!) worth of olive oil. He came first to Jerusalem; but since they could not sell him such a huge amount of oil, they advised him to go to Tyre. There, too, the available supply was inadequate, so they suggested that he should proceed to Gush Halav (or: Giscala) which had a great reputation for mass production of olive oil.

On arrival in Gush Halav, the agent was told to apply to a certain farmer whom he found working in the fields. Before attending to his customer, the farmer placidly continued the work he was doing, until he had completed it, and on his way home he was removing stones from the field as he was walking along. The agent thought the Jews were playing a practical joke on him, since the man was obviously incapable of delivering the huge quantity of oil required. However, on arrival at the man's house, the agent observed to his amazement that the maid brought him a golden bowl of oil in which he dipped his hands and feet. He was then entertained for dinner, and only after the farmer had observed all the rules of hospitality did he attend to the main business. Not only did he supply his visitor with all the olive oil for which he was able to pay, but he also added another 180,000 *manehs* worth of oil on credit. The agent had to hire — in the hyperbolic language of the story — "every horse, mule, camel and ass that he could find in all the Land of Israel".[918]

On arrival in Laodicea, accompanied by the farmer who had come to collect the debt due him, the agent was applauded by all the townspeople

---

916 T.B. B.M. 101a.
917 Gen. R. 20, 6.
918 T.B. Men. 85b; Sifre Deut. 355, edit. Friedmann 148a; edit. Horovitz-Finkelstein, p. 421.

for having brought home so much oil. However, he modestly asked them not to applaud him but the man who had sold him the oil and to whom he was still owing a good deal of money.[919]

The story is of course replete with enormous exaggerations and must not be taken literally. But it is not without some historic value. It vividly illustrates the abundance of olive oil in certain areas of Galilee. Oil was in fact a primary necessity; for it was used for lighting, cooking, cleaning (instead of soap) and perfuming.

The fame of Gush Halav as a major supplier of olive oil can be traced back to Temple times when Galilean oil was exported to neighboring countries. Once the oil of Gentiles could no longer be used for Jewish consumption,[920] Jews residing in the Diaspora (where they rarely culti-vated the olive tree) were obliged to purchase oil from the Land of Israel. At the time of the outbreak of the great Roman-Jewish war (66–70 C.E.), John of Giscala, who was an oil merchant as well as a great patriot, exported a large quantity of olive oil to Caesarea Philippi, a predomi-nantly pagan city situated on the south-western lower slopes of Mt. Hermon. The Jewish minority needed "kosher" oil. According to Jo-sephus, who was John's rival and enemy, John made a huge profit on the deal, selling the oil at eight or ten times its original cost.[921] Of course, allowing for transportation costs as well as the enormously increased war-time risks, not to mention Josephus' bias and exaggerations, John's real profit was probably not unreasonable. In any case, he seems to have used the money to defend his town against the Romans.

The export of oil from the Land of Israel to neighboring countries suffered a severe setback during the Bar-Kochba war (132–135 C.E.) when enormous damage was caused to every branch of agriculture, including the cultivation of olive trees. Even within the country there was a shortage of olives and hence of oil. However, within two or three generations the oil industry based on the mass cultivation of olives had sufficiently recovered for a third century rabbi, Simeon bar Yakim (= Eliakim), to state:

919 Ibid.; ibid.
920 Cf. *T.Y. Shab.* I, 7, 3c; *T.B. Shab.* 17b.
921 *Vita* 13, 74ff.; *Bell.* II, 21, 2, 591f.

"At first olive trees were not to be found; for the wicked Hadrian[922] had come and devastated the entire country. But now olive trees are commonly to be found".[923]

xii Horticulture

Gardening, too, was very common both in Palestine and Babylonia, but many gardeners did not own the land they were cultivating. As in all trades and professions, gardeners were extremely conscious of status. They wanted to be regarded as landowners. They would accordingly rent as many gardens as possible on terms of "half-profits", which meant in effect that they were sharecroppers who had to surrender half the crops to the landowners. Outwardly, however, they could pretend that they themselves were great squires, seeing that they gathered the produce of many gardens.

The rabbis opposed this foolish pretense, which was harmful to the true interests of the gardeners. They cited the popular proverb, "One who rents one garden eats birds; one who rents many gardens, birds eat him" (i.e., he is unable to give adequate attention to all the lands he cultivates, and in the end, the birds eat the crops). In more prosaic language, it was pointed out that "better is he who has a kitchen garden and fertilizes it and hoes it and earns his livelihood out of it, than he who takes kitchen gardens from others on terms of (surrendering) half the crops".[924]

6. Sheep and Goat Breeding

By far the most profitable aspect of farming was the breeding of sheep and goats. According to the most prominent third century Palestinian Rabbi, Johanan, "he who wishes to become rich should engage in the

---

922 Hadrian, Roman emperor from 117 to 138 C.E., put down Bar-Kochba's insurrection with great severity and outlawed the practice of Judaism. During the religious persecution of the Jews which ensued, some of the leading rabbis of the time, including R. Akiba, were cruelly put to death.
923 *T.Y. Peah* VII, 1, 20a. Cf. M. Avi-Yonah, *Bimei Roma U-Bizantyon*, 4th edit. (Jerusalem, 1970), p. 41.
924 *Lev. R.* 3, 1.

breeding of small cattle".[925] From a purely economic point of view, it was quite reasonable to advise the farmer that he should "sell his field and buy goats rather than sell his goats and buy a field".[926] It was even claimed that "it is enough for a person to sustain himself with the milk of the goats and lambs".[927]

Insofar as natural pasture land was used for sheep and goat breeding, it was a perfectly legitimate occupation, highly desirable because it brought in a maximum of profit for a minimum of investment. Thanks to the growing textile industry in the country, there was a ready market for wool, goats' hair and so on.[928]

Unfortunately, it was these very advantages of sheep and goat raising which caused a major agricultural crisis during the second and third centuries C.E. Many farmers discovered that they could earn much more and work much less by turning good soil suitable for raising crops into pasture land. In addition to the reduction of the arable land area, which in itself was bound to cause food shortages, the goats damaged whatever crops and plants were still being grown, and they also harmed the remaining forests which were steadily reduced as a result of wars and neglect.

The rabbis, accordingly, ordained that "small cattle must not be raised in the Land of Israel, but they may do so ... in the deserts of the Land of Israel".[929] One may doubt whether this prohibition was really effective; for the rabbis expressed extremely harsh opinions concerning those who engaged in such harmful activities. Eclipses of the sun or the moon, which were considered bad omens in antiquity, were attributed, among other things, to the sins of those who raised small cattle,[930] and it was said that they would never see a sign of blessing in their work.[931] Indeed, they were so hated that the rabbis decreed that, while it was not permissible to throw them into a pit, one was not morally required to bring them up if they had accidentally fallen in.[932]

925 *T.B. Hul.* 84a–b.
926 Ibid. 84a.
927 Ibid.
928 M. Avi-Yonah, *op. cit.*, p. 41.
929 Mishnah B.K. VII, 7; Tos. B.K. VIII, 10. Cf. also A. Büchler, *The Economic Conditions of Judaea after the Destruction of the Second Temple* (London, 1912), p. 45.
930 *Tos. Suk.* II, 5.
931 *T.B. Pes.* 50b.
932 *Tos. B.M.* II, 33; *T.B. A.Z.* 26a–b.

Yet, despite such strong opinions, circumstances often proved stronger than legal enactments, which could not always be justified in the face of individual needs. Even in rabbinical families the prohibition of raising small cattle was not always strictly observed. Rabbi Ishmael, an early second century Palestinian rabbi, admitted that his father's family had raised small cattle in Galilee — an offense to which he attributed the family's ruin.[933] Another rabbi, Judah ben Baba, who was considered a saintly man, was ordered by his physician to drink fresh and hot goat's milk. He, accordingly, purchased a goat and tied her to the legs of his bed, no doubt to prevent her from causing any damage. Nevertheless, when on one occasion his rabbinical colleagues wanted to visit him, they decided to cancel the visit because, as they put it, "How can we enter the house of a man who has a highwayman (*viz.*, a goat) in his home?!" Before his death, Rabbi Judah acknowledged this transgression against the decree of his colleagues.[934]

7. Medicine

i The Physician

Another example of a profession which must have been lucrative at least for experts and specialists,[935] yet was treated with considerable suspicion and disdain, was that of the physician. True, Rabbi Eleazar, a third century Palestinian rabbi, cited with approval Ben Sira's maxim, "Honor your physician even before you have need of him";[936] and, needless to say, people did have need of the physician. As a popular proverb put it, "If a man has a pain, he visits the healer".[937] Even Jesus, a faith-healer *par excellence*, stated that the sick have need of a physician.[938] Even dying patients would still have physicians visit them,[939]

933 *Tos. B.K.* VIII, 14.
934 Ibid. 13.
935 According to Julius Preuss, *Biblisch-talmudische Medizin*, 3rd edition (Berlin 1923), p. 36, physicians were poorly paid. However, the Greek analogy which Preuss adduces does not necessarily apply to Jewish society where a different scale of values prevailed. There is evidence that an expert physician was in fact well paid; Cf. Exod. R. 61, 5: "... You will be called an expert physician and receive high fees".
936 *T.Y. Taan.* III, 6, 66d; *Exod. R.* 21, 7; *Tanh. Mikketz* 10; cf. Ben Sira 38:1.
937 *T.B. B.K.* 46b.
938 Cf. *Matt.* 9:12; *Mark* 2:17; *Luke* 5:31.
939 Cf. Num. R. 18, 12: "If these people (*viz.* Korah, Dathan and Abiram) die in their beds as people ordinarily do, and physicians come up to visit them as all other

presumably in the hope that they might snatch them from the jaws of death. How important the physician was for the community can be seen in the following Midrashic parable:

"In a certain province (or city) there lived a physician. If a person was injured, the physician would heal him; if one became sick, the physician would heal him. When the physician left the province (or city) the inhabitants of the province (or city) exclaimed, 'Woe!' "[940]

The rabbis were well aware that physicians were necessary and, indeed, quite indispensable. It was even considered essential to warn scholars not to reside in a place where there was no medical doctor.[941] We also know that the rabbis did not hesitate to consult physicians on medical as well as religious-legal problems which required some medical knowledge.[942]

In the Temple of Jerusalem a physician was employed to provide medical assistance to the priests, some of whom, we are told, suffered from bowel sickness allegedly caused by their walking barefoot on the temple pavement while eating meat and drinking water.[943] We are also informed of a contemporary physician by the name of Tobiah who saw the new moon in Jerusalem together with his son and his freed slave who had evidently remained in his service as a free employee. Their testimony before a priestly court and subsequently before the High Court created something in the nature of a legal tug-of-war between the two competing courts.[944] The impression gained from this story is that Tobiah was a reasonably well-to-do middle class doctor — a status which was probably shared by most physicians of repute.

Special respect was accorded to highly skilled medical experts.[945] It was even possible for a physician to become leader or mayor of a city, though some rabbis apparently felt that such a place was likely to be poorly administered (since a physician would not be able to devote sufficient

---

sick people are visited..." The implication is clear: normally the sick have physicians visit them, and this must have been the common practice. Cf. Julius Preuss, *op. cit.*, p. 26.

940 *Tanhuma Beshallah*, edit. Buber II, 29a (57).
941 *T.Y. Kid.* IV, 12, 66d; *T.B. Sanh.* 17b.
942 *T. Ohol.* IV, 2; *T. Nid.* IV, 4; *M. Bekh.* IV, 4; *Sifre Deut.* 247, edit. Friedmann, p. 119b; edit. Horovitz-Finkelstein, p. 276; *T.Y. Ber.* I, 2, 3a; *T.B. A.Z.* 28b.
943 *M. Shek.* V, 1; *T.Y. Shek.* V, 1, 48d.
944 *Mishnah R.H.* I, 7.
945 *T.B. Sanh.* 51a.

time for the administration of the city) and therefore advised against living in such a place.[946] Respect for the healer was also implied by the presentation of Moses as a physician. According to the Midrash, Moses had claimed that God himself had made him into a doctor, and therefore, if God refused to heal Moses' sister Miriam, he, Moses, would be obliged to do so himself.[947]

Yet, in spite of this common sense approach, a lingering suspicion that the physician was really encroaching upon a divine prerogative and that healing was actually in the hands of God,[948] not of man, continued to lurk in rabbinic literature. Legally, indeed, the rabbis deduced from Exodus 21:19 ("... he shall have him thoroughly healed") that divine authority was granted to the physician to practice his healing art.[949] Pietists, nevertheless, continued to look askance at such an invasion of the realm of the divine. It was, for example, claimed that Hezekiah, King of Judah, had hidden a scroll of remedies — according to another version, a tablet on which the remedies were listed — with the approval of the sages of the day.[950] Although some commentators have suggested that the reason for this action was that the scroll or tablet had encouraged astrological, magical or idolatrous practices, the likeliest explanation is that this statement, which has no biblical support whatsoever, emanated from pietistic circles opposed to the intrusion of medical science in an area reserved for God. Man was to pray to God when he was sick, not rely on the art of the physician.

By and large, it was the educated classes which appreciated the value of the physician's services, while the less educated pietistic elements tended to avoid physicians in favor of prayer for divine healing. A very late medieval Midrash vividly depicts the ideological contrast between the two sides. According to this, R. Ishmael and R. Akiba were once walking through the streets of Jerusalem in the company of a man who was evidently a pietiest. A sick man approached them for medical advice, and they told him how to treat his malady. The pietist — or, according to another version, the patient himself — asked who had

---

946 *T.B. Pes.* 113a, and Rashbam's commentary *ad loc.*
947 *Deut. R.* 6, 13.
948 Cf. Exod. 15:26 ("... I the Lord am your healer") and II Chron. 16:12; see *supra*, p. 21.
949 *T.B. Ber.* 60a; *B.K.* 85a.
950 *M. Pes.* IV, 9; *T.Y. Pes.* IX, 1, 36c; *T.B. Ber.* 10b.

caused the illness. On their responding that it was God, the pietist (or the patient) rebuked them, saying, "you are dealing in a matter which is not your concern. He (viz. God) smote and you wish to heal?!"[951] They then asked him what his trade was, and on learning that he was an agriculturist, they asked him who had created the earth or vineyards. When he replied that it was God, they retorted that by engaging in agricultural labor he was dealing in a matter which was not his concern. When he protested that unless he plowed, fertilized and weeded the soil, it would not yield anything, the rabbis exposed him as a fool. For just as a tree cannot grow and live unless it is fertilized, weeded, hoed, and watered, so "the body is the tree, the medicine is the fertilizer, and the physician is the tiller of the earth". Duly chastened, the pietist had to ask forgiveness for his presumption.[952]

In the Middle Ages when so many Jewish physicians gained distinction by their medical practice, one would have expected a more tolerant view of the medical profession. Yet, apart from Maimonides and a few like-minded rationalists, the attitude toward physicians and their craft remained somewhat reserved, to say the least.

Abraham Ibn Ezra, the most rational Bible commentator of the Middle Ages, who flourished in the twelfth century, was of the opinion that Exodus 21:19 — "he shall have him thoroughly healed" — granted the physician license to heal only external injuries such as those mentioned in the passage cited. Internal diseases, on the other hand, remained the exclusive prerogative of the Almighty who alone would heal them if He so desired.[953]

Even more astonishing is Nachmanides' perception that, while the physician was indeed granted authorization to heal, no such permission had been extended to the patient to seek medical assistance. The truly God-fearing person will refrain from consulting a physician, but trust in God, as had been the practice of righteous men in the time of the prophets who would be consulted in times of illness, with a view to obtaining divine healing. Nachmanides concludes his lengthy discourse with the following remarkable statement: "When a man's ways please

951   This argument is more likely to have been used by a pietist. A patient who seeks medical guidance is unlikely to reject it on religious grounds.
952   Cf. *Midrash Shemuel*, ch. 4, edit. Buber, p. 54; A. Jellinek, *Bet ha-Midrasch*, Midr. Temura, ch. 2, vol. I, p. 107.
953   Cf. Ibn Ezra on Exodus 21:19.

the Lord he will have no dealings with physicians".[954] Such a disdainful attitude toward physicians is all the more surprising when one bears in mind that Nachmanides himself had originally been a physician. Perhaps he realized that the medical profession left much to be desired.

Even such a common practice as "cupping", i.e., bleeding for reasons of health,[955] was considered by some to be an act requiring, as it were, some apology. Accordingly, it was suggested that one should recite a short prayer beforehand, concluding with the words, "You are a faithful healing God, and your healing is sure, since men have no way of healing, but this practice is a habit with them". The fourth century Babylonian rabbi, Abaye, who was himself an amateur physician[956] as well as a farmer,[957] deprecated this prayer which clearly contradicted normative Judaism.[958]

In addition to religious objections, there were certain popular prejudices against the physician based no doubt on the fact that he was consulted not to prevent disease — there were, of course, no annual check-ups in those days — but to heal it when it had already afflicted the patient. The physician's appearance in the house was thus ill-omened since it was inevitably associated with sickness. If a modern proverb, "An apple a day keeps the doctor away", clearly alludes to the unwelcome nature of the physician's house call, the rabbis had a much stronger expression to indicate a similar attitude: "The door that is not opened for good deeds should be opened for the doctor".[959] This rabbinic proverb came close to being a curse upon the miser who refused to contribute his fair share to charity.

Throughout history, people tried to shun physicians as much as possible. Even the famous Egyptian physicians of antiquity were regarded as an evil visitation to be avoided if at all possible.[960] In early seventeenth century Poland, Rabbi Joshua Falk expressed his personal

---

954 Cf. Nachmanides on *Leviticus* 26:11; J. Preuss, *op. cit.*, p. 27.
955 Cf. Preuss, *op. cit.*, pp. 36 ff.
956 Cf. *T.B. Yebam.* 76a; *T.B. Ber.* 39a. Julius Preuss, *op. cit.*, p. 22, describes Abaye as "the most prominent representative" of folk medicine.
957 Cf. *T.B. Git.* 60b; *Hul.* 105a.
958 *T.B. Ber.* 60a; cf. *T.B. B.K.* 85a.
959 *Cant. R.* 6, 2, 1.
960 Cf. *Diodorus* 12:13: "We wish that we should not have need for any one of them (*viz.* the famous Egyptian physicians)".

disdain of doctors by stating, "May the Lord God protect us from the physicians".[961]

People also disliked having physicians in their neighborhood, although the presence of a doctor could in an emergency make all the difference between life and death. A physician was, as it were, a bad omen, and it was better not to have him in one's vicinity. As far as the rabbis were concerned, it was mainly the "nuisance" to the neighbors represented by a doctor's office which interested them. Since a physician was liable to be visited by a good many patients, both by day and by night, his presence in a court of houses was considered undesirable, and the other tenants could prevent him from taking up residence in their neighborhood.[962]

Those who did make use of the physician's services often doubted his capacity to help them. "Man is not privileged to be healed by everybody"[963] was evidently a common proverb indicating that in ancient as in modern times some doctors were more successful than others. Actually, of course, no physician was able to guarantee a cure. When the apocryphal Tobit suffered from "white films" in his eyes — corneal erosions according to Preuss[964] — he consulted physicians, but, in his own words, "they did not help me".[965] A Talmudic parable tells us that if a man has a pain in his eyes he pays money to a doctor for treatment; but this is no guarantee of a cure. He may be healed or, if he is unlucky, he cannot be healed.[966] On the other hand, we are told of a woman whose eyelashes fell out as a result of excessive weeping; and when she consulted a physician, he told her, "Paint your eyes with this *stibium* which I give you, and you will recover".[967]

A rather contemptuous attitude to the physician seems to be indicated in the popular proverb quoted in Luke 4:23: "Physician, heal yourself". A precise rabbinic parallel is to be found in the Midrash, where a similar popular saying is cited: "Physician, physician, heal your own limp".[968]

961 Cf. Joshua Falk, *Binyan Yehoshua* on *Aboth de-Rabbi Nathan* 36:5. Cf. Preuss, *op. cit.*, p. 27.
962 *T.B. B.B.* 21a.
963 *T.Y. Ket.* XIII, 2, 35d.
964 *Op. cit.*, p. 10.
965 *Tobit* 2:10.
966 *T.B. Ket.* 105a.
967 *Lam. R.* 2, 11, par. 15.
968 *Gen. R.* 23, 4.

Another characteristic popular saying was, "Shame on the city whose physician has the gout!"[969] A Midrashic parable tells of a doctor who was going to cure with his tongue a person who had been bitten by a snake — presumably by sucking out the poison. On the way he saw a lizard and began searching for a stick with which to kill it. People thereupon said to him, "If you cannot remove this creature, how can you offer to heal with your tongue?"[970]

There is a note of *Schadenfreude*, of ill-concealed glee, at the discomfiture of the physician who is forced to drink his own medicine; who haughtily tells others what to do, but cannot help himself.

But none of these sayings and parables can compare in antagonistic vehemence with the violent hostility implied by a rabbinic proverb mentioned in the Mishnah[971] that even "the best of physicians is destined for hell". It was probably little comfort to the physician that other professions — such as the slaughterer or the butcher (with whom he was placed in close juxtaposition[972]) — were not spared savage criticism either, and that he was only one of seven professionals who were denied a share in the world-to-come.[973]

The commentators were hard put to it to give a rational explanation for such an extreme statement, which, to be sure, was hardly meant to be taken seriously. Samuel Edels (Maharsha), in his commentary on T.B. Kiddushin 82a, and Joshua Falk, in his commentary on Aboth de-R. Nathan,[974] suggest that a physician who considers himself "best" and is too conceited to consult other doctors or to advise his patients to consult a specialist or another doctor may cause avoidable deaths — hence his severe punishment. In Edels' words, "Sometimes he errs in his assessment of the patient's constitution, and he kills the patient with his medicines..." Less convincingly, it has been conjectured that rabbinic opposition to physicians may have been due to "advanced", i.e., heretical opinions held by some doctors.[975] According to Rashi, the well-known eleventh century Bible and Talmud commentator, there were several possible reasons for the unfavorable opinions of the rabbis:

969 *Lev. R.* 5, 6.
970 *Num. R.* 20, 14.
971 *Kid.* IV, 14.
972 Ibid.
973 *Aboth R.N.*, edit. Schechter, Vers. I, ch. 36, p. 108.
974 *Ad loc.*
975 *Jewish Chronicle* (London), March 1, 1935.

1. A physician is not afraid of sickness (since he presumably knows how to deal with it), and he is therefore in the habit of eating well and enjoying life, thus refusing to "break his heart" (*viz.* by fasting) before God.

2. Sometimes he is guilty of carelessness, thus causing patients to die.

3. He is able to cure poor people, but refuses to do so — presumably preferring to treat wealthy patients rather than indigent ones.[976] Evidently, the A.M.A. had its stalwart predecessors.

The problem of medical costs was no doubt serious in an age when the vast majority of people were poor and could not afford to pay physicians. Highly skilled physicians — especially, it seems, surgeons — were paid high fees.[977] In the early second century C.E., Ben Azzai, a contemporary of Rabbi Akiba, told in one of his parables about a man who was wounded in his hand and came to a physician (or a surgeon) for treatment only to be told brusquely, "You cannot be cured. The wound is a major one, and the money (you offer) is too little". The poor fellow had to beg the doctor to take everything he had and to do him a favor and treat him at a reduced rate.[978]

It was because of this financial burden, which the poor could not easily shoulder, that people, possibly also influenced by pietists, looked to God rather than to man to cure their diseases. They appreciated the divine healer who conferred the bounty of health free of charge. A benediction to this effect — Blessed be He who heals without payment"[979] — reveals the anxiety of poor people who could not raise the money required for their treatment.

There were, no doubt, kindhearted doctors who were willing to forgo the fees due to them; but the beneficiaries and people generally would seem to have had little confidence in "socialized" medicine. On the contrary, a widely current proverb proved that, as long as they could possibly afford it, people preferred to pay the physician for his services. "A physician who heals for nothing is worth nothing"[980] was a popular

---

976 Cf. T.B. Kid. 82a and Rashi *ad loc.* Cf. also F. Delitzsch, *Jüdisches Handwerkerleben zur Zeit Jesu*, 3rd edit. (Erlangen, 1879), p. 43.
977 *Gen. R.* 61, 7.
978 *Yalk. Pss.* 764, vol. II, p. 919; cf. Midrash Pss. on Pss. 51:3, edit. Buber, p. 141a (281).
979 *T.B. Ber.* 60a.
980 *T.B. B.K.* 85a.

saying which expressed the well-known truth that the real value of the service depends on what one is prepared to pay for it.

An ingenious method of payment for the physician's services was devised in the third century C.E. by Rabbi Johanan who suggested a lump sum payment for future medical services. He advised heirs who were obligated to provide medical care for their chronically ill widowed step-mother to enter into a "health maintenance" agreement with a physician for an all-inclusive fee.[981]

Despite the reluctance of people to have a physician residing in their immediate neighborhood, they did not really want their doctors to be too far away either. In the words of another popular proverb, "If the physician is a long way off, the eye will be blind" (viz., before he arrives).[982] According to another interpretation of this saying, "A physician from afar has a 'blind eye' ", i.e., he has little concern for his patients, presumably because they are more trouble than they are worth in view of the distances he has to travel in order to visit them.

Rabbinic objections to physicians and some of their practices were to some extent reciprocated by physicians, though their reactions have for the most part remained unrecorded. Still, the attitude of the family of a fourth century Babylonian physician by the name of Benjamin is revealing and probably representative of medical impatience with non-medical rabbinic "meddling".[983] "Of what use are the rabbis to us?" asked Benjamin's family, "they have never permitted us the raven, nor forbidden us the dove". The implication was that the rabbis could only interpret the laws of the Torah, but had no power to change anything, whereas in medicine experimentation and changes in treatment were commonplace.

The rabbis did not take such criticism lying down. Whenever members of Doctor Benjamin's family brought an animal before Raba, the distinguished rabbinical authority, because, basing themselves no doubt on medical considerations, the animal appeared to be diseased and therefore trefa (ritually forbidden to be eaten by Jews), he would remark, if

---

981 Cf. T.B. Ket. 52b; Preuss, op. cit., p. 34.
982 Ibid.
983 Rabbinic "meddling" included publicizing what was supposed to be a universal bandage which threatened to reduce the practice and hence the income of Doctor Benjamin (or: Minyomi) and his family; cf. T.B. Shab. 133b; J. Preuss, op. cit., p. 20.

there were grounds for permitting it, "See, I permit you the raven". If, on the other hand, there were religious reasons to forbid the consumption of the animal, he would observe, "See, I forbid you the dove".[984] The implication was, of course, that there were many marginal areas not fully covered by the Torah, and it was then up to the rabbis to make their own decision which did not necessarily coincide with the views of competent physicians.

The most competent physicians were, of course, the specialists, and according to Herodotus,[985] in ancient Egypt there was "for every disease one physician". No such large-scale specialization was feasible in the Land of Israel, where the poor masses often had to depend on quacks. As in modern times, qualified and eminent physicians resented the competition of quack doctors.[986]

ii Pagan Physicians

Partly because of the none-too-friendly popular attitude towards physicians, partly because of the pietistic opposition to the medical profession, and partly perhaps because of lack of adequate training facilities in Palestine, recruits to the profession were few in number, and there was an acute shortage of Jewish physicians, at least during the first and second centuries C.E.[987] When R. Johanan ben Zakkai wanted to have his saintly colleague, the long-fasting and emaciated R. Zadok, healed, he had to apply to the Roman Emperor, Vespasian, for Greek or Roman physicians. By means of a carefully regulated diet they did, indeed, manage to restore R. Zadok's health.[988]

Nevertheless, later, when relations with non-Jews deteriorated still further, the problem arose whether non-Jewish doctors could be employed by Jewish patients. Pagan physicians, whatever their professional qualifications, were simply not trusted because they were suspected — like Nazi doctors in our own time — of caring so little for the lives of Jewish patients that they might deliberately administer the wrong treat-

---

984 *T.B. Sanh.* 99b–100a.
985 Herodotus, *The History* II, 84.
986 Cf. *Exod. R.* 46, 4.
987 In the Hellenistic Diaspora, Jewish physicians seem to have been more numerous, as many inscriptions, especially in Asia Minor and Syria, testify. Cf. S. Krauss, *Talm. Arch.* I, p. 265, and p. 718, note 595.
988 *T.B. Git.* 56b.

ment, with a view to poisoning the patients or killing them by other means. The rabbis therefore objected to employing a pagan doctor to treat any internal diseases or, according to one view, even to heal a scar over the puncture caused by bleeding. Even in cases where the recovery of the patient was in doubt, no pagan physician was allowed to be consulted. Only if the patient was considered beyond human help and harm could a pagan physician be allowed to try his art.[989] He could also be entrusted with the treatment of animals belonging to Jews.[990]

Despite such restrictions, sheer necessity caused some rabbis to relax the law, especially if the physician was a reputable practitioner of his craft and generally recognized as an expert.[991] In the third century C.E., when relations between Jews and pagans had somewhat improved, R. Johanan bar Nappaha not only permitted others to consult a reputable pagan physician in serious cases, but he himself sought treatment from a non-Jewish lady doctor (!) for scurvy on his gums. The treatment she prescribed would hardly pass muster in modern times, but R. Johanan was evidently satisfied and even revealed her medical secrets to his students. According to one account, she was so upset about this "breach of confidence" that she committed suicide. According to another version, however, she converted to Judaism.[992]

The medical "secrets" which were not supposed to be revealed — as we shall see, Jewish physicians were just as prone as their Gentile colleagues to keep certain techniques to themselves — are nevertheless known to us from the Talmud. The lady doctor who treated R. Johanan prescribed stones of dates, one half of which were to be burned, husks of barley, and the dried excrement of a child, all of which were to be ground together into a powder and applied to the sore gums. According to another opinion, which sounds a little more plausible, she prescribed leaven-water with olive oil and salt or, alternatively, geese-fat smeared with a goose-quill. However, in fourth century Babylonia, Abaye, who had some medical knowledge,[993] but, sad to relate, was in poor health and, among other things, needed treatment for his gums, tried all the

---

989 *T.B. A.Z.* 27a–b, 28a.
990 *Mishnah A.Z.* II, 2.
991 *T.Y. Shab.* XIV, 4, 14d; *A.Z.* II, 2, 40d.
992 Ibid.; ibid.; *T.B. A.Z.* 28a.
993 Cf. T.B. Erub. 29b; Pes. 112b; Yeb. 80a; Ket. 50a; 77b; Ned. 8b; Git. 67b; 70a; 86a; see *supra*, p. 185 and n. 956.

remedies but was not cured. Eventually, a friendly Arab advised him to get the seeds of an olive not one third ripe and burn them on a new spade and spread the ashes on his gums, which he did with excellent results.[994]

iii Judaeo-Christian Faith-Healers

While the rabbis were sometimes willing to compromise with principles insofar as pagan physicians were concerned, they would not tolerate "heretical", i.e., Judaeo-Christian faith-healers under any circumstances — no doubt because these doctors, even those that may have been skilled nature healers, invariably combined their medical "mission" with missionary activities.

Even if all hope of recovery was gone, one was not supposed to consult heretics, still less accept treatment from them. An oft-repeated story relates that Eleazar ben Dama, a nephew of R. Ishmael, was bitten by a poisonous snake, whereupon Jacob, a disciple of Jesus — identical either with James son of Alphaeus[995] or with James the Younger[996] — came to heal him in the name of Jesus. R. Ishmael would not permit this Judaeo-Christian to treat his nephew. The latter told his uncle that he could adduce proof from the Torah that it was permitted to save one's life by accepting treatment from a heretic. However, before he had time to argue his case, he expired. R. Ishmael almost breathed a sigh of relief. "Happy are you, Ben Dama", he exclaimed, "for you were pure in body, and your soul departed in purity" (or, according to another version, "you departed in peace from the world"), and you did not break down the fence (i.e., the prohibition) erected by the Sages".[997]

While in this case it would, no doubt, have made little practical difference if Jacob the disciple of Jesus had been permitted to use his faith-healing methods since Ben Dama was clearly beyond medical help, Judaeo-Christian healers did enjoy a certain reputation among the people (as we know from the New Testament), and despite strict rabbinic prohibitions, Jews continued to call upon their services.

Thus, in the third century C.E., the grandson of R. Joshua ben Levi had a choking fit. A Judaeo-Christian healer, praying in the name of

---

994 Cf. *T.B. A.Z.* 28a.
995 Cf. *Matthew* 10:3; *Mark* 3:18; *Luke* 6:15, *Acts* 1:13.
996 *Mark* 15:40.
997 *T.Y. Shab.* XIV, 4, 14d; *A.Z. II*, 2, 40d; *T.B. A.Z.* 27b; *Eccl. R.* I, 8, 3.

Jesus, managed to cure the patient. As he left, R. Joshua asked him which prayer he had used to effect the cure. On being told the truth, he indignantly exclaimed that it would have been better for the youth (or child) to have died rather than listen to such prayers. And sure enough, he did die soon after this, according to the Talmud, because of his grandfather's curse, but more probably because the healer's art was inadequate in this case.[998]

Even a leading third century rabbi, Abbahu, who frequently engaged in religious disputes with Christians, did not hesitate to call upon the services of a Judaeo-Christian by the name of Jacob, "an expert physician", to prepare a medicine for his sore leg. Whether by accident or design, Jacob's medical concoction turned out to be a poison rather than a healing salve. Rabbi Abbahu very nearly lost his leg, which was saved thanks to two colleagues of his, R. Ammi and R. Assi, who sucked the poison out of R. Abbahu's leg.[999]

iv Talmudic Medicine

The medical art as practiced in ancient Palestine and Babylonia was, to be sure, of a very inferior character, and the methods employed were often of the most doubtful type. Quite apart from faith-healing,[1000] which could at least have some psychological value, medical practitioners used all sorts of superstitions or even magic to effect so-called cures. For example, the egg of a locust was used for ear-aches; the tooth of a live fox was supposed to be a remedy for one who was an excessively heavy sleeper; and the tooth of a dead fox was a cure for insomnia. A nail from the gallows of an impaled convict was applied to inflammations or, according to other explanations, was used for healing a thistle sting or, possibly, a spider's bite. Last, but not least, strong vinegar was recommended to prolong life for a while in case one swallowed a wasp — a most unlikely contingency.[1001] Homeopathic cures were likewise frequently employed.[1002] Thus, for one who had a bone stuck in the throat the physician or, for that matter, anyone, even the patient himself, would take a bone of the same kind, place it on his head, and utter an

998 *T.Y. Shab.* ibid.; *T.Y. A.Z.* ibid.
999 *T.B. A.Z.* 28a.
1000 Cf. J. Preuss, *op. cit.*, pp. 28 f.; 164 ff.; 351 f.; 439 f.
1001 *M. Shab.* VI, 10; *T.Y. Shab.* VI, 10, 8c; *T.B. Shab.* 67a; *A.Z.* 12b.
1002 Cf. Krauss, *Talm. Arch.* I, 266 f., 720.

appropriate magic formula.[1003] A scroll or phylacteries were sometimes placed on the head of a child who was suffering from insomnia.[1004] One who was bitten by a mad dog would be given the lobe of its liver to eat.[1005] If this did not kill the patient, it would, hopefully, cure him. Whatever remedy was applied, one would never forget to attach some biblical verse or magic incantation to make it more effective.[1006] So great was the faith of some rabbis in this hocus-pocus that they permitted it to be carried on even on the Sabbath if the patient had been bitten by a snake or a scorpion or was having eye trouble.[1007] Likewise an amulet prepared by an "expert" could be carried in the street on the Sabbath.[1008] The rabbis discussed at length when an amulet could be considered reliable and effective, and when the amulet maker could be recognized as an expert. Generally, if three cures had been effected by the amulet, it was considered effective and its producer would then be a qualified "expert". Moreover, a physician was trusted implicitly if he claimed that an amulet he had been using had proven itself effective.[1009] A midrashic parable tells us about a physician who provided "proven" amulets for epilepsy patients, adding, however, a warning to one of them that he was not to visit cemeteries.[1010]

Actually, as we have seen, the rabbis were by no means ignorant of contemporary medicine. On the contrary, the evidence clearly proves that quite a few of them were skilled physicians and "had a most extensive knowledge of all parts of theoretical and practical medicine, in which they not only equalled, but in many respects surpassed their contemporaries".[1011] They were, nevertheless, products of their age, and strongly influenced by current folk medicine, including charms, amulets,[1012] incantations,[1013] and astrological associations as well as genuine

---

1003 *T.Y. Shab.* ibid.; *T.B.* ibid.
1004 *T.Y. Shab.* VI, 2, 8b; *T.Y. Erub.* X, 11, 26c.
1005 *M. Yoma* VIII, 6.
1006 Cf., e.g., *M. Sanh.* X, 1; *T.Y. Shab.* VI, 2, 8b; *T.Y. Erub.* X, 11, 26c.
1007 *T. Shab.* VII (VIII), 23.
1008 *M. Shab.* VI, 2.
1009 *T.Y. Shab.* VI, 2, 8c; *T.B. Shab.* 61a–b.
1010 *Lev. R.* 26, 5.
1011 W.M. Feldman, Appendix to Soncino edition of *T.B. Gittin* (London, 1936), p. 445.
1012 Cf. J. Preuss, *op. cit.*, pp. 167f.
1013 Cf. ibid., pp. 164–166.

medical concepts based on practical experience and rational thinking. For example, the remedies suggested for nose-bleeding[1014] are a curious mixture of superstitious practices, with the exception of one which, according to Dr. Feldman,[1015] may have done some good despite the strange methods resorted to. One was to take root of clover and the rope of an old bed, papyrus, saffron and the red part of a palm branch, and burn them all together. A fleece of wool was then to be taken, two threads of which were to be steeped in vinegar and rolled in the ashes of the above-mentioned substances. The wool threads thus treated were then to be inserted in the nostrils. The ashes of the substances in question may indeed have had some styptic action, but the efficacy of the remedy was apparently due for the most part to the fact that the nostrils were plugged by the threads, the pressure of which arrested the hemorrhage mechanically.

Many of the remedies prescribed by the rabbis must appear fantastic to the modern mind; but they can often be explained in terms of basic, though erroneous, concepts prevalent in antiquity, often continuing down to modern times and which had a logic of their own. For example, if one suffered from swelling of the spleen, "let him take seven leeches and dry them in the shade and every day drink two or three in wine. Alternatively he may take the spleen of a she-goat which has not yet had young, and stick it inside the oven and stand by it and say, 'As this spleen dries, so let the spleen of So-and-so (naming himself) son of So-and-so (naming his mother) dry up'. Or again he may dry it between the rows of bricks in a house and repeat these words. Or, alternatively, he may look out for the corpse of a man who has died on Sabbath and take his hand and put it on the spleen and say, 'As this hand is withered, so let the spleen of So-and-so son of So-and-so wither'".[1016]

While much of this sounds like sympathetic magic, it is, according to Feldman,[1017] not devoid of a substratum of reason. The human body was considered a *microcosm* containing all the qualities, including the healing properties of the *macrocosm*, i.e., the outside world. Ancient as well as modern naturalists and chemists believed in the therapeutic values of

---

1014 *T.B. Git.* 69a.
1015 *Op. cit.*, pp. 441 f.
1016 *T.B. Git.* 69b.
1017 *Op. cit.*, p. 442.

mummies, and, in our case, the corpse of a man who had died on a Sabbath, i.e., on a sacred day, was presumably meant to play on the patient's imagination and trust, thus perhaps helping to effect a cure through faith-healing. Certainly the other remedies proposed for the treatment of splenic enlargement (as well as for most other diseases) have nothing but blind faith to recommend them.

The Talmud also provides instances of cures by transference, practiced even today in some backward areas of Africa and Asia. Thus, for migraine "one should take a woodcock and cut its throat with a white zuz (a silver coin) over the side of one's own head on which he has pain, taking care that the blood does not blind him, and he should hang the bird on his doorpost so that he should rub against it when he goes in and out".[1018] Like the unfortunate rooster or hen still widely used on the eve of the Day of Atonement as *Kapparah*,[1019] the woodcock was singled out to take over one's migraine headache by frequently rubbing the head against its carcass. As Feldman puts it,[1020] "the basis of the remedy is to be found in the idea that if a person can *unconsciously* infect another, he might *consciously and deliberately* transfer his complaint to a lower animal or even to some inanimate object and thus rid himself of it altogether".

The same idea was behind a Talmudic remedy for night blindness (nyctalopia). Among the various methods prescribed, that of tying a patient's leg to the leg of a dog and blowing into the dog's eye[1021] clearly represents the idea of curing the disease by transferring it to the dog.

Animals and insects were widely used in folk remedies, and their popularity was perhaps due to the fact that they did *not* require special expertise, so that physicians could be dispensed with. People will do anything to save on expenses, and popular superstitions, however complicated the procedures required, were undoubtedly less expensive than physicians whose methods were in any case not exactly superior.

Both the Talmud[1022] and classical medicine recommend the use of animal excrement as remedial agents, originally as a method of driving

---

1018 *T.B. Git.* 68b.
1019 Lit., atonement, i.e., as the equivalent of the scapegoat which had to bear on its head the sins of the Children of Israel and carry them into the wilderness; cf. Levit. 16:21f.
1020 *Op. cit.*, p. 443.
1021 *T.B. Git.* 69a.
1022 Ibid.

away the demons who were believed to be the causes of the disease; but ultimately also because they proved effective in certain cases.[1023]

It was because of the universal belief in the demoniacal causation of diseases, physical as well as nervous, that magic formulas and incantations were everywhere resorted to. The Talmud, too, frequently recommends such methods and most of the diseases enumerated above (as well as scores of others) were supposed to be cured not only by physical substances but also by magic incantations.

Some rabbis even believed that every plant in the vegetable kingdom had its own presiding genius,[1024] which could be provoked by incantations. Eggs and oil, in particular, were used for magic purposes in folk-medicine,[1025] and the rabbis permitted to consult their spirits by means of charms. On the other hand, at least some of them had little faith in the efficacy of such incantations.[1026] It is noteworthy that the greatest rabbi of the Talmudic age, Akiba, violently opposed the use of magic formulas in healing, especially when pronounced with a biblical verse such as Exodus 15:26: "I will put none of the diseases upon you which I put upon the Egyptians; for I am the Lord your healer".[1027] R. Akiba's unmistakable disapproval of magic practices was watered down a century or more later by R. Johanan, who considered that only when one expectorated while uttering a biblical verse was the practice obnoxious and forbidden, otherwise, there was no objection to it.[1028] For eye diseases, in particular, spitting on the eye, usually with the addition of an incantation, was widely practiced, and in the second century, R. Meir used this superstition to effect a reconciliation between a wife and her estranged husband.[1029]

Magic and superstition were the handmaidens of medicine and retained their popularity among the Jewish masses right down to the nineteenth century. It was perhaps because physicians were so often mere faith-healers, quacks or worse that they were sometimes held in low esteem, and ultimately, as we have seen, they were considered to be suitable denizens of hell.

1023 Feldman, *op. cit.*
1024 *Gen. R.* 10, 6.
1025 On folk-medicine in the Talmudic age, cf. J. Preuss, *op. cit., passim.*
1026 *T.B. Sanh.* 101a.
1027 *M. Sanh.* X, 1.
1028 *T.B. Sanh.* 101a; Shevuoth 15b.
1029 *T.Y. Sot.* I, 4, 16d, *et al.*

A physician who certainly deserved to go to hell or, alternatively, to a lunatic asylum, was one mentioned in a parable about a man who had a broken leg that had healed. A physician who happened to meet him told him, "Come to me, I will break your leg anew and set it again, so that you may know that my medicaments are good".[1030]

Needless to say, not all physicians were superstitious, incompetent or grasping. We are told of a man who was suffering from heartaches. The doctors whom he consulted prescribed warm milk every morning — a remedy which was popular and reasonably effective down to modern times.[1031] The (non-Jewish) physicians who, in 70 C.E., treated R. Zadok who had become completely emaciated through prolonged fasting, ingeniously nursed him back to health by methods which even today would not be considered wrong. Thus, on the first day of treatment, they let him drink water in which bran had been soaked; on the next day water in which coarse bran mixed with flour had been put; and on the third day water in which there had been flour. In this way the patient's stomach was gradually able to absorb a normal diet.[1032]

An interesting medical case is reported in the Tosephta.[1033] A patient underwent some sort of operation near the skull, and the surgeon covered up the incision with a pumpkin-shell. The patient recovered and lived through the summer months; but during the rainy season, he caught a cold, whether through the head injury or otherwise is not clear, and died.

Another instance of relatively advanced methods used by surgeons is a story — admittedly of a legendary character — that R. Eleazar son of R. Simeon (2nd cent. C.E.) was given a sleeping draught; taken into a "marble chamber" — evidently an operating theater; and his abdomen was opened and fat removed from it.[1034] Even though the story, which has many other improbable elements, cannot be regarded as reliable history, it is significant because it indicates that drugs designed to deaden the pain were used for operations. Surgery was practiced among the Greeks with some success,[1035] and some of this medical knowledge was

1030 *T.B. M.K.* 21b.
1031 *T.B. B.K.* 80a; Tem. 15b.
1032 *T.B. Git.* 56b.
1033 *Ohol.* II, 6.
1034 *T.B. B.M.* 83b.
1035 Cf. *Enc. Brit.* (1967 edition), XI, 331.

no doubt acquired by Jewish surgeons, though their number was exceedingly small.

Unlike so many modern doctors, the ancient ones made house calls and, in addition to treating the patient, advised him or his family what to eat and drink and what to cut out from his diet. A fine Midrashic parable describes how a patient was visited by a physician who then told his family to let him eat and drink whatever he wished. He later visited another patient and warned his family not to let him eat and drink certain food items. They wondered why the first patient had been permitted to eat and drink anything he liked, while the second patient had been placed on a restricted diet. The doctor candidly told them that the first patient was not going to live, hence he might as well indulge himself while he could; "but for this one who can recover I prescribe that he should refrain from eating (certain types of food) so that he should not aggravate his illness".[1036]

Doctors also had some psychological understanding for the feelings of their patients: "It is usual when one visits a sick person to say to him, 'May heavenly mercy be vouchsafed for you'. When the physician comes to him, he tells him, 'Eat this and do not eat that; drink this and do not drink that'. Even if he sees him approaching death, he does not say to him, 'Set your house in order' (i.e., prepare your last will and testament), so that his mind should not be upset".[1037]

The dietary regime imposed by doctors was not always rigidly observed. The Talmud discusses the problem of an injured person who disobeyed the physician's medical advice, eating, for example, honey or other sweets which were believed to be harmful to a wound, causing it to become scabby.[1038] Doctors sometimes lost their patience with some careless individuals, though Hippocrates would hardly have approved of the temperamental physician who made a house-call on R. Jeremiah (3rd cent. C.E.) and, seeing a pumpkin lying there, instantly made his departure, saying "This man has the angel of death in his house (i.e., the

---

1036 *Tanh. Mishpatim* 3.
1037 *Eccl. R.* 5, 6. For a biblical precedent, cf. II Kings 8:10, where we are told that the prophet Elisha instructs Hazael to tell Ben-hadad, King of Syria, that he would recover from his disease, though "the Lord has shown me that he shall certainly die". By implication, it is indicated that a mortally sick patient should not be alarmed by being told about the hopelessness of his condition.
1038 *T.B. B.K.* 85a.

pumpkin is like poison for the patient), and yet I am supposed to come and cure him?!" The Rabbis had some difficulty explaining what was wrong with eating a pumpkin. Their conclusion was that, while the soft part of the pumpkin could be eaten and was even beneficial, the hard part was harmful.[1039]

v *Medical Equipment*

If the bedside manners of doctors were not always above reproach, the attitudes of patients and their families occasionally also left much to be desired, quite apart from disobedience of medical instructions and occasional failure to pay the physician's fee. Doctors might even be the victims of individuals who depended upon their services and did not hesitate to call upon them as soon as they needed medical aid. A Talmudic parable tells of a thief who stole a doctor's medicine chest. On leaving his victim's house, he discovered that his son had been injured and required treatment. Unabashed, the thief returned to the doctor and politely asked him to treat the boy's wound. The doctor who knew who had robbed him, calmly told the thief, "Go and bring back the medicine chest in which all kinds of medicines are kept, and then I will treat your son".[1040]

Incidentally, the medicine chest was almost the doctor's trademark, and it was not uncommon for a physician to leave it to his son as soon as he "graduated" from his medical school or, more probably, as soon as he had finished his apprenticeship with his father. For in medicine, as in other trades and professions, the son often succeeded his father's practice, and the entire profession seems to have been hereditary.[1041] Medical apprentices who were not members of the physician's family were not always taught the "copyright secrets" of the master. Exclusive methods of highly specialized treatment were often jealously guarded, and the medical student might have to plead with his teacher to initiate him into the finer points of the art of healing.[1042]

If the medicine chest was the visible trade mark of the doctor at work, individual and, possibly, guilds of physicians used special symbols as

---

1039 *T.B. Ned.* 49a.
1040 *T.Y. Ber.* V, 5, 9b; *T.Y. Taan.* I, 1, 63d.
1041 *T.Y. Rosh Hash.* I, 3, 57b.
1042 *Midr. Pss.* 25, 6, edit. Buber 106a.

their trademark. Thus, Mar Samuel (early 3rd cent. C.E.), who, as we have seen, was a skilled ophthalmologist, used the figure of a palm branch as his signature,[1043] and it is believed that this was widely used by contemporary physicians as a sign of their profession.[1044]

The essential equipment of a doctor in the Talmudic period included a leather apron[1045] used, no doubt, to protect the clothes during treatment; a metal basket and/or metal cupboard containing plasters, scissors and presumably other medical instruments;[1046] a large spoon[1047] presumably for measuring and possibly for feeding medicines to patients; a trepan or surgical drill used for operations;[1048] tongs or pincers[1049] used in surgery and dentistry; and a surgical knife required for operations and especially for circumcision.[1050] The importance of the surgical knife as well as of drugs for the practice of surgery is indicated in the following parable:

"He who studies Torah in his youth is like a physician who, when confronted with a growth, possesses a surgical knife for the operation, and drugs to heal the wound; but he who studies Torah in his old age is like a physician who, when confronted with a growth, possesses, indeed, a surgical knife for the operation, but has no drugs to heal the wound".[1051]

8. Morally Undesirable Trades — General

If a highly skilled craft like medicine was looked upon with mixed feelings, some inferior trades were despised, possibly under the influence of Hellenistic concepts of labor, or else they were considered morally unwholesome. In a society which viewed unfavorably any mingling of the sexes, a trade or profession which brought craftsmen into contact with women was *ipso facto* suspect. It was, indeed, for this reason that a bachelor, widower or even a married man whose wife was not living with him, was not supposed to be a schoolteacher because the children

---

1043 *T.Y. Git.* IX, 9, 50d.
1044 *Jew. Enc.* XI, 30.
1045 *M. Kel.* XXVI, 5; *T. Kel. B.B.* IV, 8.
1046 *M. Kel.* XII, 3; *T. Kel. B.M.* II, 9.
1047 *M. Kel.* XVII, 12.
1048 *M. Ohol.* II, 3; *T.* ibid. II, 6.
1049 *T. Kel. B.M.* III, 11.
1050 *T.Y. Shab.* XIX, 1, 16d; *T.B. Shab.* 130a–b.
1051 *Aboth R.N.*, edit. Schechter, Vers. I, chap. 23, p. 76.

were brought to school by their mothers or sisters some of whom might unduly befriend the teacher. Conversely, a woman was barred from teaching because some of her pupils might be brought to school by their fathers, and one could never be sure what some of these fathers might be up to.[1052]

It was because of such excessive moral considerations that a strong recommendation was made that "a man should not teach his son a craft which is practiced among women".[1053] Those who nevertheless did practice such crafts were advised to avoid being alone with women, no matter whether one or more.[1054] In any case, however careful they might be, they were thought to be men of bad character.[1055]

The list of these undesirable trades is formidable indeed. It includes goldsmiths who made trinkets for women; carders who combed wool for women's garments; tailors whose clientele inevitably included ladies (not all of whom would make their own dresses); handmill cleaners who would visit homes and offer their services to housewives; netmakers who presumably sold their products to women for various uses; peddlers who sold ornaments, spices and toilet articles to women; wool-dressers or weavers whose social position was extremely degraded; tanners who were socially even less acceptable; launderers whose customers were almost exclusively women; bloodletters whose moral reputation was extremely low and who were considered undesirable or at least a nuisance in good neighborhoods;[1056] barbers to whom women (who did not indeed attend beauty-parlors which were, as yet, for better or for worse, unknown to womankind) would bring their children for haircuts; and bath-attendants who prepared the public baths for female (as well as male) visitors, carried women's bathing clothes to the baths,[1057] and presumably enjoyed opportunities for peeping Tom exercises denied to ordinary mortals.[1058]

1052 *M. Kid.* IV, 13; *T. Kid.* V, 10; *T.Y. Kid.* IV, 11, 66c; *T.B. Kid.* 82a. Significantly, child-abuse and homosexual acts on the part of unmarried teachers are never mentioned as contingencies to guard against. The prevailing rabbinic view was that "Israelites (i.e. Jews) are not suspected of pederasty" (T.B. Kid. 82a). If there were any Jewish gays, they never came out of their closet.
1053 *M. Kid.* IV, 14.
1054 Ibid.; *T.Y.* ibid.
1055 *T.B. Kid.* 82a.
1056 *T.B. B.B.* 21a.
1057 Cf. *T.B. Shab.* 147b.
1058 *Tos. Kid.* V, 14; *T.B. Kid.* 82a.

The last two trades in particular were held in great contempt and considered to be utterly degrading. Thus, in the apocryphal stories told about the wicked Haman, he is represented as acting as bath-attendant and barber for Mordecai and lamenting, "The man who was esteemed by the King above all the nobles is now made a bath-attendant and barber!" Mordecai, however, reminded Haman that he had once been a village barber — indeed for no less than twenty-two years. According to another version, Haman's father had been a barber and bath-attendant as well as a maker of myrrh oil, a favorite perfume used by women.[1059]

All these trades that have been listed above were held in such low esteem that anyone practicing them was not considered fit ever to be chosen King or High Priest, not because they were necessarily "bad guys", but "because their trade is mean".[1060] According to R. Jose (mid-2nd cent. C.E.), the same holds true of the building trade, which he evidently regarded as a "mean" occupation. Since the Temple had been destroyed some two or three generations earlier, there were no High Priests in R. Jose's time, nor were there any Jewish kings. R. Jose, therefore, brought the previous ruling up to date by changing it to read that those who pursued certain undesirable professions were not to be appointed community leaders or administrators.[1061]

9. Bloodletting[1062]

Bloodletters, who usually applied leeches or incision instruments to the body to draw off blood, which was supposed to be good for one's health, were unpopular and disliked. Although people resorted to them, hoping that perhaps they could do some good, there seems to have been an underlying suspicion that they were really quacks. It did not help that conceited bloodletters pretended to be physicians (though they were paid much less than physicians)[1063] and gave themselves haughty airs while walking and sitting. The bloodletter was supposed to be a miser; to have an evil eye which he cast on healthy people so that they might get sick and need his services; to be a glutton enjoying the good meals usually

---

1059 *T.B. Meg.* 16a; *Lev. R.* 28, 6; *et al.*
1060 *T.B. Kid.* 82a.
1061 *Der. Er. Z.* X, 2.
1062 On bloodletting in ancient times, and on the professional activities and social position of the bloodletter, cf. J. Preuss, *op. cit.*, pp. 36–39; 289–300.
1063 Cf. J. Preuss, *op. cit.*, p. 39.

eaten by his patients after the "operation". He was also suspected of taking advantage of female patients and committing adultery with them; robbing their husbands by charging more than he ought to; and of "bloodshed", presumably through excessive bleeding, thereby endangering the lives of his clients.[1064]

Like all generalizations, this, too, was not always true. In fourth century Babylonia, a certain Abba the Bloodletter was highly commended as a saintly man who was privileged to receive daily greetings from the heavenly academy, while leading rabbis had to content themselves with much rarer communications from the Great Beyond. Unlike other members of his profession, Abba was a highly moral person of unimpeachable character. Moreover, he saw to it that his clients' morality should be equally safeguarded. He accordingly segregated the sexes in his surgery, keeping the men in one room and the women in another. He had a special garment with numerous slits which his female patients had to wear during the bleeding operation. Through the slits in the garment he was able to insert surgical instruments without looking at the bare body of any female client. He was also very charitably disposed. Outside his consultation room he had a box where his fees were to be deposited. "Whoever had money would put it in; but whoever had no money could come in without feeling embarrassed. When he saw a person who was in no position to pay, he would give him some money" and tell him to buy himself a good meal, which was medically advisable after bleeding.

In addition, Abba held men of learning in high regard. On one occasion, two scholars were sent to him to find out the truth about him. He invited them to his home; gave them to eat and to drink; and laid cushions before them to sleep on. Next morning the two scholars wanted to test his sincerity, took the cushions with them and brought them to the market place. Abba was sent for and asked to appraise the value of his own missing cushions. He claimed no more than he had paid for them. Asked about his feelings concerning what looked like an unmistakable theft, he replied that he assumed that the two scholars were in need of money for some charitable purpose but were too embarrassed to ask him for a contribution. When they wanted to return the cushions, he refused to take them because he had already consecrated them for charity.[1065] The generalized criticism leveled against "bleeders" clearly did not apply in his case.

1064 Ibid.
1065 *T.B. Taan.* 21b–22a.

10. Prison Administration

Another unlikely saint turned out to be a Babylonian Jewish jailer. He, too, had a high sense of moral propriety, and took good care to keep male and female prisoners segregated. Since facilities for complete isolation of female prisoners were inadequate, the jailer would place at night his own bed between the men and the women "so that no wrong be committed". He would specially guard Jewish female prisoners and even risk his life to preserve their honor if the pagans (who generally regarded prison inmates as fair game) had "fixed their eyes" on them. One day a betrothed girl was brought to the prison, and the pagan prison officials were getting ready to rape her. The Jewish jailer managed by a ruse to make her appear extremely unattractive, thereby saving her from the unwanted attention of the pagans.

This jailer was apparently a man of some influence. He dressed like a Gentile and did not wear the ritual fringes habitually worn by other Jews. In fact, outwardly, he lived like a pagan and was believed to be such by the authorities. Thanks to his official connections, he was able to learn in advance about various anti-Jewish measures or plots, and to warn the rabbis concerning the impending danger. Since the Babylonian Jews were generally able to take care of themselves, such warning served a useful purpose, and the perils threatening the community were averted.[1066]

For all that, it is doubtful whether the rabbis would have considered a career in jail administration to be a desirable profession. The average jailer was far from being a saint; the daily duties of such an official were obviously incompatible with a genuinely Jewish religious life; and the temptations offered to a person in such a position were clearly too dangerous.

11. Peddling

Particularly exposed to temptation were peddlers — the commercial travelers of antiquity whose profession survived down to the twentieth century. They would go from door to door, usually during the day while the husbands were away at work. Women would eagerly purchase the trinkets, spices and perfumes offered by the peddlers, and the friendly

1066 Ibid. 22a.

relations established between housewives and peddlers whose natural gift of the gab could equally be used for noncommercial purposes would all-to-often degenerate into illicit love and adultery.

As early as the time of Ben Sira (c. 200 B.C.E.), the moral reputation of the peddlers was none-too-high, as we have seen in an earlier chapter. In a passage no longer extant in the Greek version but to be found in a corrupt form in the Hebrew original discovered in the Cairo Genizah, it would appear that the peddler was indeed regarded as a sinner and seducer of married women:

> "Not every man is brought into the house,
> And how numerous are the wounds of the peddler".[1067]

It is not quite clear what is meant by "the wounds of the peddler". It could refer to the moral injuries inflicted by the peddler upon his unsuspecting female customers, who are warned accordingly not to let any peddlers enter their home. However, it may be a reference to the wounds sustained by the peddler at the hands of jealous husbands. Of considerable interest, too, is the Talmudic version of this quotation:

> "Many were the wounds of the peddler
> That lead on to lewdness
> Like a spark that lights the coal".[1068]

Despite such prejudice, the rabbis recognized the essential usefulness of the peddler whose profession was such an old-established institution that the rabbis attributed its origin to Ezra. According to them, Ezra had ordained that peddlers should be able to travel about in the small towns (where shopping facilities were limited) to provide toilet articles and ornaments for women, " so that they should not be repulsive in the eyes of their husbands".[1069] With this in view, the rabbis insisted on free competition, and one peddler could not prevent another from encroaching on his "territory".[1070]

The itinerant spice and perfume peddler was indeed a welcome figure wherever he made his appearance. He was after all the only purveyor of beauty preparations, and women in antiquity were no less anxious to enhance their attractiveness than their modern descendants. A parable describes how an itinerant perfume peddler "takes his chest and enters a

---

1067 *Ecclus.*, Heb. edit., 11:29.
1068 *T.B. Yeb.* 63b; *Sanh.* 100b.
1069 *T.B. B.K.* 82b.
1070 *T.B. B.B.* 22a.

town (i.e., a large village). The townsfolk come and enquire, 'Have you got any fine oil? Have you got any spikenard oil? Have you got any balsam oil?' They then find that he has everything (they require)".[1071]

12. Tanners

Although the wandering perfumer and spice dealer was welcome wherever he went, and consequently must have conducted a highly profitable business, the profession of the settled perfumer who sold his fragrant wares in his own store was much more desirable. In a pungent saying, already cited in a different context, R. Meir or, according to another version, Rabbi Judah the Patriarch (d. 219 C.E.) asserted that "the (civilized) world cannot exist without a perfume-maker and without a tanner; but happy is he whose craft is that of a perfume-maker and woe to him who is a tanner by trade".[1072]

An apposite parable describes customers who visit the store of a perfume-maker and a tannery, respectively. When a man enters a spice store or perfumery, even if he buys nothing, the scent of the perfumes and spices clings to him and his clothes long after he has left. Conversely, when one visits a tannery, even if nothing is bought or sold, the unpleasant odor of the skins clings to the body and to one's clothes even after leaving the place.[1073]

If perfumers and spice merchants were thus held in high esteem as long as they had their own stores and did not become itinerant peddlers, tanners, whose trade was so noticeably unpleasant, tended to be despised. It has also been suggested that the strict concepts of (ritually) clean and unclean in the Law of Moses inevitably created an antipathy to unclean trades, the bad odor of which would often cling to one's clothes and body throughout one's working life.[1074] This did not deter the apostle Peter from staying at the sea-shore home of a tanner at Jaffa.[1075] But then, of course, it is a fact that the early Christians associated mainly with the lower classes and even with the outcasts of society among whom they found their most ardent supporters.

1071 *Aboth R.N.* Vers. I, ch. 18, edit. Schechter, p. 67.
1072 *T.Y. Kid.* IV, 11, 66d; *T. Kid.* V, 14; *T.B. Kid.* 82b, *et al.*
1073 *Aboth R. Nathan,* edit. Schechter, Vers. II, ch. 11, p. 28.
1074 F. Delitzsch, *Jüdisches Handwerkerleben zur Zeit Jesu,* 3rd edit. (Erlangen, 1879), p. 39.
1075 *Acts* 9:43; 10:6, 32.

The rabbis, who were concerned with the legal and religious aspects of incompatible marriages, sought to protect the rights of the wives of craftsmen and physically repulsive men who for one reason or another had become unendurable to their spouses. Accordingly, a woman married to a tanner — or for that matter, to a copper-miner or a collector of dogs' excrement which served as raw material for the tanning of hides[1076] — could demand a divorce. According to one view, the offensive odor of such workmen constituted plausible grounds for divorce even if they had been engaged in the same trade at the time of the marriage. Even if this had been expressly stipulated in the marriage contract, the wife could nevertheless plead, "I thought I would be able to endure him, but now I cannot bear it".[1077] Although the majority of rabbis disagreed on this point, the general liberality of the divorce law in matters of this type can hardly be disputed.

An actual case of such liberality was reported from Zidon in Phoenicia, which seems to have been a major center of tanneries.[1078] A tanner happened to die there without children, leaving a widow who was supposed to contract a levirate marriage with her deceased husband's brother[1079] who was likewise a tanner by trade. The rabbis decided that she could reject her brother-in-law, even though her late husband had been in the same trade; for she could tell her prospective husband, "I was able to endure your brother, but I cannot endure you".[1080]

On account of their malodorous occupations, tanners as well as copper-miners and collectors of dogs' excrement were also socially and religiously disadvantaged. In an age when pilgrimages to the Temple of Jerusalem were both a religious obligation[1081] and a social privilege, they were exempt because other pilgrims would be inconvenienced by their offensive odor,[1082] and perhaps also because their presence in the holiest place of Judaism was regarded as unseemly. The ritual ablutions performed by all who entered the sacred Temple area also had a cleansing effect; but tanners and others engaged in such obnoxious trades simply could not rid themselves of the unpleasant smell caused by their occupations unless they abandoned or interrupted them for a lengthy period.

Because of the stench of a tannery, it could not be set up anywhere within a town, but at a distance of at least fifty cubits, and then only east

---

1076 Cf. *T.B. Ber.* 25a.
1077 *M. Ket.* VII, 10; *T. Ket.* VII, 11.
1078 *T. Ohol.* XVIII, 2.
1079 Cf. Deut. 25:5ff.
1080 *M. Ket.* VII, 10.
1081 Cf. Exod. 23:17; 34:23; Deut. 16:16; *M. Hag.* I, 1.
1082 *T.B. Hag.* 4a; 7b.

of the town, since the prevailing wind in Palestine is from the north-west.[1083] Similar "environmental" laws for the protection of the citizens against air pollution and other nuisances existed also in Athens where, for example, traders in (strong-smelling) cheese and honey (which attracts bees and wasps) had to do their business outside the city.[1084]

In view of the extreme unpleasantness of the tanner's work and his low social status, it is surprising that anyone was willing to devote his career to such a despised trade. This can be explained partly by the fact that this craft, like most others, was to a considerable extent hereditary and thus self-perpetuating. Economic mobility was far from adequate, and inevitably a son would follow his father's occupation. Another reason for the survival of tanneries may have been the relatively good income derived from this work. We do not hear of unemployed, poverty-stricken or starving tanners, and precisely because it was not an attractive occupation, competition was evidently light and work plentiful.

13. Weavers

In Palestine, though not in Babylonia, the trade of the weaver was no less despised than that of the tanner. This may have been due to the fact that, like spinning, it had once been an almost exclusively female occupation, and was still widely practiced by women.[1085] A Midrashic parable even speaks of a woman who became rich through diligent spinning, which she was therefore determined never to abandon.[1086]

Weaving, on the other hand, does not seem to have ever been a profitable occupation. In Babylonia, to be sure, spinning and weaving were not considered degrading trades even for men,[1087] and the cities of Borsippa and Nearda were in fact major centers of the textile industry.[1088] Yet, even in Babylonia it was apparently only poor people and orphans who were apprenticed to learn the weaving trade,[1089] although

---

1083 *M. Baba Bathra* II, 9.
1084 Cf. Krauss, *Talm. Arch.* II, 626, n. 81.
1085 Cf., e.g., Exod. 35:25f.; II Kings 23:7; Prov. 31:19; *Mishnah B.K.* X, 9; *T.Y. Shek.* IV, 3, 48a; *T.Y. Sot.* III, 3, 19a; *T.B. Yoma* 66b; *M.K.* 21b; *Ket.* 86b; 106a; *Pesik. R.*, edit. Friedmann, 131a.
1086 *Gen. R.* 56, 11.
1087 Cf. Josephus, *Ant.* XVIII, 9, 1, 314.
1088 *Strabo* XVI, 39; F.M. Heichelheim, "Roman Syria", in T. Frank, *An Economic Survey of Ancient Rome*, IV, (Baltimore, 1938), p. 191.
1089 Josephus, ibid.

the sons of weavers presumably followed their fathers' trade, as was customary in all handicrafts.

In Palestine, weaving was one of the humblest of trades, and in Jerusalem the social status of the weavers was especially degraded as we learn in connection with the testimony of two weavers whose trade center was the so-called Dung Gate:

"There is no more degraded craft than that of the weaver, and there is no more despised place in Jerusalem than the Dung Gate" (near which the trash of the city was deposited — hence its name).[1090]

The rabbis, who did not always share the prejudices of their contemporaries, accepted the statements of the above-mentioned two weavers, and decided a doubtful religious question in accordance with their testimony; for low in status though they were, they had evidently studied under two leading scholars, Shemaiah and Abtalyon.[1091]

Such scholarly weavers must have been the exception rather than the rule. A more characteristic example of a weaver was an extreme Zealot by the name of Jonathan who fled from Jerusalem after the capture of the city in 70 C.E. He came to Cyrene in North Africa where he stirred up a popular movement among the poorer Jews against the Romans. Like all such efforts, this, too, was doomed to failure, and Jonathan the weaver was captured, and eventually, after causing major disasters to the wealthier elements among the Jews, he was brought to Rome, tortured, and burnt alive.[1092]

Bad luck generally seems to have pursued Jewish weavers. A Talmudic story, told with a good deal of unconscious humor, relates how R. Menashi, a disciple of the third century Babylonian teacher, Rab Judah, once encountered a gang of thieves on a journey. When they asked him where he was going, he pretended that he was traveling to a distant place, his purpose being to gain time, since they might not be in such a hurry to rob him if he was going their way. However, on his arrival at his real destination, he parted from them. Since they were in a town, which was presumably policed, they could not rob him as they had planned. But, chagrined as they were, they insulted him and his teacher, saying, "You are a disciple of Judah the deceiver". R. Menashi could not forgive them the insult to his master, and he solemnly put them under the ban. The effect was devastating. For the next twenty-two years, the gang went on thieving, but luck had turned against them, and their crooked efforts

---

1090 T. Eduyoth I, 3.
1091 Ibid.; M. Ed. I, 3.
1092 Josephus, Bell. VII, 11, 1–3, 437–450.

met with no success. Appalled at their constant failures, they resolved to apologize and ask for annulment of the ban, to which they attributed their misfortunes. We are not told whether their request was granted — in the interest of law and order it would presumably have been wiser to be adamant. However, one of them, a weaver by trade, who evidently felt that robbery was more profitable than labor, refused even to apply for the removal of the ban. He was duly devoured by a lion — not, mind you, because of his criminal activities, but because he had neglected to request that the ban be lifted.[1093]

It was this incident that gave rise to a popular proverb, the meaning of which is not altogether clear: "If the weaver refuses to be humble, the ban will shorten his years".[1094] According to another translation, "If the weaver does not humble himself one year, he shortens (all) his years". A third rendering reads: "If the weaver is not humble, curse his years!" Finally, a fourth translation, which radically differs from the previous ones, proposes this reading: "A year's scanty earnings will change (i.e., improve) a weaver, if he is not a proud fool". Whatever the meaning of the proverb, it is clearly uncomplimentary to the weaver.

Weavers were also considered to be frivolous in their singing, and because of the mourning following the national calamities their light-hearted songs were excluded from places of feasting. It has been surmised that the weavers' songs may have been objectionable to the neighbors.[1095] In contrast, the singing of sailors and ploughmen which was supposed to help them in their work was permitted.[1096]

Legally, too, weavers were placed under certain restrictions as regards setting up workshops at their homes. If the neighbors objected, there was nothing they could do about it, and likewise landlords were not permitted to rent them workshops in a courtyard — presumably if the neighbors objected.[1097] True, the same restrictions were placed on physicians, bloodletters and certain types of schoolteachers;[1098] but whereas the practice of these professions could be a real nuisance to neighbors because of the noise made by the coming and going of patients or schoolchildren, a weaver's workshop was no worse than that of any other craftsman. In all probability it was singled out because weavers repre-

---

1093 *T.B. A.Z.* 26a.
1094 Ibid.
1095 Cf. M. Wischnitzer, *op. cit.*, p. 47.
1096 *T.B. Sot.* 48a.
1097 *T.B. B.B.* 21a.
1098 Ibid.

sented a despised social class whose presence was resented because it lowered the tone of the neighborhood.

Even in the Middle Ages, weavers continued to be an inferior social class, and in France there were Jewish communities in which the testimony of weavers was not admitted in court.[1099]

Contemptible though the weaver was in the eyes of society, in his own home he was king, and his wife and children evidently honored and respected him: "Even a common weaver must be master in his own house".[1100] A similar proverb regarding a carder, whose occupation also was very humble, was current in Babylonia where it was said, "Though her husband be a carder (lit., a flaxbeater), she calls him to the threshold and sits down with him",[1101] no doubt to demonstrate her pride in being a married woman, in spite of her husband's lowly social status. According to another explanation, this proverb refers to a watchman of vegetables,[1102] also a somewhat despised occupation.

14. Artistic Weavers

On a rather higher social level were the artistic weavers (טרסיים) who, it seems, used metallic threads for their work.[1103] Although in some passages the functions of the "Tarsiim" would appear to have been rather different — they may have been simple metal workers, copper smiths or miners,[1104] most passages point to highly skilled craftsmen engaged in artistic weaving with golden or silver threads, possibly using work methods and skills originally developed in Tarsus, Cilicia (in Asia Minor), but flourishing also elsewhere, especially in Egypt. The "Tarsiim" in Palestine were in all probability Jewish craftsmen originating in Alexandria,[1105] a great industrial center from which other craftsmen, too, were occasionally imported to the Holy Land.[1106]

These "Tarsian" weavers formed well-organized guilds which had their own synagogues in places as far apart as Jerusalem, Lod (Lydda),

---

1099 Cf. Krauss, *op. cit.*, II, 560, n. 274.
1100 *T.B. Meg.* 12b.
1101 *T.B. Yeb.* 118b; *Ket.* 75a.   1102 Cf., *Arukh* s.v. נפס.
1103 Cf. Jastrow, *A Dictionary of the Targumim* etc., p. 555, s.v. טרסי; Kohut, *Aruch* IV, 87, s.v. טרסי).
1104 Cf. *Hul.* 57b and *Tosafot A.Z.* 17b, s.v. רבן.
1105 Cf. S. Krauss, *Synagogale Altertümer*, p. 201; *Talm. Arch.* II, 625, n. 67a.
1106 Cf., e.g., *T. Yom Hakip.* II, 5; *T.Y. Yoma* III, 9, 41a; *T.Y. Shek.* V, 2, 48d-49a; *T.B. Yoma* 38a.

and Tiberias. They were headed by presidents who bore the title "Rab" (master) similar to the well-known rabbinical title. This could sometimes confuse the Roman authorities and actually helped to save R. Eleazar ben Perata's life during the Hadrianic persecution (135–138 C.E.). When charged with being called "Rabbi", which implied that he was illegally teaching the proscribed Jewish religion, he blandly replied, "I am a master (Rab) of *Tarsiim*". The Romans were not so easily fooled, and they tested him by requiring him to identify which of two coils was for the warp and which for the woof. Miraculously, he found the right answer, thus escaping death.[1107]

The synagogues of the artistic weavers served social and economic as well as religious purposes. They were in effect trade union centers, and, as we have seen in Chapter Four, in the great synagogue of Alexandria the "Tarsiim" had a special section of the building assigned to themselves. There they would carefully sit apart from the socially inferior common weavers. At the same time they assisted poor immigrant fellow craftsmen to obtain work and lodging, and generally to be integrated in the community.[1108]

Perhaps because these craft guild synagogues largely served secular purposes, they were not always treated with the reverence due to a house of prayer despite the fact that occasionally important rabbis would honor them with visits, teach there and deliver public sermons.[1109] The "Tarsian" synagogue in Jerusalem, described as a very small building, was sold to R. Eliezer who had no compunction about using it for all kinds of secular purposes.[1110] R. Eliezer was certainly not lacking in reverence, but he evidently regarded the synagogue in question primarily as a secular house of assembly used only incidentally for religious services. Consequently, he felt free to use it in any way that suited him.

Although we are not told why the "Tarsiim" sold their synagogue, the parallel accounts in other sources[1111] provide significant clues. There we are informed that it was the "Alexandrians" who sold their synagogue in Jerusalem to R. Eleazar son of R. Zadok whose name in Hebrew is almost identical with Eliezer. It may be surmised that during the troubled years preceding the destruction of the Second Temple, most, perhaps all, of the foreign craftsmen who resided in Jerusalem decided to

1107 *T.B. A.Z.* 17b.
1108 *T. Suk.* IV, 6; *T.Y. Suk.* V, 1, 55a–b; *T.B. Suk.* 51b.
1109 Cf., e.g., *Lev. R.* 35, 12; *T.B. Yeb.* 96b *et al.*
1110 *T.B. Meg.* 26a.
1111 *T. Meg.* III (II), 6; *T.Y. Meg.* III, 1, 73d. Cf. also S. Krauss, *Talmudische Archäologie*, vol. II (Leipzig, 1911), p. 258 and p. 625, notes 67a–69.

leave the doomed city. Prior to their departure they would naturally try to dispose of their private and communal properties, and since they were not the only ones, there must have been a catastrophic decline in real estate values. Hence it became possible for a rabbi, who was certainly not renowned for his wealth, to purchase a synagogue, albeit a small one, in Jerusalem.

The "Tarsian" synagogue in Lod (Lydda) was also treated, on at least one occasion, with a remarkable lack of reverence. For no apparent reason, a basket full of human bones was taken into the synagogue, and although the precaution was taken to place the basket under an opening in the roof to prevent ritual uncleanness, it required the testimony of a group of physicians, led by a certain Theodos or Theodoros the Physician, concerning the state of the human bones in the basket to avoid defilement of the synagogue.[1112]

By far the most scandalous event known to have occurred in a "Tarsian" synagogue is reported to have taken place in Tiberias. There, we are told, two second century rabbis were once engaged in a heated dispute concerning a point of religious law which would hardly arouse much excitement even among ultra-orthodox Jews in modern times. In the Tiberias synagogue, however, the contestants became so furious that they tore a Torah scroll, probably inadvertently, while no doubt trying to prove their respective views from different biblical verses. A third rabbi, R. Jose ben Kisma, who was present, was so disgusted with this outburst that he somberly predicted that the desecrated synagogue would be turned into a house of idolatry.[1113] While we do not know the background of this incident, the manifest disrespect shown within a sacred edifice by prominent rabbis who should have known better can be explained only if we bear in mind that a trade union synagogue was perhaps regarded as a secular rather than religious building.

15. Launderers

The launderers or fullers, whom we have already met in biblical times,[1114] were on a slightly higher social level than one would expect, mainly because some of them attained scholarly proficiency; but the trade itself,

---

1112 *T. Ohol.* IV, 2; *T.B. Nazir* 52a.
1113 *T.Y. Shek.* II, 7, 47a; *T.B. Yeb.* 96b; Cf. also *M. Erubin* X, 10, where the Torah scroll incident is omitted.
1114 Cf. *Isaiah* 7:3. See *supra*, p. 18.

though by no means unskilled, was, as we have seen, considered undesirable.[1115] It involved frequent contact with women, and it was practiced by women[1116] as well as men, and in a male-dominated society this in itself was sufficient to degrade such an occupation. Washing dirty linen and clothes was not exactly the cleanest trade either, and this may have given rise to many jests and parables, presumably at the expense of the launderers' dignity.[1117] Among the Romans, the launderer was invariably a ridiculous figure and hence a favorite character in popular comedies.[1118]

Nevertheless, fullers appear to have been organized in guilds,[1119] which at any rate afforded them some economic protection, and in Jerusalem there was even a monument called the Monument of the Fuller.[1120] While we cannot be sure that it was erected in honor of someone who was a fuller and had somehow deserved well of the city or the people, the fact that it is mentioned together with monuments of Queen Helena, a highly respected convert to Judaism, tends to favor this interpretation.[1121]

In rabbinic circles launderers were treated with considerable respect, and pious as well as learned launderers were familiar figures in scholarly circles. One of them, a learned fuller by the name of Abba Hoshaya (or: Yeshayah) of Tiryah in Galilee, would insist on wearing only one girdle made of only one kind of wool, so as to avoid any suspicion that he was using for himself strips of the clothes given to him for washing.[1122] Another fuller was sent by the rabbis on a confidential mission to R. Eleazar ben Azariah (c. 100 C.E.) to inform him that his predecessor, Rabban Gamaliel II, was going to be reinstated as President of the Sanhedrin.[1123] The fuller in question must have been a man of learning and discretion to be entrusted with such an important and delicate mission. Indeed, according to another version, it was R. Akiba (who is not known ever to have been a fuller) who carried out this task.[1124]

Another fuller distinguished himself during an argument with a heretic — probably a Judaeo-Christian — who had asked R. Ishmael ben Jose to

---

1115 *T.B. Kid.* 82b.
1116 Cf., e.g., *M. Ket.* V, 5; *T. Nid.* VI, 12; *T.Y. Ned.* V, 1, 39b; *T.Y. B.B.* I, 7, 13a; *T.Y. Sanh.* X, 2, 29b; *T.B. B.B.* 57b; *Mak.* 24a.
1117 *T.B. Suk.* 28a; *B.B.* 134a; cf., Krauss, *Talm. Arch.* I, p. 153.
1118 Cf. Speck, *Handelsgeschichte des Altertums* 3, 2, 245.
1119 Cf. Krauss, ibid.
1120 Josephus, *Bell.* V, 4, 2 (147).
1121 Cf., Krauss, *op. cit.*, p. 571, n. 325 for a different explanation.
1122 *T.Y. B.K.* X, 11, 7c; *T.* ibid. XI, 14.
1123 *T.B. Ber.* 28a; *T.Y. Ber.* IV, I, 7d; *T.Y. Taan.* IV, 1, 67d.
1124 *T.Y. Ber.* ibid.; *T.Y. Taan.* ibid.

explain a difficult biblical passage. The unnamed fuller asked for permission to answer, and his rational explanation, which was based on comparative scriptural idioms, would probably meet with approval among modern commentators.[1125]

But it was above all at the semi-royal household of R. Judah the Patriarch that learned fullers, or plain launderers, who had nevertheless picked up a good deal of knowledge were to be found. This is not surprising when it is borne in mind that even one of R. Judah's maidservants had a great reputation for learning.[1126] One of the fullers, who was apparently working at R. Judah's household, once helped the Patriarch to recall the legal-religious material he had forgotten during a serious illness. The most interesting aspect of this incident is the fact that R. Judah had never taught this material to anyone, but had apparently often repeated it aloud to himself. The fuller had overheard it; evidently understood it; memorized it; and was able to recall it when the Patriarch himself could do so no longer.[1127]

It may have been the same fuller or a colleague of his who came to a tragic end at the time of R. Judah the Patriarch's death. The mourning was so intense that people thought they heard the echo of a heavenly voice announcing that everybody who had been present at the time of his death — or, according to another version, who had participated in the funeral mourning rites — was assured of life in the world-to-come, except for one fuller who used to pay daily visits to the Patriarch, but had failed to appear on that day. The fuller, we are told, was so upset about this that he threw himself to his death from the top of a roof; whereupon a heavenly voice duly included him among those assured of eternal salvation.[1128]

While such legends must be taken with a grain of salt — the fuller's suicide would have been contrary to Jewish law and tradition and would hardly have earned him a share in the future bliss — yet the tale is not without historical value. It demonstrates close relations between the Patriarch and an ordinary fuller who frequently visited him; probably learned a great deal from him; and may indeed have committed suicide as a result of the overwhelming shock at his revered teacher's decease.

While some fullers might be learned men, others could be ruffians capable of criminal acts. In the Christian tradition, James the Just was

1125 *T.B. Sanh.* 38b.
1126 *T.B. Erub.* 53b; *R.H.* 26b; *Meg.* 18a; *T.Y. Meg.* II, 2, 73a.
1127 *T.B. Ned.* 41a.
1128 *T.B. Ket.* 103b; *T.Y. Ket.* XII, 3, 35a; *T.Y. Kil.* IX, 4, 32b; *Eccl. R.* 7, 12; 9, 10, 3.

murdered by a fuller.[1129] Of course, such an isolated instance could hardly be regarded as general evidence; but it reinforces the impression that the fuller's trade was a rough one, and that its practitioners were not all gentle characters.

The skilled fuller was more than a mere washerman. His function was not merely to wash garments, but also to tread, beat, scour, stretch, scrape, brush, press and trim, i.e., cut away loose threads.[1130] He used a specially constructed pit into which the laundry was placed. The pit was then filled with warm water, and various lyes or detergents were added which, hopefully, dissolved stains, dirt, etc.[1131] However, to make sure that the cleaning was really thorough, the fuller would tread the garment with his bare feet — presumably like the treading of grapes to make wine — while the wash was in the warm water-filled pit.[1132] In this manner the entire weight of the fuller was used to scrape out any stains which the water would not otherwise cleanse thoroughly. With such rough treatment, it is a miracle that any garments survived the laundry at all. Indeed, the very name given to the fuller in Hebrew (*Koves*, i.e., one who presses) and Aramaic (*Katzra*, one who shortens, i.e., shrinks) indicate that the treatment accorded by him to the laundry was none too gentle.[1133] However, since garments were manufactured by hand, and were designed to last a long time — most people could not afford to buy new garments at frequent intervals — the greater part of the laundry survived, perhaps somewhat shrunken, but still usable for some considerable time.

Another factor that probably saved clothes from too rapid shrinking and disintegration was the relatively infrequent laundering to which they were subjected. True, washing one's garments was considered more important than washing the body;[1134] but hygienic standards were inevitably lower than in modern times, and it would seem that most garments were worn for an entire week and then washed — usually on Thursday in honor of the Sabbath when clean garments were considered essential.[1135] The same held true also for festivals;[1136] and on the eve of

1129 Eusebius, quoting Hegesippus, *Hist. Eccl.* II, 23.
1130 Krauss, *op. cit.*, pp. 154, 571ff.; 580.
1131 Ibid. pp. 154ff.; 571f., n. 333, where the sources are cited in great detail.
1132 Krauss, *op. cit.*, pp. 153; 571, n. 330.
1133 Cf., *T.B. Taan.* 29b, and Rashi *ad loc.*, s.v. צרי.
1134 *T.Y. Ned.* XI, 1, 42c; *T.Y. Sheviith* VIII, 5, 38b.
1135 *Mekil.* on Exod. 20:11–12, edit. Friedmann, 70a; M. Taan. II, 7; Gen. R. 2, 2; Deut. R. 3, 1.
1136 *Mekil.* on Exod. 12:16, edit. Friedmann 9a; edit. Horovitz-Rabin, p. 30; *Sifra*, edit. Weiss, 102a; *Sifre* on *Num.* 28:18, No. 147, edit. Friedmann, 54b; edit. Horovitz, p. 194; *T.B. Shab.* 119a.

the Passover, fullers (as well as ordinary launderers), tailors, barbers and, according to one opinion, cobblers were permitted to work until noontime, because their services were badly needed by pilgrims many of whom would come from distant countries. Other craftsmen were not permitted to work on Passover eve or, in many cases, during the intermediate days of the festival; but fullers and the other tradesmen mentioned above who were performing vital services that could not be postponed were allowed to work during the intermediate days of Passover and Succot.[1137] On the other hand, during the week preceding the fast of the 9th of Ab, fullers were usually idle, especially if they were employed by scholars and pious people who would not have their garments washed during the period of mourning.[1138]

While fullers might be rough with the garments entrusted to them, they took good care not to mix them up, and the same procedure, incidentally, was also followed by weavers who did bespoke or repair work.[1139] Garments torn in the course of washing, cleaning, treading, stretching, etc., had to be repaired, and usually patches were sewn on. Great care had to be taken to make sure that the patch was not made of new cloth. As two parallel New Testament passages point out, "no one puts a piece of unshrunk cloth on an old garment, for the patch tears away from the garment, and a worse tear is made".[1140] According to another version, "no one tears a piece from a new garment and puts it upon an old garment; if he does, he will tear the new, and the piece from the new will not match the old".[1141]

Such parables indicate that clothing repair problems caused in the main by rough handling during washing and cleaning were of some importance in the life of the people. Not everybody, however, could afford the expense of professional laundering and the inevitable repair costs that would follow. In most households, accordingly, women would do the family wash themselves, for the most part in the courtyard, which, if it was owned by two or more partners, had to be available for washing the laundry. While joint owners could stop one another from using the courtyard for any kind of work, they could not stop women from doing their laundry there, "since it is not fitting that the daughters of Israel should expose themselves to the public gaze (lit., to be disgraced) while

1137 *M. Pes.* IV, 6; *T.* ibid. II (III), 18.
1138 *T.B. Taan.* 29b.
1139 *M. Kil.* IX, 10.
1140 *Matt.* 9:16; *Mark* 2:21.
1141 *Luke* 5:36.

washing clothes".[1142] The "respect due to the daughters of Israel" was in the Puritan society of ancient Palestine and Babylonia a major consideration, and it was felt necessary to warn men *not* to watch women who had to do their laundering outside their homes or courtyards (e.g., at a river or a well). In fact, any man who could go on a different road and deliberately failed to do so in order to have an opportunity to look at women who were busily washing their garments was described as "wicked".[1143]

There are some indications that the number of Jewish launderers was inadequate to meet the needs of the population, so that it became necessary to use the services of Gentile launderers or fullers. It would seem that even in Jerusalem there were pagan fullers in the market of the Upper City;[1144] but the passage in question is doubtful and the reference may be to Roman soldiers stationed in the area.[1145] By the first century C.E., however, pagan launderers were definitely in business in Jewish Palestine,[1146] and even the Patriarch, Rabban Gamaliel II, and his household used the services of non-Jewish launderers.[1147]

Despite the somewhat lowly occupation of the fuller or launderer, whether male or female, the cleaning of garments was not only considered necessary and meritorious, but also served as material for parables of moral-religious significance:

"Just as when a garment becomes soiled, it can be made white again, so can Israel return unto God after they have sinned".[1148] In a similar mood, it was said that the sacrificial lambs offered in the Temple "press down" and "wash out" the sins of Israel.[1149]

Finally, the fact that during the rainy season it was difficult to dry the laundered garments in the open, was utilized by a preacher to point out the kindness of God in His ordering of Nature:

"In the ordinary way when a man washes his cloak during the rainy season, how much trouble he must go through before he can dry it! Yet, people sleep in their beds and the Holy One, blessed be He, brings out a little wind and dries the earth".[1150]

1142 *T.B. B.B.* 57b; *T.Y. Ned.* V, 1, 39a; *T.Y. B.B.* I, 7, 13a.
1143 *T.B. B.B.* 57b.
1144 *T.Y. Shek.* VIII, 1, 51a.
1145 Cf. Krauss, *op. cit.*, I, 571, n. 328.
1146 *M. Shab.* I, 8.
1147 Ibid. I, 9.
1148 *Exod. R.* 23, 10.
1149 *Pesik, R.K.* 6, edit. Buber, p. 61b.
1150 *Lev. R.* 28, 2.

16. Transport Workers — Ass-Drivers and Camel-Drivers

Occupations in which fraudulent practices or any kind of dishonesty were frequent were frowned upon by the rabbis, who advised that such trades should be avoided:

"One should not teach his son to be an ass-driver, camel-driver, wagoner (or, according to another reading, potter), sailor,[1151] shepherd or storekeeper, for their trade is that of robbers".[1152] According to the commentaries, the first four, being constantly on the move and sleeping away from home, tended to be careless about other people's property. For example, when they were sent by their employers on long journeys, they would take timber and fruit from private vineyards. Furthermore, when hired by people, they did not keep to the arrangements agreed upon which presumably means that they would either fail to carry out their side of the bargain or else they would end up charging more than was originally stipulated.

On the other hand, it must be borne in mind that these occupations were often extremely hazardous, unpleasant, and physically exerting. Sailors were exposed to the perils of the sea as well as to assaults by pirates. The drivers had to brave mountains and deserts, not to mention inadequate roads, and they were also exposed to attacks by highwaymen. To safeguard their interests, it became necessary to establish drivers' guilds which organized armed caravans to insure the safety of the drivers and of the goods shipped by them.[1153]

The loads carried by donkeys, mules and camels and consisting of grain, wine, oil as well as a variety of other goods were sometimes quite heavy, so that loading and unloading could be a hard task requiring a good deal of physical strength.[1154]

Most of the international and inter-urban trade of the ancient world depended on the services of ass-drivers, muleteers and camel-drivers who would often hire out their animals to merchants to transport their goods. Usually, the owners, who were familiar with roads and traveling-

---

1151 The reading of the Mishnah editions — *Sappar* (barber) is probably an error for *Sappan* (sailor).
1152 *T.B. Kid.*, 82a; *M. Kid.* IV, 14.
1153 Krauss, *op. cit.*, II, 334, 677, notes 162 ff.
1154 Cf. *M. Zab.* III, 2; *Tos. B.M.* VII, 10 f.; Krauss, *op. cit.*, II, 333, 676, n. 154.

conditions, would be hired along with the animals.[1155] Galilean drivers would often go to the Phoenician ports of Tyre and Sidon which they supplied with grain, oil, honey and balsam from Palestine.[1156] There were indeed cities and provinces which were totally dependent on grain transported by ass-drivers, and grain-prices would accordingly be subject to daily fluctuations.[1157]

Apparently ass-drivers were also employed for pilgrimages to Jerusalem, and, possibly, other holy places.[1158] Nevertheless, because of the relatively shorter distances normally traversed by them, they were expected to visit their wives at least once a week. The wives of camel-drivers, on the other hand, whose journeys across the desert would take considerably longer, had to be satisfied with one visit every thirty days. Still, they were lucky compared to sailors' wives who often did not see their husbands for as long as six months at a stretch.[1159] Although it was more profitable to be a camel-driver, an ass-driver's wife could legally prevent her husband from changing his occupation to one which would deprive her of his company for much longer periods. As a popular proverb put it, "a woman prefers one *kab* (a measure of grain, i.e., a scanty livelihood) with sexual indulgence to ten *kab* (i.e., wealth) with abstinence".[1160]

The bad reputation of camel-drivers and ass-drivers was also due to the nature of their trade which involved prolonged riding on their animals. The friction on the male organ was apt to engender heat resulting in an emission of semen. Although this could be regarded as involuntary and accidental, the prolonged absence from their wives rendered them suspect of deliberately practicing masturbation while riding. Such acts were sharply frowned upon by some rabbis who accordingly declared that "all camel-drivers are wicked", though "among the ass-drivers some are wicked and others righteous" depending on the manner of riding.[1161] Others, however, took the opposite view, declaring

---

1155 Krauss, *op. cit.*, II, 333, 677, notes 157 and 158; cf. especially *T.B. Men.* 85b.
1156 Cf. I Kings 5:25; Ezek. 27:17; *Acts* 12:20; *Tos. Demai* I, 10; Krauss, *op. cit.*, II, 335.
1157 Cf. *Gen. R.* 8, 2.
1158 Cf. *T.Y. Ber.* IX, 3, 13d.
1159 *M. Ket.* V, 6.
1160 *T.B. Ket.* 62b.
1161 *T.B. Nid.* 14a.

that "most ass-drivers are wicked" (according to Rashi, "because they are robbers"), while "most of the camel-drivers are worthy men".[1162] The reason given for this opposing viewpoint is that the immense dangers lurking in the desert[1163] where camel-drivers have to make their way cause them to fear for their lives, so that "they break their heart before God".[1164] Camel-drivers as well as others who had to travel frequently through the desert were indeed pitied, so much so that it was said that their lives were not worth living. Because of their prolonged absence from home, the fidelity of their wives was doubted, and a shadow was cast on the legitimacy of their children.[1165]

Ass-drivers occasionally showed little respect to scholars. Hillel, who flourished shortly before the beginning of the Common Era and was recognized as the greatest sage of his time, was once approached by an ass-driver:

"Rabbi", he said, "See how superior we ass-drivers are as compared to you scholars; for you have to trouble yourselves walking all this long way from Babylonia (Hillel was a Babylonian by birth) to Jerusalem. But I go out from the door of my house (i.e., riding on my donkey) and arrive at the gate of Jerusalem in time to lodge there overnight". For the ass-driver his donkey was clearly a status-symbol, on which he prided himself, especially when talking to poverty-stricken pedestrians. Hillel, however, gave the ignorant man a sensible, dignified answer. Asking him how much he charged for hiring out his donkey to carry a load to various towns, the ass-driver explained that the charge depended on the distance involved, the longer the distance the greater the cost. Hillel thereupon retorted, "Surely the divine reward for wearing out my feet going to Jerusalem should be no less than the charge for the feet of your animal!"[1166]

1162 *T.B. Kid.* 82a.
1163 Cf., e.g., *Tos. B.M.* VII, 13; *T.B. Erub.* 55b; *Der. Er. Z.* 10, 2.
1164 *Rashi* on *T.B. Kid.* 82a.
1165 *T.B. Erub.* 55b *et al.*
1166 *Aboth R.N.* Vers. II, ch. 27, edit. Schechter, pp. 55f. Cf. *T.B. Hag.* 9b, where we learn that Hillel was familiar with the ass-drivers' market (presumably in Jerusalem) and knew the precise charges for given distances. Thus, one had to pay one *zuz* (= one denarius) for the ass-driver's services for a journey of ten parasangs (=63 kilometers); but for eleven parasangs the cost doubled to two *zuz*; cf. F.M. Heichelheim, *op. cit.*, p. 210.

That rabbis and ass-drivers did not always see eye to eye is illustrated by the following story:

Some ass-drivers came to the house of R. Simeon (2nd cent. C.E.) where they stayed while waiting to buy grain in town. His wife was baking small loaves or rolls, and their son, Eleazar, was sitting by the baking-oven. Endowed as he was with an enormous appetite, he swallowed one freshly baked roll after another, leaving none for the ass-drivers who had apparently hoped to be offered some. Annoyed with the voracious young fellow, they said, "For shame! An evil snake is lodged in the belly of this boy. It appears that he will bring famine upon the world". Eleazar felt offended, and when they left to make their purchases, he took their donkeys, and brought them up to the roof. When the ass-drivers returned, they could not find their donkeys. Eventually, they discovered them on the roof, but they had no idea how to bring them down. When they complained to Eleazar's father, R. Simeon rebuked them severely, and completely took the side of his son:

"Why were you so grudging and ill-natured towards him? Did he eat what was yours? Or do *you* have to provide his food? Did not He that created him provide food for him? All the same, go and tell him in my name that he should bring the asses down to you". Eleazar thereupon kindly consented to bring down the asses from the roof.[1167]

It was because of the supreme importance of their animals to ass-drivers, muleteers and camel-drivers that the conditions of hiring such animals were carefully regulated, with a view to safeguarding the health of the animals and the interests of their owners. Overloading of the animals was forbidden — as was cruelty to animals generally — and other regulations were enacted to cover various business contingencies. Above all, ass-driver guilds as well as mariners' guilds established a remarkable insurance system, whereby losses caused by highwaymen, pirates, tempests and other unavoidable causes were to be made good by the members of the guilds.[1168] The guilds also enabled their members to have special markets or market-sections allocated to them, so that they could easily be found when required for hire. Thus, we hear of a mule-drivers' market,[1169] and there were almost certainly special market areas

---

1167 *Gen. R.* 5, 14, 3; *Pesik. R. K.* X, edit. Buber, pp. 90bf.
1168 *T.B. B.K.* 116b; Krauss, *op. cit.*, II, 333f.; Delitzsch, *op. cit.*, p. 37.
1169 *T.B. Hag.* 9b.

for ass-drivers and camel-drivers. The guilds seem to have regulated working conditions in great detail, so that we are remarkably well informed on the wage and hire system prevailing in certain areas.[1170]

To many drivers their animals became as dear as the personalized car to the modern motorist. In reference to Exodus 17:3 (where we meet with special concern for cattle), it was said that the ancient Israelites had made their animals equal to themselves in importance, saying, "A man's beast is as his life. If a man travels on the road and has not his beast with him he suffers".[1171]

17. Herdsmen and Shepherds

Whatever the faults of drivers, it was the shepherds and "cowboys" who were often regarded with far more jaundiced eyes, and some people seem to have disliked them intensely. They were frequently guilty of allowing the animals entrusted to their care to graze in privately owned fields, thus robbing people and damaging their crops. That this was a real problem causing a great deal of anxiety and ill-will is indicated in the Midrashic stories concerning Abraham and Lot. Accordingly, Abraham's herds used to be muzzled while moving from one pasture area to another so as to prevent them from grazing in the fields of others. Lot's herdsmen, on the other hand, did not bother to muzzle their animals — hence the quarrel between Abraham's honest and Lot's dishonest herdsmen.[1172]

According to the Midrash,[1173] Abraham's camels were distinguishable wherever they went because they, too, were muzzled to prevent any damage to the property of others. Likewise, Moses and David had led their sheep into the wilderness[1174] in order to keep them from despoiling private fields.[1175] There is no doubt that these didactic stories were designed to serve as relevant instruction relating to current problems.

1170 Ibid.; *Aboth R.N. ad loc.*
1171 *Mekil.* on Exod. 17:3, edit. Friedmann 52a; edit. Lauterbach II, 130; edit. Horovitz-Rabin, p. 174.
1172 *Gen. R.* 41, 5; cf. Gen. 13:7.
1173 *Gen. R.* 59, 11.
1174 Cf. Exod. 3:1, I Sam. 17:28.
1175 *Exod. R.* 2, 3.

It was probably because of the perennial friction caused by careless herdsmen and shepherds who permitted or even encouraged their animals to destroy or at least damage the crops produced by hard-working farmers that the latter assumed an attitude of hostility and contempt towards the former. Even in biblical times, the story of Cain and Abel reflects the deadly animosity of the tiller of the soil toward the "parasitical" herdsman, though at that time the ancient nomadic traditions of the Hebrews inclined them to favor the herdsman. In the Talmudic age, however, the shepherd, whose function in the economy of Palestine was becoming, as we have seen, increasingly harmful, was extremely despised: "No craft in the world is held in greater contempt than that of the shepherd".[1176] The author of this statement found it difficult to understand how David could have said, "The Lord is my Shepherd ..."[1177] Significantly, the Aramaic translation of this verse reads, "The Lord fed His people in the wilderness; they were not in want of anything" — thus avoiding any association between God and the despised shepherd.

It was probably because of the low esteem in which herdsmen were held that Jacob's "dwelling in tents",[1178] which clearly implies that he was a shepherd, was homiletically rendered by the Aramaic translations: "who ministered in the house of study." In the view of the translators it was quite unbecoming for the ancestor of the people of Israel to be depicted as a nomadic tent-dwelling shepherd.

Josephus, who was himself an aristocratic priest and very proud of his distinguished ancestry,[1179] displays unmistakable signs of contempt towards Athronges, the leader of an anti-Roman rebellion (in 4 B.C.E.) who happened to be a shepherd. According to Josephus, he was a man "distinguished neither by the dignity of his ancestors nor by the excellence of his character, nor for any great wealth, but merely a shepherd completely unknown to everybody....This man had the temerity to aspire to the kingship. ..."[1180] In reality Athronges' humble calling was perhaps politically advantageous. If King David had been a shepherd, why not the Messianic deliverer of Israel?

1176 *Midr. Pss.* 23, 2, edit. Buber, p. 198.
1177 Pss. 23:1.
1178 Gen. 25:27.
1179 *Vita* I, 1 ff.
1180 *Ant.* XVII, 10, 7, 278; cf. *Bell.* II, 4, 3, 60.

Since most shepherds and herdsmen were employed by sheep and cattle breeders to look after the animals, the herdsmen were not infrequently suspected of dishonest practices, sometimes even of outright deceit. It was therefore forbidden to buy wool, milk or kids from hired shepherds who were apt to steal from their employers.[1181] It was apparently common practice for shepherds to use some of the milk of the goats and sheep which they tended for others: "Who feeds a flock without getting some of the milk?"[1182] asked the apostle to the Gentiles. This was probably in accordance with Pharisaic *Halacha*. Like the laborer in the fields and vineyard,[1183] the shepherd was allowed to use the product of his labor for his personal sustenance, but not for trading purposes or even to take home for his family.

Some shepherds were, it seems, easily provoked to anger even by the dumb animals under their care. A proverb cited by a Galilean preacher shows up an unfaithful shepherd at his worst: "When the shepherd becomes angry with his flock he appoints a blind animal as leader".[1184] No doubt, this would happen only if the shepherd was a hired hand. He would look better after his own.

The Talmud records the case of a hired shepherd who tried to deny that any animals had been entrusted to his care, though witnesses testified that he had eaten two of them.[1185] Even shepherd priests could not be trusted when their own interests were at stake.[1186] So deep was the distrust of, and scorn for, shepherds — some of whom, we are told, deliberately drove their animals to graze in fields belonging to others — that they were classed with robbers, usurers, tax collectors, publicans and habitual gamblers as unfit to act as witnesses before a court of law.[1187]

Such contempt for the shepherd was, however, by no means universal. After all, not only had Akiba, the great rabbi of the Talmudic age, begun his meteoric career as a poor shepherd,[1188] but even the most important biblical figures — such as Jacob, Joseph and his brothers, Moses and

1181 *M. Baba Kama* X, 9; *Tos. B.K.* XI, 9.
1182 I Cor. 9:7.
1183 Deut. 23:25f.; *T.B. B.M.* 87b; *T.Y. Maas.* II, 6, 50a.
1184 *T.B. B.K.* 52a.
1185 *T.B. B.M.* 5a.
1186 *M. Bekhor.* V, 4; *Tos.* ibid. III, 19.
1187 *T.B. Sanh.* 25b; *Tos.* ibid. V, 5.
1188 *T.B. Ket.* 62b.

David — had all been shepherds. To regard the craft of the shepherd as despicable would inevitably reflect upon the ancestors and heroes of Israel. Care was, therefore, taken by the rabbis to make a clear distinction between the wicked or careless shepherd who deserved to be despised and condemned and the good, faithful shepherd who was highly praised for his devotion.

Particularly instructive are the stories related in the Midrash concerning Moses — the "faithful shepherd" *par excellence,*[1189] — and David who had been taken "from the sheepfolds ... to feed Jacob his people, and Israel his inheritance".[1190] Both these leaders of Israel were tested by God as to their worthiness of assuming the mantle of leadership. The manner in which they discharged their duties to their flocks was to show whether they were fit to rule Israel.

In the case of Moses, the Midrashic tale relates, a little kid once ran away from his flock. Moses ran after it until it reached a shady spot where there was a pool of water. There the kid stopped to drink. Moses, realizing that the kid had not been trying to run away but had merely sought to quench its thirst, humbly "apologized": "I did not know that you were running away because of thirst. You must be tired out". So he placed the kid on his shoulder and brought it back to the flock. God thereupon told Moses, "Because you are compassionate in leading the flock of a mortal (lit. flesh and blood), you will assuredly tend my flock Israel".[1191]

David, too, showed himself thoughtful and considerate in looking after his father's flocks. He used to stop the bigger sheep from going out before the smaller ones whom he would bring out first, so that they should graze upon the tender grass. The older sheep were next in line, and they would feed on ordinary, average grass. Lastly, he would lead out the young, tough sheep to eat the tougher grass. In David's case, too, God commented appropriately, "He who knows how to look after sheep, bestowing upon each the care it requires, let him come and tend my people".[1192] No doubt, this description of David's methods of feeding the sheep corresponded to the age-old practice of sensible, experienced shepherds.

1189 *Esther R.* 7, 13.
1190 Pss. 78:70–71.
1191 *Exod. R.* 2, 2.
1192 Ibid.

Shepherds who fail to protect and care for their flocks are castigated in several biblical parables which, while no doubt alluding to evil kings and leaders of Israel, also portray the practices of bad shepherds. Thus Ezekiel faithfully depicts the duties of the shepherd which the careless shepherd neglects to perform. Rhetorically, the prophet asks: "Should not shepherds feed the sheep?"[1193] But in fact, Ezekiel concludes, they are falling down on their job:

"You eat the fat, you clothe yourselves with the wool, you slaughter the fatlings; but you do not feed the sheep. The weak you have not strengthened, the sick you have not healed, the crippled you have not bound up, the strayed you have not brought back, the lost you have not sought, and with force and harshness you have ruled them. So they were scattered because there was no shepherd; and they became food for all the wild beasts".[1194]

In contrast to such bad shepherds, the good shepherd (viz. God) searches for his sheep, rescues them, feeds them on fat pasture land where they lie down to graze, and all the duties which the bad shepherds have neglected are conscientiously performed by the good shepherd.[1195]

Worthless shepherds (i.e., rulers) who "have no pity" on their flocks are also condemned in what is probably a late addition to the book of Zechariah. Some of these shepherds buy the sheep in order to kill them, while others sell them, saying, "Blessed be the Lord, I have become rich".[1196] Zechariah, too, enumerates the sins of omission perpetrated by the worthless shepherd who "does not care for the perishing (viz. sheep), or seek the wandering, or heal the maimed, or nourish the sound, but devours the flesh of the fat ones, tearing off even their hoofs".[1197] Zechariah concludes with a powerful curse upon "the worthless shepherd who deserts the flock: "May the sword smite his arm and his right eye! Let his arm be wholly withered, and his right eye utterly blinded".[1198]

In the New Testament, too, a distinction is made between the good shepherd who cares for his flock and the bad, negligent one. The good shepherd goes before the flock, "and the sheep follow him, for they know

---

1193 Ezek. 34:2.
1194 Ibid. 34:3–5.
1195 Ibid. 34:10–31.
1196 Zech. 11:5.
1197 Ibid. 11:15.
1198 Ibid. 11:16.

his voice... The good shepherd lays down his life for the sheep. He who is a hireling and not a shepherd, whose own the sheep are not, sees the wolf coming and leaves the sheep and flees; and the wolf snatches them and scatters them. He flees because he is a hireling and cares nothing for the sheep".[1199]

The first and foremost duty of the good shepherd was, of course, to protect the sheep against thieves, and especially against wolves, occasionally also against bears, lions and other wild animals.[1200] Shepherds, who lived in the open and ate simple, wholesome fare, were as a rule endowed with great physical strength[1201] as well as excellent eyesight,[1202] and thus well matched against any beast or man attacking the flock. Shepherds were also equipped with sticks and stones to defend themselves and their sheep.[1203]

Legally, shepherds who were given charge of other people's flocks were held responsible for any negligence or losses they could have prevented.[1204] Very high standards were set for any paid bailee, including herdsmen, who were expected to emulate Jacob's example in guarding his flocks round the clock, claiming that "by day the heat consumed me, and the cold by night, and my sleep fled from my eyes".[1205]

Some shepherds did indeed live up to high religious and moral standards, and the rabbis would then unstintingly accord them approval and praise. Thus, in third century Babylonia, a certain Benjamin the shepherd, who was apparently not familiar with the standard Hebrew text of the blessings would recite a brief grace over bread, in Aramaic: "Blessed be the Master of this bread". Although the rabbis were generally punctilious about the correct traditional version of the blessings, Rab had no hesitation in declaring that Benjamin had adequately performed his duty and did not need recite the usual grace.[1206]

Again, we are told of an old shepherd whose testimony induced R. Judah the Patriarch to permit a certain doubtful practice on the

---

1199 *John* 10:4, 11–13.
1200 I Sam. 17:34f.; *Mekil.* on Exod. 22:12, edit. Friedmann 93b; edit. Horovitz-Rabin, pp. 305–306; *Mishnah B.M.* VII, 9; *T.B.* ibid. 93b; *T. Yeb.* III, 4; *T.B. Yoma* 66b.
1201 Cf., e.g., I Sam. 17:34ff.; Josephus, *Ant.* XVII, 10, 7, 278; *Bell.* II, 4, 3, 60.
1202 *T.B. Bekhor.* 54b.
1203 I Sam. 17:40ff.; *T.B. B.M.* 93b.
1204 Ibid.; *Mekil. op. cit.*; *Mishnah B.K.* VI, 2; *B.M.* VII, 9; cf. also Gen. 31:39.
1205 Gen. 31:40; *T.B. B.M.* 93b.
1206 *T.B. Ber.* 40b.

Sabbath.[1207] Cowherds, in particular, whose activities were generally less harmful than those of shepherds, were accordingly more trusted — indeed so much so that on the basis of a chance conversation of three cowherds which some rabbis had overheard it was resolved to intercalate the year.[1208] Furthermore, cowherds were not only trusted as witnesses but could form an arbitration court if the two sides to a dispute agreed to submit to its decision, which was then legally binding.[1209] Some rabbis did not deem it beneath their dignity to spend a good deal of time with shepherds in order to learn matters of halachic importance. Thus, Rab spent eighteen months with a shepherd in order to learn the various types of blemishes to which animals were subject.[1210]

Perhaps the most saintly of all the shepherds mentioned in rabbinic literature was a young man who came to the High Priest Simeon the Just (c. 200 B.C.E.) because he had taken a Nazirite vow but had become defiled so that he had to bring a guilt offering to the Temple. Noticing that he had beautiful eyes and was of handsome appearance, with thick locks of curly hair, the High Priest asked him why he had made a Nazirite vow which, since it was of limited duration, would mean that he would eventually have to sacrifice his fine hair.[1211] The Nazirite gave this remarkable explanation:

"I was a shepherd in my native town. Once I went to draw water from a well and gazed at my reflection (in the water). Thereupon my evil impulse overwhelmed me, seeking to drive me from the world (through sin). So I said to my evil inclination, 'You wicked wretch! You had nothing with which to vaunt yourself except with that which is not your own, with that which is destined to be worms and maggots?!' " He vowed, accordingly, to dedicate his beautiful hair to the altar of God. Simeon the Just was so impressed by the chaste young shepherd that he kissed him on his head, saying, 'May there be many like you in Israel who do the will of God'".[1212]

Such stories, isolated though they may be, indicate nevertheless that the low esteem in which herdsmen as a class were held was far from uni-

---

1207 *Tos. Erub.* VI (V), 13.
1208 *T.B. Sanh.* 18b; *T.Y.* ibid. I, 2, 18c; *T.Y. R.H.* II, 6, 58b.
1209 *M. Sanh.* III, 2; *Tos.* ibid. V, 1.
1210 *T.B. Sanh.* 5b.
1211 Cf. Num. 6:18.
1212 *T. Naz.* IV, 7; *T.B.* ibid. 4b; *Ned.* 9b; *T.Y.* ibid. I, 1, 36d; *T.Y. Naz.* II, 6, 51c; *Sifre Num.* 22, edit. Friedmann 7a–b; edit. Horovitz, p. 26; *Num. R.* 10, 7.

versal; that much of the criticism directed against shepherds was due to the agrarian problems of Palestine which caused sheep-breeding to be regarded as a menace to the future of the Jewish community; [1213] and that individual shepherds who had anything to contribute to the religious-moral life of the country were welcomed with open arms.

18. Storekeepers

If shepherds were sometimes disliked and distrusted because of the special economic problems raised at various times by their activities, storekeepers seem to have been uniformly unpopular throughout antiquity. As already pointed out in Chapter Five, the storekeeper's reputation was none too high. According to Rashi, [1214] the storekeeper was in the habit of employing fraudulent practices, such as diluting wine with water [1215] and mixing pebbles with grain sold to customers. While Rashi was no doubt thinking of his own time — eleventh century France — it is safe to assume that such fraudulent practices were always and everywhere familiar and, indeed, commonplace.

Since storekeepers would also sell liquor, they had a vested interest in drunkenness. A Midrashic interpretation of Proverbs 23:31: "Do not look at wine when it is red, when it sparkles in the cup" pointedly states, "While he (the drinker) directs his eye at the cup (Hebrew: *kos*), the storekeeper directs his eye at the purse" (Hebrew: *kis*). [1216]

If the treatment of customers by storekeepers left much to be desired, mutual relations between shopkeepers were even more strained. In addition to the usual competition and price-cutting, which has already been referred to, there were occasional attempts to ruin one's competitor altogether (the same problem, incidentally, also existed among competing shipowners), though the means employed to this end can only be conjectured. [1217] In addition, neighbors could object to a store being opened in a residential area because the coming and going of customers represented a nuisance. [1218]

1213 Cf. Krauss, *op. cit.*, II, 142.
1214 *T.B. Kid.* 82a, s.v. חנוני.
1215 A practice not unknown even in biblical times; cf. Isaiah 1:22.
1216 *Lev. R.* 12, 1.
1217 *T.Y. B.M.* V, 5, 10b.
1218 *Mishnah B.B.* II, 3; *Tos.* ibid. I, 4.

In view of the unequivocal Talmudic opposition to storekeeping and its built-in temptations to defraud customers and ruin competitors, it may seem surprising that in medieval and modern times no religious or moral objections to this popular Jewish occupation were raised by rabbis, many of whom were themselves storeowners. This is, however, simply another illustration of the decisive character of economics in determining the Jewish *Halacha* (law). Once the Jews were deprived of alternative economic opportunities, it became impossible to follow the letter of the law. Jews had to undertake whatever could provide them with a livelihood. In the nineteenth and twentieth centuries when legal restrictions on Jewish vocational training and employment were for the most part removed, it was too late to alter fundamentally the long-established Jewish occupational structure. Only major upheavals and emigration to overseas countries, especially to Palestine, could bring about decisive changes in this area.

19. Sailors

Not everybody agreed with the unfavorable verdict rendered against the occupations discussed above. We have already seen some revised judgments on ass-drivers and camel-drivers. But the most extreme opposing view is that rendered concerning sailors who are depicted as mostly pious[1219] or even as "altogether righteous"[1220] — a verdict with which few modern observers would agree. It seems, however, that ancient Jewish mariners were in fact scrupulously Puritan in their morals, and, as we have already seen,[1220a] there were indeed sailors whose strict adherence to Sabbath observance came close to risking their own as well as their passengers' lives. Rashi attributes their piety to the perils of the sea, and he may well be right. Ancient sailors may have been reckless adventurers; but more often than not they were likely to find a watery grave in the end. Such a prospect could hardly fail to induce a contemplative, religious spirit, so that, in Rashi's words, "they would direct their hearts to their father in heaven".[1221]

1219 *T.B. Kid.* 82a.
1220 *T.B. Nid.* 14a.
1220a See *supra*, pp. 154–155.
1221 Cf. *T.B. Nid.* 14a.

There was, however, another overriding consideration in the rabbinic opposition to training one's son for life at sea. The prolonged absence from home made it difficult, if not impossible, to study Torah, which, according to the Midrash, "does not dwell among those that sail the seas. Why so? One goes away for a six months' voyage, and it takes another six months to return. One cannot therefore study Torah".[1222] Even those who were sailing on coastal routes, such as the Acco (Acre)–Jaffa line, which ideally did not involve any prolonged absence from home,[1223] were apparently unable to find the time and effort to study.[1224] For the rabbis this was a sufficient reason, quite apart from any other considerations, to avoid such a vocation.

20. Ritual Slaughterers and Butchers

Although this concludes the list of undesirable and potentially dishonest trades which should, preferably, not be taught to one's son, there are scattered references to a few other crafts which, by implication, were to be shunned. Among these was that of the ritual slaughterer who, in antiquity, often combined this function with the closely related trades of the butcher and the cook (significantly, all three are rendered *Tabbah* in Hebrew). None of these crafts was particularly pleasant, and this in itself was enough to repel sensitive people, though in ancient times such delicate feelings were conspicuous by their rarity.

More decisive was the friction which frequently marked the relations between the rabbis and the ritual slaughterers. The latter were supposed to be under strict rabbinical supervision. They were required to present, periodically, their slaughtering knives for inspection by a rabbi who, on his part, had to make sure that the knives were sharp and without any notch (which would have rendered the animals slaughtered with them ritually unfit for Jewish consumption).[1225] There were slaughterers who resented rabbinical supervision and, if they did not refuse outright to submit to inspection, they would studiously neglect to present their

1222 *Deut. R. Nitzavim* 6, edit. Liebermann, p. 119.
1223 Cf. *M. Ned.* III, 6.
1224 Ibid.
1225 *T.B. Hul.* 17b.

slaughtering knives to a rabbi. This was considered an act of gross disrespect, and in Babylonia the rabbis would retaliate by placing such a recalcitrant slaughterer under the ban, a strict form of excommunication revocable only after submission by the offender. This penalty would be imposed even if the knife was found to be perfectly satisfactory. If it was discovered that the slaughtering knife was faulty, its owner would have his license to act as ritual slaughterer revoked, and a public announcement would be made that his meat was *trefah*, i.e., unfit for consumption by Jews. As an additional penalty, the meat was to be soiled with dung so that it should be unfit for sale to Gentiles.[1226] The form of the announcement, incidentally, points to the fact that the slaughterer and butcher were for the most part identical.

In real life, the severity of the rabbinic regulations was often relaxed in favor of humanitarian considerations, as is indicated by the following story. A certain slaughterer in fourth century Babylonia failed to present his knife for inspection to Raba bar Hinena, the local rabbi, who thereupon excommunicated him, removed him from his position, and announced publicly that his meat was *trefah*. Having performed his legal-religious duty, Raba instructed two junior colleagues to look into the case, since the slaughterer was the father of young children whom he would not be able to support if he were deprived of his livelihood. One of the two rabbis examined the knife and, finding it satisfactory, he declared the slaughterer fit to follow his trade. The other rabbi thought that it might be inappropriate to overrule Raba; but he was reassured that Raba's instructions to find mitigating circumstances were in fact carried out.[1227]

Such cases notwithstanding, friction between rabbis and ritual slaughterers and/or butchers continued throughout the Middle Ages, indeed, right down to the twentieth century. The vast mass of Responsa literature testifies to innumerable cases of unsatisfactory or religiously deficient slaughterers and of *trefah* meat being sold as kosher by unscrupulous butchers. The latter were also notorious for their unrefined manners and the coarseness with which they would at times treat their customers. A characteristic story is told of a third century Palestinian butcher who refused to sell meat to R. Zera, who had just arrived from

1226 Ibid. 18a.
1227 Ibid.

Babylonia, unless he submitted to a blow with a strap. The purpose of this "practical joke" was no doubt to humiliate the "greenhorn". R. Zera, who had never experienced such treatment, complained to the local rabbis who summoned the butcher to answer for his conduct. However, when the summons was served on him, he was already dead. His sudden decease was attributed to the insulting treatment he had accorded to R. Zera. The latter, however, protested that he had borne no personal grudge against the butcher, but had been under the impression that his act was a local custom — a sort of "hazing" of newcomers.[1228]

It may have been partly because of such ruffians and partly because of the religious unreliability of greedy and unscrupulous slaughterers and butchers that the rabbis denied to the slaughterer (or butcher) a share in the world-to-come.[1229] Hyperbolically, it was said, "The worthiest of butchers is Amalek's partner".[1230]

In some places, slaughterers and butchers formed well-organized associations, presumably to protect their interests and keep the price of meat high — of course, at the expense of the consumer. If this was indeed the case, we can readily understand why the rabbis consigned slaughterers and butchers to eternal damnation. An example of such a trade association was furnished by the Galilean hill-town of Sepphoris where there was a "chief of the slaughterers" by the name of Nathan bar Shila.[1231] He must have been the president of the slaughterers' (and butchers') union.

The same source, however, also indicates that slaughterers could be quite scholarly, at least in the sphere of animal anatomy. Nathan bar Shila, for example, is reported to have testified on a question of this type before Judah the Patriarch, citing R. Nathan (mid-2nd cent. C.E.) as his authority.[1232] During the Middle Ages, too, and right down to our own time, *Shochetim* (ritual slaughterers), and occasionally also butchers who did not themselves slaughter the animals, were, and still are, scholarly men, well-versed in Talmudic learning, and often indeed functioning as qualified rabbis.

1228 *T.Y. Ber.* II, 8, 5c.
1229 *Aboth R.N.*, Vers. I, ch. 36, edit. Schechter, p. 108.
1230 *T.B. Kid.* 82a; *T.Y.* ibid. IV, 11, 66c.
1231 *T. Hul.* III, 2; *T. B. Hul.* 50b.
1232 Ibid.; ibid.

21. Hunters

If nevertheless a streak of cruelty inevitably attached itself to the slaughterer, it was almost the hallmark of the hunter. As a sport, hunting was totally alien to the spirit of Judaism, just as the cruel arena shows introduced by King Herod of Judaea were bitterly resented by the Jewish population.[1233] Even the very terms for hunt or hunter used in much of rabbinic literature were frequently the Greek equivalents rather than the Hebrew expressions used in the Bible and the Mishnah.

Hunting as a profession, while not actually outlawed, was considered wrong and strongly discouraged.[1234] Dislike of hunting is evident in the Aramaic translations of the biblical description of Nimrod's accomplishments. "He was a mighty hunter before the Lord"[1235] was no doubt meant as a compliment to Nimrod's prowess. The Aramaic translations, however, render either "He was a mighty potentate etc." — thus omitting the implied praise of hunting — or "He was a mighty and rebellious (or: faithless) man ... mighty in the hunt and rebelliousness"; or: "He was mighty in sinful hunting etc.". Thus, Nimrod's agility in hunting, clearly emphasized in the Bible, was deliberately suppressed or played down by the translators because they did not wish to dignify hunting by providing biblical support for a disliked and despised sport.

There is nothing in the story of Moses to suggest that he was a hunter. Nevertheless, the Talmud asks incredulously, almost indignantly, "Was Moses a hunter or an archer?"[1236] The form of the question is such that a decisive negative answer is clearly implied. Obviously, hunting was not in keeping with Moses' dignity, and the very idea of such a possibility is implicitly rejected.

From the point of view of the rabbis, to attend wild beast hunts was equivalent to standing "in the way of sinners".[1237] Since there were nevertheless some Jews who did show some interest in this blood sport, they were promised an alternative — a super-contest in the world-to-come:

1233 Cf. Josephus, *Ant.* XV, 8, 1, 274f.
1234 *M. Sheviith* VII, 4.
1235 Gen. 10:9.
1236 *T.B. Hul.* 60b.
1237 *T.B. A.Z.* 18b; cf. Pss. 1:1.

Behemoth and Leviathan are to be the beasts of chase of the righteous in the Time-to-Come, and whoever has not been a spectator at the hunts (or: wild beast shows) of the pagan nations in this world will be accorded the boon of seeing one in the world-to-come.[1238]

One cannot escape the impression that this fanciful description was designed as a concession to young Jews who were attracted to the ways of the Gentiles. It is, however, equally obvious that the rabbis used their imagination to impress upon the people the desirability of suppressing any evil desire for blood sports. The promise of the great fight in the world-to-come was, of course, not binding either legally or morally.

Ishmael, a negative character in both biblical and Talmudic literature, is homiletically depicted as hunting for grasshoppers which he would burn for idolatrous purposes.[1239] Thus, Ishmael's many sins are compounded by his childish hunting expeditions — a description which is more suited to the Talmudic age.

Rabbinic opposition to hunting is also evident in some of the popular proverbs cited in the Talmud. "The cunning hunter will not live long"[1240] makes no pretense of expressing much liking for the hunter. A certain malicious joy at the hunter's occasional discomfiture is at the back of some of the proverbs preserved in rabbinic literature. "O hunter, how have you become hunted!"[1241] conveys a picture of a devotee of the chase whose weapons fail him, so that he himself must run for his life, with some enraged beast hotly pursuing him. Similarly, "the archer is killed by his own arrows"[1242] somehow suggests a *schlemiel* who tries to be a hunter or a fowler but shoots in the wrong direction.

Somewhat more complimentary is a proverb stating that "the cunning (i.e., skillful) hunter has prey to roast".[1243] A parable concerning a fowler who breaks the wings of each bird as soon as he catches it to prevent it from flying away[1244] indicates rabbinic recognition, if not exactly approval, of the fowler's skillful professional methods.

1238 *Lev. R.* 13, 3.
1239 *Tos. Sot.* V, 12.
1240 *Erub. 54b.*
1241 *Gen. R.* 67, 2.
1242 *T.B. Pes.* 28a.
1243 *T.B. A.Z.* 19a; cf. *Erub.* 54b.
1244 *T.B. A.Z.* 19a.

A legendary story concerning R. Simeon bar Yohai who, as we have seen, was an uncompromising proponent of exclusive Torah study and had no use for agricultural pursuits, suggests that he raised no objections to the activities of a fowler whom he noticed laying his snare near a cave.[1245] Presumably, he considered this not unduly time-consuming, so that there was still plenty of time left for the study of the Torah.

If R. Simeon held this view, it was not shared by R. Eleazar ben Hakappar (c. 200 C.E.) who maintained that knowledge of the Torah is not to be found among fowlers.[1246] He may have had in mind the difficulty of observing the dietary laws when birds — or, for that matter, animals — were chased, injured and killed in a manner inconsistent with Jewish ritual requirements.

There were, nevertheless, pious hunters and fowlers who were not only acquainted with Jewish religious law, but even went beyond the requirements of the law. Thus, although permitted to pursue their vocation unobtrusively during the intermediate days of the festivals of Passover and Tabernacles, they would adopt a stricter rule and altogether abstain from work during the entire holiday period.[1247]

The rabbis, moreover, had no hesitation in relying on the expertise of fowlers to determine whether any given bird was ritually clean or not.[1248] The legal rights of hunters and fowlers as well as fishermen were carefully preserved, and whatever was caught in their traps, snares or nets rightfully belonged to them. For a stranger to take the prey or the catch was an act of robbery.[1249] Hunters, fowlers and fishermen were permitted to sell non-kosher animals, birds or fish which they had caught to Gentiles, although trading in "unclean" animals etc. was generally discouraged.[1250] On the other hand, it was permitted to hunt a snake either to use it as a remedy for certain skin diseases[1251] or to prevent it from biting. The latter was permitted even on the Sabbath.[1252]

Hunting must have been sufficiently popular to be included among the thirty-nine categories of work forbidden on the Sabbath;[1253] and it is

1245 *T.Y. Sheviith* IX, 1, 38d.
1246 *Deut. R.*, Nitzavim 6, edit. Liebermann, p. 119.
1247 *Mishnah M.K.* II, 5.
1248 *T.B. Hul.* 63b.
1249 *M. Git.* V, 8.   1250 *M. Sheviith* VII, 4.
1251 Cf. *T.B. Shab.* 105b.   1252 *M. Ed.* II, 5.
1253 *M. Shab.* I, 6; VII, 2; XIII, 5ff.; XIV, 1; *Tos.* ibid. XII [XIII], 2.

even listed among the relatively small number of types of work forbidden on the festivals.[1254] Even in the enumeration of a few sample trades, hunting is duly included.[1255] In an age of extreme poverty when the wolf was never far from the door, hunting and fowling, pursued as a livelihood rather than a disreputable sport, played a significant role in the economy of the country, and was, therefore, tolerated and protected by the rabbis.

22. Fishermen

No stigma whatsoever was attached to fishing, no matter what the purpose, and it was even maintained that Joshua had stipulated after the conquest of Canaan that fishing with an angle in the Lake of Tiberias must be free and unrestricted.[1256] In practice this meant that since time immemorial everyone had the right to fish in the lake and, of course, along the entire sea shore, although, theoretically, certain exclusive tribal fishing rights had to be respected.[1257] There was also complete freedom of fishing in all the streams of the Holy Land.[1258] The spreading of sails, on the other hand, was restricted since it was liable to interfere with navigation.[1259]

Fishermen were generally poor, and Tiberias, which was the center of the Galilean fishing industry,[1260] also played a prominent part in the social and political troubles of the Roman-Jewish wars.[1261] It was not by accident that the first disciples who followed Jesus' revolutionary gospel were simple Galilean fishermen. Despite good catches, vividly described in the New Testament,[1262] fishermen were poor and hence easily attracted by any movement that promised to ease their lot.

Another important fishing center was Tarichaea or Migdal Nunya (= Magdala), a few miles north of Tiberias. Both the Greek and Hebrew-

---

1254 *M. Bez.* III, 1–2; *T. Yom Tov* III, 1, 4.
1255 *T.Y. Hag.* II, 1, 77b.
1256 *T.B. B.K.* 80b–81a.
1257 *Tos. B.K.* VIII, 17–18.
1258 Ibid. VIII, 17.
1259 Ibid.; *T.B. B.K.* 81b.
1260 Cf., e.g., *Tos. B.M.* VI, 5.
1261 Cf. Josephus, *Vita* 9 (35ff.); 17 (87ff.); 54ff. (276ff.) *et al.*
1262 Cf., e.g., *Matt.* 13:47f.; cf. also Krauss, *op. cit.*, II, 145f.

Aramaic names of the place testify to its close association with the fishing industry. The fish of Tarichaea were used not only for local consumption or for sale at near-by markets, but also for export abroad. For this purpose, the fish were salted and dried.[1263] Although the town is said to have been wealthy,[1264] it was drawn into the rising against the Romans in 67 C.E.,[1265] with terrible consequences for the inhabitants.[1266] The rabbis attributed the ruin of Magdala (which was, incidentally, the home of Mary Magdalene, Jesus' faithful follower) to the prevalence of immorality in the town — a natural phenomenon in a fishing port.[1267]

Although the Lake of Galilee was by far the most important fishing area, other waters were also utilized for fishing. These included the Jordan and Mediterranean coast-line, especially in the north between Haifa and Acco.[1268] Large-size fish, which were cut up and sold in smaller sections, were imported to northern Palestine from the Red Sea port of Elath, where many Jews resided down to the time of the Arab conquest.[1269]

1263 Strabo XVI, 2, 45; Allon, op. cit., p. 101; S. Klein, Eretz Ha-Galil (Jerusalem, 1946), pp. 49, 211.
1264 T.Y. Taan. IV, 8, 69a; Lam. R. 2, 2, 4.
1265 Josephus, Bell. III, 9, 7 (445).
1266 Ibid. III, 10, 1–10 (462–542).
1267 T.Y. Taan. ibid.; Lam. R. ibid.
1268 Cf. Allon, ibid.
1269 Ibid.; M. Makshirin VI, 3; Tos. Kel. B.M. V, 7.

Chapter Seven

Vocational Training — Masters and Apprentices

1. Biblical and Hellenistic Periods

During the biblical and Hellenistic periods we hear virtually nothing about apprentices learning a trade. No doubt there were apprentices here and there; but by and large, arts and crafts were hereditary family monopolies, so that sons or sons-in-law would automatically succeed their fathers or fathers-in-law, simultaneously inheriting the jealously guarded trade secrets of the family.

2. Shepherd Apprentices

The only system of apprenticeship which undoubtedly existed since very early times was that of shepherds who taught their none-too-easy trade to boys, not necessarily members of their own family. It was customary to entrust the apprentice shepherds with the care of the flocks whenever the master had to go away. This could, however, bring about legal complications if animals were stolen or lost while the less than fully competent apprentices were in charge.[1270]

3. Roman Age

During the Roman period, the immense growth of urban centers, and the development of trade and industry, brought about a much wider distribution of crafts among the urban masses, and this, in turn, made it possible, and, indeed, necessary, to transform family-centered domestic

1270 *Mekil.* on Exod. 22:11, edit. Friedmann, 93a; edit. Horovitz-Rabin, p. 305; T.B. B.K. 56b.

crafts into general industries, open to all young males whose parents were willing to apprentice them to a craftsman. This was true not only of Palestine, but also of all the major Diaspora centers.

4. Apprenticeship Agreements

It would seem that most boys in urban centers were apprenticed to a craftsman as soon as they left school, usually at the age of thirteen,[1271] often no doubt earlier when they were still minors.[1272] The parents of the boy would negotiate terms with a master craftsman who would undertake to teach him certain skills within a given period of time. Such was the importance attributed to these negotiations that they were permitted even on the Sabbath when business talks in general were frowned upon.[1273] To apprentice a boy to learn a trade was considered a meritorious act — indeed, the fulfillment of a divine precept — which took precedence even over the sanctity of the Sabbath. In the words of the famous medieval commentator Rashi, "To teach a boy a craft is a religious precept....(It is) the learning of a trade by which to maintain oneself".[1274]

Once an agreement between the master craftsman and the father (or, in the case of orphans, the mother or guardian) of the apprentice had been concluded, it was legally binding on both parties, involving the penalty of "forfeiture", if either party broke it.[1275] Judging by what is known about similar practices in Egypt, it would seem that compensation had to be paid by the guilty party if either the master failed to instruct the boy fully in accordance with his undertaking or if the apprentice was recalled by his parents or otherwise failed to complete the specified period of service.[1276]

1271 *Gen. R.* 63, 10.
1272 *T.Y. Git.* V, 8, 47b.
1273 *T.B. Shab.* 150a; *Ket.* 5a; cf. Isaiah 58:13.
1274 Rashi on *T.B. Ket.* 5a, s.v. ללמדו אומנות.
1275 Cf. *T.Y. Git.* V, 8, 47b; *T.Y. B.B.* X, 5, 17c; S. Lieberman, *Greek in Jewish Palestine* (New York, 1942), p. 4.
1276 Lieberman, *op. cit.*

5. Unsuitable Applicants for Apprenticeship

Not every master would necessarily agree to teach his craft, even for payment. If, for example, he found the boy unsuitable for the trade in question, he might refuse to take him on. Thus, we are told in a parable of a father who wanted to have his son taught the dyer's trade. However, when the master craftsman saw that the boy had some fingers — according to another account, one finger — missing, he told the boy's father that he could not teach him a trade for which the use of all the fingers was required.[1277]

6. Duration of Apprenticeship

Apprentices would learn their trade for several years. There were, no doubt, considerable variations as between different trades, and even in the same trade the practice was not always the same. Much would depend on the thoroughness of the master and the degree of specialization on the part of the apprentice. Specialized apprenticeship seems to have been a wearisome process,[1278] involving as it did many years of learning and practice. We hear, for example, of a woman who asked a baker in Caesarea to teach his trade to her son, and was told by him that the boy would have to stay with him for five years during which time, he would teach him five hundred (!) confections with wheat. At the end of that period, the baker offered to keep the young fellow for another five years, and to teach him another five hundred wheat confection baking recipes.[1279]

Of another Caesarean woman it was told that she applied to a cook to accept her son as an apprentice. He stayed with him some four or five years, learning to make a hundred different egg dishes. Here, again, the master eventually suggested continuing the apprenticeship for another four or five years so that the boy should learn another hundred egg recipes.[1280]

1277 *Pesik. R.* 25, edit. Friedmann, p. 128a; *Midr. Pss.* VIII, 2, edit. Buber 37b.
1278 Cf. *Eccl. R.* I, 8, 2.
1279 Ibid.; *Lam. R.* 3, 17.
1280 Ibid.; ibid.

7. Relationship between Master and Apprentice

While we may discount round exaggerated figures, these stories undoubtedly reflect current practices in apprenticing, indicating an extraordinary degree of specialization attainable by hard-working apprentices who were willing to learn their chosen craft for sufficiently long periods. The young apprentice would live with his master and would be expected to do any work required of him. Like orphans raised by guardians or foster parents, an apprentice might, for instance, be asked to clear a space for a meal, to bring along a jar of water or to chop wood.[1281] If he found any article which legally belonged to the finder, he had to surrender it to his master.[1282] In return, he had to be maintained by his master and might, in addition, be paid a fair wage once he had completed his apprenticeship.[1283]

The relationship between master and apprentice was not always smooth. Sometimes, the latter would be given a sound beating — a practice considered so perfectly normal that even accidental death as a result of such blows was not legally punishable.[1284]

Traditionally, apprentices have often been exploited by their masters, and not infrequently ill-treated. Jewish apprentices were, in this respect, no exception. We hear of two brothers named Asinai and Anilai (or: Asineus and Anileus), who were apprenticed to a weaver in Babylonia around the middle of the first century C.E. They were ill-treated by their master, ran away from him, and formed an entire army of Jewish outlaws. They managed to defeat all the regular troops sent against them by the Parthians, who ruled the country. Though, eventually, they met their doom, their activities brought terror to the Parthian empire, and very disagreeable consequences for the Babylonian Jews.[1285]

Some unhappy apprentices apparently resorted to stealing from their master. A midrashic parable tells us about a potter's apprentice who stole a lump of clay from his master. When the latter detected the theft, he made the stolen clay into a vessel and hung it up before the apprentice, so that he should know that he had been caught red-handed.[1286]

1281 *Deut. R.* 3, 4.
1282 *T.Y. Git.* V, 8, 47b.
1283 *Deut. R.* 3, 4; *Yalkut* I, p. 586, par. 848; cf. *T.B. Shab.* 78a and Rashi *ad loc.*
1284 Cf. *T.B. Mak.* 8b.
1285 Josephus, *Ant.* XVIII, 9, 1 (310ff.).
1286 *Lev. R.* 23, 12.

There are many indications that the intense respect accorded to rabbis by their disciples was not shared by master-craftsmen whose apprentices all too frequently behaved disrespectfully towards their masters. Alternatively, they were on terms of all too easy familiarity which, as we know, could breed contempt. We are told, for example, that a carpenter's apprentice might enjoy the privilege of reclining on the first night of Passover in his master's presence, which was not permitted to a student in his teacher's presence.[1287]

A tragic and shocking story is told in the Talmud concerning a carpenter's apprentice who had apparently saved enough money to become independent. Once his master, finding himself short of money, applied to him for a loan. The apprentice agreed, but cunningly asked that the master should send his wife to collect the money. Suspecting nothing, the master consented. The apprentice seduced her, in accordance with his preconceived plan, and she stayed with him for three days. Her husband was worried about her failure to come home, and eventually he went to his apprentice and asked him what had happened to his wife. The apprentice pretended that he had sent her back immediately, but that he had heard that on her way home she had been sexually abused by some young men. The husband did not know what to do about his wife, and asked his apprentice for advice. Since the latter wanted her for himself, he suggested that the master should divorce her, which must have appeared quite reasonable since the strict morality of the Jews did not favor the continuance of a marriage if the slightest shadow of doubt was cast on the wife's fidelity. The master agreed to divorce his wife, but found himself unable to pay her considerable marriage settlement to which she was entitled in case of a divorce. The scheming apprentice blandly offered to lend him the money required.

No sooner had the divorce been carried through than the apprentice married his master's ex-wife himself. Having inveigled the master into getting into debt, which he had no chance to repay, the ruthless apprentice demanded his pound of flesh when the time for payment arrived. He insisted that, since the master could not pay him, he must enter his service and stay with him until he had worked off his debt. The master's tragedy was now compounded by the heartless couple who would sit at the table and eat, drink and enjoy themselves while the ex-master had to

1287 *T.B. Pes.* 108a.

stand and wait on his alienated wife and his former apprentice. The Talmudic story depicts the pathetic scene. The ex-master who had fallen into the most humiliating servitude would weep while he was pouring the wine for them, and his tears would fall into the wine cups. According to the Talmud, it was at that moment of inhuman degradation and cruelty that the divine decree for the destruction of the Temple and of Jerusalem was promulgated.[1288]

On the whole, it appears that the master, no matter how harsh he might be in other respects, faithfully carried out his side of the bargain and instructed his apprentice to the best of his ability. An example of such instruction is furnished in a parable of a changer of money and valuables who told his apprentice that while he (viz. the apprentice) could exchange coins himself, he should not handle any transactions in pearls and precious stones but consult him first to get proper advice.[1289] It might, however, happen that the master-banker himself would not be too sure and, consequently, would have to refer the matter to greater experts.[1290]

8. Refusal to Teach a Craft

i Temple Craftsmen

There were sometimes cases when highly skilled craftsmen would refuse to teach outsiders certain family secrets. Temple-craftsmen, for example, whose expertise was irreplaceable, successfully resisted all efforts to induce them to teach their trade secrets. Thus, a priestly family known as the House of Garmu enjoyed the monopoly of preparing the showbread which had to be baked once a week for display in the sanctuary.[1291] They adamantly refused to teach the finer points of their craft to outsiders. Exasperated, the rabbis who controlled the Temple Administration sent for specialists from Alexandria in Egypt to replace the uncooperative Garmu family. The Alexandrian specialists — who, it has been surmised, may have been employed at the Temple of Onias at Leonto-

---

1288 T.B. Git. 58a.
1289 Num. R. 21, 12; Tanh. Pinchas 8.
1290 Ibid.; ibid.
1291 Cf. Levit. 24:5-9; M. Shek. VI, 4; M. Men. XI, 7-8.

polis[1292] — were excellent bakers, but they did not know the art of removing the thin loaves from the oven without breaking them — which rendered them unsuitable for display in the Temple. The Alexandrians also used faulty heating methods, with the result that their bread, which was supposed to keep reasonably fresh during the week it was on display, became moldy. The rabbis, thereupon, relented and invited the House of Garmu to resume their work in the Temple. The triumphant family, well aware that they had the public at their mercy, refused to return to office. The Temple administrators had no alternative but to offer them a huge salary raise — it was in fact double — and only then did they graciously consent to end their strike.

After their restoration to office, and possibly after the destruction of the Temple in 70 C.E., they were discreetly asked why they had refused to teach their art to outsiders. They ingeniously replied that they knew (or had known) that the Temple was destined to be destroyed, and if an unworthy man were to learn the art of baking the showbread, he might then use his knowledge for idolatrous purposes.

While the family of Garmu could be ruthless in defense of their monopolistic interests, they had a strict code of honor. To avoid any suspicion that they might be misappropriating some of the flour used in preparation of the showbread, even their children would never be permitted to have fine bread in their hands.[1293]

Another priestly family, the House of Abtinas, specialized in the preparation of the incense used in the Temple. They, too, refused to teach their art to others. The rabbis who were in charge of the Temple Administration experimented once again with Alexandrian experts[1294] who could indeed compound the incense as well as the family of Abtinas. They did not know, however, how to make the smoke go up in the right direction. While the priests of the House of Abtinas knew a plant which would make the incense smoke go up straight as a stick, the smoke produced by the incense prepared by the Alexandrian experts would scatter in every direction. Since this disturbed the beauty of the incense-

1292 Cf. M. Wischnitzer, op. cit., pp. 50, 292, n. 39.
1293 Tos. Yom Hakip. II, 5; T.Y. Yoma III, 9, 41a; T.Y. Shek. V, 2, 48d–49a; T.B. Yoma 38a.
1294 The reason for summoning Alexandrian experts may have been the same as in the case of the showbread bakers — namely previous experience at the Temple of Onias; see supra, n. 1292.

burning ceremony, the Temple Administrators had no alternative but to recall the Abtinas family. They, too, held out for higher wages, and only when their salary was doubled did they return to duty.

Like the House of Garmu, the Abtinas family, too, justified their refusal to teach their craft to strangers on the ground that it might be abused by unworthy men for serving idols. They also had their code of honor, and their brides would never go out perfumed so as to avoid suspicion of misappropriating spices belonging to the Temple.

Even after the destruction of the Temple, the survivors of the House of Abtinas continued to guard jealously the secret of their craft, refusing to initiate any outsider, however distinguished. During the second century C.E., however, the family seems to have died out, and one of the last survivors reluctantly consented to give R. Johanan ben Nuri a scroll containing the prescriptions for preparing incense. But before surrendering the scroll, the old man asked R. Johanan to take great care not to let the long-cherished secret fall into the wrong hands.[1295]

Less useful but more intricate was the accomplishment of a certain scribe, Ben Kamtzar, who was apparently also employed at the Temple. He had deft fingers and was able to hold four pens between his fingers and write four letters simultaneously. He, too, refused to teach his technique to others — possibly because he felt that one must be born with such a talent, which could not really be taught or communicated to others. But for one reason or another, he failed to explain his refusal to teach his skill, and was, therefore, condemned by the rabbis in far stronger terms than the other Temple artists who had at least produced some plausible excuse for their conduct.[1296]

ii Physicians

Such secretiveness was strongly deplored by the rabbis who considered it incumbent on anyone endowed with skill to teach it to others. Sometimes students or apprentices would beg the master to change his mind and teach them the secret of his art or craft. A Midrashic parable tells of a physician who had a pupil whom he taught methods of curing all sorts of diseases except one. The student doctor then said to his master, "You

1295 *Tos. Yom Hakip.* II, 6; *T.Y. Yoma* III, 9, 41a; *T.Y. Shek.* V, 2, 49a; *T.B. Yoma* 38a.
1296 *M. Yoma* III, 11; *Tos. Yom Hakip.* III, 8; *T.Y. Yoma* III, 9, 41b; *T.B. Yoma* 38b.

have revealed to me all the curative treatments in the world except for the cure of such and such a disease. I pray you, reveal it to me".[1297] We are not told whether the master physician acceded to his pupil's request.

Another parable of a student doctor who is about to become an independent physician is told in the Midrash. The student's sister is suffering from some disease, and he brings her to his teacher for treatment. However, he feels confident enough to say, "Master, you have already taught me the complete list of remedies. If you will heal her, good and well; but if not, I will cure her myself".[1298]

As already pointed out in Chapter Six,[1299] there are strong indications that the medical profession was hereditary. A physician's son would therefore become his father's apprentice until he had mastered his father's medical skill. However, not every physician's son wanted to follow in his father's footsteps, especially if the father was no longer alive and able to put pressure on his son to stick to the family profession.

A Midrashic parable tells us about a physician's widow who vainly tried to get her orphaned son apprenticed to a master craftsman or, alternatively, to get him to study at a synagogue school. He ran away from both craftsmen and schoolteachers. Eventually, his mother brought him to a colleague of her late husband and begged him to teach the boy his father's profession. The physician agreed to do so. He was unaware of what he was letting himself into. Sure enough, whenever the apprentice "doctor" was told to treat a patient and scrape away the top of an abscess (or of an ulcerous growth), he would throw the physician's instructions to the wind and scrape away the bottom of the abscess. When asked to scrape away the bottom, he would do the opposite. At long last the physician lost his patience and brought the wayward boy back to his mother. "Take him", he told her angrily, "and bury him (i.e., give up all hope of reforming him); for he has abandoned (lit., transgressed) his father's profession".[1300]

Significantly, it was an accepted rabbinic view that one should not change his occupation or that of his ancestors,[1301] presumably because of

1297 *Midr. Pss.* 25, 6, edit. Buber 106a.
1298 *Deut. R.* 6, 13.
1299 See *supra*, p. 200.
1300 *Midrash Samuel* on Sam. 8:19, edit. Buber, pp. 84f. (42b–43a); *Yalkut* II, 720, par. 106. S. Krauss (*Talm. Arch.*, vol. II, p. 255) and M. Wischnitzer (*op. cit.*, pp. 35f.) give different — and erroneous — interpretations of this Midrashic parable.
1301 *T.B. Arakhin* 16b. See *supra*, p. 31, on Ben Sira's similar view.

the economic disruption that might ensue if young people did not continue in their fathers' trades and crafts. The same problem might also result if people changed occupations in quest of a successful career in a different direction. For example, exchanging hard agricultural labor for a relatively easier urban job — if carried out on a large scale — could have had serious consequences resulting in grain shortages and higher food prices. It was thus the social factor rather than the individual's personal advantage that was the decisive consideration in rabbinic thinking.

In line with this social ideology, it was maintained that the Almighty had made everyone's trade seem beautiful in his own eyes;[1302] for only pride in, and satisfaction with, one's calling could ensure continuity and economic stability.

1302 *T.B. Ber.* 43b.

Bibliography

a. Primary Sources

Biblia Hebraica, edit. R. Kittel and P. Kahle, 3rd edit., Stuttgart, 1937; 7th edit., Leipzig, Halle, Oxford, 1951. Reprinted Stuttgart, 1973.

The Holy Bible. Revised Standard Version, New York, Glasgow, London, Toronto, Sydney, Auckland, 1973.

The Torah — The Five Books of Moses, J.P.S.A., Philadelphia, 1962.

The Prophets — Nevi'im, J.P.S.A., Philadelphia, 1978.

The Writings — Kethubim, J.P.S.A., Philadelphia, 1982.

The Apocrypha and Pseudepigrapha, edit. and transl. R.H. Charles,
Vol. I Apocrypha, Oxford, 1913. Reprinted Oxford, 1963.
Vol. II Pseudepigrapha, Oxford, 1913. Reprinted Oxford, 1963, 1964, 1966.

Ha-Sefarim ha-Hitzonim, edit. A. Kahana, two volumes, Tel-Aviv, 1959.

Sefer Ben-Sira ha-Shalem, edit. M.Z. Segal, 2nd edit., Jerusalem, 1972.

Philo, Works, Loeb Classical Library, 10 Vols., London and Cambridge, Mass., 1929–1962.

Josephus, Works, Loeb Classical Library, 9 Vols., London and Cambridge, Mass., 1926–1965.

Shisha Sidrei Mishnah, with Commentary by C. Albeck, Jerusalem and Tel-Aviv, 1958.

Mekhilta, edit. M. Friedmann, Vienna, 1870. Reprinted New York, 1947;
idem, edit. J.Z. Lauterbach, 3 Vols., Philadelphia, 1933;
idem, edit. H.S. Horovitz–I.A. Rabin, 2nd edit., Jerusalem, 1970.

Sifra, edit. H. Weiss, Vienna, 1862. Reprinted New York, 1946;
idem, edit. L. Finkelstein, 5 Vols., Jerusalem and New York, 1983–1991.

Sifrei, edit. M. Friedmann, Vienna, 1864. Reprinted New York, 1948;
idem, on Numbers, edit. H.S. Horovitz, Leipzig, 1917;
idem, on Deuteronomy, edit. H.S. Horovitz–L. Finkelstein, Berlin, 1939. Reprinted New York, 1969.

Tosefta, edit. M.S. Zuckermandel, 2nd edit. with Supplement by S. Lieberman, Jerusalem, 1975.

Tosefta ve-Tosefta ki-fshutah, edit. S. Lieberman, 10 Volumes, New York, 1955–1988.

Aboth de-Rabbi Nathan, edit. S. Schechter, corrected edition, New York, 1967.

Talmud Yerushalmi, Krotoschin, 1866;
idem, with Commentaries, 5 Vols., Montreal, New York, Tel-Aviv, 1949.

Talmud Bavli, Shulsinger edition, 20 Vols., New York, 1948.

Der babylonische Talmud, L. Goldschmidt edition, Text, German translation and notes, 9 Vols., Berlin, Leipzig, The Hague, 1897–1935.

The Babylonian Talmud, edit. I. Epstein, English translation and notes, The Soncino Press, 35 Vols., London, 1935–1952.

Midrash Rabbah on the Pentateuch, with Commentary by M.A. Mirkin, 11 Vols., Tel-Aviv, 1977–1982.

Midrash Rabbah on the Pentateuch and the Five Megillot, Vilna, 1909–1911.

Midrasch Bereschit Rabba (on Genesis), edit. J. Theodor–C. Albeck, 2 Vols., Berlin, 1912–1927.

Midrash Wayyikra Rabbah (on Leviticus), edit. M. Margulies, 5 Vols., Jerusalem, 1953–1960.

Midrash Debarim Rabbah (on Deuteronomy), edit. S. Lieberman, Jerusalem, 1940.

Midrash Tannaim (on Deuteronomy), edit. D.Z. Hoffman, Berlin, 1908–1909.

Midrash Tanhuma on the Pentateuch, with Commentary by C. Zundel, New York, 1924. Reprinted Jerusalem, 1962.

Midrash Tanhuma, edit. S. Buber, 2nd edit., 2 Vols., New York, 1946.

Pesikta de-Rab Kahana, edit. S. Buber, Lyck, 1868. Reprinted New York, 1949.

Pesikta Rabbati, edit. M. Friedmann, Vienna, 1880.

Midrash Zuta (on Canticles, Ruth, Lamentations and Ecclesiastes), edit. S. Buber, Berlin, 1894.

Midrash Tehillim (= Shoher Tov) on Psalms, edit. S. Buber, Vilna, 1891. Reprinted New York, 1947.

Midrash Shemuel (on Samuel), edit. S. Buber, Krakau, 1893. Reprinted Jerusalem, 1965.

Midrash Mishle (on Proverbs), edit. S. Buber, Vilna, 1893. Reprinted Jerusalem, 1965.

Seder Eliahu Rabba and Seder Eliahu Zuta (Tanna d'be Eliahu), edit. M. Friedmann, Wien, 1904. Reprinted Jerusalem, 1960.

b. *Modern Literature*

Albright, W.F., *From the Stone Age to Christianity*, Baltimore, 1940;
idem, *Archaeology and the Religion of Israel*, Baltimore, 1942;
idem, *The Archaeology of Palestine*, London, 1949. Revised and reprinted, 1960.

Allon, G., *Toledot ha-Yehudim be-Eretz Yisrael bi-Tekufat ha-Mishnah ve-ha-Talmud*, 2 Vols., Tel-Aviv, 1953–1956;
idem, Mehkarim be-Toledot Yisrael bi-Ymei Bayit Sheni u-vi-Tekufat ha-Mishnah ve-ha-Talmud, 2 Vols., Tel-Aviv, 1957–1958.

Avigad, N., "Baruch the Scribe and Jerahmeel the King's Son", in *Israel Exploration Journal*, Vol. 28 (1978), pp. 52 ff.

Avi-Yonah, M., *Bi-Ymei Roma u-Bizantion*, 4th edit., Jerusalem, 1970.

Bacher, W., *Die Agada der Tannaiten*, 2nd edit., 2 Vols., Straßburg, 1903;
idem, Die Agada der palästinensischen Amoräer, 3 Vols., Straßburg, 1892-1899.

Baron, S.W., *The Jewish Community*, Vol. I, Philadelphia, 1942;
idem, A Social and Religious History of the Jews, 2nd edit., Vols. I and II, Philadelphia, 1952.

Beer, M., *Amora'ey Bavel — Perakim be-Hayyey ha-Kalkalah*, Ramat-Gan, 1975.

Büchler, A., *Der galiläische Am-ha-Areṣ des zweiten Jahrhunderts*, Wien, 1906;
idem, The Political and Social Leaders of the Jewish Community of Sepphoris in the Second and Third Centuries, London, 1909;
idem, The Economic Conditions of Judaea after the Destruction of the Second Temple, London, 1912.

Delitzsch, F., *Jüdisches Handwerkerleben zur Zeit Jesu*, 3rd edit., Erlangen, 1879.

Dubnow, S., *Weltgeschichte des jüdischen Volkes*, Vols. I-III, Berlin, 1925-1926.

Encyclopaedia Biblica (Heb. *Entsiklopedia Mikrait*), 8 Vols., Jerusalem, 1965-1982.

Encyclopaedia Judaica, 16 Vols., Jerusalem, 1971.

Farmer, W.R., *Maccabees, Zealots, and Josephus*, New York, 1956.

Feldman, W.M., "Notes on the various remedies recommended in Folios 68b-70b(Tractate Gittin)". Appendix to Soncino edition of *The Babylonian Talmud-Gittin*, London, 1936, pp. 441-445.

Finkelstein, L., *The Pharisees*, 2 Vols., Philadelphia, 1938.

Gafni, Y., *Yehudey Bavel bi-Tekufat ha-Talmud*, Jerusalem, 1990.

Glueck, N., "The Excavations of Solomon's Seaport: Ezion-Geber" in *Annual Report of the Smithsonian Institution*, 1941, pp. 453-478.

Grayzel, S., *A History of the Jews*, Philadelphia, 1947.

Guignebert, C., *The Jewish World in the Time of Jesus*, New York, 1939.

Heichelheim, F.M., "Roman Syria" in An *Economic Survey of Ancient Rome*, T. Frank edit., 2 Vols., Baltimore, 1938.

Herz, J., "Großgrundbesitz in Palästina im Zeitalter Jesu" in *Palästina Jahrbuch* XXIV, 1928, pp. 98-113.

Herzfeld, L., *Handelsgeschichte der Juden des Altertums*, 2nd edit., Braunschweig, 1894.

Hyman, A., *Toledot Tannaim va-Amoraim*, 3 Vols., London, 1910.

The Interpreter's Dictionary of the Bible, Vols. I-IV, Nashville-New York, 1962.
idem, Supplementary Volume, Nashville, 1976.

Jastrow, M., *A Dictionary of the Targumim, the Talmud Babli and Yeru-shalmi, and the Midrashic Literature*, 2 Vols., New York, 1950.

Jewish Encyclopedia, 12 Vols., New York, 1901-1907.

Jones, A.H.M., "The Urbanization of Palestine", in *Journal of Roman Studies* XXI, 1931, pp. 78-85;
idem, The Herods of Judea, Oxford, 1938.

Juster, J., *Les Juifs dans l'Empire romain*, 2 Vols., Paris, 1914.

Kanael, B., *Altjüdische Münzen*. Sonderdruck aus *Jahrbuch für Numismatik und Geldgeschichte*, 17. Jahrgang,. 1967.

Kelso, J.L., art. "Pottery", in *The Interpreter's Dictionary of the Bible*, Vol. 3 (Nashville-New York, 1962), pp. 846-853.

Klausner, J., *Ha-Bayit ha-Sheni bi-Gedulato*, Tel-Aviv, 1930, pp. 42-104;
idem, Historia shel ha-Bayit ha-Sheni, 5th edit., 5 Vols., Jerusalem, 1958.

Klein, S., *Eretz Yehudah*, Tel-Aviv, 1939;
idem, Eretz ha-Galil, Jerusalem, 1946.

Krauss, S., *Talmudische Archäologie*, 3 Vols., Leipzig, 1910-1912;
idem, Synagogale Altertümer, Berlin-Vienna, 1922.

Landes, G.M., *The Interpreter's Dictionary of the Bible*, Vol. 3, s.v. Kenites, pp. 6-7.

Leiman, S.Z., "The Camel in the Patriarchal Narrative", in *Yavneh Review*, 1967, pp. 16-26.

Leon, H.J., *The Jews of Ancient Rome*, Philadelphia, 1960.

Levy, J., *Chaldäisches Wörterbuch über die Targumim*, 3rd edit., Leipzig, 1881;
idem, Wörterbuch über die Talmudim und Midraschim, 2nd edit., 4 Vols., Berlin-Vienna, 1924. Reprinted Darmstadt, 1963.

Lieberman, S., *Greek in Jewish Palestine*, New York, 1942;
idem, Hellenism in Jewish Palestine, New York, 1950.

Löw, L., "Graphische Requisiten und Erzeugnisse bei den Juden", in *Gesammelte Schriften*, Szegedin, 1889-1900.

Margalioth, M., *Entsiklopedia le-Hakhemei ha-Talmud ve-ha-Geonim*, 2 Vols., Tel-Aviv, 1946.

Margolis, M.L. and Marx, A., *A History of the Jewish People*, Philadelphia, 1927.

Mendelsohn, I., "Guilds in Ancient Palestine", in *Bulletin of the American School of Oriental Research*, No. 8, 1940, pp. 17-21;
idem, "State Slavery in Ancient Israel", in *Bulletin of the American School of Oriental Research*, No. 85, 1942, pp. 14-17;
idem, Slavery in the Ancient Near East, New York, 1949.

Montefiore, C.G., and Loewe, H., *A Rabbinic Anthology*, London, 1938. Reprinted Philadelphia, 1960.

Moore, G.F., *Judaism in the First Centuries of the Christian Era*, 3 Vols., Cambridge, Mass., 1927-1930.

Neusner, J., *A History of the Jews in Babylonia*, Leiden, 1965.

Newman, J., *The Agricultural Life of the Jews in Babylonia*, London, 1932.

Parkes, J., *The Conflict of the Church and the Synagogue*, London, 1934.

Preuss, J., *Biblisch-talmudische Medizin*, 3rd edit., Berlin, 1923.

Pritchard, J.B., *The Ancient Near East: An Anthology of Texts and Pictures*, Princeton, 1958;
idem, *Ancient Near Eastern Texts relating to the Old Testament*, 3rd edit., Princeton, 1969;
idem, in *The Interpreter's Dictionary of the Bible*, Vol. 2 (Nashville–New York, 1962), s.v. Ivory, pp. 773–775.

Radin, M., *The Life of the People in Biblical Times*, Philadelphia, 1943;
idem, *The Jews among the Greeks and Romans*, Philadelphia, 1915.

Reifenberg, A., *Ancient Hebrew Arts*, New York, 1950.

Rostovtzeff, M.I., *The Social and Economic History of the Roman Empire*, Oxford, 1926. 2nd revised edit. by P.M. Fraser, Oxford, 1957;
idem, *The Social and Economic History of the Hellenistic World*, Oxford, 1941.

Sachar, A.L., *A History of the Jews*, New York, 1940; 5th edit. — revised and enlarged, 1965.

Schalit, A., *Hordos ha-Melekh*, Jerusalem, 1960.

Schechter, S., "A Glimpse of the Social Life of the Jews in the Age of Jesus the son of Sirach," in *Studies in Judaism*, Second Series, pp. 55–101, Philadelphia, 1908. Reprinted 1945.

Schürer, E., *The History of the Jewish People in the Age of Jesus Christ*, 2 Vols.; A new English version revised and edited by Geza Vermes, Fergus Millar and Matthew Black. Edinburgh, 1973 and 1979.

Tcherikover, V., *Hellenistic Civilization and the Jews*, Philadelphia, 1959;
idem, *Ha-Yehudim be-Mitzrayim ba-Tekufah ha-Hellenistit—ha-Romit le-Or ha-Papyrologiya*, 2nd edit., Jerusalem, 1963.

Vaux, Roland de, *Ancient Israel*, Vol. I, Engl. Transl., New York, 1961.

Vogelstein, H., *History of the Jews in Rome*, Engl. transl., Philadelphia, 1940.

Winnett, F.V., *The Interpreter's Dictionary of the Bible*, Vol. 1, s.v. Bronze, p. 467.

Wischnitzer, M., *A History of Jewish Crafts and Guilds*, New York, 1965.

Yadin, Y., "The Fourth Season of Excavations at Hazor", in *Biblical Archaeologist XXII*, 1 (Feb. 1959), fig. 11.

Zeitlin, S., *The Rise and Fall of the Judaean State*, 3 Vols., Philadelphia, 1962–1978.

List of Abbreviations

Ab. — Aboth
Ant. — Antiquities
Arak. — Arakhin
Arch. — Archaeology
(or [German] Archäologie)
ARN — Aboth de-Rabbi Nathan
A.Z. — Abodah Zarah
B.B. — Baba Bathra
Bekh. — Bekhoroth
Bell. — Bellum Iudaicum
Ber. — Berakhoth
Bez. — Bezah
Bik. — Bikkurim
B.K. Baba Kamma
B.M. — Baba Metsia
Cant. — Canticles
Cor. — Corinthians
Der. Er. Z. — Derekh Eretz Zuta
Deut. — Deuteronomy
Eccl. — Ecclesiastes
Ecclus. — Ecclesiasticus
Erub. — Erubin
Exod. — Exodus
Ezek. — Ezekiel
Gen. — Genesis
Git. — Gittin
Hag. — Haggai or Hagigah
Hakip. — Hakippurim
Hash. — Hashanah
Hil. — Hilkhoth
Hist. Eccl. — Historia Ecclesiastica
Hor. — Horayoth
Hos. — Hosea

Hul. — Hullin
Is. — Isaiah
J.E. — Jewish Encyclopedia
Jer. — Jeremiah
Jos. — Joshua
Jud. — Judges
Kel. — Kelim
Ket. — Ketuboth
Kid. — Kiddushin
Kil. — Kilayim
Lam. — Lamentation
Lev. — Leviticus
M. — Mishnah
Maas. — Maasroth
Mak. — Makkoth
Mal. — Malachi
Matt. — Matthew
Mekil. — Mekhilta (or: Mekilta)
Men. — Menahoth
Mic. — Micah
Midr. — Midrash
M.K. — Moed Katan
Nah. — Nahum
Ned. — Nedarim
Neh. — Nehemiah
Nid. — Niddah
Num. — Numbers
Ohol. — Oholoth
Pal. Am. — Palästinensischen
Amoräer
Pes. — Pesahim
Pesik. R. — Pesikta Rabbati
Pesik. R.K. — Pesikta de-Rab Kahana

PRE — Pirkei de-Rabbi Eliezer
Prov. — Proverbs
Pss. — Psalms
R. — Rabbi or (Midrash) Rabba
R.H. — Rosh Hashanah
R.N. — Rabbi Nathan
Sam. — Samuel
Sanh. — Sanhedrin
Shab. — Shabbath
Sheb. — Shebiith
Sot. — Sotah
T. — Tosefta
Taan. — Taanith

Talm. Arch. — Talmudische
  Archäologie
Tanh. — (Midrash) Tanhuma
T.B. — Talmud Babli
Tem. — Temurah
Ter. — Terumoth
Thessal. — Thessalonians
T.Y. — Talmud Yerushalmi
Vers. — Version
Yeb. — Yebamoth
Zab. — Zabim
Zeb. — Zebahim
Zech. — Zechariah

General Index

Aaron, Moses' brother 1 2
Abaye, see: Abbaye
Abba, Rabbi 59
Abba bar Abba (father of Samuel Yarhina'a) 42–43 58–59 143
Abba bar Abina, Rabbi 44
Abba bar Zemina, Rabbi 84
Abba, the Bloodletter 204
Abba Hilkiah 39 40
Abba Hoshaya (or: Yeshayah) of Tiryah 215
Abba Shaul ben Botnith 62
Abbahu, Rabbi 61 193
Ab[b]aye, Babylonian *Amora* 43–44 118 185 190–191
Abdima, Rabbi 63
Abdominal Operations 198
Abel, brother of Cain 3 225
Abimelech, king of Shechem 5–6
Abin, the Carpenter, Rabbi 82
Abiram, rebel against Moses 181
Ablutions 208
Abraham, the patriarch 5 57 93 95 224
Abtalyon, a leader of the Pharisees 210
Abtinas, House of 247–248
Academies 59 73 92 119 169, see also: Schools
Academy, Heavenly 204
Accidents 49 162–163 244
Acco (= Acre, Ptolemais) 66 136 153 233 240
Accountancy and Accountants 164
Actors 156–157

Adam 3 17 94 132
Adda, Rab 55
Adda bar Abba, Rab 64–65
Addaeus, the Apostle 60
Adiabene, Kingdom of 60 129
Administrators 127 203 205
Adultery 204 206 245
Advertising 48
Aesop's Fables 103
Afforestation 99
Africa 154 156 196 210
Aggadah 95
Agriculture and Agricultural Laborers IX–X 1 3–7 11 27 29 30 38 39–55 57 58 77 80 81 96 101 104 105 110 111 114 118 126 127 131 133 155 159 160 164–170 171 173–176 178 180 184 225 226 231 238 250
Agrippa I, king of Judaea 128
Agrippa II, king of Judaea 128 129
Aha bar Jacob, Rab 73–74
Ahab, king of Israel 13
Aibu, son of Rab 160
Air and Air Pollution 78 209
Akiba, Rabbi 55–56 72 84 120 122 124 179 183–184 188 197 215 226
Albright, W.F. 2 9
Alexander the Great 30 152
Alexandria 29 30 100 133 151–155 157 212 213 246–247
Aliens 120 150 169
Alityros (= Aliturus), the actor 157

Almonds 147
Amalek 235
Amarantus, a shipowner 154
America 143 150 152
American Medical Association (=
  A.M.A.) 188
Am Ha-'Areş 111 166 175
Amida prayer 130
Ammi, Rabbi 73 112 193
Ammonites 9
Amos, the prophet 13
Amulets 194
Ananias (= Hananiah), merchant
  and missionary 60
Anatomy 235
Angels 5 94 199
Anger 226
Anilai (= Anileus), leader of
  outlaws' army 244
Animals and Animal Hire
  Service 56–57 121 129 145 160
  163 189 191 196 220 221 222
  223–229 230 233 235 238 241
Antioch, Syria 66
Antisemitism and Antisemites IX
  155 205
Ants 26 105
Apothecaries, see: Pharmacists
Appeals, for assistance 119
Apples 147 185
Apprentices and Apprenticeship 83
  108–109 135 200 209 241–250
Aprons 201
Arab, a town in Galilee 72
Arabs and Arabia 58 62 72 127
  192 240
Aramaic 15 58 118 137 147 164
  217 225 229 236 240
Aram Naharaim (=
  Mesopotamia) 95
Aram Nahor (= Syria) 95
Aravah 8 9
Arbel, a town in Galilee 133
Arbitration 230
Archaeology and Archaeologists 7
  9 13 136 137 142 155 157 158

Archers 236 237
Architects 9 130
Aristeas, Letter of 29 30
Aristocrats and Aristocracy 12 30
  35 36 92 156 157 159 174 225
Arms (= Weapons) and
  Armorers 6 11 88 140–141 237
Artisans 4 14 29 34 37 99 107 130
  136
Arts and Artists 7–19 29 34 153
  156 212–213
Asa, king of Judah 20–21
Ashes 192 195
Ashi, Rab 138–139
Asia, Continent of 196
Asia, Province of 75
Asia, Western or Minor 60 133
  190 212
Asinai (= Asineus), leader of
  outlaws' army 244
Assembly, Men of the Great, see:
  Men of the Great Assembly
Asses and Ass Drivers 2 56–57 62
  94 103 170 172 177 220–224 232
Assi, Rab 43 193
Assyria and Assyrians 13
Astrology 183 194
Astronomers 43 77
Athens 100 209
Athronges, rebel against the
  Romans 225
Atonement, Day of 17 142 156 196
Austria X
Automation 110 111

Baalei Battim 166
Babylonia and Babylonians 5 11
  12 19 38 39 43 44 45 46 47 50 51
  52 53 54 55 58 59 61 64 65 68 69
  73 75 77 78 80 81 85 86 91 106
  107 118 126 127 138 142 143 146
  150 164 165 166 168 169 170 171
  172 176 179 185 189 191 193 204
  205 209 210 212 219 222 229 234
  235 244
Bailees, paid 229

Baking and Bakers   4–5 18 19 41
  102 109 134 135 142 148 223 243
  246–247
Balaam, the sorcerer   67
Balsam (= Balm)   20 174 207 221
Ban, rabbinic   210–211 234, see
  also: Excommunication
Bandages   189
Bandits, see: Robbers
Banking and Money-changing   IX–X
  48 49 65–68 99 100 120 142 147
  155 246, see also: Money-lenders
Barbers   202–203 218 220
Bar Kochba   122 131 141 157 178
Barley   4 103 166 169 170 191
Baruch the Scribe, son of
  Neriah   13 25
Baruch, Syriac Apocalypse of   132
Basilicas   151
Baskets and Basketsellers   106 139
  150 201 214
Bathing, Bathhouses and Bath-
  attendants   78 79 149 202–203
Beams   106 130
Bears   229
Beasts, wild   88 108 172 228 229
  236–237
Beds   139
Beer   47–48 161
Bees   209
Beggars   157
Behemoth, a mythical beast   237
Belus, a stream   136 137
Ben Azzai, Simeon   123 188
Benedictions   188 229
Ben-Gurion, David   xi
Ben-Hadad, king of Syria   199
Benjamin (= Minyomi), the
  physician   189
Benjamin, the shepherd   229
Ben Kamtzar, the scribe   248
Ben Karara (or: Kadara), the
  scribe   72
Ben Sira (= Ecclesiasticus)   29–37
  114 181 206 249
Ben Zoma, Simeon   116

Beth (Ha)Midrash   61 89, see also:
  Study, House of
Bethlehem, Galilee   135
Bethlehem, Judah   22 134 135
Beth Mehoza, a town in
  Galilee   132
Beth Midrash   61 89, see also:
  Study, House of
Beth Shean (= Scythopolis), a city
  in N.E. Israel   132–133
Betrothed Girls   205
Bezalel, son of Uri   9–10
Bibi, Rabbi   132
Bibi bar Abaye, Rab   50–51
Bible, Hebrew (= Old
  Testament)   XI 1 10 12 24 25 33
  58 60 69 70 75 85 91 105 137 144
  147 155 157 165 167 169 183 184
  187 194 197 199 214 216 225 228
  236 237 241
Biblical Age   1 3 18 20 22 137 147
  167 169 225 241
Birds   52 121 160 161 179 196 237
  238
Blacksmiths   8 11 12 14 35 83 138
  140 152
Blasphemy   89
Bleeding and Bleeders (=
  Cuppers)   44 149 185 191 202–
  205 211
Blemishes   230
Blessings, divine   75 91–92 93 94
  95 105 109 120 163 164 180, see
  also: Benedictions
Blindness and the Blind   139 196
  226 228
Bloodletters, see: Bleeding and
  Bleeders
Blows   235
Boatmen   44 49
Bones   193 214
Bookkeeping and Bookkeepers   164
Borsippa, a city in Babylonia   209
Bostra, a town in Transjordan   70
Bottles (= Flasks)   17 137
Bowel Sickness   182

Boys 223 241 242 243, see also: Children
Bran 198
Bread 4 19 40 57 75 94 109 123 125 133 165 167 175 229 246 247
Breweries 161, see also: Beer
Bribery 54 67
Bricks and Brickmakers 1 130 131 195
Brides 17 248
Brigands, see: Robbers
Bronze 8 9 153 154
Buber, Solomon 116
Building and Builders 11 12 37 81–82 113 127–131 203
Bureaucracy 7
Burglars 86–87
Businessmen, see: a) Merchants; b) Trade and Traders
Butchers, see Slaughterers
Buying and Selling 144–145 161–162

Caesarea 127 142 243
Caesarea Philippi 178
Cain, brother of Abel 3 8 175–176 225
Cairo Genizah 206
Calendar 77 81 230
Calves 5, see also: Golden Calf
Camels and Camel Drivers 2 129 177 220–224 232
Canaan, Land of 2 24 95 96 239
Canaanites 4 6 15 18 23
Canals 44 49
Cantors 151
Capitalism and Capitalists x 162 163
Captives, see: Prisons and Prisoners
Caravans 220
Carders 202 212
Carobs 93 118
Carpenters 12 14 82 90 99 113 128 130 245
Cars 224

Cattle, Raising of 1–3 7 34 45 46 47 50 169 170 180 181 224 226
Catullus, Roman governor of Cyrene 155–156
Cedars 11
Cemeteries 194
Champagne, French province 48
Charcoal 83
Charity and Public Assistance 72 92 110 139 159 185 204 213
Charles, R.H. 34–35
Cheese 209
Chemists 195
Chicks and Chickens 97
Children 4 69–70 75 143 165 169 170 191 194 201–202 208 211 212 222 223 234 242 247, see also: Boys
China ix
Christ, see: Jesus
Christianity and Christians ix 25 60 89–90 147 192–193 207 215 216–217 239 240
Christian Scientists 21 32
Cilicia, Asia Minor 212
Circumcision 60 81 171 201
Circus Games 88–89
Cities 30 41 126 127 128 131 176 182–183 209 221 241 242
"Class Struggle" and Class Solidarity 83 171
Clean and Unclean, ritual concepts 207 214 238
Cleaning and Cleaners 178 202 217–219
Clement of Alexandria 133
Climate 99
Clothing 6 10 17 48 52–53 75 82 96 99 122 123 128 131 132 133 138 141 145 156 163 201 202 204 205 207 215 217–219
Clover 195
Coals 14 134 206
Cobblers and Shoemakers 84–85 218
Codes, rabbinic 142

Coins and Coinage　37 65–66 145
160 196 246
Colds　79 106 198 229
Comedies　215
Commandments, religious, see:
Religion and Religious Laws and
Customs
Commerce　IX 27 29 30 31–32 34
37 46 48 49 50 68 81 118–119
120 121 126 142 144–147 155
157 160–163, see also: Trade and
Traders
Commercial Travelers, see: Peddlers
Commodities, sacred　163–164
Commonwealth, First, see: First
Commonwealth
Commonwealth, Second, see:
Second Commonwealth
Competition, fair and unfair　143–
144 148–151 231 232
Construction Workers　81–82, see
also: Building and Builders
Contractors　130
Converts and Conversions　38 59–
61 65 82 89–90 171 191 215
Cooks and Cooking　5 18 102 132
142 178 233 243
Copper, Copper Mining and
Coppersmiths　8 9 12 140 153
154 208 212
Corinth, a city in Greece　153
Corporal Punishment　69 244
Corpses　195–196
Courts, Jewish religious　40 46 65
72 182 212 226 230
Courtyards　83 105 148 186 211
218–219
Covenant, between God and
Israel　117
Cowboys, Cowherds, see: Herdsmen
Crafts, Craftsmen and
Craftsmanship　ix–x 4 6–19 22
29 34 35 36 37 38 39 81–85 91
99–101 102 104 107–109 110 111
113 121 126 127 130 136 138 142
148 149 152 153 155 159–160

166 201 202 207 208 209 210 211
212 213 218 225 233 241–242
244 246–248 249–250
Credit Sales　49 64 161
Cress　79
Crime and Criminals　39 40 127
190–191 193 210–211 216–217
220 244, see also: a) Robbers and
Robbery; b) Burglars; c) Thieves;
d) Highwaymen
Crop Rotation　176
Crucifixions　87 193
Crusades　x
Cultivation, improved methods
of　45
Cumin　142
Cupboards　201
Cuppers, see: Bleeding and Bleeders
Curses　3 94 120 160 165 185 193
211 228
Curtains　153
Cushions　204
Customs Officers　155
Cymbals　153–154
Cyrene　154 155–156 210
Cyrus, king of Persia　16

Daniel bar Rab Ketina, Rab　54
Dankcho, the money-changer　68
Dates and Date Trees (= Palm
Trees)　43 44 46–48 50 51 52
101 123 161 169 191 201
Dathan, rebel against Moses　181
David, king of Israel　2 3 7 9 11 15
75 163 224 225 227
Days, division of　110
Dead Sea　174
Death　97–98 103 124–125 142 182
186 187 199 213 216 235 244
Debir, a city in Judah　24
Deborah's Song　10
Deception and Deceivers　144 145
147 210 226
Decorations　13
Deer　121
Demons　197

Dentists and Dentistry 201
Deserts and Wilderness 96 155 180
220 221 222 224 225
Detectives 86–87
Diaspora, Jewish xi 31 119 126
128 140 151–158 178 190 242
Diet 78 89 190 198 199–200
Dignity, of Man, Labor, etc. 91 92
95 98 99 100 105 107 115 116
120 215 225 230 236
Dimi, Rab (of Nehardea) 64–65
Diocletian, Roman emperor 132
Disease, see: a) Physicians;
b) Medicines
Dishonesty 220 224 226
Divorce and Bills of Divorce 72 76
208 245
Dogs 194 196 208
Donkeys, see: Asses
Doors and Doorposts 196
Dothan, a town in N. Samaria 2
Doves 189–190, see also: Pigeons
Drugs 198 201
Drunkenness 176 231
Dung Gate 210
Dyers and Dyeing 10 99 148 174
243

Ears 193
Earth 3 27 134 175 184 219
Eating and Drinking 28 89 93 94
95 101 103 104 115–116 119 167
182 188 194 199 200 203 204 223
226 228 229 245
Ecclesiastes, Book of 28 29
Ecclesiasticus, see: Ben Sira
Eclipses, of the sun or moon 180
Economic Crises 42 102 122 142
143 145
Edels, Rabbi Samuel (=
Maharsha) 48 187
Edessa, a city in the upper Euphrates
Valley 60
Education and Educators 36 56
68–70 108 112 115 119 160–163,
see also: a) Study, of Torah, and

Students; b) Teaching and Teachers
Eggs 135 143 193 197 243
Egypt and Egyptians 1 2 3 11 19
21 29 30 132 133 151 152 154
155 169 173 185 190 197 212 242
246
Ein Gedi 174
Ekron, a Philistine city 7
Elath, a city in the southern
Negev 240
Eleazar ben Arach, Rabbi 113
Eleazar ben Azariah, Rabbi 40 99
172 215
Eleazar ben Dama 192
Eleazar ben Hakappar, Rabbi 238
Eleazar ben Harsom, Rabbi 41
Eleazar ben Pedath, Rabbi 66–67
117 166 175 181
Eleazar ben Perata, Rabbi 213
Eleazar ben Rabbi Simeon,
Rabbi 86 113–114 119 198 223
Eleazar ben Rabbi Zadok,
Rabbi 62 213
Eliezer ben Hyrcanus, Rabbi 40 94
102 115–116 213
Elijah, the prophet 87
Elisha, the prophet 199
Elisha ben Abuyah 113
Emancipation, Jewish x
Embalming 19
Embroidery 10 11 159
Embryology 80
Emigration (from Eretz Israel) 166
168
Emperors x 98 179 190
Employers 128 148 169–170 220 226
England 156
Engraving and Engravers 12 34
Ephesus, a city in Asia Minor 15
Epidemics 79
Epilepsy 194
Equality 111
Eretz Israel, see Israel, Land of
Esther, Book of 75
Ethics 27 38 50–53 61–64 79 144–
146, see also: Morality

Euphrates, river   60
Europe   ix–x 118–119 120 157
Eusebius, a Roman Jew   158
Eve, Adam's wife   3 17 132
Evil Impulse (= Inclination)   230
Excommunication   234, see also:
   Ban, rabbinic
Exercise   78
Excrement   191 196–197 208
Exilarchs   64 146
Exploitation   244
Export—Import Business   64 240
Eye — "Evil Eye"   74 163 176 203
Eyes and Eye Diseases   20 77–78
   80–81 114 163 173 176 186 189
   194 196 197 203 228 229 230, see
   also: a) Eye — "Evil Eye";
   b) Ophthalmology
Ezekiel, the prophet   11 228
Ezion-Geber   9
Ezra, the Scribe   36 76 206

Factories   7 110
Faith-Healers   181 192–193 196 197
Falk, Rabbi Joshua   185 187
Famine and Starvation   35 89 107
   115 223
Farmers and Landowners   3 4 7 27
   34 36 38 40–55 56 57 58 66 68 77
   105 141 143 162 164–166 168
   169–170 171 172 174 175 176
   177 179 180 225, see also: Tenant
   Farmers
Fasts and Fasting   76 188 190 198
   218
Fat, goose and sheep   191 228
Fat, human   198
Feasts, see: Festivals, Feasts and
   Festivities
Fathers and Sons   87 108 138 159
   160 200 202 220 223 234 241–
   243 249
Fees   77 181 188 200 203 204
Feldman, Dr. W.M.   195 196
Festivals, Feasts and Festivities   4 6
   115 132 138 148 211 217–218 239

Fevers   79 80 81
Fields, see: Agriculture
Figs, Fig-leaves and Fig trees   17 20
   40 57 64–65 98
Fingers   6 243 248
First Commonwealth   12 14 15
First Fruits   100
Fishing and Fishermen   90 156 174
   238–240
Flasks, see: Bottles
Flax   62
Flood   101
Flour   5 40 109 143 198 247
Fodder   50 70 103
Food   48 52 57 101 103 104 118
   131 133 141 142 143 145 146 148
   165–166 167 180 199 223 228
   250
Fools   104 110 123 184 211
Foreigners, see: Aliens
Forests   44–45 180
Fortune-tellers   157
Fowlers   237 238–239
Foxes   121 158 193
France   ix 48 212 231
Fraud and Fraudulent
   Practices   144 145 146 220 231
   232
Free Enterprise, see: Private
   Enterprise
Fridays   154
Fringes, ritual   205
Fullers   18 87 142 214–219
Funerals   216

Galilee and Galileans   25 70 72 79
   83 90 126 127 131 132 133 134
   135 141 147 169 170 178 181 215
   221 226 235 239 240
Galilee, Sea of (= Tiberias, Lake
   of)   90 127 239–240
Gallows   193
Gamaliel II, the Patriarch,
   Rabban   83 108 171–172 215 219
Gamaliel III, the Patriarch,
   Rabban   102 109–110

Gamaliel VI, the Patriarch 80
Gamblers 226
Garden of Eden 94 97
Gardens and Gardeners 51 52 54
55 69 105 168 179
Garments, see: Clothing
Garmu, House of 246–248
Gaza, a city 5
Geese and Goose-quills 191
Generations, differences
between 116
Genizah, Cairo 206
Gentiles 42 60 62 82 84 119–120
130 132 141 171 178 190–191
192 198 205 219 226 234 237
238
Gerasa, a city in Transjordan 134
Germany ix–x
Ghetto Jews 156
Gifts 114
Gilead 20
Girdles 6 17 23 215
Gisc(h)ala, see: Gush Halav
Gittlen, Dr. Barry M. 7
Gladiators 87–89
Glass and Glaziers 136–140 149
Gluttons, see: Eating
Goats and Goat Breeding 5 179–
181 195 196 226
God and Fear of God 2 3 4 11 14
17 18 20 21 27 29 31 32 33 60 62
63 75 87 91 92–93 94 95 97 99
107 109 111 114 116 117 120 121
122 124 132 139 183 184–185
186 188 197 199 219 222 225 227
228 230 232 236 250
Golan Heights 127
Gold 9 11 56 132 137 138 140 151
152 153
Golden Calf 22
Goldsmiths 14 136 138 140 152
202
Goose, see: Geese
Gordon, Aharon David xi
Goshen, Land of 1
Gout 187

Grain 4 5 54 143 165 166 167 176
220 221 223 231 250
Grasshoppers 237
Greece and Greeks 28 32 152 155
181 190 198, see also: a) Greek —
Language, Concepts, etc.;
b) Hellenistic Age; c) Hellenistic
Cities and Empires
Greek — Language, Concepts,
Values and Influence 27 28 31
34 36 38 91 106 116 126 130 131
132 142 151–156 169 175 181
190 201 206 236 239 241
Grinding 5 102 149
Grocers 146, see also: Stores and
Storekeepers
Guerillas 87
Guides 18
Guilds ix 152 200 212–213 215
220 223–224, see also: Trade
Unions
Gums 191 192
"Gun Control" 141
Gush Halav (Gisc[h]ala) 132 133
177 178

Hadrian, Roman emperor 66 98
179, see also: Hadrianic
Persecution
Hadrianic Persecution 72 84 124
213
Hagira, family of 71
Haifa 240
Hair 230
Halacha 226 230 232
Halutzim (= Pioneers) iii
Hama, Rab 64
Haman 203
Hametz (= Leavened Food) 146
Hammurabi, Code of 20
Hana, Rab, the money-changer 68
100
Hananel, Rab 74 75
Hananiah (= Ananias), a merchant
and missionary 60
Handmills 149 202

Hands   188 195
Hanina, Rabbi   61 79 80 84
Hanina ben Dosa, Rabbi   93–94
Hanina bar Sisi, Rabbi   107
Hanina the Writer, Rabbi   74
Hanseatic League   ix
Hardware Dealers   146
Harlots, see: Prostitutes
Haroseth   147
Harvests (= Crops)   4 118 167 168
Hasmoneans and Hasmonean
   Age   37
Hazael, king of Syria   199
Headaches   196
Health   48 69 78 188 189 190 191
   198 203 223, see also: Mental
   Health
Hearts and Heartaches   198
Heat   229
Hebrew   8 15 16 152 158 206 213
   217 229 233 236 239
Hebrews, see: Israelites
Hebron   1
Hegra, a town in Arabia   58
Helena, queen of Adiabene   129
   215
Hell   34 187 197–198
Hellenistic Age   27 28–37 169 241
Hellenistic — Concepts, Values and
   Influence, see: Greek —
   Language, Concepts, etc.
Hellenistic Cities and Empires   30
   67 130 131 151 190
Hens   97 196
Herdsmen   3 45 224—226 229 230
Heresy and Heretics   187 215
Hermon, Mount   178
Herod, king of Judaea   127 128 236
Herodotus, Greek historian   190
Hezekiah, king of Judah   13 19–20
   183
Hezekiah, son of Rabbi Hiyya   41–
   42
Highwaymen   220 223, see also:
   Robbers and Robbery
Hilazon (= Purple Fish)   174

Hilkiah bar Tobi   45
Hillel, the Elder   56 82 117 122 222
Hinnom, Valley of   16
Hippocrates, Greek physician   199
Hiram (or Huram), Tyrian
   craftsman   9
Hisda, Rab   44 46–48
History and Historians   xi 126 190
Hitler, Adolf   x
Hiyya, Rabbi   41–42 58 66 68–69
   80–81
Hiyya bar Abba, Rabbi   156
Hiyya bar Adda, Rabbi   54–55
Hiyya bar Joseph, Rabbi   63–64
Hoarding   143
"Holy Brotherhood"   109 110
Holy Places   142 208 221
Homes   85 110 206 212 219, see
   also: Houses
Homo Economicus   104
Homosexuals   202
Honey   3–4 61 199 209 221
Honor   105–106 247 248
Horses   177
Horticulture, see: Gardens and
   Gardeners
Hosea, the prophet   23
Hospitality   177
House-calls, Doctors'   199
Houses and Houseowners   83 149
   195 206 222, see also: Homes
Humility   211
Humor   34 210
Huna, Rab   45–46 73–74 82
Huna son of Rab Joshua, Rab   49–
   50 51
Hunger, see: Famine
Hunters   113 236–239
Hygiene   78 141 217
Hyrcanus, Rabbi Eliezer's
   father   40

Ibn Ezra, Abraham   184
Idleness   25–27 28–30 92 94 102–
   103
Idiocy   102

Idols and Idolatry   14 15 183 214
237 247 248
Ikkarim (= landless farm
laborers)   168–169
Ilfa, a scholar and businessman   61
117
Immorality   102 171 204–206 240
Incantations   194 197
Incense   154 176 247–248
India   ix 132 153
Indolence   25–27 105 171 174
Industriousness (= Diligence)   25–
30 174
Industry   i 6 7 8 11 28 39 49 58
127 131–141 149 209 239–240
241–242
Inflammations   80 193
Inflation   132–133 153
Injuries, see: Wounds
Insects, 196
Inspection of Property, 43
Insomnia   193 194
Insurance — Accident
Insurance   49 223
Intercalation, of the year   230
Investments   162
Iraq   60
Iron and Iron Smiths   8 11 14 35
Irrigation   43 44 46
Isaac, the patriarch   57 93 95
Isaiah, the prophet   10 19–20
Isaiah — Deutero-Isaiah   14 16 27
Ishmael, son of Abraham and
Hagar   237
Ishmael son of Elisha, Rabbi   74
118 192
Ishmael son of Rabbi Jose,
Rabbi   54 84 86–87 181 183–
184
Israel, Land of   xi–xii 3 4 10 11 15
19 22 29 30 37 38 39 45 54 58 59
61 63 66 73 74 77 78 79 80 81 86
88 93 95 96 97 99 100 106 109
112 126 127 131 133 134 136 137
139 140 141 142 143 145 146 151
156 157 158 164 166 168 170 171

176 177 178 179 180 181 190 193
209 210 212 219 221 225 231 232
234 239 240 242, see also:
Canaan, Land of
Israel, State of   ix xi 127
Israelites (= Hebrews) and
Jews   ix–xi 1–4 7 8 9 10 11 12 18
19 20 21 23 84 95–97 114 115
117 119–120 128 131 137 140
151 152 156–158 163 166 167
169 196 202 219 224 225 227 228
230 232 234 236 237 240 244
Issur, the money-changer   65 68
Issur, the Proselyte   65
Italy   ix 157
Ivory   13

Jabbok, river   9
Jabez, a town in Judah and center of
a family of scribes   24
Jabneh, a town in Judah   111
Jacob, the patriarch   1–3 19 22 57
225 226 229
Jacob bar Aha, Rabbi   63
Jacob, a disciple of Jesus   192
Jacob, a Judaeo–Christian
physician   193
Jaffa, a city   37 142 207 233
James son of Alphaeus   192
James the Just   216–217
James the Younger   192
Jannai, Rabbi   54
Jars   52 134 135 163 244, see also:
Pitchers
Jaundice   80
Jealousy   206
Jerahmeel the King's son   13
Jeremiah, the prophet   3 13 16 17
19 20 22 25 115
Jeremiah, Rabbi   199
Jericho, a city in the Land of
Benjamin   174
Jerome, St.   158
Jerusalem   10 11 12 16 19 24 29 40
53 56 59 62 65 71 93–94 100 127
128 131 133 136 141 145 146 147

151 153 177 182 183 208 210 212
213 214 215 219 221 222 246, see
also: Zion
"Jerusalem of Gold"   56 140
Jerusalem Talmud, see: Talmud,
Babli and Yerushalmi
Jesus   60 67 90 147 181 192–193
239 240
Jewels and Jewellery   11 56 137
Jewish National Fund   99
Jews, see: Israelites and Jews
Job, Book of   20 137
Jobs   22 110 128
Johanan ben Mathia, Rabbi   57
Johanan bar Nappaha, Rabbi   42
53 63–64 71 80 81 83 89 100
106–107 112 117 176 179 189
191 197
Johanan ben Nuri, Rabbi   248
Johanan ben Zakkai, Rabbi   40 58
113 190
Johanan the Sandal-maker,
Rabbi   84
John of Gisc[h]ala, oil merchant and
Zealot leader   178
Jonathan, Moses' grandson   22
Jonathan, Rabbi   79
Jonathan, the Potter   136
Jonathan, the Weaver   155–156
210
Jordan, river   9 129 240
Jordan, valley   9 127
Jose ben Halafta, Rabbi   84 141
203
Jose bar Hanina, Rabbi   53 61
Jose ben Kisma, Rabbi   214
Jose ben Meshullam, Rabbi   110
118
Jose of Yodkart, Rabbi   56–57
Joseph, son of Jacob   1 2 19 44 164
173 226
Joseph, father of Jesus   90
Joseph, Rab   44 51–52 54 55 65
106
Josephus Flavius   126 128 136 141
178 225

Joshua ben Hananiah, Rabbi   83
111 116
Joshua ben Korha, Rabbi   87
Joshua ben Levi, Rabbi   192–193
Joshua son of Nun   239
Josiah, king of Judah   12
Josiah, Rabbi   96
Jubal, a descendant of Cain   8
Judaea   30 33 37 126 127 134 236,
see also: Judah, Land of
Judah ha-Nasi (= the Patriarch),
Rabbi   35 69 70–71 78 85 101
107 109 159 207 216 229 235
Judah Nesiah, Rabbi (son of Rabban
Gamaliel III)   70
Judah, Land of   7 8 13 15 22 24
134 176, see also: Judaea
Judah ben Baba, Rabbi   181
Judah ben Bathyra II, Rabbi   58–59
Judah, son of Rabbi Hiyya   41
Judah bar Ilai, Rabbi   106 116 117
143 145 162
Judah, Rab   55 80 81 176 210
Judah the Circumciser, Rab   81
Judah the Tailor, Rabbi   84–85
Judah, tribe of   8 24
Judaism   ix 27 33 36 60 82 91 175
179 185 191 208 236
Judan, Rabbi   81
Judges   36 46 50–54 70 96 109
Junk Dealers   142

Kahana III, Rab   80
Kahana IV, Rab   150–151
Kapparah   196
Katzenelson, Berl   xi
Kenites   8
Kephar Hananiah, village in
Galilee   134
Kephar Shihin, village in
Galilee   134
Kephar Signa, village in
Galilee   134
Kiddush (sanctification blessing)   50
Kings   ix 12 15 16 24 32 67 174
203 212 228

Kiriath Sepher, a city in Judah 24
Knives 201 233-234
Koheleth, see: Ecclesiastes
Korah, rebel against Moses 181
Kurdistan 60

Labor — General ix-xi 12 25-30
39 45 91-121 128 129 130 131
138 142 148 160 167 201 213
238-239
Labor — Agricultural Laborers, see:
Agriculture, etc.
Labor, division of 104
Labor — Forced Labor 41
Lamb, Poor man's 4
Lamentation 21-22
Lamps 134
Land-clearing 44-45
Landlords x 211, see also: Farmers
and Landowners
Landowners, see: Farmers and
Landowners
Landsmanshaften 152
Land Surveyors 55
Laodicea, a city in Syria 156
177
Latin 131
Launderers 18 102 202 214-219
Law, see: a) Legal; b) Torah
Laxatives 78
Lead, metal 140
Leaders and Leadership 106 182
203 226 227 228
Leaseholders 167 174
Leaven-water 191
Lebanon, mountains of 11 14
Leeches 195 203
Leeks 134
Legacies 65
Legal Problems, Devices and
Documents 44 50 51 52 53 57
62-63 65 76 100-101 102 121
141 142 143 144-146 148-151
154 172-173 181 182 183 186
208 209 211 214 216 221 223 229
231 238 241 242 244

Legs 193 196 198
Leisure 110 111
Leontopolis, a city in Egypt 246-
247
Leprosy 19
Leviathan, a mythical sea
monster 237
Levi bar Sisi 70-71
Levirate Marriage 208
Levites 22 24
Libya 154
Life, eternal and temporary 114
116 117
Life-saving and prolonging 79 80
102-103 107
Lighting 178
Lime Burners 156
Linen 6 10 11 23 41 48 61 62 132-
133 138 142
Lions 27 121 158 211 229
Liquors 231, see also: a) Wine; b)
Beer
Litigation, see: Legal Problems, etc.
Liturgy 17
Liver, lobe of 194
Lizards 187
Locusts 193, see also:
Grasshoppers
Lod (= Lydda), a city in the Land of
Benjamin 133 134 135 146 212
214
Logic 195
Lord, the, see: God
Lordship 103
Lot, Abraham's nephew 224
Ludarii 88-89
Luke, gospel writer 90
Lunatics 198
Luxury 13 14 162
Lydda (= Lod), a city in the Land of
Benjamin 133 134 135 146 212
214
Lyres 8

Macrocosm 195
Madison Avenue 48

Magdala (= Migdal Nunya), a city in Galilee   239 240

Magic and Magicians   19 137 183 193 194 195–197, see also: Sorcerers

Maharsha (= Samuel Edels)   48 187

Maimonides (= Rabbi Moshe ben Maimon)   56 110–111 184

Man — General   104 105 112 120 139 160

Manasseh (= Mniaseas), Roman synagogue leader   158

Manna   97 115 119

Manufacture and Manufacturing   xii 104 127 137 138 140–141 149, see also: Industry

Manure   174

Mariners, see: Sailors

Markets and Market Privileges   23 48 58 64–65 67 72 92 131 133 136 141 142 143 144–146 149 150 151–152 162 163 165–166 204 219 222 223 240

Marriage and Marriage Counselors   49 102 110 121 208 245, see also: Matchmakers

Martyrs and Martyrdom   72 120 124–125

Mar Ukba   80 81

Mary Magdalene   240

Masada, a fortress near the Dead Sea   127

Masons, see: Stonemasons

Masters and Apprentices, see: Apprentices and Apprenticeship

Masturbation   221

Matchmakers   17

Mats and Mattresses   133

Mattia (= Mattithya) ben Cheresh, Rabbi   157–158

Mausoleums   129

Mayors   182

Measures, see: Weights and Measures

Meat   4 63 84 141 156 160 182 234 235

Medical, see: a) Physicians; b) Medicines

Medicines and Remedies   19 21 32 77–81 183 184 187 188 191 192 193–201 238 249

Mediterranean, sea and coast-line   240

Meir, Rabbi   74–75 159–160 197 207

Men of the Great Assembly   75–76

Menashi, Rabbi   210

Mental Health   69–70

Merchants and Merchandise   ix–x 6 11 23 31 41 51 58–68 80 117 118 119 145 146–149 161–164 178 220

Mercy   199 227 228

Merit, of fathers, labor, etc.   92–93

Mesopotamia   95

Messiah and Messianic   25 147 225

Metals and Metal Workers   8 9 86 139 140 152 201 212

Mezuzzot   164

Microcosm   195

Middle Ages (= Dark Ages)   ix–x 77 120 121 142 149 184 212 232 234 235

Middlemen   143

Midrash   39 67 92 93 95 97 98 130 131 135 136 138 139 152 169 174 182 183 186 187 188 194 199 207 219 224 227 231 233 237 244 246 248–249

Migdal Nunya (= Magdala), a city in Galilee   239

Migraine   196

Milk   3–4 180 181 198 226

Mills and Millstones   5 6 106 163, see also: Handmills

Mines and Mining   ix 8

Miracles   ix 39 57 93–94 153

Miriam, Moses' sister   183

Mirrors   137 140

Misers   185 203

Mishnah 69 70 109 112 187 236
Missionaries 59–60 89–90 192–193
Modiin, a town in the Land of Benjamin 37
Money — General ii 49 62 65 93 98 99 101 104 107 110 128 138 147 150 161 162 163 164–165 168 169 170 173 177–178 186 188 189 200 204 245
Money-changing, see: Banking and Money-changing
Money-lenders 62 155 245
Monopolies 241 247
Monotony, of labor 104
Monuments 215
Moon 180
Morality 52 102 136 163 175 201 202 204 205 206 219 229 230 231 232 245, see also: Ethics
Mordecai, Esther's cousin 203
Mortars 154
Moses 1 2 8 22 97 122 123 131 153 154 183 207 224 226 227 236
Mothers 165 172 242
Mountains 126 129 220, see also: a) Sinai, Mount; b) Temple Mount
Mourning 138–139 172 211 216 218
Mouths 114
Mules and Muleteers 79 129 177 220 223
Mummies 196
Murder 216–217
Music 8
Muzzling, of animals 224
Myrrh Oil 203
Myrtle dealers 146

Naaran, a town in the Land of Benjamin 134
Nachmanides (= Rabbi Moshe ben Nachman) 184–185
Nahum, "the Libellar(ius)" 71–72
Nails 193

Nakai, the Scribe 72–73
Naples 157
Nathan, Rabbi 235
Nathan bar Shila, "chief of the slaughterers" 235
Navigation and Navicularii (= shipowners) 154 157 239
Nazirites 230
Nazis 190
Neapolis (= Nablus), a city in Samaria 127
Near East, Ancient 9 11 152
Nebuchadnezzar, king of Babylonia 12
Needles and Needlemakers 83 99 140
Negev 8
Nehardea (= Nearda), a city in Babylonia 64 77 209
Nehemiah, governor of Judah 23 29
Nehorai, Rabbi 114–115
Neriah, father of Baruch 13
Nero, Roman emperor 157
Netmakers 202
Newcastle 134
"New Deal" 128
New Moon 182
New Testament 24 71 90 121 192 218 228 239
Nicanor and Nicanor Gate 153
Nimrod, a king and "mighty hunter" 236
Nisan, month of 53 118
Nisibis, a city in South Anatolia 59
Noah 176
Nobles, see: Aristocrats
Noise, nuisance of 148 149
North Africa 154 156 210
Nose-bleeding 195
Nursing Mothers 165
Nuts 143–144 147
Nyctalopia (= Night Blindness) 196

Occupation, a worldly 102 109 111 113 117 118 120 122

Occupational Structure, of the
  Jews   126–158 232
Occupations, recommended   159
  160 161 164 165 166
Occupations, undesirable   159 160
  162 163 164 166 167 168 169
  201–239
Occupations, hereditary —
  Continuity and Change   22 24
  30–31 108–109 110 200 209 210
  241 249–250
Occupations, rabbinical   36 38–89
Odor, offensive   207–209
Oesterley, W.O.E.   33–34
Officials, of the government   85 155
Oholiab, son of Ahisamach   9–10
Oil   19 79 142 143 177–178 197
  203 207 220 221, see also: Olives,
  Olive Presses and Olive Oil
Old Age   115 201
Olives, Olive Presses and Olive
  Oil   7 14 42 79 118 170 176
  177–179 191 192
Onassis, a shipping magnate   41
Onias, Temple of   246–247
Onkelos, Targum   164
Operations, surgical   20 198 201
  204
Ophir   132
Ophthalmology and
  Ophthalmologists   77–78 201
Oral Law   157
Orchards   54
Ordination, rabbinical   107
Ornaments   10 11 59 137 139 140
  202 206
Orphans   69 163 209 242 244 249
Oshaia, Rabbi   84–85
Ossuaries   136
Ostia, a city near Rome   157
Outlaws   244
Ovens   134 135 223 247
Oxen   5 47 70, see also: Cattle
Oxford, a city in England   156

Pagans, see: Gentiles

Pain   196
Painters   156
Palaces   13 129
Palestine, see: Israel, Land of
Palm Trees, see: Dates and Date
  Trees
Papa, Rab   48–50
Papi, Rab   50
Papyri   155 195
Parables   4 36 67 97 99 103 129
  135 136 138 139 174 182 186 187
  188 194 198 199 200 201 206 207
  209 215 218 219 228 237 243 244
  245 248 249
Paradise   94
Parasitism   ix
Parchment   73
Parthia and Parthians   65 244
Partnerships   49
Passover festival   66 135 146 147
  148 218 238 245
Pasture land   1 2 133 180 224 228
Patience   199
Paul, the Apostle   15 60 90 226
Paulus, Roman jurist   144
Pearls and Precious Stones   137
  246
Peasants   23 30 111 127 175
Pedagogy and Pedagogues   68–70
Peddlers   23 84 147 150–151 156
  157 163 202 205–207
Pederasty   202
Pelusium, a city in N.E. Egypt   132
Pens and Reed Pens   99 248
Pentateuch   69
Pentecost (= Shavuoth) festival   66
Perfumes and Perfumers   18 21 159
  178 203 205 206 207 248
Persecutions, religious   72 84 124
  157 179 213
Persia and Persians   16 27 86
Peter, the Apostle   207
Pharaoh   1 2
Pharisees   24–25 71 103 226
Pharmacists   32
Philanthropy   46

Philistia and Philistines 7 11
Philosophy and Philosophers 91
  104
Phoenicia and Phoenicians 6 11 14
  23 31 131 136 208 221
Phylacteries 164 172 194
Physicians 18 19–21 32–33 43 77–
  81 90 149 181–191 193–201 211
  214 248–249
Piety and Pietists 3–4 20 85 92
  154 170 171—172 175 183–184
  188 190 215 232 238
Pigeons 44, see also: Doves
Pilgrims and Pilgrim Festivals 4 65
  66 100 147 208 218 221
Pilots, ships' 154–155
Pincers (= Tongs) 138 201
Piracy and Pirates 162 220 223
Pitchers 134 166, see also: Jars
Pits 180
Plants, Planting and Planters 96–
  99 168 180 197 247
Plasterers 130
Pliny, a Roman writer 174
Ploughing and Ploughmen 8 114
  211
Plums 144
Poetry and Poets 13 17 156
Poisons and Poisoning 187 191
  192 193 200
Poland 185
Police Officers 86 155
Poor, see: Poverty and the Poor
Poppaea Sabina, a Roman
  empress 157
Porters 14 52–53 93–94 130 131
Portus, Roman harbor city 157
Potiphar, an Egyptian officer 164
Potters and Pottery 4 5 15–17 35
  53 134–136 138 149 220 244
Poverty and the Poor 4 35 45 52–
  53 56 66 68 75 76 88–89 93 106
  113 119 121–125 130 139 142
  144 151 155–156 157 159 160
  163–164 166–168 170 188 190
  209 210 213 221 222 239

Powders 191
Power 103
Prayer 21 32 39 50 110 130 142
  152 163 173 183 185 192 193 213
Preachers and Preaching 33 39 40
  70 71 100 219 226
Prejudices 171 185 206 210
Price Control and Price-
  cutting 133 142–146 231
Pride 99 211 212
Priests 12 19 22–23 24 35 73 74 82
  92 120 128 142 182 203 225 226
  230 246–248
Prisons and Prisoners 88 124 174
  205
Private Enterprise 148–151
Profiteering 143 144 146 147
Proletariate 128
Promised Land 95 97
Prophets and Prophetic
  Movement 15 25 33 60 184 228
Proselytes, see: Converts, etc.
Prostitutes and Prostitution 85 157
Proverbs — General 32 33 107
  130 134 161–162 165 166 173
  175 179 181 185 186 187 188–
  189 211 212 221 226 237
Proverbs, Book of 25–27 33 105
Psalms, Book of 13 33 85 123
Psychology 96 193 199
Ptolemaic — Dynasty and
  Government 30
Ptolemais (= Acco), a city in
  Western Galilee 136
Publicans 226
"Puddings" 141
Pulse (= Legumes) 57
Pumbeditha, a city in Babylonia 51
  65 169
Pum Nahara, a city in
  Babylonia 150
Pumpkins 198 199–200
Punishment, see: a) Reward and
  Punishment; b) Corporal
  Punishment
Purim 75

Purity, Ritual   19 73 207
Purses   161 231
Puteoli, a city near Naples   157

Quack Doctors   33 190 197 203

"Rab" — title   213
Rab (= Rabbi Abba bar Aibu)   45
    52–53 54 66 69–70 78 92 99 146
    160 176 229 230
Raba   52 53 118 160 189–190
Raba bar Rab Hanan   52
Raba bar Hinena   234
Rabbah bar Rab Huna   44–45 80
    81
Rabbah bar Rab Nahman   45
Rabbinate — General   38 107
Rabbinic — Attitudes and Views on
    Labor, Study, etc.   xi 40 42 68 69
    70 75–76 83–84 88 91–125 134
    136 141 142 143–146 148–151
    173 174–177 180 181 182 183–
    185 187 189 192–193 194 197
    208 210 215 220 223 229–239
    245 246–250
Rabina   52 54 150
Radanites   ix
Radin, Max   6
Rain and Rainmakers   39 54 135
    198 219
Ransoming   88 173
Rape and Rapists   205
Rashi (= Rabbi Solomon ben
    Isaac)   48 187 222 231 232 242
Rationalism and Rationalists   184
    194
Ravens   189–190
Real Estate   162 214
Reaping   114
Rechabites   3–4 24
Red Sea   240
Reed-mats   133
Religion and Religious Laws and
    Customs   xi 84 111 146–147 156
    175 205 213 214 216 229 231 232
    238 242

Renaissance   x
Repentance   219
Resh Lakish, see: Simeon ben
    Lakish, Rabbi
Resh Galuta, see Exilarchs
Respect toward Teachers   45
Responsa Literature, Rabbinic   142
    234
Resurrection of the Dead   139
Retailers   143 145
Reward and Punishment   98 222
Riches, see: Wealth
Riding   221
Robbers and Robbery   89 101 108
    116 127 147 162 171 210–211
    220 222 223 224 226 238
Roman Age   3 31 136 169 241
Roman Empire   42 65 102 122 130
    132 134 145 151–158 153 157
Romans   41 83 86–87 104 113 120
    124 128 129 131 132 136 141 144
    152 154 155 156 167 169 170 178
    190 210 213 215 219 225 239 240
    241
Rome   84 100 151 154 156–158
    210
Roofs   223
Roosters   196
Rothschild, banking family   x

Sabbath   38 80 82 96 99 122 131
    154–155 156 194 195–196 217
    229–230 232 238 242
Sabbatical Year   163
Sacred Commodities and
    Literature   163–164
Sacrifices, Animal   219
Sacrifices, Human   16
Saffron   55 89 195
Safra, Rab   65
Sailors   154 211 220 221 223 232–
    233
Sails   239
Saints and Saintly Persons   39 40
    109 110 114 181 190 204 205 230
Salaries, see: Wages

Salt 63 123 160 175 191 216
Samaria, a city in Central
  Palestine 127
Samaritans 89
Samson, a judge of Israel 5
Samuel, a judge and prophet of
  Israel 18
Samuel, Yarhina'a, Mar 42–43 46
  77–78 79 80 81 106 143 146 201
Samuel bar Shilath, Rab 69–70
Sand 136 137 138 161
Sandalmakers 84 142
Sanhedrin 40 58 83 215
Sarah, Abraham's wife 5
Satire 27
Saturnalia 132
Saul, king of Israel 18
Sausages and Sausage-sellers 156
Scapegoats 196
Scent 207
Scholars and Scholarship 40 41 59
  61 64 65 68 73 74 75 76 80 83 85
  86 100 101 111 112 113 114 115
  117 118 119 120 121 122 123 124
  157 158 160 172 175 182 204 210
  214–216 218 222 235
Schools 68–70 82 151 202 242
  249, see also: Academies
Schoolteachers, see: Teaching and
  Teachers
Scientists 91
Scorpions 81 194
Scribes 24–25 33–34 71–77 85 99
  109 159 164 248
Scriptures, see: Bible, Hebrew
Sculptors 37
Scurvy 191
Scythopolis, see: Beth Shean
Seals 12–13
Seas 14 90 104 126 134 153 154–
  155 162 220 232 233 239 240
Seats and Sitting 106
Second Commonwealth 24 132
Secretaries 24 164
Sects and Sectarian 92
Seder 147

Seduction 206 245
Selling and Buying 144–145 161–
  162
Semen 221
Sennacherib, king of Assyria 13
Sepphoris, a city in Galilee 61 79
  141 235
Serfs 173–175
Sermons 163 213
Serpents, see: Snakes
Servants, domestic and
  agricultural 4–5 38 40 41 47 105
  156 167 216
Sesame 49
Sewing 6 131
Sex and Sexual Intercourse 172
  221 245
Shammai, the Elder 81–82
Sharecroppers 42 50 54 167–168
  179
Sharon, Plain of 135
Shavuoth (= Pentecost) festival 66
Shechem 1 2 5
Sheep (= Flocks) and
  Shepherds 1–3 4 6 12 55 120
  169 179–181 220 224–231 241
Shema, a Torah reading and
  prayer 112 130
Shemayah, a leader of the
  Pharisees 103 210
Shepherds, see: Sheep and
  Shepherds
Shesheth, Rab 106
Shimi ben Ashi, Rab 43–44
Ships, Shipping and Shipowners 37
  41 49 137 153 154–155 157 231
Shivers 81
Shoemaker, see: Cobblers and
  Shoemakers
Shops and Shopkeepers, see: Stores
  and Storekeepers
Showbread 246–247
Sidon and Sidonians 11 208 221
Silk and Silk Trade 11 41 45 58–60
  66 68 132 133
Silver 9 11 152 196

Silversmiths   14 140 152
Simeon ben Eleazar, Rabbi   94 105
   120–121
Simeon ben Gamaliel II,
   Rabban   102
Simeon ben Halafta, Rabbi   41 58
Simeon ben Rabbi Judah Ha-Nasi,
   Rabbi   58 85
Simeon ben Lakish, Rabbi   55 66
   87–89
Simeon ben Manasia, Rabbi   110
   118
Simeon ben Shetah, a leader of the
   Pharisees   62
Simeon bar Yakim (= Elkyakim),
   Rabbi   178
Simeon ben Yohai, Rabbi   73 86–
   87 106 112–120 124 223 238
Simeon the Just, a high priest   230
Simeon, tribe of   22
Simon, the Hasmonean   37
Simon, Rabbi   42 117
Simonia, a town in Galilee   70
Sinai Desert   1
Sinai, Mount   114
Singing, see: Songs
Sins and Sinners   31 33 39 87 102
   109 120 121 160 196 206 219 228
   230 236 237
Sisera, a Canaanite general   10 18
Skin Diseases   78 238
Skins, of animals   207
Skulls   198
Slaughterers (= Butchers)   18 52 63
   156 187 228 233–236
Slaves and Slavery   1 5 9 28 38 88
   91 102 131 157 165 170–174 175
   182 245–246
Sleep   28 123 124 148 171 193 194
   198 204 219 220 229
Smelters   140
Smiths, see: a) Blacksmiths;
   b) Goldsmiths; c) Silversmiths
Smoke   247
Snakes (= Serpents)   8 187 192 194
   223 238

Soap   178
Social Security   107–108
Soil Erosion   99
Soldiers   62 155 219
Solomon, King of Israel   8 9 11 12
   13 14 15 28 57
Song of Songs, Book of   12
Songs   211
Sorcerers   156, see also: Magic and
   Magicians
Sowing   114 165
Sows   103
Spain   i
Spices and Spicesellers   21 141 150
   202 205 206 207 248
Spiders   193
Spinning   6 102 131 209
Spitting   197
Spleen   80 195 196
Spoons   201
Sport   236 237 239
Stealing   42 43 46 47 59 135 169
   171 176 200 204 210 226 241
   244, see also: Thieves
Stepmothers   189
Sticks   139 229
Stock Exchange   162
Stone(s) and Stonemasons   11 12
   14 93–94 127–130 177 229
Stores and Storekeepers   62 121 139
   143–145 148 149 207 220 231–232
Storms   153 154–155 223
Straps   235
Straw   174
Strikes   1 167 247
Students, see: Study (of Torah) and
   Students
Study (of Torah) and Students   40
   41 42 43 45 46 48 50 53 56 59 61
   65 68–70 77 89 100 101 102 108
   109–125 150 157 158 161 191
   200 233 238 245 248–249
Study, House of (= *Beth
   Midrash*)   61 89 106 111 225
Succot festival (= Tabernacles)   66
   146 148 218 238

Succoth, a town in Transjordan 9
Suffering 114 115 121-124
Suicide 191 216
Summers 110 136 198
Sun 180
Superstitions 77 193 195-198
Sura, a city in Babylonia 46 73 92
Surgeons and Surgery 20 188 198-
199 201 204
Surveyors, Land, see: Land
Surveyors
Swords 8 88 228
Synagogues 33 70 133 151-152
157 158 163 212-214 249
Synesius, Bishop of Cyrene 154
Syria 20 59 66 95 134 156 177 190
199

Tabernacle, Israelite Santuary 9 10
95-96
Tabernacles (= Succot), a
festival 66 146 148 218 238
Tabi, Rabban Gamaliel's (II)
slave 172
Tables 139
Tailors 17 84-85 99 113 149 156
202 218
Talebearing 23 85
Talmid Hakham 158
Talmud (Babli and Yerushalmi) and
Talmudic 39 51 53 62 69 73 77
79 109 114 119 123 129 131 137
142 148 157 164 169 186 187 191
193 196 197 199 200 206 210 226
232 235 236 237 245-246
Talmudic Age 38 68 77 91 109 122
126 127 136 137 169 197 201 225
226 237
Tanners 84 149 159 202 207-209
Tarfon, Rabbi 40-41 105 146 165
171
Targum, see: Aramaic
Tarichaea, a city in Galilee 239-
240
Tarsiim (= artistic weavers) 133
212-214

Tarsus, a city in Asia Minor 133
212
Taverns 86
Taxes and Tax-collectors 64 85-86
90 101 127 150 152 168 226
Teaching and Teachers 24 33 43
44 50 52 54 55 56 61 68-70 74 76
80 89 100 108 109 112 115 116
124 158 159 160 175 200 201 202
210 211 213 216 220 233 245
246-249
Tears, see: Weeping and Tears
Tell el-Kheleifeh, archaeological
site 9
Tel Miqne, archaeological site 7
Temple, First (Solomon's) 8 9 11
12 14 176
Temple, Second 14 23 24 59 65 66
67 71 93 100 101 127-128 138
139 142 147 153 155 178 182 203
208 213 219 246-248
Temple Mount 130
Tenant Farmers 40 43 44 46 47 50
51 54 105 167-168 172
Tenants, of a house, courtyard,
etc. 148-149 186
Tent of Assembly, see: Tabernacle,
Israelite Sanctuary
Tents and Tent-makers 90 156 225
Testimonies 210 212 226 229 230
235
Textiles and Textile Industry 131-
133 153 180 209
Thaddeus (= Theodos) of
Rome 157
Thebez, a town in Central Israel 5
Theft, see: Stealing
Theodos (= Thaddeus) of
Rome 157
Theodosius I, Roman emperor 154
Thieves 40 86-87 176 200 210-
211 229, see also: Stealing
Thirst 227
Thistles 94 193
Thomson, W.M. 17
Thorns 81 94

Threshing 114
Tiberias, a city in Galilee 72–73
133 137 148 213 214
Tiberias, Lake of (= Galilee, Sea
of) 90 239–240
Timber 11 14 47 50 220
Tiryah, a town in Galilee 215
Tisha b'Ab (9th of Ab) 218
Tishri, month of 53 118
Tobiah, the physician 182
Tobit (Apocrypha) 186
Tombstones 142 156 158
Tongs, see: Pincers
Tools 12
Toothaches 81
Torah and Torah Scrolls 33 36 39
40 41 42 60 69 71–76 82 91 109–
110 111 112 114–125 137 166
167 171 175 189 190 192 201 207
214 238
Torah, Study of, see: Study, of
Torah
Tosephta 198
Tourists 100
Towns, small 150 206 207 208 209
210, see also: Cities
Trachonitis, a district in N.
Transjordan 127
Trade and Traders 23–24 28 ff. 37
38 39 42 53 58–68 75 76 79 117
141 142 144–151 159 ff. 161 162
163–164 165 226 241, see also:
a) Commerce; b) Crafts
Trade Unions 151–152 213 214
235, see also: Guilds
Trading Stamps 143
Transference, cures by 196
Transjordan 20 70 127 134
Transportation and Transport
Workers 14 44 49 52–53 163
178 220–224
Trees and Tree-Planing 50 94 96–
99 184
Tribes 18 22
Troyes, French town 48
Tubal-Cain, a descendant of Cain 8

Tubes 138
Turkey 75
Tyre and Tyrians 9 11 58 133 140
177 221
Tyre, Promontory of 95

Ugarit, a city in Syria 20
Ulla, a Babylonian *Amora* 91
Unemployment 22 96 128 166 209
United Jewish Appeal 151
Urbanization 27 30 33 109 141
142 160 166 241
Usha, a city in Galilee 83 132 133
Usury and Usurers x 226
Uzziah, king of Judah 7 169 176

Vegetables 133 160 162 168 175
197 212
Veils 61
Vespasian, Roman emperor 190
Villages and Villagers ix 4 30 41
126 139 203 207
Vinegar 46 87 161 193 195
Vineyards and Viniculture 3 42 43
46 47 48 52 54–55 87 108 165
169 170 171 176 220 226
Virgins 132
Vocational Careers and
Training 112–113 232 241–250
Voices, heavenly 216
Volga, river 44
Vows 230

Wages (= Salaries) 29 53 70–71 75
88 101 104 128 130 159 167 170
174 224 244 247 248
Wagons and Wagoners 127 129
220
Wailing Women 21–22
Wall, third (of Jerusalem) 128
Wars and Warriors 18 41 129 131
136 141 157 167 170 178 180 225
239 244
Washermen and Washerwomen, see:
Launderers
Wasps 81 193 209

Watchmen 212
Water 32 48 76 78 81 104 118 123
134 182 198 217 227 230 231 240
244
Wealth 13–14 30 35 40 41 45–49
51 54 56 58 67 70 73 76 83 102
121 123 151 155–156 157 160
164 165 171 172 181 188 209 210
214 221 228 240
Weapons, see: Arms
Weavers and Weaving 6 10 99 102
131 132 133 149 152 153 155 202
209–214 218 244
Weddings 13 138 139
Weeping and Tears 21–22 94 122
137 186 246
Weights and Measures 145 161
165 171 221
Western Wall (of the Temple
Mount) 127
Wheat 4 45 62 102 169 170 243
Wholesalers 143 145
Widowers 201
Widows 208 249
Wills 199
Winds 78 114 137 209 219
Wine and Winecups 43 45 46 48
52 55 62 79 87 134 135 137 141
142 143 160 161 195 217 220 231
246
Winnowing 114
Winters 6 79 110
Wisdom (Literature) 25 26 27 28
137
Wolves 229
"Woman of Worth (or Valor)" 6 23
25
Witnesses, testimony of 210 212
226 229 230
Women 4 5 6 9 10 11 18 21–22 23
28 50–51 56 66 75 91 98 102 110
121 131 132 136 150 154 157 163
164 165 169 171 173 186 189 191

197 201 202 203 204 205 206 208
209 212 215 216 218–219 221
222 223 242 243 245–246 249
Wood — "Hewers of Wood and
Drawers of Water" 76
Woodcocks 196
Woodwork and Woodcutters 8 9
11 14 55–56 107 244, see also:
Timber
Wool 6 18 99 102 131 132 133 150
180 195 202 215 226 228
Work and Workers, see: Labor —
General
Workday 111
Work Ethic 27 102–106
Workshops 110 136 211
World-to-come 76–77 115 116 123
124 187 216 235 236–237
Worms and Maggots 230
Wounds (= Injuries) 78 79 80 173
182 184 188 198 199 200 201 206
Wrestling 87
Writing and Writers 74 248, see
also: Scribes

Yavneh 58
Yeshebab the Scribe, Rabbi 72
Yeshivot 119, see also: Academies
Yitzhak Nappaha, Rabbi 83
Yitzhaki, Rabbi Solomon, see: Rashi
Youth 201

Zadok, Rabbi 190 198
Zarethan, a town in Transjordan 9
Zealots 155 210
Zebid, Rab 169
Zebulun, tribe of 137
Zechariah, Book of 147 228
Zera, Rabbi 61 85 132 234–235
Zidon, see: Sidon
Zion 10, see also: Jerusalem
Zionism iii 99
Zoroastrianism 27

Sources

HEBREW BIBLE

GENESIS
2:2   92 99
2:8   97
2:15   94
2:16   94
2:18–22   17
3:7   18
3:17   3
3:18   94
3:19   94
3:21   17 132
4:2 ff.   3 176
4:8   176
4:21   8
4:22   8
5:29   3
9:20   176
9:21   176
10:9   236
12:16   2
13:2   2
13:5 ff.   1
13:7   224
18:6   5
18:7–8   5
24:10–46   2
25:27   225
26:12   1 95
26:14   2
26:24   95
30:43   2
31:17   2
31:19   6
31:39   229

31:40   229
32:8   2
32:15   2
32:16   2
33:19   1
36:6 ff.   1
37:7   1
37:13   2
37:17   2
38:18   12
38:25   12
39:11   164
45:10   2
46:32   2
46:33   2
46:34   2 3
47:1   2
47:4   2
48:15   3
49:5 ff.   22
50:2   19
50:8   2

EXODUS
2:11   131
3:1   2 224
5:4 f.   1
5:6 ff.   1
5:7 ff.   1
9:1–7   169
9:4 ff.   2
10:9   2
11:5   5
12:32   2

12:36   152
12:38   2
13:21   18
14:14   18
14:25   18
15:3   18
15:26   21 183 197
15:27   18
16:33   115
17:3   224
20:9   96
21:2   173
21:19   183 184
21:26 f.   173
23:17   208
25:8   96
25:38   12
26:1 ff.   10
26:31–37   10
28:11   12 14
28:21   12
28:36   12
31:2 ff.   9
31:5   14
32:4   12
32:26 ff.   22
34:1 ff.   12
34:23   208
35:5   10
35:23–26   10
35:25 f.   209
35:30–33   9
35:33   14
35:34   10

35:35 10
36:8ff. 10
36:35 10
37:23 12
38:9ff.
38:23 10
39:1ff. 10
39:6 12
39:14 12
39:22-29 10
39:30 12

LEVITICUS
16:21f. 196
19:23 97
24:5-9 246
25:14 144
25:55 167
26:11 185

NUMBERS
4:9 12
6:18 230
15:38 174
21:6-9 8
23:9 7
27:17 3

DEUTERONOMY
5:13 96
6:4-9 112
8:9 12
15:12 173
15:13-15 173
15:18 169
16:16 208
19:5 12
20:19 12
23:25f. 167 226
23:39 21
24:6 5
24:14-15 167
25:5ff. 208
28:66 165
30:13 117
30:19 107

33:8 23
33:19 137 140

JOSHUA
1:8 112
9:23-27 76
15:15f. 24

JUDGES
1:11 24
1:16 8
4:11 8
4:21 12
5:20 18
5:30 10
10:53 6
16:21 5
chs. 17-18 22
17:4 14

I SAMUEL
8:13 18
9:23f. 18
13:19 11
13:20 11
15:6 8
16:11 2
16:19 2
17:15 2
17:28 2 224
17:34ff. 2 229
17:40ff. 229
25:2ff. 6
25:36 6

II SAMUEL
5:2 2
5:11 11 14
7:7 3
7:8 2
12:1-4 4
12:31 9

I KINGS
5:20 11
5:25 221

5:29 12
5:32[18] 14
6:7 12
7:13 9 11
7:14 9
7:15ff. 8 9
7:45-46 9
7:47 9
7:49 12
10:18 13
21:8 12
22:17 3
22:39 13

II KINGS
8:10 199
12:2 12
12:12 14
12:13 12
20:6f. 20
22:5 12
22:6 12
23:7 209
24:14 12
24:16 12

ISAIAH
1:6 19
1:22 231
3:16 10
3:18-24 11
6:6 12
7:3 18 214
8:1 12
10:15 12
16:14 169
30:14 15
38:1 20
38:5 20
38:21 20
40:11 3
40:19 14
40:20 14
41:7 12
41:25 16
44:12f. 12 14

44:13 14
44:20 3
45:7 17
45:9 17
45:18 27
46:6 14
47:2 5
54:16 14
58:13 242
61:5f. 120 169
63:11 3
64:7 17

JEREMIAH
2:2 4
2:8 3
3:15 3
6:29 12 14
8:22 20
10:3f. 12 14
10:9 14
10:14 14
10:20f. 22
10:21 3
13:17 3
18:3–6 17
19:2 16
19:3ff. 16
19:10–11 16
22:24 12
23:1ff. 3
23:29 12
25:34ff. 3
29:2 12
31:10 3
32:7ff. 3
32:15f. 3
32:43f. 3
35:1ff. 24
35:6ff. 3
35:13ff. 4
36:32 25
37:21 18 19
50:6 3
51:7 14

EZEKIEL
16:10–13 11
27:17 221
34:2–31 3 228
34:3–5 228
34:10–31 228
34:11ff. 3
37:24 3

HOSEA
4:16 3
12:8 23,147

AMOS
3:15 13
4:1 13
6:4 13
8:4ff. 147

MICAH
5:4 3
6:11 147
7:14 3

NAHUM
3:18 3

HAGGAI
2:23 12

ZECHARIAH
10:2f. 3
11:3–17 3
11:5 228
11:15 228
11:16 228
13:7 3
14:21 147

MALACHI
3:3 14

PSALMS
1:1 236
2:9 15

23:1 3 225
37:25 75
45:9 13
56:8 137
74:1 3
77:21 2
78:70f. 2
78:71 227
79:13 3
80:2 3
95:7 3
100:3 3
104:23 57
107:17–19 21
119:71 123

PROVERBS
2:20 53
6:6 105
6:6–8 26
6:9–11 26
10:4 25
10:5 26
10:26 25
12:11 27
13:4 27
19:15 25
20:4 26
20:13 26
22:13 27
23:31 231
24:30f. 26
24:33f. 26
25:4 14
25:31 231
26:14 26
26:16 27
31:13 6
31:15 25
31:18 25
31:19 209
31:19–24 6
31:21 6
31:24 23
31:27 25

JOB
1:10 93
5:18 21
13:4 20
28:17 137

CANTICLES
8:6 12

LAMENTATIONS
1:14 165
3:27 110
4:2 15

ESTHER
3:12 12
8:8 12
8:10 12

ECCLESIASTES
1:1 28
3:11 99
5:9 147
5:11 28
7:18 118
9:16 35

10:18 28
11:4 28
11:6 28
12:8 28

DANIEL
12:3 69

EZRA
3:7 12 14
7:1-6 24

NEHEMIAH
chs. 3-4 29
3:8 14 18
3:31 14 24
3:32 14

I CHRONICLES
2:55 24
4:9f. 24
4:23 16
11:2 2
14:1 14
17:6 3
17:7 2

22:15 14
24:6 24
27:25-31 7
29:5 14

II CHRONICLES
2:1 12
2:6 11
2:7f. 11
2:12f. 9 11
2:17 12
3:15ff. 8 9
4:1ff. 8 9
4:17 9
4:18 9
4:29 12
9:17 13
16:12f. 20 32 183
16:13 21
16:14 21
18:16 3
24:12f. 12 14
26:10 7 169 176
26:16ff. 176
34:11 12
34:13 24

APOCRYPHA and PSEUDEPIGRAPHA

ECCLESIASTICUS
(BEN SIRA)
7:11 30
7:15 29-30
11:1 35
11:10 31
11:20 31
11:29 (Heb. edit). 206
18:19 32
22:1-2 30
26:29 31
27:1-3 31
37:11 31

38:1-15 33 181
38:24 34
38:25-34 36

I MACCABEES
13:29 37
14:5 37
14:34 37

TOBIT
2:10 186

THE LETTER OF
ARISTEAS
107 29
108 29 30
109ff. 30
114 29
258 29
259 29

THE SYRIAC
APOCALYPSE
OF BARUCH
10, 19 132

NEW TESTAMENT

MATTHEW
4:18ff.   90
6:25—34   93
6:26ff.   121
9:12   181
9:16   218
10:3   90 192
11:15ff.   147
13:47f.   239
13:55   90
20:1-7   166
21:12f.   65 67 147
ch. 23   24 71

MARK
2:17   181
2:21   218

3:18   192
6:3   90
11:15   65 67
15:40   192

LUKE
4:23   186
5:31   181
5:36   218
6:15   192
19:45f.   147

JOHN
2:14ff.   67 147
2:15f.   65
10:4   229
10:11-13   229

ACTS
1:13   192
9:43   207
10:6   207
10:32   207
12:20   221
18:3   90
19:23ff.   15

I CORINTHIANS
9:7   226

COLOSSIANS
4:14   90

II THESSALONIANS
3:10   104

HELLENISTIC-JEWISH LITERATURE

PHILO
De Legibus
XX, 98   96

In Flaccum
Par. 8   151
Par. 57   155

JOSEPHUS — THE JEWISH WAR (BELLUM IUDAICUM)
I, 6, 6 (138)   174
I, 18, 5 (361)   174
II, 4, 3 (60)   225 229
II, 10, 2 (190)   137
II, 11, 6 (218)   128
II, 21, 2 (591f.)   178
II, 21, 2 (592)   170
II, 22, 1 (646)   141
III, 3, 2 (42ff.)   170
III, 3, 2 (43)   126

III, 3, 3 (44)   126
III, 9, 7 (445)   240
III, 10, 1-10 (462–542)   240
IV, 8, 3 (469)   174
V, 1, 5 (36)   129
V, 2, 2 (55)   129
V, 4, 2 (147–155)   128 129 215
V, 5, 3 (201)   153
V, 8, 1 (331)   131 133
VII, 11, 1-2 (437–446)   156
VII, 11, 1-3 (437–450)   210

JOSEPHUS — THE ANTIQUITIES OF THE JEWS
IX, 1, 2 (7)   174
XIV, 4, 1 (54)   174
XV, 4, 2 (96)   174

XV, 8, 1 (274f.)   88, 236
XV, 11, 2 (390)   128
XVII, 2, 1-2 (23ff.)   127
XVII, 10, 7 (278)   225 229
XVIII, 2, 2 (38)   73
XVIII, 9, 1 (310ff.)   244
XVIII, 9, 1 (314)   209
XIX, 7, 2 (326f.)   128
XX, 2, 3 (34f.)   60
XX, 2, 4 (38–42)   60
XX, 9, 7 (219ff.)   128
XX, 9, 7 (220)   128

*JOSEPHUS —
I APION*
12 (60) 126

*JOSEPHUS — THE
LIFE (VITA)*
1 (1 ff.) 225
3 (16) 157

9 (35) 239
13 (74 ff.) 178
17 (87 ff.) 239
54 ff. (276 ff.) 239

RABBINIC LITERATURE

MISHNAH

BERAKHOTH
II, 4 130
II, 7 172

PEAH
II, 6 72

DEMAI
I, 2 175
I, 3 175
III, 1 172

KILAYIM
IX, 10 218

SHEBIITH
III, 9 130
VII, 4 236 238

MAASROTH
III, 7 136

BIKKURIM
III, 3 100

SHABBATH
I, 3 99
I, 6 238
I, 8 219
I, 9 219
VI, 1 140
VI, 2 194

VI, 10 193
VII, 2 131, 238
XII, 1 129
XIII, 5 ff. 238
XIV, 1 238

ERUBIN
X, 9 131
X, 10 214

PESAHIM
III, 4 135
IV, 6 218
IV, 9 183
X, 3 147

SHEKALIM
I, 3 147
IV, 9 147
V, 1 182
VI, 4 246
VII, 2 147

YOMA
I, 3 35
I, 6 35
III, 7 132
III, 11 248
VIII, 6 194

SUKKAH
II, 1 172

BEZAH
III, 1 239
III, 2 239
III, 8 62

ROSH HASHANAH
I, 7 182

TAANITH
II, 7 217
III, 8 135

MOED KATAN
II, 5 238

KETUBOTH
V, 5 102 132 215
V, 6 221
VII, 10 140 208

NEDARIM
III, 6 233

GITTIN
III, 1 72
IV, 4 173
V, 8 238

KIDDUSHIN
I, 10 109
IV, 13 202
IV, 14 33 115 121

136 159 160 187
202 220

BABA KAMMA
VI, 2 229
VII, 7 180
X, 9 132 209 226

BABA METSIA
II, 8 138
II, 9 166
IV, 3 146
IV, 4 145
IV, 12 143 145
V, 8 172
VII, 1 57 167
VII, 2 167
VII, 5 167
VII, 9 229
IX, 1 167

BABA BATHRA
II, 3 148 149 231
II, 9 209
VI, 2 135

SANHEDRIN
III, 2 230
IV, 3 72
X, 1 194, 197

EDUYOTH
I, 3 210
I, 13 173
II, 5 238

ABODAH ZARAH
I, 7 141
I, 10 103
II, 2 191

ABOTH
II, 2 102 109
II, 5 34 117
II, 6 175
II, 7 171
II, 8 113
II, 9 113
II, 15 105
III, 17 40 109
IV, 5 39 76
IV, 7 56
IV, 10 34 117
IV, 14 115
IV, 15 158
V, 23 123
VI, 5 123
VI, 6 34 117

MENAHOTH
VIII, 2 45

XI, 7 246
XI, 8 246

BEKHOROTH
IV, 4 182
V, 4 226

MIDDOTH
I, 4 153

KELIM
II, 2 135
V, 4 134
XI, 8 137, 140
XII, 3 201
XVII, 12 201
XXIV, 8 139
XXVI, 5 201
XXIX, 6 140
XXX, 1-4 140
XXX, 2 140

NIDDAH
II, 7 135

MAKSHIRIN
VI, 3 240

ZABIM
III, 2 220

TOSEFTA

BERAKHOTH
VI, 2 116
VII (VI), 8 95 159

PEAH
IV, 10 139
IV, 11 139
IV, 12 139

DEMAI
I, 10 221

II, 2 175

MAASER RISHON
II, 21 136

BIKKURIM
II, 15 75 163 164
II, 16 163

SHABBATH
I, 8 99

VII (VIII), 23 194
XII (XIII), 2 238
XV (XVI), 16 155

ERUBIN
VI (V), 13 230
VII, 7 83

PESAHIM
II (III), 18 218

YOM HA-KIPPURIM
II, 4   153
II, 5   212 247
II, 6   248
III, 8   248

SUKKAH
II, 5   180
IV, 6   152 213

YOM TOB
III, 1   239
III, 4   239
III, 8   62

MEGILLAH
III (II), 6   213

YEBAMOTH
III, 4   229

KETUBOTH
IV, 7   121
VII, 11   208

NAZIR
IV, 7   230

SOTAH
V, 12   237

GITTIN
II, 10   72

KIDDUSHIN
I, 11   108 159
I, 16   109
V, 10   202
V, 14   107 159 202
      207
V, 15   115 121 159

BABA KAMMA
VIII, 10   180
VIII, 13   181
VIII, 14   181
VIII, 17   239
VIII, 18   239
X, 10   66
XI, 9   226
XI, 14   215

BABA METSIA
III, 19   147
VI, 3   134
VI, 5   239
VI, 14   145
VII, 10f.   220
VII, 13   222
VIII, 8   167
VIII, 27   134
IX, 1ff.   167
IX, 17   168
IX, 18   168
XI, 5   129
XI, 9   169

BABA BATHRA
I, 4   149 231

SANHEDRIN
V, 1   230
V, 5   226

EDUYOTH
I, 3   210

ABODAH ZARAH
II, 4   141
IV (V), 1   143
IV (V), 2   143

MENAHOTH
IX, 3   45

HULLIN
III, 2   235

BEKHOROTH
III, 19   226

ARAKHIN
II, 3   154
II, 4   154

KELIM —
BABA KAMMA
VII, 17   135

KELIM —
BABA METSIA
I, 3   135
II, 9   201
III, 10   138
III, 11   138 201
IV, 6   129
V, 7   240

KELIM —
BABA BATHRA
II, 2   130
IV, 8   201

OHOLOTH
II, 3   201
II, 6   198, 201
IV, 2   182, 214
XVIII, 2   208

NIDDAH
IV, 4   182
VI, 12   215

HALAKHIC MIDRASHIM

MEKHILTA de-RABBI
YISHMAEL
on Exod. 12:16   217
on Exod. 13:13   108
on Exod. 13:17   119
on Exod. 14:7   120
on Exod. 15:4   111
on Exod. 16:4   119
on Exod. 16:33   115
on Exod. 17:3   224
on Exod. 20:11   217
on Exod. 20:12   217
on Exod. 21:26   173
on Exod. 21:27   173

on Exod. 22:11   241
on Exod. 22:12   229
on Exod. 31:13   155

MEKHILTA de-RABBI
SIMEON, edit.
EPSTEIN
on Exod. 20:9   96

SIFRA
(TORATH KOHANIM)
Shemini VII, 3   135
Emor XII, 4   217

SIFRE(I) —
NUMBERS
Par. 22   230
Par. 147   217

SIFRE(I) —
DEUTERONOMY
Par. 13   67
Par. 118   173
Par. 247   182
Par. 269   72
Par. 306   105 122
   123
Par. 355   170 177 178
Par. 357   58

TALMUD YERUSHALMI

BERAKHOTH
I, 2, 3a   182
II, 5, 5a   167
II, 8, 5b   172
II, 8, 5c   235
IV, 1, 7d   83 215
V, 5, 9b   200
IX, 1, 13a   130
IX, 3, 13d   221
IX, 5, 14d   117

PEAH
I, 1, 15b   72
I, 1, 15c   107
VII, 1, 20a   179
VII, 4, 20b   61

DEMAI
VI, 1, 25a–b   42

KILAYIM
VII, 4, 31d   66
IX, 4, 32b   216
IX, 5, 32d   84

SHEBIITH
IV, 2, 35a   84
IV, 2, 35b   41 84
VI, 1, 36d   70
VIII, 5, 38b   217
IX, 1, 38d   114 238

TERUMOTH
VIII, 5, 45d   886

MAASROTH
II, 6, 50a   101 226

BIKKURIM
III, 3, 65c   100

SHABBATH
I, 2, 3a   114
I, 2, 3b   114
I, 7, 3c   178
VI, 1, 7d   56 140
VI, 2, 8b   194
VI, 2, 8c   194
VI, 10, 8c   193 194

VII, 4, 10d   138
XIV, 3, 14c   79
XIV, 4, 14d   78 79
   80 191 192 193
XIX, 1, 16d   81 201

ERUBIN
X, 1, 26a   172
X, 11, 26c   194

PESAHIM
VII, 1, 34a   157
IX, 1, 36c   183

SHEKALIM
IV, 3, 48a   209
V, 1, 48d   182
V, 2, 48d   212 247
V, 2, 49a   212 247
   248
VIII, 1, 51a   165 219

YOMA
III, 9, 41a   212 247 248

III, 9, 41b   248
V, 3, 42c   142

SUKKAH
I, 2, 52c   133
II, 1, 52d   172
IV, 7, 54d   138
V, 1, 55a   71 152 213
V, 1, 55b   152 213

BEZAH
III, 9, 62b   62

ROSH HASHANAH
I, 3, 57b   200
II, 6, 58b   230
III, 9, 59a   81

TAANITH
I, 1, 63d   200
I, 1, 64a   74
III, 6, 66d   32 181
IV, 1, 67d   215
IV, 8, 69a   41 240

MEGILLAH
I, 7, 71a   81
I, 11, 71d   71
II, 2, 73a   216
II, 7, 47a   214
III, 1, 73d   213

MOED KATAN
III, 1, 81c   35
III, 5, 82b   169
III, 7, 83b   89

HAGIGAH
II, 1, 77b   113 239
III, 1, 78d   84

YEBAMOTH
XII, 6, 12d   84
XII, 6, 13a   71

KETUBOTH
V, 2, 29d   121
VII, 9, 31c   132
XII, 3, 35a   216
XIII, 2, 35d   186

NEDARIM
I, 1, 36d   230
V, 1, 39a   18 219
V, 1, 39b   215
XI, 1, 42c   217

NAZIR
II, 6, 51c   230

SOTAH
I, 4, 16d   197
III, 3, 19a   209
IX, 10, 23c   116

GITTIN
IV, 4, 45d   173
IV, 9, 46b   88
V, 6, 47b   168
V, 8, 47b   242 244
IX, 9, 50d   201

KIDDUSHIN
II, 5, 62c   132
IV, 11, 66c   202 235
IV, 11, 66d   159 160
    207
IV, 12, 66d   182

BABA KAMMA
X, 11, 7c   215

BABA METSIA
I, 4, 7d   44
I, 4, 8a   44
II, 5, 8c   62 63
IV, 9, 9d   61 63
V, 5, 10b   231
V, 8, 10c   41
VI, 1, 10d   41
VI, 8, 11a   53
X, 7, 12c   129

BABA BATHRA
I, 7, 13a   215 219
V, 11, 15a   146
V, 11, 15b   146
X, 5, 17c   242

SANHEDRIN
I, 1, 18b   46
I, 218c   230
II, 1, 19d   74
II, 6, 20c   107
II, 6, 20d   107
X, 2, 29b   215

ABODAH ZARAH
I, 2, 39c   132
II, 2, 40d   78 79 80
    191 192 193

NIDDAH
I, 5, 49b   172
II, 6, 50b   137

TALMUD BABLI

BERAKHOTH
5a   114
5b   46, 66

8a   91
10b   183
16a   167

16b   172
17a   111
18b   42

22a   84
25a   208
27b   40
28a   83 215
31a   139
35b   54 114 116 117 118
   120
39a   185
40b   229
43b   99 250
44a   170
45b   43
47b   173
58a   116
58b   77
60a   183 185 188
61b   124
63a   159 161
63b   125

SHABBATH
11b   99
15b   140
17b   178
23b   82
25b   122 165 171
26a   174
26b   174
31a   82
33b   114 120
49a   84
49b   84
59a   56 140
59b   56 140
67a   193 194
78a   78 244
83b   125
105b   238
108a   78
108b   78
110b   80
119a   65 217
119b   69
120b   134
127b   170
130a   201

130b   81 201
133b   78 189
140b   48 49
147b   113 202
149a   140
150a   108 242

ERUBIN
13a   74 159
29b   191
53b   216
54b   237
55a   117
55b   222

PESAHIM
28a   237
30a   146
49a   175
49b   175
50b   75 76 162 163 164
   180
53a   157
53b   157
88b   172
108a   245
112a   124
112b   191
113a   47 49 92 161 173
   183
113b   85 171
116a   146 173
118a   94

YOMA
35b   41 56
38a   153 212 247 248
38b   248
49a   79
66b   209 229
85a   155
87a   172

SUKKAH
8b   136
20a   133

20b   133
28a   215
34b   146
51b   152 213

BEZAH
15b   116
29a   62
32b   159

ROSH HASHANAH
20b   77
26b   216
29b   50
31b   58

TAANITH
8b   162
9b   47 54
21a   61 117
21b   204
22a   204 205
23a   39
23b   39
29b   217 218

MEGILLAH
6a   137
12b   212
16a   172 203
18a   216
18b   75
26a   133 213
27b   45
28a   45

MOED KATAN
13b   148
21b   198 209

HAGIGAH
4a   171 208
5b   112 122
7b   208
9b   112 222 223 224
15a   137

YEBAMOTH
62a 172
63a 130 160 165 175
63b 165 206
76a 185
80a 191
96b 213 214
118b 212

KETUBOTH
5a 108 242
23a 65
50a 70 72 191
52b 189
60b 43
62b 56 221 226
63a 56
75a 212
86b 209
103b 69 216
105a 46 186
105b 54
106a 46
111b 55

NEDARIM
8b 191
9b 230
37a 68
41a 123 216
49a 200
49b 106 116
50a 56
50b 56
62a 41

NAZIR
4b 230
31b 47
52a 214

SOTAH
11a 130
20a 74 159
21b 123
48a 211

48b 138
49a 163
49b 140

GITTIN
46b 88
47a 88 89
56a 47
56b 190 198
57b 125
58a 246
60b 44 185
67b 106 191
68b 196
69a 80 81 195 196
69b 195
70a 81 191
73a 49
84b 72
86a 191

KIDDUSHIN
22b 167
23b 172
29a 108 116 159
30b 42 108 159 162
33a 100
49b 40 171
59a 59
70a 106
82a 159 188 202 203
    220 222 231 232 235
82b 107 115 121 159
    207 215

BABA KAMMA
31a 138
39a 53
46b 181
52a 226
56b 241
79b 159
80a 198
80b 239
81a 239
81b 239

82b 206
85a 183 185 188 199
92a 43 47
99b 65 66 68
100a 66
116b 167 223
117b 59
119a 44 47

BABA METSIA
5a 226
10a 167
21b 81 138
30b 53
31b 65
32a 65
38a 165
40b 162 163
42a 162
46a 48
48b 64
50b 144
51a 145 162
59a 166
60a 144
65a 49 64
74a 134 135
83a 53
83b 57 86 87 198
84a 87 89
85b 69 77 78
86a 167
86b 57 171
87b 226
93b 229
101a 17
107a 170 176
107b 45 48 55 78
    176
109a 50 51 52 168
109b 52 168
113b 78

BABA BATHRA
4a 171
8b 69

14a   54 71 73 74
21a   68 70 149 186
      202 211
21b   68 149 150
22a   65 150 151 206
22b   44
23a   44
26a   50 52
26b   50
57b   215 219
75b   141
89a   140 145
89b   145
90b   143
91a   142 143
110a   92
134a   215
137b   51
144a   65
146a   78
149a   65
164b   85

SANHEDRIN
5b   230
17b   76 182
18b   230
20a   122
25b   86 226
26a   86
26b   169
29a   35 107
32b   157
38b   216
41a   58
51a   182

58b   175
91a   139 152
99b   190
100a   190
100b   206
101a   197

MAKKOTH
8b   244
24a   18 215

SHEBUOTH
15b   197

ABODAH ZARAH
3a   104
12b   193
17b   212 213
18a   124
18b   236
19a   237
26a   180 211
26b   180
27a   191
27b   191 192
28a   78 80 191 192 193
28b   78 81 182

HORAYOTH
10b   49

ZEBAHIM
5a   89

MENAHOTH
16b   108

85a   162
85b   45 170 177 178 221
87a   55
99b   112
103b   165

HULLIN
17b   233
18a   234
24b   79
50b   235
54b   68 100
57b   212
60b   236
63b   238
84a   180
84b   138 162 180
95b   77
105a   43 185

BEKHOROTH
54b   229

ARAKHIN
10b   154
16b   108 249

TEMURAH
15b   198

NIDDAH
14a   221 232
17a   172
21a   135 137
25a   80
63b   80

MINOR TRACTATES

ABOTH de-RABBI
NATHAN —
VERSION I
ch. 1   94
ch. 6   40 56 115 129 140

ch. 11   94 96 101 103
         105 123
ch. 14   113
ch. 18   207
ch. 23   201

ch. 27   104
ch. 28   116
ch. 30   165
ch. 36   76 186 187 235

ABOTH de-RABBI
NATHAN —
VERSION II
ch. 11   207
ch. 12   129

ch. 21   94 96 99 101 103
          105 107 115
ch. 27   222 224

DEREKH ERETZ
ZUTA
X, 2   203 222

AGGADIC MIDRASHIM

MIDRASH RABBAH
— GENESIS
2, 2   217
5, 14   223
8, 2   221
9, 5   74
10, 6   197
11, 4   156
19, 1   132 133
19, 6   139
20, 6   177
20, 12   74 132
21, 12   132
22, 3   3 176
23, 4   186
24, 1   130
32, 3   135
34, 2   135
36, 3   3
39, 8   95
41, 5   224
42, 1   40
56, 11   209
61, 7   152 188
63, 10   242
64, 10   66
67, 2   237
68, 4   17
74, 12   93
76, 3   162
77, 2   41 58
79, 6   73
79, 7   58

81, 2   71
86, 5   134
87, 7   164
98, 11   71

MIDRASH RABBAH
— EXODUS
1, 10   130
1, 27   131
2, 2   174 227
2, 3   224
9, 4   162
21, 7   32 181
23, 10   219
46, 4   190
47, 5   42 117

MIDRASH RABBAH
— LEVITICUS
3, 1   179
5, 4   70
5, 6   187
8, 1   17
9, 5   171
12, 1   231
13, 3   237
23, 12   135 244
25, 5   97 98
26, 5   194
28, 2   219
28, 6   203
30, 1   42 117
35, 12   213

MIDRASH RABBAH
— NUMBERS
2, 13   138
2, 17   136 138
4, 8   67
8, 4   76
10, 7   230
16, 12   162
18, 12   181
20, 7   67
20, 14   187
20, 18   67
21, 12   246

MIDRASH RABBAH
— DEUTERONOMY
3, 1   217
3, 3   62
3, 4   244
3, 17   76
6, 13   183 249
edit. Liebermann
Nitzavim 6
    (119)   233 238

MIDRASH RABBAH
— CANTICLES
1, 1   164 173
6, 2   185
8, 7, 1   42

MIDRASH RABBAH
— RUTH
5, 12   41

MIDRASH RABBAH
— ESTHER
7, 1   103
7, 13   227

MIDRASH RABBAH
— LAMENTATIONS
2, 2   72 240
2, 11   186
3, 16   70
3, 17   142 243
3, 27   110

MIDRASH RABBAH
— ECCLESIASTES
1, 1   94
1, 8   142 243
1, 15   104
1, 18   132 133
2, 2   98
2, 8   132
2, 18   75 159
5, 6   199
5, 8   165
6, 8   107
7, 2   17
7, 3   17
7, 7   113
7, 12   216
8, 2   132
9, 9   109 110
9, 10   216

MIDRASH TANHUMA
(YELAMDENU)
Noah 3   124
Noah 13   3
Wayetse 13   93

Mikketz 10   32 181
Beshallah 20   111 119
Beshallah 21   115
Mishpatim 3   199
Mishpatim 5   161
Kedoshim 8   97 98
Naso 5   130
Naso 12   96
Shelach 6   162
Balak 4   67
Balak 12   67
Pinchas 8   246

MIDRASH TANHUMA,
edit. BUBER
Bereshith 24   132
Beshallach 6   182
Ki Tissa 19   42
Naso 8   130
Balak 4   67
Balak 12   67

PESIKTA de-RAB
KAHANA
ch. 6   219
ch. 10   223
ch. 28   117

PESIKTA RABBATI,
edit. M. FRIEDMANN
V, 20b   96
XXV, 128   243
XXVI, 131a   209

MIDRASH SAMUEL
(SHEMUEL)
4, 1   184
8, 19   249
10, 3   59

MIDRASH TEHILLIM
on PSALMS
(SHOHER TOV)
1:17   116
8:2   243
23:2   3 225
25:6   200 249
51:3   188
75:4   137
136:10   92

MIDRASH
MISHLE(I)
on PROVERBS
ch. 6   104
ch. 9   172

MIDRASH ZUTA —
LAMENTATIONS
I, 5   134

TANNA debei
ELIAHU
Seder Eliahu Rabbah
ch. 14   92

YALKUT SHIMONI
I, 586, par. 848   244
II, 899, par. 690   92
II, 919, par. 765   188
II, 973, par. 934   124
II, 1039, par. 597   124

PIRKEI de-RABBI
ELIEZER
ch. 1   40
ch. 29   171

BET ha-MIDRASCH,
edit. JELLINEK
MIDRASH TEMURA
ch. 2, vol. I, 107   184

DATE DUE